Understanding Corporate Bonds

Harold Kerzner

LIBERTY HALL
PRESS™

This publication is designed to provide accurate and authoritative information in regard to the subject matter covered. It is sold with the understanding that the publisher is not engaged in rendering legal, accounting or other professional service. If legal advice or other expert assistance is required, the services of a competent professional person should be sought.

—from a declaration of principles jointly adopted by a committee of the American Bar Association and a committee of publishers.

First Edition
First Printing

Library of Congress Cataloging-in-Publication Data

Kerzner, Harold.
Understanding corporate bonds / by Harold Kerzner.
p. cm.
ISBN 0-8306-8058-6
1. Bonds. I. Title.
HG4651.K42 1990
332.63'234—dc20 89-29874
CIP

TAB BOOKS offers software for sale.
For information and a catalog, please contact:

TAB Software Department
Blue Ridge Summit, PA 17294-0850

Questions regarding the content of this book should be addressed to:

Reader Inquiry Branch
TAB BOOKS
Blue Ridge Summit, PA 17294-0214

Vice President & Editorial Director: David J. Conti
Book Editor: Lori Flaherty
Production: Katherine Brown

Contents

Dedication

To my number one student,
Geraldine Klass

Acknowledgments

Special thanks to those people who have provided me with support and criticism during this undertaking. To my wife, Jo Ellyn, I am eternally grateful for her assistance in updating the portfolio test cases, the constructive criticism of each chapter, and finally, for her patience and understanding during the many hours I was away from home conducting research. To my friend and bond advisor, Richard Chernus (vice president, Merrill Lynch), many thanks for the wisdom you have given me over the past 13 years.

Introduction

IN AN ENVIRONMENT CHARACTERIZED BY UNSETTLED ECONOMIC CONDITIONS, investors need sound investment advice on how to build and preserve wealth. Today's environment has seen significant evolution in the introduction of new debt instruments. Matching the right investment strategy to the right investor has become a perilous business. Simply following the herd might provide some degree of near-term profitability but cannot guarantee continued financial success.

Perhaps the ideal investment for those who want to plan for their own financial security is the corporate bond market, which is based on fixed-income securities. Playing the field of corporate bonds is all too often misunderstood, because the dollar and cents associated with bonds do not always tell the true story, especially the associated benefits and risks. Stockbrokers might not take the time to explain the benefits and risks, nor encourage bond investments primarily because of the low commissions. Therefore, many bond investors might find themselves on their own.

The purpose of this book is to take the mystique out of the corporate bond market. It is ideal for those who have as little as $800 to invest, or for those who want to establish a portfolio of $10,000 or more. It is written for the novice or intermediate investor, although advanced investors will find it useful as well. This book provides a practical approach to financial decision-making in the corporate bond market and is based upon my 20 years of involvement in the marketplace.

In the last ten years there have been tremendous changes in the bond market. Rarely does a day go by without the newspapers talking about takeovers, restructuring, leveraged buy outs, and the introduction of billions of dollars of junk bond debt. With this recent glut of junk bonds, the investor has numerous opportunities to increase his wealth based upon the amount of risk the investor is willing to incur. The material in this book provides the investor with ways to evaluate risk, methodologies for selecting the proper portfolio strategy, and ways to implement the strategy.

Chapter 1 introduces the reader to the corporate bond market, including risks and rewards. Chapter 2 describes the terminology of the bond market, and Chapter 3 explains how the bond market works. Chapters 4 and 5 describe the methodologies for assigning risk to bonds and the various types of corporate bonds. Chapter 6 discusses how the junk bond market works and the advantages and disadvantages of junk bond ownership. Chapter 7 shows you how to increase your return on an investment by using margin leveraging on corporate bonds. Chapter 8 identifies the most commonly used strategies for managing your own bond portfolio including the benefits of using the portfolio management software offered in this book. Chapter 9 shows you how to select and work with a bond broker. Finally, Chapter 10 introduces you to the easy-to-use mathematical formulas that you can use to select and manage bond portfolios.

1

Introduction to Corporate Bonds

TODAY'S MARKETPLACE OFFERS THE AVERAGE INDIVIDUAL MANY investment opportunities. An investor must decide how much to invest, the risks to be taken, the type of investment, and the objectives of the investment. The average investor does not perceive that he has the time necessary to understand or manage his investments and relies heavily upon financial advisors and stockbrokers. As one former executive once said, "The average person is too busy working for a living instead of learning how to make money." There are, however, several investment instruments that can be easily understood, easily "tracked" on a daily basis, and offers a wide selection of opportunities and risks. One investment opportunity is the corporate bond market.

The concept of corporate bonds is a relatively simple one. Corporate bonds are debt obligations issued in the form of certificates. When you buy a corporate bond you are, in fact, lending money to the corporation. In return for the loan, the corporation agrees to pay you interest on the loan and to repay the loan at a predetermined time. Today, there are trillions of dollars in outstanding bonds in the form of government bonds, corporate bonds, and municipal bonds.

When you purchase stock, you are part owner of the business. The corporation promises you nothing, and your stock might even depreciate. When you purchase a bond, you are a creditor rather than a part owner, and the company promises you the face value of the bond at maturity, together with semiannual interest payments. If the company were to dissolve, creditors (i.e., bondholders) most often get paid before stockholders do.

Stocks and bonds do have similarities, however. Both can be used for income as well as capital gains. You can also take as much, or as little, risk as you want with both. For example, you could buy "blue chip" bonds the same way you would buy blue chip stocks. The difference with stocks is that you have an equity position and own part of the company. With bonds, however, all you have is a promise (i.e., I.O.U.) of a set dollar amount to be paid to you each year.

There are three ways to make money with stocks and bonds: interest, interest-on-interest, and capital gains. In general, stocks generate profits mainly from dividends and capital gains whereas bonds emphasize interest and interest-on-interest.

Corporate bonds can be very advantageous to the issuer because the principal on the bond might not have to be repaid for 20 or 30 years, unlike bank loans, which require *both* principal and interest to be repaid periodically. For the privilege of using your money for 20 to 30 years, the issuer agrees to pay you semiannual interest, which might be three or four percentage points greater than bank certificates of deposit. In other words, if certificates of deposit pay seven percent, then you might find quality corporate bonds paying about 10 to 11 percent.

If corporate bonds are so good, then why doesn't everyone invest in them? There are two reasons. First, corporate bonds are instruments of indebtedness, where a company agrees to repay you for your loan at a given point in time. What if the company cannot repay you? What if the company stops making interest payments to you because of an erosion of their earnings? What if the company files for bankruptcy? Needless to say, corporate bonds run the risk of defaulting on payments. Because of this risk, corporations offer you a higher interest rate than government securities. High-risk companies must pay very high interest rates to attract investors, whereas low-risk companies can offer lower interest rates because of the reduced risk to the lender.

Both Amoco Oil Company and Pan Am Airlines have corporate bonds maturing in 2004. The current return on investment for the Amoco bond is 9.4 percent a year, whereas the Pan Am bond is 23 percent. The reason for this difference is because Amoco is regarded as a very low-risk company and Pan Am as a high-risk company. For high-risk companies, there is a concern about the ability for a company to continue paying interest and, eventually, to repay the principal.

The second reason corporate bonds lack popularity is because brokerage house account executives (AE's) make very little commission on the sale of a bond. Consider a 20-year bond that sells for $1,000. If you buy the bond and hold it until maturity, then the AE would receive a $10 commission at the purchase, nothing for the next 20 years, and perhaps even no commission at maturity. Consequently, it's no surprise that AE's have an incentive to offer you other investment opportunities where your cash is "turned over" regularly at higher commissions. Good AE's might recommend a diversified portfolio for safety. This might include bonds, stocks, and other financial instruments.

BOND BENEFITS

Corporate bonds are generally fixed-income securities that have a fixed-interest rate until the bond matures. For example, consider a corporate bond that is issued at $1,000 purchase price and has a 30-year maturity at a 9 percent interest (or coupon) rate. The interest rate of 9 percent is fixed and is referred to as the coupon rate. For the next 30 years, the issuer will pay you nine percent interest on $1,000 or $90 per year. Because most bonds pay the interest semiannually, you will receive $45 each six-month period. Regardless of the selling price of the bond, your $90 per year coupon is fixed.

Table 1-1, column one indicates that if you invest $2,000 each year (as you might in an IRA account) in this bond, and reinvest the coupon interest income in the same bond or a similar investment at the same 9 percent, at the end of 30 years your total cash value would be $297,113. At 10 percent and 11 percent coupon rates, your cash value would be $361,853 and $441,753, respectively.

Simply put, fixed-income securities allow you to project exactly what your income will be at a given point in time. Unlike stocks, which pay variable dividends based on performance, fixed-income debt securities are good income-forecasting instruments. Suppose, for example, you feel that your financial needs will require $830,000 in 30 years when you get ready to retire, you can then manage your portfolio to achieve this goal.

If we invest $3,000 a year (instead of $2,000), the 30-year cash value will be $542,768 as shown in column five of Table 1-1. Because this does not satisfy your financial requirements, you have two alternatives:

- Invest in bonds with higher coupons (i.e., lower-quality) bonds.
- Increase the annual contributions to the account.

If you invest $500 in year one, $1,000 in year two, $1,500 in year three, and so on for 30 years, the cash value will be $830,126 as shown in column six of Table 1-1. These are the types of calculations that pension plan administrators use to project retirement income for their plan members.

INTEREST-ON-INTEREST

Because the interest payment dates of bonds are semiannual, it is important to recognize the need for calculating interest-on-interest returns. For example, a couple invests $2000 on January 1 of each year into an IRA account. Table 1-2 shows the 30-year cash value for 9 and 11 percent portfolio returns. A 9 percent return with semiannual reinvestment will provide them with an additional $12,069. With an 11 percent portfolio return, the difference is $27,776. In this case, assuming they wanted to withdraw the interest each year after 30 years, their retirement income would be $3,055 more each year because of the semiannual interest-on-interest calculation.

TABLE 1-1
Wealth Accumulation (Assuming Deposits made on January 1)

End of Year	*$2000 Annual Savings at 9%*	*10%*	*11%*	*$3000 Savings at 10%*	*Arithmetic Savings at 10%**
1	2180	2200	2220	3300	550
2	4556	4620	4684	6930	1705
3	7146	7282	7419	10923	3525
4	9969	10210	10455	15315	6077
5	13046	13431	13825	20146	9434
6	16400	16974	17565	25460	13677
7	20056	20871	21717	31306	18894
8	24041	25158	26325	37736	25183
9	28384	29873	31440	44809	32651
10	33118	35060	37118	52589	41416
11	38278	40766	43420	61147	51607
12	43903	47042	50416	70561	63367
13	50034	53946	58181	80917	76853
14	56717	61540	66800	92308	92238
15	64001	69894	76368	104838	109711
16	71941	79083	86988	118621	129482
17	80595	89191	98776	133783	151780
18	90028	100310	111861	150461	176858
19	100310	112541	126385	168807	204993
20	111517	125995	142507	188987	236492
21	123733	140794	160402	211185	271691
22	137048	157073	180266	235603	310960
23	151562	174980	202315	262463	354706
24	167382	194678	226789	292009	403376
25	184626	216345	253955	324509	457463
26	203422	240179	284110	360259	517509
27	223909	266396	317582	399584	584109
28	246240	295235	354736	442842	657919
29	270581	326958	395976	490426	739660
30	297113	361853	441753	542768	830126

*Note: Arithmetic Savings are $500 for year 1, $1,000 for year 2, increasing each year by $500.

Further impact of compounded interest can be seen by investing $2,000 each year for 30 years into a security earning 11 percent interest. Figure 1-1 shows that the interest-on-interest calculation greatly exceeds the simple interest calculation the longer the duration of the investment.

TABLE 1-2
Effect of Semiannual Compounding

End of Year	*9% Compounded Annually*	*9% Compounded Semiannually*	*11% Compounded Annually*	*11% Compounded Semiannually*
1	2180	2184	2220	2226
2	4556	4569	4684	4703
3	7146	7173	7419	7461
4	9969	10017	10455	10530
5	13046	13123	13825	13947
6	16400	16515	17565	17749
7	20056	20219	21717	21981
8	24041	24264	26325	26692
9	28384	28681	31440	31935
10	33118	33504	37118	37770
11	38278	38771	43420	44265
12	43903	44523	50416	51494
13	50034	50805	58181	59541
14	56717	57664	66800	68496
15	64001	65155	76368	78464
16	71941	73335	86988	89559
17	80595	82268	98776	101907
18	90028	92022	111861	115651
19	100310	102675	126385	130949
20	111517	114307	142507	147976
21	123733	127011	160402	166927
22	137048	140883	180266	188020
23	151562	156032	202315	211497
24	167382	172575	226789	237627
25	184626	190640	253955	266711
26	203422	210368	284110	299082
27	223909	231911	317582	335112
28	246240	255437	354736	375214
29	270581	281127	395976	419849
30	297113	309182	441753	469529

INFLATION PROTECTION

Corporate bonds can provide good protection against inflation. If the inflation rate is 5.4 percent and your bonds are paying 10.36 percent, then you appear to be in a favorable financial position. But what if the inflation rate increases to 9.5 percent ten years from now? If you had been saving $3,000 per year and investing in 10 percent bonds, then in the tenth year, your coupon interest available for reinvestment would be $5,259 (see Table 1-1). Adding your $3,000 annual contribution to this, you have a total of $8,259 to invest.

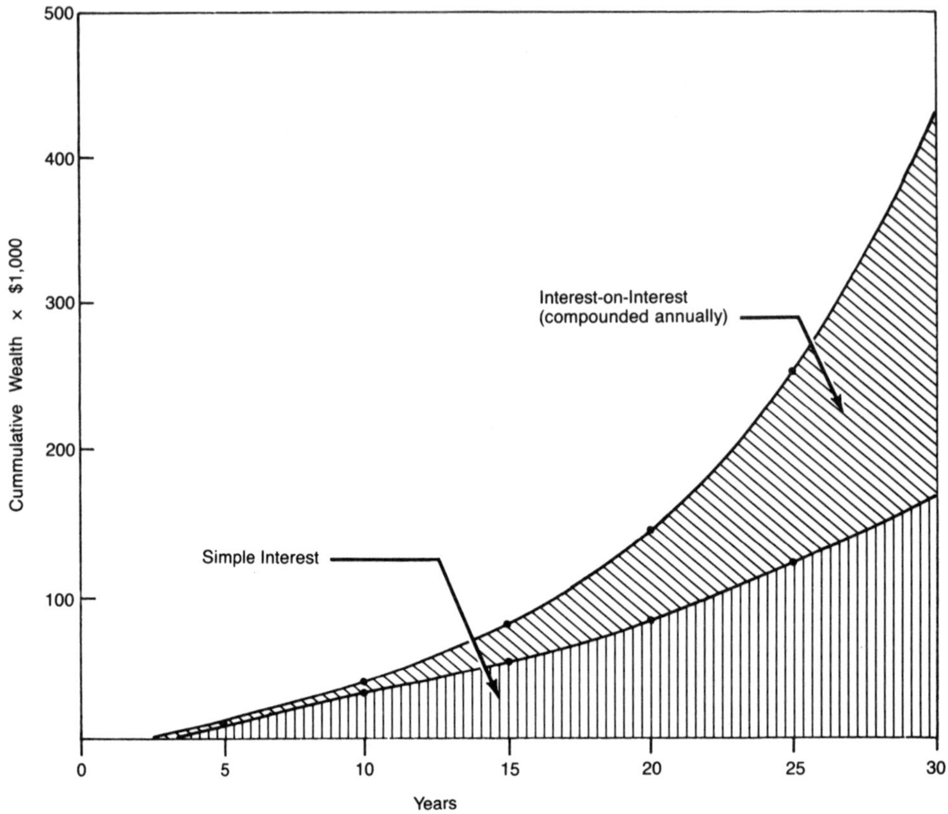

Fig. 1-1. *An IRA deposit of $2,000, invested annually at 11 percent.*

Inflation has a tendency to erode the purchasing power of the principal because of higher interest rates. If the inflation rate is 10 percent, corporate bond rates will more than likely be selling at a lower price so that the return on investment will be 12 to 13 percent. Therefore, the $8,259 available to you can be invested at 13 percent. And if you are still worried, then perhaps you can invest more than $3,000 each year. The conclusion to be drawn from this example is that corporate bonds are long-term investments and, as such, your primary objective should be the ***preservation of your capital investment*** (i.e., your original investment) and its ***purchasing power.***

Corporate bonds do not always provide a hedge against inflation. Once you purchase the bond, the coupon or interest payment is fixed through to maturity. Even large financial institutions that once purchased and then held all bonds until maturity, are now looking for profits as well as interest payments. This has resulted in a very active bond market where large profits (and hedges against inflation) are possible.

To understand the benefits of corporate bonds, you must remember that corporate bonds are long-term investments and were once considered well suited only for pension plans, profit-sharing plans, IRA's, Keogh's, and retirement savings. In recent years, there have been numerous bonds issued with coupons ranging from 10 to 15 percent, making them extremely attractive for short-term investing and the average investor. With these coupons, you can *double* your investment in five years and *triple* your investment in eight to nine years. And if the bonds are held within a qualified retirement plan (i.e., IRA, pension plan, etc.) the money grows tax-free until withdrawal. With that in mind, consider the following benefits:

- **Fixed Income**: Most corporate bonds provide fixed coupon rates. *Regardless* of the selling price of the bonds, the coupon rate is fixed so long as the companies remain solvent.
- **Income Projections**: Fixed coupon rates allow you to project, with a reasonable amount of certainty, what your gross savings will be at any point in time.
- **Preservation of Capital**: By investing in corporations with good credit ratings, you can preserve your capital and earn good income. There are many bonds that provide high returns with minimum-risk.
- **Collateral**: Bonds can be used as collateral for other financial needs.

Bond markets generally do well, regardless of the interest rates. Consider the Moody's Corporate Aaa rated bonds shown in Fig. 1-2. (Bond ratings are explained in Chapter 4.) Corporate bonds offer higher yields than municipal bonds and 10-year treasury bonds. If lower quality but higher yield bonds were included in Fig. 1-2, the spread between these lower quality bonds and the treasury/municipal bonds would have been greater.

DISADVANTAGES

As with any type of investment, there are limitations as well as benefits. Some people consider the large denominations of issues that exist with a wide variation of yields, maturities and risks, as being a disadvantage. Other limitations are:

- Interest rates. Although the coupon rate of the bond is fixed, the selling price is extremely sensitive to government and bank interest rates. The selling price of the bonds and the interest rates move in opposite directions. When interest rates drop, the selling price of the bond increases. When interest rates rise, the selling price of the bond decreases.

  For example, you have just purchased a 9 percent coupon bond for \$800. This gives you a yield (ROI) of 11.25 percent (\$90/\$800 × 100) on your investment. If interest rates increase, your bond might be selling for \$750, which would give you a 12 percent yield (i.e., to compensate for increasing interest rates). However, if interest rates fall, your bond might increase in price to \$850 giving you a yield of 10.6 percent. This example

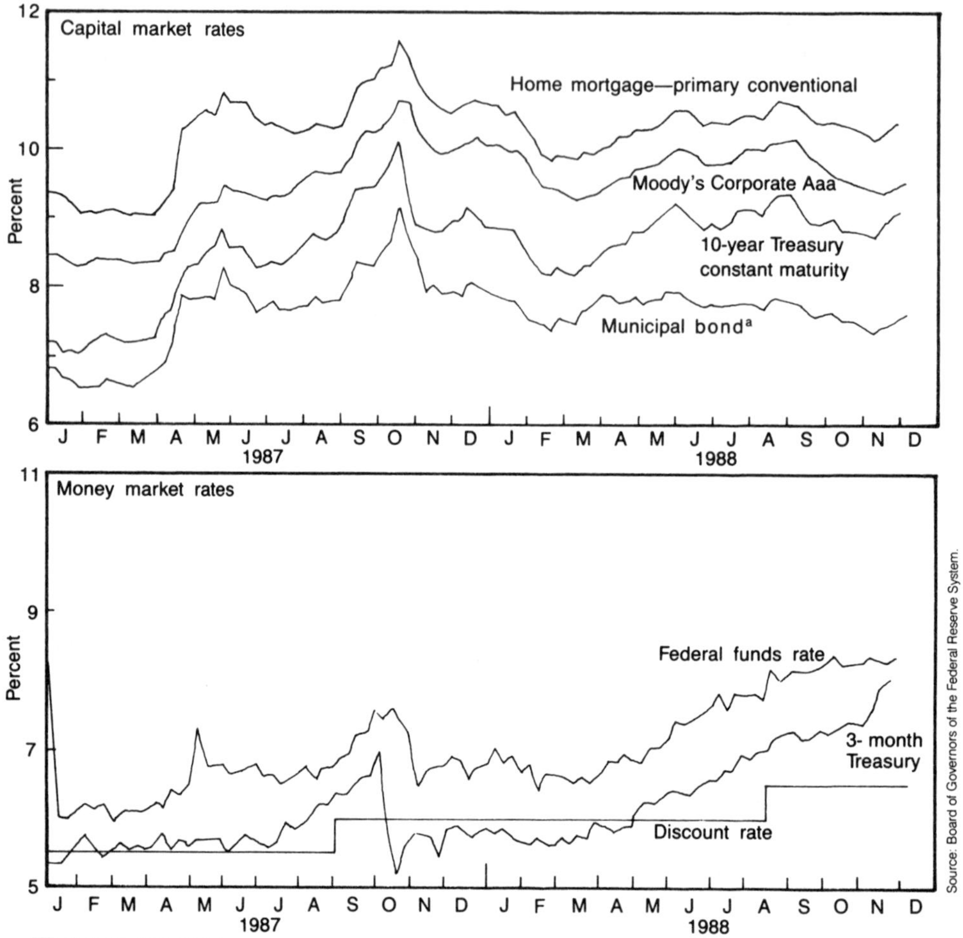

[a]Bond Buyer Index, general obligation, 20 years to maturity, mixed quality.

Fig. 1-2. *Interest rate percents, weekly averages.*

also illustrates the importance of timing when it comes to buying and selling bonds.

- Maximization of wealth. Bonds are generally a conservative investment instrument but can provide good yields at a low risk. For maximization of wealth, other investment instruments such as the stock, real estate, or commodity markets might provide more opportunities but at differing degrees of risk.
- Liquidation. Liquidation refers to how quickly you can sell an asset. For most people, bonds are long-term investment instruments and, as such, the price of the bond *at maturity* is fixed. However, selling the bonds before maturity might require a sale at a price substantially below what

you paid for it. This is particularly true during periods of rising interest rates.

Bonds traded on the New York Stock Exchange and the American Stock Exchange are generally highly liquid, whereas over-the-counter bonds are not. (Bond types are discussed in more detail in Chapter 3.) In other words, when you buy a bond, you must consider how difficult it will be to find a buyer for the bond should you want to sell in a hurry.

- Reinvestment. Let us assume that during the recession of the early 1980's, you invested your entire savings in a quality bond paying 13 percent interest and maturing in 1989. As you enter 1989, you realize that the bonds will mature in two months and to replace the bonds with new bonds of similar quality will generate only 9 percent. This is considered as the maturity reinvestment risk, where your only options are at lower coupon rates than you desire. Reinvestment risks also include your inability to reinvest coupon interest payments (during the time you hold the bond) at desired returns.

  The solution to reinvestment risks is to diversify the maturity years of the bonds you purchase. True, this is easier said than done, but your exposure to lower interest rate periods will be lessened.

- Purchasing power. Let us assume that you buy some bonds at a substantial discount, say at $700 per bond. The bonds have a coupon of 10 percent and mature in 1989. If you bought the bonds in 1982, your yield was 14.28 percent (100/700 × 100 percent). But as the bonds approach maturity, the selling price of the bonds approaches $1,000.

  Let us assume further that, in January of 1989 (the year of maturity), the bond is selling at $980. Your yield right now is 10.2 percent. If you can find bonds of comparable quality paying 11 to 12 percent coupons, then by holding on to your existing bonds your *purchasing power* is diminished. In general, holding quality bonds to maturity is advisable *as long as your purchasing power is not diminished*. This example implies that bonds should not necessarily be held to maturity. Most monthly brokerage houses' statements print out the current yield.

- Call risk. Call risks are the risk of early redemption by the issuer. Some bonds cannot be redeemed prior to the planned maturity date but other bonds have special provisions allowing for early redemption (Chapter 3 contains more detailed information on call risks). Bonds that are retired from circulation early usually pay the bondholder a premium such as $1,050 per bond rather than the expected $1,000. This may seem good for the bondholder, but more often than not, the bonds are being refinanced with the lower yield bonds. Consequentially, the bondholder might find that he has not planned for the reinvestment of the funds, and opportunities for reinvestment are available only at lower yields.

- Default risk. Default risk falls into two categories. First, because of cash flow problems, the company defaults on its semiannual payment. The second category, and the more serious one, is when the company files for bankruptcy protection under Chapter 11. Payment defaults might be temporary, whereas Chapter 11 recovery could be three or four years. If the company does not recover from Chapter 11, then the bonds can become totally worthless.

BOND VOLATILITY

There appears to be a misconception that bonds are not necessarily as volatile as stocks, and when you purchase a bond, your return is based simply upon the interest you receive. Nothing could be further from the truth. Bonds can and do fluctuate, but perhaps not in the proportions that stocks do.

Table 1-3 shows that corporate bonds can appreciate in value as well as paying a fixed interest rate. Flow General closed out in 1987 selling for $850. During

TABLE 1-3
Appreciating Bonds

Bond	*Year*	*Coupon, %*	*1988 Appreciation, $*	*1988 Appreciation, %*	*Total Return (Coupon and Appreciation), %*
Allegheny Int.*	1999	10.75	513.75	135.00	135.00
American Cyan.	2001	7.375	95.00	11.50	20.45
Assoc. Corp. N.A.	2001	6.0	156.25	26.90	37.30
Bank America	2005	8.875	91.25	11.80	23.26
Bethlehem Steel	1992	5.4	92.50	12.00	19.03
Brown Group	1998	7.375	120.00	14.03	22.66
Carter Hawley	1996	12.25	135.00	16.07	30.65
Citicorp	1998	8.30**	108.75	12.79	22.56
Duquesne Light	2009	10.125	60.00	6.38	17.15
Flow General	2004	14.30	146.25	17.20	34.02
Gulf Resources	2004	12.5	90.00	10.59	25.29
Home Shopping	1996	11.75	192.50	28.30	47.69
Navistar	2004	9.0	142.50	18.87	30.79
Reliance Group	1998	9.875	97.50	13.52	27.20
Resorts Int.	2004	16.625	172.50	21.77	42.74
Union Carbide	2006	7.5	110.00	15.71	26.43
Williams Co.	1996	9.4	148.75	17.92	29.25

*Trading without interest payments.

**Floating rate.

***Changes based on 1987 year-end closing price compared to 1988 year-end closing price.

1988, not only did Flow General pay $143 per bond in interest, but also appreciated in price to $996.25. Therefore, had you purchased the bond for $850 on January 1, 1988 and sold the bond for $996.25 on December 31, 1988, you would have earned $143 in interest plus $146.25 in appreciation for a total return of 34.02 percent. Even if the bond had not appreciated, your return would still have been 16.82 percent.

The downside risks are just as great because if a company goes bankrupt, your loss could be as much as 100 percent of your investment. Even if the bond decreases in price, however, the coupon payments are still payed as long as the company remains solvent.

People invest in stocks for dividends (usually a 2 to 4 percent return) and capital gains (i.e., where a selling price, less purchase prices results in a positive value or profit). People invest in bonds for future guaranteed income, and perhaps, little capital gains. As a result, most people, when buying bonds, plan on holding the bonds for a long time, perhaps until maturity as long as you have quality bonds that provide a hedge against inflation. If you need cash for other purposes, use the coupon interest as it becomes available rather than liquidating the bonds.

A lot of people feel a compulsion to ''dabble'' in the investment markets and fantasize about hitting it big with high-risk investments. Often it may be better and simpler to maintain two investment strategies: a retirement savings plan diversified with corporate bonds and other investment instruments and a ''mad money'' account for speculation.

2

Bond Terminology

CORPORATE BONDS HAVE THEIR OWN TERMINOLOGY, JUST AS STOCKS OR ANY other investment instruments do. The purpose of this chapter is to introduce you to bond terminology and its meaning.

PAR

The word "par" as used in bonds refers to the par value of the bond at maturity which is $1,000. Bonds selling over par, are selling over $1,000. Bonds selling under par might be selling for $800, $750, or even less. Most bonds are initially issued below par. Because par is determined by prevailing interest rates, however, the selling price might fluctuate over and under par hundreds of times until the bond matures.

BOND PRICE FLUCTUATIONS

Bond prices fluctuate on a daily basis the same way that stock prices do. Although stock prices can fluctuate as much as 5 to 10 percent daily, whereas bond prices fluctuate 1 to 2 percent. Bond prices are normally expressed as 10 percent of their actual value. For example, a bond listed at 98 actually means $980. A bond listed at 93 5/8 would be $936.25. Other examples are:

Bond Quote	*Dollar Value*
87 7/8	$878.75
101 1/8	$1011.25
96 3/4	$967.50
73 1/2	$735.00
79	$790.00

Most bonds are listed in eighths of a unit, as indicated above. One eighth indicates one-eighth of \$10 or \$1.25. Five eighths would be \$6.25. Therefore a bond quoted at $87\,^7/_8$ would be:

$$\begin{array}{lcr} 87 \quad \times 10 & = & \$870 \\ \underline{\;\;^7/_8 \times 10} & = & \underline{\;\;8.75} \\ 87\,^7/_8 & & \$878.75 \end{array}$$

Bonds that are within one year of maturity or are not paying interest (either because of bankruptcy or default) might be trading in increments of sixteenths. Therefore, when your account executive tells you that your bond is trading between $88\,^5/_8$ and $90\,^1/_4$, what he really means is \$886.25 to \$902.50.

Low-quality bonds have high yields because of the risk to the investors. These bonds are known and expected to fluctuate dramatically in price because of their sensitivity to interest rate changes. With the large volume of bonds that now exist, however, even high-quality bonds can fluctuate, perhaps more so than stocks. See Fig. 2-1.

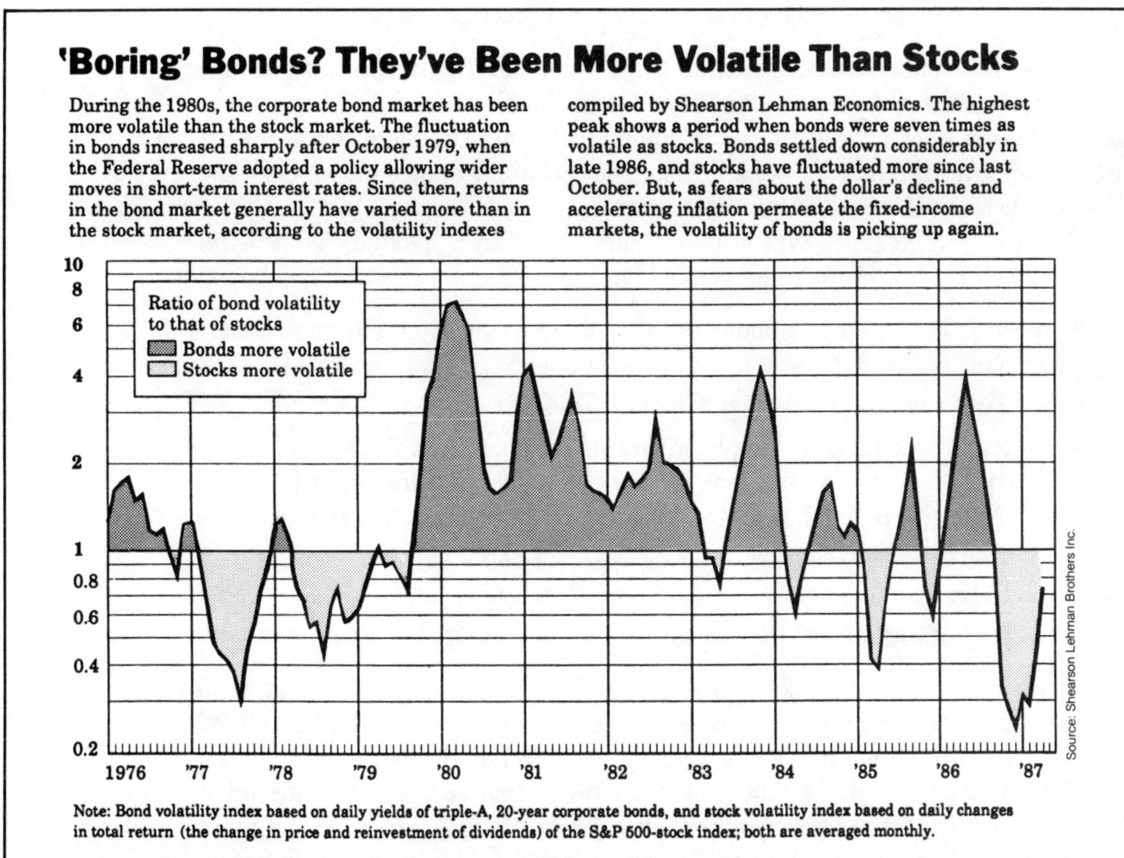

Fig. 2-1. Bond fluctuations and volatility trends compared with stocks.

UNDERSTANDING BOND QUOTES

A typical bond quote as it might appear in a newspaper would be:

			Cur Yld	*Vol*	*High*	*Low*	*Close*	*Net Chg*
DuPont	$8^1/_2$	06	9.6	35	$90^1/_4$	$88^3/_4$	$88^7/_8$	$-^1/_8$

Below is an explanation of what each item means.

DuPont	:	Bond Title
$8^1/_2$	:	Coupon is $8^1/_2$ percent
06	:	Maturity year is 2006
9.6	:	Current return is 9.6 percent
35	:	Volume of bonds traded this day
$90^1/_4$	:	Highest price paid this day, $902.50
$88^3/_4$	:	Lowest price paid this day, $887.50
$88^7/_8$	:	Last price paid this day, $888.75
$-^1/_8$	:	Last price paid was $1.25 lower than the last price quoted the previous day.

Not all newspapers contain each of these columns. *The Wall Street Journal*, for example, does not include the "high" and "low" columns. On the other hand, *Baron's Weekly* includes two additional columns; the highest and lowest selling price over the past 52 weeks. Also, since *Baron's* comes out weekly, the "Net Change" is the change from last week.

Figure 2-2 represents typical bond quotes as they appeared in *The Wall Street Journal* May 24, 1988. The symbols in the table are explained as follows:

- cv—Bonds that have coupons but can also be converted into stock, i.e., convertible bonds.
- zr—Zero Coupon Bonds (see Chapter 5)
- s —Has no meaning. It simply separates coupons from the year of maturity, i.e., 10.4s03 means 10.4 percent coupon maturing in 2003. Note that $8^1/_4$03 has no "s," since it can only mean $8^1/_4$ percent coupon maturing in 2003.
- vj—In bankruptcy, receivership, or under reorganization.
- f —Traded without accrued interest. (i.e., trading flat)

Read bond quotes carefully. Consider the Citicorp bond, which has an 8.45 percent coupon that matures in 2007. At a price of $85^1/_4$, you feel that this bond is an excellent buy. But when you ask your broker to buy this bond, he tells you that the asking price is $87^1/_2$. The reason for this is that *no* bonds are offered at the price you are willing to pay. Notice that only four of these bonds were traded. Perhaps the seller was in a hurry to raise cash and couldn't wait for a better

CORPORATION BONDS
Volume, $26,390,000

Bonds	Cur Yld	Vol	Close	Net Chg.
Advst 9s08	cv	60	78¼	...
AetnLf 8⅛07	9.2	15	88	+1
AirbF 7½11	cv	35	87	...
AlaP 9s2000	9.7	3	92¾	−¼
AlaP 8½s01	9.8	10	86¾	+1¼
AlaP 7⅞s02	9.3	5	85	...
AlaP 9½08	10.3	15	92⅝	+⅛
AlaP 12⅝10	11.9	39	106	+½
AlskH 17¾91	15.3	18	116	+½
vjAlgl 10¾99f	...	3	54¼	...
vjAlgl 10.4s02f	...	58	52	−1
AlldC zr92	...	5	67¼	−¼
AlldC zr98	...	11	38¾	+¾
AlldC zr2000	...	45	31½	+1⅛
AldC dc6s90	6.4	53	93¾	...
AlldC zr95	...	15	51	−2½
AlldC zr99	...	30	35¾	...
AlldC zr09	...	110	11½	...
AldSig 9⅞02	9.9	2	100	+1
AMAX 14¼90	13.2	5	107⅝	−⅝
AMAX 14½94	12.5	10	116	+⅜
AForP 5s30	10.0	6	50⅛	−2⅞
ABrnd 8⅝90	8.7	25	99½	+1
ACeM 6¾91	cv	9	48	−1
AmMed 9½01	cv	20	97	+¼
ATT 3⅞s90	4.1	65	93⅜	−⅛
ATT 6s00	8.2	17	73	...
ATT 8¾00	9.3	202	93¾	...
ATT 7s01	8.8	23	79⅜	+¾
ATT 7⅛03	9.1	58	78⅛	−¼
ATT 8.80s05	9.6	166	91¾	+⅝
ATT 8⅝s07	9.6	68	89½	−⅛
ATT 8⅝26	10.2	510	84¾	−¼
Amfac 5¼94	cv	93	110¾	+3¾
Amoco 6s98	7.4	2	81¼	−⅜
Amoco 9.2s04	9.7	30	95	+¾
Amoco 8⅜05	9.5	10	88½	−⅛
Amoco 7⅞96	8.7	15	90⅞	+⅜
Amoco 8⅝16	9.9	11	87	+¼
Ancp 13⅞02f	cv	12	107	+½
Andarko 5¾12	cv	95	93	...
Anhr 8s96	8.8	36	91⅛	+⅛
Anhr 5.45s91	5.9	5	91⅝	−⅝
ArizP 10⅝00	10.5	8	101⅛	−1⅜
ArkBst 7s11	7.3	41	96	+½
Arml 8½01	10.4	4	82⅛	...
ARch 10⅜95	10.0	370	104	−⅜
ARch 9¾89	9.5	2	102¼	−¼
ARch 9½96	9.5	75	99⅞	+⅛
ARch 9⅞16	10.1	90	98¼	−¾
AutDt 6½11	cv	35	110	−1
BRE 9½08	cv	65	104½	−1½
BakrHgh 9½06	cv	9	97	...
Bally 6s98	cv	20	75½	−½
Bally 10s06	cv	20	89½	−¼
BalGE 3s89	3.2	5	95	−½
BkNY 8¼10	cv	136	103	...
Banka 8¾01	10.7	4	82	−1
Bkam 8.35s07	10.9	2	76⅞	...
Bkam zr92s	...	139	65	...
Bkam zr91s	...	31	77⅛	−⅞
Bkam zr93s	...	19	61¾	+¼
BarcA 7.95s92	8.2	5	97½	−⅛
vjBASIX 8¾05	cv	2	35	...
vjBeker 15⅞03f	...	25	47¼	...
BellCn 8¾06	9.7	2	90	+¾
BellPa 8⅝06	9.8	6	88⅜	−½
BellPa 7½13	9.6	7	78	...
BellPa 9⅝14	10.1	120	95½	+¼
BellPa 9¼19	10.2	25	91	−⅞
BenCp 8.4s07	10.2	7	82¼	...
BestPr 12⅝96	12.5	60	100¾	−⅛
BethSt 4½90	4.8	33	93	+¼
BethSt 5.4s92	6.4	1	84¾	...
BethSt 9s00	10.5	12	85½	−1½
BethSt 8.45s05	10.5	258	80⅝	+⅛
BethSt 8⅜01	10.3	20	81⅜	+⅞
Bevrly 7⅝03	cv	28	55	+¾
Beverly zr03	...	208	28	+⅛
Boeing 8⅜96	8.9	68	93⅞	−½
BoisC 7s16	cv	10	111½	...
BorgW dc6s01	9.0	4	66½	−2⅞
BwnSh 9¼05	cv	12	98⅛	−⅜
BwnFer 6¼12	cv	130	84	+⅜
BurNo 10s97	9.9	40	101½	−1½
CBS 10⅞95	10.4	7	104⅛	...
CIT 9½95	9.5	30	99⅝	−⅛
CIT 8.8s93	8.9	2	98½	...
CSX 9½16	10.2	3	93	...
CPC 4sr	9.9	5	40¼	...
CaroFrt 6¼11	cv	26	79	...
CaroT 9s08	10.1	7	89	−1½
Carsn 7½11	6.9	2	108½	−1½
CartHaw 12¼96	13.1	75	93¾	−1¾
Caterp 12½90	12.3	20	101⅝	+⅛
CATS zr11-02	...	5	26¼	−1¾
CATS zr2006-11	...	5	18½	−1
Champ 6½11	cv	23	109¼	−¾
ChartC 12s99	12.7	15	94⅛	−⅛
vjChmtrn 9s94f	...	14	73¼	+¼
ChNY 8.4s99	9.5	10	88	−¾
CPoV 7¼12	9.5	5	76	+⅜
CPWV 7¼13	9.4	10	77	...
ChvrnC 11¾88	11.6	50	101⅝	−1/32
ChvrnC 11s90	10.8	40	102	...
Chvrn 5¾92	6.4	60	90⅛	+¼
Chvrn 8¾05	9.6	8	91⅜	...
Chvrn 8½95	8.9	2	95⅝	−⅝
Chvrn 8¾96	9.2	25	95⅝	−⅛
Chvrn 9⅜16	9.9	2	94⅝	+¼
ChckFul 7s12	cv	1	96½	+1½
Chryslr 8s98	9.0	29	89	+⅜
Chryslr 12¾92	11.5	15	111	+1
Chryslr 10.95s17	11.1	14	98⅝	+⅝
ChryF 11½97	11.9	1	97	...
ChryF 9⅜91	9.3	69	100½	+⅛
ChrvF 9¼91	9.2	100	100⅛	−⅞
CirclK 7¼06	cv	34	98	...
CirclK 13s97	12.9	35	101⅛	−⅞
Citicp 6.60s89t	6.6	8	100	+¼
Citicp 8.45s07	9.9	4	85⅛	−2⅛
Citicp 8⅛07	10.0	2	81⅛	−⅞
Citicp 12¼93	12.0	40	102⅛	+⅛
Citicp 12½93	12.2	10	102⅝	−⅛
CitSvG 13s05	12.4	20	105	+1
ClevEl 7⅛90	7.3	5	97	...
ClevEl 8⅜91	8.6	51	97⅞	+½
ClevEl 8¾05	10.3	25	85	−⅜
ClevEl 9¼09	10.6	5	87½	+⅜
ClevEl 9.85s10	10.7	10	92	−¼
ClevEl 8⅜12	10.3	1	81	−1½
Coastl 11¼96	11.3	5	99½	...
Coastl 11¾06	11.9	34	99	...
Coastl 8.48s91	8.9	78	95⅜	...
Coleco 14⅜02f	...	15	21¼	−1⅜
Coleco 11s89f	cv	45	21⅛	−¼
Coleco 11⅛01f	...	35	21	+⅝
Coltln 10⅛95	10.8	20	94	−¼
Coltln 11¼15	12.1	10	93	−3¼
Coltln 12½01	12.4	10	101	−¼

Source: *The Wall Street Journal*, May 24, 1988.

Fig. 2-2. Wall Street Journal *bond quotes.*

price. The point is that you cannot always buy/sell according to the newspaper quotes.

INTEREST PAYMENT DATES

Companies issuing corporate bonds are required to pay the bondholders interest. Payments are normally semiannual at precise six month intervals. These dates are referred to as Interest Payment Dates (IPD's). Most IPD's are on the 1st or 15th of the month, although there are some exceptions.

Interest payment dates can be obtained from account executives or by reading bond guides such as the Standard and Poors Bond Guide. Typical IPD's are shown in Table 2-1. Most IPD's list two months. The month identified in "bold" print or capitalized is the month for the bond's final maturity. If the IPD has a number following the two months, then the number represents the day of the

TABLE 2-1
Typical IPD's

Bond	*Coupon*	*Maturity*	*IPD*	*Remarks*
Alabama Power	7.5%	2002	Jj	Interest paid on Jan – Jul 1. Last payment on Jan 1, 2002.
Atlantic Richfield	9.25	1993	Fa15	Interest paid on February and August 15.
Consumer Power	9.0	2008	mS15	Interest paid on March and September 15, with last payment September 15, 2008.
Ford Motor Credit	8.7	1999	Ao	Interest paid on April and October 1.
Marriott Corporation	9.875	1997	Mn	Interest paid on May and November 1.
Texaco, Inc.	7.75	2001	Jd	Interest paid on June and December 1, with last payment June 1, 2001.

month when payment will be made. If there is no number following the two months, then the payment date is the 1st of the month.

Read IPD's carefully. For example, the letter "J" can mean January, June or July. The letter "A" can be April or August, and the letter "M" can be March or May. However, since the IPD's identify two months exactly six months apart, then there can be one and only one meaning of each letter. For example, "Jj" must be January to July and "Mn" must be May to November.

Although most bonds have IPD's on the 1st and 15th of the month, there are exceptions as shown in Table 2-2. Also, there are corporations that have several issues or series of bonds maturing on a regular basis over the next 30 years. Such companies include Alabama Power, General Motors Acceptance Corporation, Commonwealth Edison, Philadelphia Electric, and Chrysler. Companies with multiple bond issues usually spread out their IPD's over several different months because of cash flow. An example of this would be the Connecticut Light and Power bonds shown in Table 2-3. On the 1st of each month, Connecticut Light and Power has coupon payments to make to investors.

TABLE 2-2
Example of Nonstandard IPD's

Bond	*Coupon*	*Maturity*	*IPD**	*Remarks*
CitiCorp	9.0%	1993	Ao14	Interest paid April and October 14
Private Export Funding	8.55	1993	Mn31	Interest paid May and November 31
Marriott Corporation	9.0	1995	Mn24	Interest paid May and November 24
GATX Corporation	11.5	1996	Jd30	Interest paid June and December 30
Holiday Inns	15.0	1992	QNov15	Interest paid quarterly on Nov.15, Feb. 15, May 15, and Aug. 15, with final interest paid Nov. 15, 1992
National Medical Enterprises	12.5	2000	QMy15	Interest paid quarterly on May 15, Aug. 15, November 15, and February 15

*Note: There are also bonds with monthly IPD's, but they are very uncommon.

In recent years, with the rapid growth of the high-risk, high-yield bond market (i.e., junk bond market), underwriters have found new and intriguing ways of offering corporate bonds. One way is to defer the coupon payments until a later date, say six years from now. Another way is to vary the coupon at specified increments towards maturity, have the coupon payment based upon earnings, or have coupon payments paid with debt rather than cash. As an example, consider that on May 15, 1988 Bell and Howell issued $225.2 million of 8.25 percent senior subordinated debenture bonds. The bonds mature in 10 years and were initially offered below par at $888 per bond. Three years from the date of issue, the coupon on the bond will be increased from 8.25 to 12.875 percent. Beginning May 15, 1991, however, Bell and Howell has the right to redeem the bonds.

In 1986, National Gypsum offered more than $800 million of subordinated debenture bonds that would mature in the year 2004. The coupon on the bond is 15.5 percent, but interest does not accrue until July 1, 1991. (IPD is June 30, December 31). The bonds have traded from a low of $402.50 to a recent high of $650.

TABLE 2-3
Connecticut Power and Light Bonds

Coupon	*Year of Issue*	*Maturity*	*IPD*
4.875%	1960	1990	Fa
12.25	1983	1993	jJ
8.5	1988	1993	Ao
12.375	1984	1994	Jj
9.75	1987	1994	Mn
10.0	1987	1995	aO
8.875	1986	1996	mS
9.125	1987	1997	Ao
6.0	1967	1997	Mn
6.5	1967	1998	Jj
6.875	1968	1998	aO
8.75	1969	2000	Jj
8.875	1970	2000	aO
11.0	1975	2000	mS
7.375	1971	2001	jD
7.625	1972	2002	fA
7.625	1973	2003	Ao
8.75	1974	2004	Ms
8.875	1977	2007	Mn
9.25	1978	2008	Ms
15.0	1982	2012	aO

Also in 1986, Eckerd Holdings issued more than $340 million discounted subordinated debenture bonds that matured in 2006. Interest accrues at 13 percent from May 1, 1991 with IPD's of May and November 1. The market price has varied from $520 to $670.

All of these three cases are examples of speculative bonds with a high degree of risk in the ability of the issuer to pay semiannual interest as well as principal at maturity. These three situations can occur as a result of leveraged buy outs, reorganization, or expansion where companies feel that near-term cash flow might be critical.

BOND YIELDS

Once a bond begins to trade on the open market, the selling price can fluctuate because of supply and demand, risk, coupon percentage, interest rates, and even industry trends. Some bonds will increase while others will decrease. Quality bonds might increase by 5 percent whereas high-risk bonds might decrease from 10 to 20 percent.

The average investor needs some sort of quantitative measure to assist in selecting a bond. With all other factors being equal, the two most common measures are: Current yield and yield to maturity.

The current yield, or current return on investment, is the annual coupon payment divided by the purchase price. For example, Duquesne Light has a bond with a 9 percent coupon maturing in 2006. The selling price of the bond is currently $925. Therefore, the current yield can be calculated as follows:

$$\text{Current Yield (CY)} = \frac{\$90}{\$925} \times 100\% = 9.73\%$$

Suppose, however, that your minimum acceptable return is 10.2 percent. This means that the selling price of the bond would have to drop to $881.25 for you to achieve your 10.2 percent return. If you have a love affair with this bond, then you might wish to purchase it at the existing price or simply tell your broker to place a buy order at $88^1/_8$. If the selling price fluctuates enough, you might get lucky and buy your bond quickly.

For bonds selling over par, the current yield is calculated the same way. For example, Fruit of the Loom has a $12^3/_8$ percent coupon bond maturing in 2003 and was selling at $102. The current yield would be 12.13 percent.

The current yield identifies your return on investment **today**. But as I mentioned in Chapter 1, most bondholders consider holding their bonds until maturity. Is it wise to hold the bond to maturity? What measurement can I make to assist me in making a decision? The answer to these two questions requires the calculation of the yield to maturity (YTM). Consider the three bonds shown below, simply labeled A, B, and C.

Title	*Coupon, %*	*Current Selling Price*	*Current Yield, %*
A	9	$88^1/_8$	10.2
B	10.8	98	11.0
C	13	$106^1/_2$	12.2

Assume that your minimum acceptable return is 10 percent. All three bonds satisfy your requirements but, being a shrewd investor, you want to maximize your return. Which bond is best? If you simply use the current yield, you would select Bond C. But a better measure would be the YTM, especially if you plan on holding the bond.

To calculate the yield to maturity, you must use the year of maturity together with the information previously shown. Assume that it is now 1989 and all three bonds mature three years from now in 1992. The following steps can be used to calculate the YTM: (Example here is for Bond A)

Step 1: Subtract the current selling price of $881.25 from $1,000. This gives you $118.75. In other words, Bond A will *appreciate* in value by $118.75 between now and maturity. (Note that Bond C, which is currently selling over par, will *depreciate* by $65 between now and maturity.)

Step 2: Determine the annual appreciation or depreciation by dividing your answer in Step 1 by the remaining years to maturity. Since there are three years to maturity, Bond A will appreciate by $39.58 each year.[1] (Note that for Bond C, the annual appreciation is negative.) The value you calculate here is your annual expected capital gain.

Step 3: Add the annual capital gain to the annual coupon to obtain your annual return (i.e., $90 + 39.58 = $129.58). This is your total earnings each year to maturity.

Step 4: Divide your annual return to maturity of $129.58 by the *current* selling price of $881.25. This will give you a return of 14.7 percent.

For a quick and dirty calculation of YTM, steps 1–4 will suffice. This is where most investors stop in their calculations; and this is acceptable if you simply wish to compare various bonds. For a more precise calculation, however, there are three additional steps. The problem with stopping at Step 4 is that as you approach maturity, the selling price of the bond will either increase or decrease towards par of $1,000.

Step 5: Calculate the selling price of the bond in the year before maturity. In other words, subtract your answer in Step 2 from $1,000 to give you a selling price of $960.42 in the year 1991. (If the bond were selling over par, you would *add* this value to $1,000.)

Step 6: Calculate the annual return on investment for 1991 by dividing your annual return of $129.58 by the expected selling price of $960.42. This gives you a 13.5 percent yield for 1991.

Step 7: Take the average value of steps 4 and 6, (i.e., [14.7% + 13.5%] ÷ 2 = 14.1%). This is your average annual return until maturity.

Calculate all seven steps for each of the three bonds, and you'll find that the bond with the smallest current yield had the best YTM. This is not always the case.

---

[1]Actual maturity curves are not linear. But for YTM calculations, it is common practice to assume linearity.

Bond	*Current Yield*	*Yield To Maturity*
A	10.2%	14.1 %
B	11.0	11.32
C	12.2	10.375

Simply stated, as a bond approaches maturity, your current yield will change because the selling price will approach $1,000. The yield to maturity, therefore, provides you with an *average current yield* for each year.

The yield to maturity is often considered to be a better measure for bond selection than the current yield. Because the selling price of bonds fluctuate, however, you should recalculate the yield to maturity. For example, suppose your bond has dramatically increased in price to the point where your yield to maturity has *decreased* from 11.45 percent to 10.3 percent. If you can find other bonds that provide a greater YTM than 10.3 percent, then you might want to sell your existing bonds and purchase the others.

This example does not necessarily hold true for current yield calculations, because, although your current yield might *decrease* as the bond prices increase, you might find that other bonds with higher current yields still cannot give you the same yield to maturity.

ACCRUED INTEREST

When a bondholder sells his bonds between interest payment dates, he is entitled to the accrued or earned interest from the last IPD. The corporation that originally issued the bond pledges to pay on the IPD. Therefore, the buyer must pay to the seller the accrued interest. The buyer is then "reimbursed" for the accrued interest payment on the next semiannual interest payment date. In order to understand accrued interest, two dates must be defined:

- Transaction Date. This is the date when the transaction to buy or sell the bond was made and ownership changes hands.
- Settlement Date. The settlement date is the date where the new owner *begins* earning interest.

Settlement dates are five working days (seven calendar days) after the transaction date unless a holiday occurs in between. Five days is the standard for settlement dates. These five days include:

- Processing and mailing the confirmation slips to the buyer and seller.
- Delivery of the certificates by the seller.
- Transferring the required funds by the buyer.

When a bond is sold, the seller receives accrued interest up to, but *not* including, the settlement date. The buyer begins receiving interest *on* the settlement. Note that the transaction date is not included in calculating accrued interest. Also, unlike many certificates of deposit, there are no penalties for buying/selling between IPD's.

When investing in bonds, it is good practice to understand how accrued interest is calculated, not only to verify the amounts in the confirmation slips, but to determine beforehand exactly how much money you must come up with in order to make the purchase. There are three guidelines you should follow to calculate accrued interest:

- Each year has 360 days.
- The 360 days are broken down into 12 months and each month has 30 days.
- The settlement date is *not* included in the calculation of accrued interest.

To illustrate the calculation of accrued interest, consider the following bond data:

Title: Best Products
Coupon: 12⅝ percent
IPD's: June, December 1st
Bond Cost: $982.50
Transaction Date: October 3
Broker Commission: $10.00/bond
Brokerage Handling Cost: $2.35/transaction

Step 1. Calculate the daily interest by dividing the coupon rate by 360 days:

$$\$126.25 \div 360 \text{ days} = 35.069¢/\text{day}$$

Therefore, for each day you own the bond, you will earn approximately 35 cents.

Step 2. Calculate the number of days from the last IPD to the settlement date. If the transaction date is October 3, then the settlement date is October 10. The accrued interest must be paid up to, but *not* including, the settlement day (i.e., through October 9th.).

Month	*Days of Accrued Interest*
June	30
July	30
August	30
September	30
October	9
	129

Step 3. Calculate the accrued interest by multiplying the daily interest rate by the number of days.

$$(\$.35069/\text{day}) \times (129 \text{ days}) = \$45.24$$

Therefore, the seller is entitled to $45.24 in accrued interest to be paid by the buyer. On December 1st (the IPD), Best Products will pay you the semiannual interest of $63.13. The IRS considers the entire $63.13 taxable but allows you to subtract the accrued interest paid as long as you receive paid, rather than accrued interest from this bond in the same year. In the case of the Best Products bond, since interest was paid on December 1, you pay tax on the difference between the paid interest by Best Products and the accrued interest you paid the seller. Had you purchased the bond in October, but the IPD was February 1, the accrued interest is *not* deductible until the year in which the next IPD occurs. Use the following tax guidelines:

- For the seller, the accrued interest is taxable in the year of the sale because the accrued interest was paid.
- For the buyer, the accrued interest paid is a deductible expense only if an IPD occurs within the same year following the settlement date. Otherwise, the accrued interest must be expensed the following year.

Returning to the Best Products bond, you can now calculate the total cost to the buyer:

Purchase Price:	$982.50
Accrued Interest:	45.24
Commission:	10.00
Handling Cost:	2.35
	$1040.09

The seller will receive the following:

Selling Price:	$982.50
Accrued Interest:	45.24
	$1027.74
Less Commission:	10.00
Less Handling Cost:	2.35
	$1015.39

MATURITY

The expiration date on a bond is the maturity date where the issuer promises to repay the bondholder the face value of the bond. Before the maturity date, the selling price of the bond might fluctuate well above or below the face value of $1,000 per bond.

When bonds are first issued, the maturity date of the bond is specified. Utility bonds are issued for 25 to 30 years before maturity. Intermediate maturities might run from 10 to 20 years, or even less. Bonds issued with maturities of less than 10 years are referred to as notes. Although rare, some railroad bonds have been issued with 50 years until maturity.

The length of maturity of a bond is determined by the corporation's need for cash and the current or predicted market conditions. Companies needing cash to expand might want to offer 25 to 30 year bonds, whereas companies with short-term financial woes might issue 5 to 10 year notes. Corporations want to provide the lowest acceptable coupon and lock the investor into this coupon for the maximum number of years. On the other hand, the investor wants the largest coupon rate. Based on current economic conditions, investors might purchase a five-year note with a coupon rate based upon the risk the investor is willing to incur.

- If the prime rate is 9 percent and expected to increase, investors are unlikely to purchase 30-year notes with a nine percent coupon.
- If the prime rate is 9 percent and expected to decrease, investors might accept a 30-year note at perhaps a 10 to 10.5 percent coupon.
- If the prime rate is 9 percent and expected to decrease, investors accept a five-year note with a 9.5 percent coupon.

Of course, the quality of the bond and company repayment history play an important role.

When prime lending rates are low, corporations flood the floor of the exchanges with new issues at low coupon rates trying to lock the investors in for 20 to 30 years. The smart investor, however, realizes that over the long run, this investment might not provide a hedge against inflation and might look for higher yield (i.e., lower quality) bonds or bonds with less than five years to maturity. Of course, if the prime lending rates were to decrease further, then the investor will see further benefits.

EARLY REDEMPTION

In practice, a large percentage of corporate bonds are paid off well before they ever reach maturity. When a corporation issues a bond, it will be stated either on the bond itself or in the prospectus that the bond is subject to early redemption. This is referred to as the "call" feature of the bond and means that the bond could be called in by the issuer prior to maturity and providing that certain conditions exist.

Today, almost all bonds have call features. If a bond has a 30-year maturity date, then the corporation might promise that the bonds will not be callable for five or ten years after the date of issue. Bonds with high coupons, especially those that sell over par, must have at least five to ten years of noncallable protection in order to attract investors. The bond issuer has the right to exercise the call option at *any* time on or after the call date. Some call dates are never exercised at all.

When a bond is called, the issuer pays the bondholder at least the face value of the bond or more. Most often, when a company identifies the call date, it will also identify the call price. Bonds with low coupons will most often be called at par (i.e., $1,000). Bonds with double-digit coupons might be called at a premium of 2 to 10 percent over par based upon the terms and conditions of the indenture. If the call date is relatively close to the issue date, then the call premium might be one year's interest. Table 2-3 identifies bonds that have been called in and the call premium. Table 2-3 can tell us quite a bit about prevailing interest rates:

- If interest rates are low and the bond's coupon is high, the bonds almost assuredly will be called in as early as possible.
- When the risk of being called in is great, the bond's selling price will approach the call price.
- If the interest rates are high, the risk of a call still exists for high coupon bonds, but perhaps to a lesser degree.

When interest rates are low, investors can loose large sums of money because of a call. For example, Collins Food was called in at $100 and the month before was selling for $109 1/4. Minnesota Power and Light was selling at $114 and two months later was called in at $106.52. Calling in a bond can also be favorable as in the Valero bond, which was selling at $101 1/2 in January and four months later was called in at $110.948.

There are four reasons why a company might want to retire the bonds earlier than maturity:

- To refinance the bonds at a lower interest rate.
- To reduce the debt in an orderly fashion, perhaps because of improved cash flow conditions.
- To eliminate the entire debt if funds are available.
- To get out of restrictive covenants (i.e., agreements in the way the company will conduct business until the bonds are out of circulation).

TABLE 2-4
Executed Call Dates

Bond	*Call Date*	*Call* Price*	*Remarks*
Collins Food 12% 2008	04-30-87	100	Selling at $109^1/_4$ prior month
Minnesota Power & Light $10^1/_2$ 2005	04-22-87	106.52	Selling at 114 2/87
Valero Natural Gas $13^1/_2$ 2003	05-22-87	110.948	Selling at $101^1/_2$ Jan. 87
Tennessee Gas Pipeline $14^1/_2$% 1991	06-01-88	100	High for 1988 was 103
Atlantic Richfield $11^3/_8$% 2010	05-2-88	107.57	High for 1988 was 108
Dayton Hudson $14^3/_4$% 2012	06-01-88	100	High for 1988 was 111
Eastern Edison $12^1/_4$% 2013	05-01-88	109.48	Month before selling for $106^1/_8$
Xerox Credit $15^1/_4$% 1991	05-05-88	100	1988 high was $103^1/_2$ 1987 high was $111^1/_2$

*Note: Call price generally does not include accrued interest, which is paid up through the call date.

Consider a company that, during the recession of the early 1980's, issued $300 million in bonds with a 12 percent coupon. Following the recession, the interest rates had dropped such that the same bonds could now be issued with a 10 percent coupon. With a 12 percent coupon, the company's annual interest payment is $36 million. If it could refinance the debt with a 10 percent coupon, the company would save $6 million a year. This savings would more than offset the administration and underwriting cost of financing a new issue.

The company issuing this bond must provide the investor with some degree of "call protection." A five year time limit is relatively typical. When companies issue bonds, they must declare in the prospectus how the money will be used. In other words, they must declare in the new issue that the money is to be used to refinance existing debt at a lower interest rate. Issuing false statements in an attempt to deceive investors can lead to legal battles.

To reduce debt in an orderly fashion, some companies use a "sinking fund." A sinking fund is controlled by the bond's trustee, who must act to protect the interests of the investors. The sinking fund might specify exactly how many bonds (i.e., dollars) can be retired each year, or might simply be open-ended based on cash flow and profitability.

For example, Charter Medical Corporation has a 12.875 percent coupon bond maturing in 2005. The prospectus stated that the bonds are redeemable at the company's option on or after June 1, 1990 at the following prices, expressed as percentages of the principal amount:

Date	*Percent of Principal*
1990	106.4375*
1991	105.1500
1992	103.8625
1993	102.5750
1994	101.2875
1995	100.0000

*The percentage column reads: 106.4375 percent, which means 106.4375 percent × $1,000 = $1064.375

Figures 2-3 and 2-4 identify typical prospectus summaries. In Fig. 2-4, Eastern Airlines called in the bonds at par on October 15, 1987. Note that Fig. 2-4, Western Airlines, was acquired by Delta Airline. The Western Airline Bonds were then upgraded in quality from speculative to investment grade and the bonds were called in at par on June 15, 1988. In Fig. 2-5, the Beverly bond was redeemed in February 1986 for $1,000. Unfortunately, the day before the redemption announcement, the bonds were selling at $1,050. The trustee of a sinking fund has two choices to reduce debt: Call in a certain number of bonds by lottery; or purchase the bonds in the open market.

The lottery usually occurs on, or slightly before, each interest payment date. If the bonds are selling below par, or if the market price is over par but less than the sinking fund redemption price, then it benefits the trustee to purchase the bonds on the open market.

Bondholders can benefit from sinking funds. First, sinking funds reduce the company's outstanding debt, thereby lowering the bondholder's risk. Second, if the bonds are selling below the sinking fund call price, then the sinking fund will maintain the market price close to the call price.

Market equilibrium around the call price will not occur if the bond's selling price is drastically depressed. For example, consider the prospectus summary shown in Figure 2-6 for Pan American World Airways. In April, 1988 the bond was selling at $650. Since the redemption is optional until 1994, it seems very unlikely that Pan American would redeem bonds at $1,060 when they could buy them at $650 on the exchange floor.

The disadvantage of the sinking fund is when the bonds are selling well above the sinking fund price. Alaska Housing (rated AAA by Standard and

Company:	Eastern Airlines
Coupon:	16.125%
Maturity:	October 15, 2002
Amount Issued:	$188 million
Amount Outstanding:	$188 million
Issue Date:	October 7, 1982
Type:	Secured Equipment Certificates, Series C
Average Life:	12.7 years
Current Ratings:	B3/CCC
Interest Payable:	April 15 and October 15
Use of Proceeds:	To finance 51 – 53% of the equipment cost of the underlying collateral, described below.
Security:	Secured by 10 new B757-225 aircraft. Fifteen new B-757-225 were scheduled to be delivered to the Company during 1982 – 1983 and prices ranging from $29.5 mil. to $35 mil. per aircraft.
Mandatory Redemption:	Through operation of a sinking fund, beginning October 15, 1993 and continuing through October 15, 2001. The principal amount to be redeemed each year is set forth below:

Date	Percent
October 15, 1993	10.0000%
October 15, 1994	11.1111%
October 15, 1995	12.5000%
October 15, 1996	14.2857%
October 15, 1997	16.6667%
October 15, 1998	20.0000%
October 15, 1999	25.0000%
October 15, 2000	33.3333%
October 15, 2001	50.5000%
October 15, 2002	100.0000%

The sinking fund is calculated to retire 90% of the issue prior to maturity.

Optional Redemption:	The Certificates are redeemable at 100% of principal amount plus accrued interest at the option Eastern on or after October 15, 1987.
Price Yield at 8/13/85:	107.50/14.89%

Fig. 2-3. *An Eastern Airlines prospectus.*

Company:	Western Airlines
Coupon:	10.75%
Maturity:	June 15, 1998
Amount Issued:	$90 million
Amount Outstanding:	$90 million
Issue Date:	June 16, 1983
Type:	Senior Secured Trust Notes with Common Stock and Warrants
Average Life:	8.5 years
Current Ratings:	B2/B –
Interest Payable:	June 15 and December 15
Use of Proceeds:	Prepayment of approximately $78 mil. of existing indebtedness with the balance to be used for general corporate purposes.
Security:	Title to 3 used MD DC-10-10 aircraft and 4 used B-727-200ADV aircraft with an appraised value of approximately $90.4 mil. at 6/1/83.
Mandatory Redemption:	The Company must retire $9 mil. principal amount of the Trust Notes each June 15 1989 – 1997 at par plus accrued interest, calculated to retire 90% prior to maturity.
Optional Redemption:	Redeemable at any time at the Company's option at par plus accrued interest provided that the Notes are not redeemed prior to June 15, 1988 using borrowed funds having an interest cost of less than 10.75%.
Description of the Unit:	The issue was a unit with each unit consisting of a $1000 principal mount 10 3/4% Senior Secured Note due 1998, 36 shares of common stock of Western Airlines and warrants to purchase 100 shares of common stock at $9.50 per share. The warrants expire June 15, 1993 but this date may be accelerated by Western to as early as June 15, 1988 in the event the common stock trades at 125% of the then effective exercise price of the warrants for at least 30 consecutive trading days. The warrants are callable by Western at $3.00 per share on or after June 15, 1986 if the price of the common stock is at least 125% of the then effective price of the warrant.
Price/Yield at 8/13/85:	82.25/13.72%

Fig. 2-4. *A Western Airlines prospectus.*

Company:	Beverly Enterprises
Coupon:	15%
Maturity:	June 15, 2002
Amount Issued:	$70 million
Issue Date:	June 7, 1982
Type:	Subordinated Debentures
Offering Price Yield:	85.023/17.75%
Current Price Yield:	106.50/13.979%
Ratings at Issuance:	Ba3/B +
Current Ratings:	Ba3/BB –
Interest Payable:	June 15 and December 15
Use of Proceeds:	Added to working capital and primarily used to finance acquisition of additional facilities and retirement living units.
Mandatory Redemption:	Annual sinking fund payments of $10 million will commence June 15, 1993, calculated to retire 90% of the issue prior to maturity.
Optional Redemption:	Redeemable at any time at par accrued. Not refundable prior to June 15, 1987.

Fig. 2-5. *A Beverly prospectus.*

Poor's) had a bond selling at $1,180 and was called in at $1,000. These investors suddenly found that they lost 15 to 18 percent of their initial investment in *one day* on an AAA-rated bond. The moral to the story is to avoid buying or holding on to bonds that are selling above the call price and beyond the early redemption date. The risks might be great.

The third way of reducing debt is to call in the entire issue with funds from profits. Calling in the entire issue is not the same as refinancing, because the company does not issue new securities. Figure 2-7 shows examples taken from Standard and Poor's *Bond Guide*.

In the case of the Atlantic Richfield bond, the footnote "13" indicates that the bond cannot be refinanced until on or after May 1, 1990 and that each bondholder will receive $1,066.80. Footnote "14" indicates that the sinking fund cannot begin until May 1, 1991 and the bonds will be called in at $1,000. The last column, entitled "Regular," is used to call in the entire issue for retirement, not refunding. The symbol "±" indicates that the redemption price will change periodically, usually to a lower value approaching par of $1,000. In the Blair and Company bond, the regular redemption price is fixed at $1,045.60 and the sinking fund cannot begin until January 15, 1993. Note also that the Blair and Company bond has no provision for refunding.

Company:	Pan American World Airways
Coupon:	15.00%
Maturity:	April 15, 2004
Amount Issued:	$130 million
Amount Outstanding:	$130 million
Issue Date:	March 30, 1984
Type:	Senior Debentures
Average Life:	14.9 years
Current Ratings:	B3/B –
Interest Payment Dates:	April 15 and October 15
Use of Proceeds:	To be used for general corporate purposes, which includes working capital and capital expenditures.
Security:	Unsecured
Mandatory Redemption:	Pursuant to the operation of a sinking fund, $9.75 million to be retired annually beginning April 15, 1994, calculated to retire 75% of the issue prior to maturity.
Optional Redemption:	Redeemable at the Company's option at any time at whole or in part at the redemption prices set forth below plus accrued interest. The prices are 110% initially, expressed as a percentage of principal amount, and as follows for the following years: April 15, 1985 109% April 15, 1986 108% April 15, 1987 107% April 15, 1988 106% April 15, 1989 105% April 15, 1990 104% April 15, 1991 103% April 15, 1992 102% April 15, 1993 101% Thereafter at 100% provided that the Debentures are not redeemed prior to April 15, 1989 using borrowed funds having an interest cost of less than 15%.
Price/Yield at 8/13/85:	102.75/14.56%

Fig. 2-6. *A Pan Am prospectus.*

In the Southern Union bond, the symbol "NC" stands for noncallable. This bond cannot be redeemed until the year of maturity, 1994. The Detroit Edison bond has no provision for refinancing or sinking fund, and the regular redemption price will change as the maturity year approaches.

Bond			Refund Earliest/ Other	Redemption Provisions Call Price For S.F.	Regular
			13	14	
Atlantic Richfield			106.68	100	± 108.01
	$11\frac{3}{8}\%$	2010			
Blair and Co.	$13\frac{5}{8}\%$	1998		25	
				100	104.56
					32
Capital Holding	12.15%	1992			100
Detroit Edison	$10\frac{7}{8}\%$	2009			± 106.86
Southern Union	$10\frac{1}{8}\%$	1994			NC

13. 5-1-90 14. 5-1-91 25. 1-15-93 32. 1-15-90

Fig. 2-7. *A corporation can reduce a debt by using profits to call in the entire issue.*

BUYING BONDS OVER PAR

The years 1984 to 1986 proved to be lucrative years for corporate bond attorneys. During the early 1980's, company's flooded the marketplace with high coupon bonds thinking that double-digit interest rates would continue, gasoline would cost $2 a gallon by 1985, nuclear power would be readily accepted by all, and that construction costs of nuclear power plants were predictable within acceptable tolerances. Unfortunately for these corporations, gasoline prices dropped to 80 cents a gallon, interest rates decreased, and perhaps 80 percent of all nuclear power plants were terminated, even after 80 to 90 percent of the construction was completed.

As a result, corporations were hiring financial attorneys looking for ways to call in bonds early, even though the prospectus clearly indicated the terms and conditions. Numerous law suits occurred because investors who thought that they were "protected," suddenly found their cash flow lowered by as much as 40 to 50 percent. In addition, many investors took large losses because the bonds were called in at a price substantially lower than the current market price.

By the early 1990's, perhaps as much as $10 billion worth of corporate bonds will be available for recall. This is particularly true if interest rates continue to drop. Bondholders run a risk if interest rates drop and the bonds are called in. Although the bondholders get their money back plus perhaps a premium, their cash flow may be dramatically reduced if lower yield bonds are the only ones available. Perhaps the investor should sell his callable bonds while there still exist good investment opportunities in noncallable bonds or bonds that do not mature in the near term.

Neither the average investor nor the account executive has the time to review the prospectus for all bonds. As a result, the average investor may be better off investing in bonds selling below par provided that the company's performance is not overly poor. If the bonds are called, there will be a capital gain.

Also, bonds selling below par are less likely to be called making it easier to forecast cash flow. It is true, however, that for this protection against calls, the investor might have to accept a somewhat lower cash flow.

3

How the Bond Market Works

THE BOND MARKET OFTEN FASCINATES THE AVERAGE INVESTOR WHO, MORE often than not, has a poor understanding of how bonds are issued and make it to the marketplace. The purpose of this chapter is to solve the mystery.

THE INITIAL OFFERING

Virtually every corporation that wants to raise cash through the sale of bonds goes through an "investment banker." These investment bankers are not only financial institutions, but brokerage houses as well. Today, brokerage houses are offering many of the same services as banks do.

The investment banker will agree to purchase all of the securities being offered and then sell the securities to their clients. If the initial offering is large or is a high risk, then several investment bankers and securities brokerage houses will team up or syndicate to purchase the initial offering. The more widely known the corporation making the offer, the more important it is to use nationally recognized securities brokers and investment bankers. For the small or locally known issues, a local investment banker might be advantageous.

The investment banker receives a commission from the issuer for the sale of each bond. Typical commissions are $8.75 to $10 for each $1,000 bond. If the bond is high risk or could prove difficult to sell, then the investment banker might negotiate a higher commission, say $11 to $12 per bond. To illustrate the process of bond sales, consider the following scenario:

1. Company X wishes to raise $300 million for either plant expansion or acquisition.

2. Company X then solicits advice from an investment banker on the coupon for the bond, the years to maturity, and other such factors.
3. The investment banker provides advice, recommendations and alternatives to Company X, based on the prevailing interest rates and the company's past history in repaying debt. This advice involves how much money it can potentially raise, the interest rate it must pay, and how to advertise.
4. After an agreement is reached, the investment banker purchases the issue and tries to solicit sales from its clients.

These four steps are referred to as "underwriting a bond issue." Underwriters are committed to finding homes for all, or part, of the issue. For both large and small issues, underwriters first approach pension fund managers who control billions of dollars in retirement monies in hopes of placing a large percentage of the issue.This process is referred to as the *initial offering,* and it is not uncommon for some underwriters to require a minimum purchase of $100,000. For bonds that are difficult to place, brokerage houses might ask their account executives to contact small clients and offer them the bonds in increments of $10,000 or less. Unfortunately, more often than not, the small investor might not be invited to participate in the initial offering.

Because the coupon rates on today's bonds are extremely attractive and institutional demand for corporate bonds is so great, an underwriter might place an entire issue of $150 million or more with just one or two clients. This is referred to as "private placement" and might very well account for as much as 30 to 40 percent of all bond offerings. Companies do not necessarily need underwriters, however, for private placement. Underwriters prefer this approach because it also eliminates their advertising and distribution costs. Private placement usually goes to high-volume bond purchasers such as institutional investors, pension funds, banks, charitable foundations, and insurance companies.

If your broker calls you to purchase initial offering bonds, he will tell you that you will *not* have to pay any commission, and the accrued interest from the date of issue might be small. To illustrate where the investment banker makes its money, look at the table below where the underwriters agree to a commission of $8.75 for each bond (assume a company wished to raise $291 million).

	Price to Public	*Underwriter's Commission*	*Proceeds to Company X*
Per Bond	981.25	8.75	$972.50
Total	$294,370,000	$2,625,000	$291,750,000

These examples illustrate several key points:

- The underwriter's commission is paid out of the sale of the bonds. The company had to offer $300 million at maturity to raise $294 million gross in order to net $291 million.
- The price to the public could be well below par, or even above par, based on the coupon, risk, and years to maturity. Most offerings are near par.
- The underwriter's commission is generally three quarters to one percent of the gross offering.

If the initial offering is not sold out, then the underwriters might be at risk for the unsold bonds. Some underwriters might buy perhaps 5 to 10 percent of the bonds for their own portfolios, whereas other underwriters might hold the bonds for a short period of time anticipating that the selling price of the bond will increase.

If the underwriter cannot sell the bonds, then he might offer salesmen increased commissions for soliciting orders. As an example, consider the following:

"Oversupply jitters also arose in the tax-exempt sector on Tuesday when an icy reception was accorded to $125 million of Connecticut bonds priced to yield between 5.4 percent in 1980 and 6.05 percent in 1999. Only $55 million of the double-A securities were retailed today. Eventually, however, the remainder sold briskly owing to a determined effort by salesmen who had been offered an increased commission fee for soliciting orders."[1]

"Bond salesmen were inspired by a sizeable $11 credit for every $1,000 of new Louisiana Power & Light Co. bonds they could retail. Thus, in the face of a very weak market for older utility bonds, this $45 million issue was said to be 75 percent placed by last night."[2]

The role of investment bankers and underwriters can be expected to diminish over the next several years. The Securities and Exchange Commission (SEC) has authorized a regulation known as the "Shelf Rule" or "Rule 415." This allows companies to file a registration form (with the SEC) stating the amount of bonds they want to sell over the next year or two. It also allows the company to eliminate the underwriting costs and market the securities any way they want.

PROSPECTUS SUMMARY INFORMATION

To understand what a prospectus is, consider the prospectus for the 14 percent first mortgage bonds for the Trump Taj Mahal underwritten by Merrill Lynch on

---

[1] *Barron's* Weekly Bond Column, March 5, 1979.

[2] *Wall Street Journal*, April 27, 1979.

November 9, 1988. The following information appeared on the cover page of the prospectus:

$675,000,000
Trump Taj Mahal Funding, Inc.
14% First Mortgage Bonds, Series A, due 1998
Guaranty of Payment by
Trump Taj Mahal Associates Limited Partnership

The 14% First Mortgage Bonds, Series A, due 1998 (the "Bonds") are being issued by Trump Taj Mahal Funding, Inc., (the "Company") and will be secured by an assignment of a promissory note (the "Note") of Trump Taj Mahal Associates Limited Partnership (the "Partnership"), in the aggregate amount of $675,000,000, evidencing the loan to it by the Company of the gross proceeds of this offering, and a mortgage on and other documents evidencing a security interest in (the "Mortgage") the casino/hotel and convention center complex to be acquired by the Partnership from Resorts International, Inc. and certain of its subsidiaries, which is being constructed on The Boardwalk in Atlantic City, New Jersey (the "Taj Mahal"), and certain other property herein described. The Collateral for the Bonds will not include cash and Permitted Investments of the Partnership, including any proceeds from the sale of the Bonds held by the Partnership until expended. The Partnership expects substantially all of the Taj Mahal will be open to the public for gaming business on or about February 15, 1990. See "Properties of the Partnership—Appraisals" for a description of appraisals of the Taj Mahal as of March 31, 1988 (as an uncompleted facility) and as of February 15, 1990 (assuming completion and opening of the Taj Mahal). The appraisals, in the opinion of the appraisers, conform with the guidelines regarding appraisal procedures set forth in regulations governing Federal savings institutions.

The Partnership will issue a guaranty of the payment of the principal of, premium, if any, and interest on the Bonds (the "Guaranty"). The Bondholders and the Company will have recourse to all of the assets of the Partnership excluding cash permitted to be distributed by the Indenture, regardless of whether such cash has been distributed. Cash is not distributable by the Partnership to its Partners unless certain coverage tests are satisfied. The Bonds, the Note, the Mortgage and the Guaranty will be non-recourse to the Partners of the Partnership, the shareholders of the Company and to all other persons and entities whatsoever (other than the Company, the Partnership and, with respect to the Trump Completion Guaranty and the Trump Line of Credit, Donald J. Trump). To the extent set forth in the Trump Completion Guaranty, Donald J. Trump will guarantee that construction of the Taj Mahal will be substantially completed in accordance with the plans and specifications therefore by March 1, 1991, subject to extension by reason of Force Majeure Delays. See "Trump Completion Guaranty and Line of Credit."

Interest on the Bonds will be payable semiannually, commencing May 15, 1989. The Bonds are redeemable at any time on or after November 15, 1993, at the option of the Company, in whole or in part, at the prices set forth herein, together with accrued interest to the redemption date. The Bonds are not entitled to the benefit of any sinking fund.

The Partnership will use the net proceeds of this offering to repay the interim financing incurred to pay the cash portion of the purchase price of the Taj Mahal and certain other assets, including interest thereon, and, together with funds from other sources, to finance the cost of completing and opening the Taj Mahal, including funding interest on the Bonds for fifteen months from the date of issuance.

The Bonds are being sold pursuant to delayed delivery contracts and will be delivered against payment therefore at such time as certain conditions are satisfied, including those described below. In connection with the delayed delivery contracts, certain fees will be paid to the purchasers of the Bonds. See "Underwriting."

The sale of the Bonds is conditioned upon the occurrence by December 7, 1988 of the closing of the purchase by the Partnership of the Taj Mahal and certain other assets and the receipt by the Partnership of a capital contribution of $75,000,000 from Donald J. Trump.

The Bonds have been approved for listing on the American Stock Exchange, subject to official notice of issuance.

Certain capitalized terms used herein are defined in the "Glossary" or the "Description of the Bonds—Certain Definitions," included elsewhere in this Prospectus.

See "Special Considerations" for a discussion of certain factors to be considered by potential investors.

THESE SECURITIES HAVE NOT BEEN APPROVED OR DISAPPROVED BY THE SECURITIES AND EXCHANGE COMMISSION NOR HAS THE COMMISSION PASSED UPON THE ACCURACY OR ADEQUACY OF THIS PROSPECTUS. ANY REPRESENTATION TO THE CONTRARY IS A CRIMINAL OFFENSE.

THE ATTORNEY GENERAL OF THE STATE OF NEW YORK HAS NOT PASSED ON OR ENDORSED THE MERITS OF THIS OFFERING. ANY REPRESENTATION TO THE CONTRARY IS UNLAWFUL.

	Price to Public	Underwriting Discount (1)	Proceeds to Company/ Partnership (1)(2)
Per Bond	100%	3%	97%
Total	$675,000,000	$20,250,000	$654,750,000

In addition to the title page, the body of the prospectus contained the following:

- Prospectus Summary
- Summary Historical and Pro Forma Financial Information
- Special Considerations
- The Company
- The Partnership
- The Acquisition
- The Financing
- Use of Proceeds
- Capitalization
- Selected Historical and Pro Forma Financial Data
- Management's Discussion and Analysis of Financial Condition and Results of Operations of the Partnership and the Company
- Combined Pro Forma Balance Sheet
- Business of the Partnership
- Properties of the Partnership
- Management
- Description of the Bonds
- Trump Completion Guaranty and Line of Credit
- Management Agreement
- Certain United States Tax Considerations
- Underwriting
- Legal Matters
- Experts
- Glossary
- Index to Financial Statements

BOND COVENANTS

Long-term debt agreements include both standard and restrictive debt provisions. Standard debt provisions specify that the company will maintain satisfactory methods of accounting and recordkeeping in compliance with generally accepted accounting principles. Typical, debt provisions include paying all liabilities, including taxes, supplying audited financial statements to the lenders, adhering to state and local government regulations, and ensuring the company's existence for the long-term.

Long-term debt agreements also include restrictive covenants that provide protection to the lender by imposing financial constraints on the borrower. According to Gitman:[3]

> "Since the lender is committing funds for a long period, it of course seeks to protect itself. Restrictive covenants, coupled with standard debt provisions, allow the lender to monitor and control the borrower's activities in order to protect itself against the agency problem created by the relationship between owners and lenders. Without these provisions the borrower could "take advantage" of the lender by acting to increase the firm's risk while not being required to pay the lender an increased return (interest)."

1. The borrower is required to maintain a minimum level of net working capital. Net working capital below the minimum is considered indicative of inadequate liquidity, a common precursor to loan default and ultimate failure.
2. Borrowers are prohibited from selling accounts receivable to generate cash because using proceeds to meet current obligations could cause a long-run cash shortage.
3. Long-term lenders commonly impose fixed-asset restrictions on the firm. These constrain the firm's liquidation, acquisition, and encumbrance of fixed assets, because any of these actions could damage the firm's ability to repay its debt.
4. Many debt agreements constrain subsequent borrowing by prohibiting additional long-term debt, or by requiring that additional borrowing be "subordinated" to the original loan. Subordination means that all subsequent or less important creditors agree to wait until all claims of the senior debt are satisfied before satisfying their claims.
5. Borrowers can be prohibited from entering into certain types of leases in order to limit additional, fixed-payment obligations.

---

[3]L.J. Gitman, *Principles of Managerial Finance*, Fifth Edition, Harper and Row, 1988, pp. 576–577. Restrictive covenants remain in force for the life of the debt agreement. The most common restrictive covenants are listed below.

6. Occasionally, the lender prohibits combinations by requiring the borrower to agree not to consolidate, merge, or combine in any way with another firm, because it could significantly change the borrower's business and financial risk.
7. To prevent liquidation of assets because of large salary payments, the lender might prohibit or limit salary increases for specified employees.
8. The lender might include management restrictions requiring the borrower to maintain certain "key employees," without whom the future success of the firm would be uncertain.
9. Occasionally, the lender includes a covenant limiting the borrower's security investment alternatives. This restriction protects the lender by controlling the risk and marketability of the borrower's security investments.
10. Occasionally, a covenant specifically requires the borrower to spend the borrowed funds on a proven financial need.
11. A relatively common provision limits the firm's annual cash dividend payments to a maximum of 50 to 70 percent of its net earnings, or a specified dollar amount.

An example of a restrictive covenant is the Best Product Bond, which matures in 1996 with a coupon of 12.625 percent had a restrictive covenant that stipulated that $20 million of these bonds must be repurchased each year if the tangible net worth fell below $250 million. To remove the covenant, Best Products offered the bondholders an increase in coupon. Unfortunately, for Best Products, the bondholders felt more comfortable retaining the restrictive covenant.

OBSTACLES TO FINDING NEW OFFERINGS

The average investor often finds it stimulating to tell friends that he has just purchased a "new bond offering," but the problem the average investor has is how to find out about new offerings. There are three ways to find out about new bond offerings. The first is from advertisements in the Wall Street Journal, such as the one shown in Fig. 3-1. The underwriters are identified in the bottom of the ad. For the most part, this type of ad is referred to as a "tombstone" ad because, by the time the ad is placed, the entire initial offering might have been sold out.

The second source is from publications such as Standard and Poor's *Bond Guide* (see Fig. 3-2). The difficulty with this method is that the Guide comes out on the 20th of each month and, as in the first method, the bonds might not be available.

The third method, and probably the best, is to work through your account executive. Ideally, your account executive should inform you of new offerings.

This announcement is under no circumstances to be construed as an offer to sell or as a solicitation of an offer to buy any of these securities. The offering is made only by the Prospectus. The Attorney General of the State of New York has not passed on or endorsed the merits of this offering.

NEW ISSUE

May 26, 1988

$100,000,000

Lomas & Nettleton Mortgage Investors

10½% Subordinated Notes due 1993

Price 100%

(Plus accrued interest, if any, from June 6, 1988.)

Copies of the Prospectus may be obtained in any State in which this announcement is circulated from only such of the undersigned or other dealers or brokers as may lawfully offer these securities in such State.

Merrill Lynch Capital Markets

Donaldson, Lufkin & Jenrette
Securities Corporation

Source: *The Wall Street Journal*, May 26, 1988.

Fig. 3-1. *A Lomas and Nettleton "tombstone" ad.*

The obstacles are:

- Your account executive might have access to only those new offerings in which his brokerage house is participating as an investment banker.
- If the account executive is not actively involved in the bond market, then he might not want to spend his time soliciting for small commissions.
- Your account executive might not inform you of the bonds if he is unfamiliar with your buying habits, financial constraints, or quality constraints, or if the bonds must be purchased in large, minimum quantity limits and his philosophy is to diversify your account with small quantities of several different types of bonds.

The best bet is to inform your account executive of your desire to purchase new offerings and to provide him with your requirements and constraints. The account executive will then be able to screen the offerings for you.

CALENDAR OF NEW OFFERINGS

Date Off'd	Company & Issue	Int. Dates	Ind'ty Code	Amt. Mil$	S & P Rating	Bank Status	Off'g Price	Yield to Mty.	Underwriter
Oct 12	Ingles Markets, Cv Sub Reset Deb, 9s, 2008	aO15	58c	50.0	B+	Y	100.000	9.00	Drexel Burnham
Oct 12	Marley Co., Sr Sub Ext'd Reset Notes (13s, '91), 1998	aO15	42	125.0	B−	Y	100.000	...	Drexel Burnham
Oct 13	Elizabethtown Water Co., Deb, 10 1/8s, 2018	aO15	74	20.0	A+	X	99.795	10.15	L.F. Rothschild
Oct 13	Student Loan Marketing Assn, Reverse PERLS, 11 3/8s, 1993	aO15	26	60.0	NR	...	99.875	...	Morgan Stanley
Oct 13	Welbilt Corp, Sr Sub Notes, 13 3/4s, 1998	aO15	32c	75.0	B−	Y	100.000	13.75	Kidder Peabody
Oct 17	American Shared Hospital Services, Sr Sub Exch Reset Notes (14s, '89) 1996	aO15	43	30.0	CCC+	Y	100.000	...	Drexel Burnham
Oct 18	Dayton Hudson, Notes, 9 3/4s, 1998	mN	58	100.0	A+	X	99.875	9.77	Goldman Sachs
Oct 18	Panhandle Eastern Pipe Line, SF Deb, 9 7/8s, 1996	aO15	73a	250.0	BBB−	X	100.000	9.88	Kidder Peabody
Oct 20	Arkla Inc, Notes, 9.45s, 1995	aO15	73b	150.0	A	X	100.000	9.45	Kidder Peabody
Oct 20	Morgan Guaranty Trust Co. of N.Y., Notes, 8.7s, 1990	mN	10	100.0	AAA	X	100.000	8.70	Nomura Securities
Oct 21	Eastman Kodak, Notes, 9 7/8s, 2004	mN	40d	300.0	A−	X	99.800	9.90	First Boston
Oct 21	Grant Street Nat'l Bank (In Liquidation), Extendible Pay-Thru Notes Ser A (10 1/4s, '91), 1992	mN	10	225.0	BBB−	X	100.000	...	Drexel Burnham
Oct 21	Grant Street Nat'l Bank (In Liquidation), Extendible Pay-Thru Notes Ser B (14 1/4%, '93), 1994	mN	10	288.0	B−	Y	100.000	...	Drexel Burnham
Oct 21	Lomas & Nettleton Financial, Sub Notes, 11 3/8s, 1995	aO15	26f	175.0	BBB	X	100.000	11.38	Salomon Bros
Oct 21	Seamen's Capital, Mtg-Backed Bonds, 9 3/4s, 1998	mN	26	200.0	NR	...	99.792	9.78	Merrill Lynch
Oct 25	Florida Power & Light, 1st Mtg, 9.8s, 2018	mN	72a	125.0	AA−	X	99.625	9.84	Salomon Bros
Oct 25	Fort Howard Corp, Jr Sub Deb, 14 5/8s, 2004	mN	50	300.0	B	Y	100.000	14.63	Morgan Stanley
Oct 25	Fort Howard Corp, Jr Sub Disc Deb (14 1/8s fr 11-1-94), 2004	mN	50	703.0	B	Y	44.091	14.13	Morgan Stanley
Oct 25	Fort Howard Corp, Sr Sub Notes, 12 3/8s, 1997	mN	50	355.0	B+	Y	100.000	12.38	Morgan Stanley
Oct 25	Fort Howard Corp, Sub Deb, 12 5/8s, 2000	mN	50	355.0	B	Y	100.000	12.63	Morgan Stanley
Oct 25	Waste Management, Zero Cpn Cv Sub, Notes, 2012 (Apr 13)	...	22	1600.0	AA−	Y	25.000	6.00	Merrill Lynch
Oct 26	Avalon Marketing, Sr Sub Notes, 14s, 1998	mN	59	100.0	CCC+	Y	98.687	14.25	Drexel Burnham
Oct 26	Chrysler Financial, Sub Step-Down F/R Notes, 1991 (Nov 15)	Mthly	26a	200.0	NR	...	100.000	...	Merrill Lynch
Oct 26	Private Export Funding, Sec Notes Ser BB, 9.1s, 1998	aO30	26	100.0	AAA	X	99.966	9.11	Citibank, N.A.
Oct 27	Arkansas Best, Sr Sub Notes, 14s, 1998	mN	71	125.0	B−	Y	100.000	14.00	First Boston
Oct 27	Chemical Banking, Sub Cap Notes, 10 1/8s, 2000	mN	10	150.0	A−	X	99.250	10.24	Salomon Bros
Oct 27	Citicorp, Notes, 9s, 1991	mN15	10	250.0	AA	X	100.000	9.00	Merrill Lynch
Oct 27	Utilicorp United, Mtg Bonds (Ser 1), 9 7/8s, 1998	aO15	75	75.0	BBB−	X	100.000	9.88	Drexel Burnham

Source: Standard and Poor's *Bond Guide*, November 1988.

Fig. 3-2. *Calendar of new offerings.*

NEW OFFERINGS AND THE SECONDARY MARKETS

As defined previously, the "primary" market for bonds is when the underwriters place their bonds with their clients. Once the bonds have been placed, the investor must rely upon the "secondary" market for purchases. The secondary market consists of:

- New York Stock Exchange (NYSE)
- American Stock Exchange (AMEX)
- Regional Stock Exchange
- Over-the-Counter (OTC)

Bonds that are traded on the NYSE and AMEX are "listed" bonds whereas, OTC bonds are nonlisted. For listed bonds, your broker can obtain an instantaneous quote on bonds offered, offering price, and asking price. Listed bonds can be used as collateral and are easily marketed. Nonlisted bonds have no collateral value and might not be able to be liquidated quickly enough without taking a substantial loss. When you read the bond activity columns in *The Wall Street Journal*, you are actually seeing the listed bonds as they are traded in the secondary market.

There are two reasons why an investor would buy new issue bonds. First of all, the bonds have a coupon higher than prevailing interest rates and, even if the bond is high risk, the danger of appreciable near-term volatility might be lower. In this case, the purchaser might want to hold the bonds until this first or second interest payment and then offer them for resale on the secondary market at a higher price.

The second reason is in the hope that the secondary market will drive up the price of the bond and the investor can make a quick profit. For example, ARMCO initially offered a bond with a 13½ percent coupon near par and the secondary market drove the price up to $1,060 within a short period of time. Control Data Corporation's initial offering of a 12¾ percent coupon bond near par rapidly rose to $1,070 on the secondary market. In both cases, investors who took part in the initial offering made wise decisions.

There are also volatility risks on the down side. Some bonds might drop in price by as much as $20 to $30 per bond within days of being listed on the exchanges. Some bonds have a waiting period of 30 to 60 days between the initial offering and being listed on the exchanges.The most common reasons for a sudden decrease in price would include:

- The interest rates increase.
- The economic conditions of the company deteriorated.
- Industry volatility.
- The company's bond rating changed.
- A large volume of the issue is being offered for sale on the secondary market.
- Public disclosure of prospectus terms and conditions.

These last two elements require further comment. The initial offering price of the bonds is fixed for all marketing activities during the primary market function. If an underwriter cannot sell the entire bond issue at the initial terms, then the underwriter sells the unsold portion on the secondary market at a lower price, which might be more acceptable to secondary-market investors. This process is often referred to as "unloading" or "dumping" the issue. Large volume sales immediately after listing on the exchanges are characteristic of dumping.

The last element involves the prospectus. During the initial offering of a bond, perspective buyers are given the prospectus of the bonds, which indicate what the money will be used for, special terms and conditions, and criteria for early recall. The primary market for bonds is generally pension plan administrators, who are extremely knowledgeable in understanding the information in a 50- to 100-page perspectus. Unfortunately, some organizations buy the bonds during the primary marketing function and later recognize that the terms and conditions are not in the best interest of the pension plan. They then dump the bonds onto the secondary market at a low price. An astute investor might find good buys when new bonds are first listed on the secondary markets.

BUYING LISTED BONDS

The most common way to find listed bonds is in newspapers such as *The Wall Street Journal*. Let us assume that you read the newspaper and see the Philadelphia Electric Bond, $8^1/_2$ percent-2004, selling for $782.50. You then call your account executive and he gives you the following information:

$$80^1/_4 \text{ to } 81^1/_8,\ 4 \times 7$$

This means that the current bid price is $802.25 (this is the price being offered by a buyer) and the seller is asking for $811.25. The buyers are offering to purchase four bonds at $802.25, but the sellers are offering seven bonds at $811.25. If you place an order at $782.50 (i.e., the price you read in the newspaper), you might have to wait until the price comes down. You could, however, immediately purchase seven bonds if you are willing to pay $811.25.

If a buyer wants to purchase a bond at the current asking price, then his broker will place a ''market order,'' which means that the buy order will be processed at the lowest asking price when it arrives at the floor of the exchange. The buyer might also want to place a ''limit'' order that limits the amount the buyer is willing to pay.

It is common practice, however, to place a ''discretionary'' order. In this case, the buyer states the quantity of bonds to be purchased as well as the target price. The broker is given the discretion, however, to increase the offering price by as much as $^1/_8$, $^1/_4$, or even $^1/_2$ a point.

4

Bond Ratings

WHEN IT COMES TO INVESTING IN STOCKS AND BONDS, THE MORE information you have, the more often you'll make wise decisions. Major brokerage houses employ experts who follow certain stocks and industries, and can provide you with detailed advice on such issues as earnings, profits, growth potential, assets, and liabilities. When buying bonds, however, this type of information is normally not available.

UNDERSTANDING RATINGS

The most commonly used parameter in assessing the worthiness of a bond is its rating (i.e., quality rating). The rating is an indication of the firm's ability to pay semiannual interest and principal at maturity. These bond ratings are often the only parameter considered in purchasing bonds. There are five main organizations in the United States that rate corporate bonds:

- Standard and Poor's Corporation
- Moody's Investor Services
- McCarthy, Crisanti, and Maffei
- Duff and Phelps
- Fitch Investors Service

Moody's Investor Service and Standard and Poor's Corporation are the two largest and widely publicized agencies. A good rating by one of these agencies allows a corporation to borrow money at a lower interest rate. Ratings by these agencies reflect current assessments of the corporation's creditworthiness with respect to a specific debt obligation. The ratings should *not* be interpreted as a recommendation to purchase, hold, or sell bonds. The ratings are also *not* based on the current market price. According to Standard and Poor's:

> "The ratings are based upon current information furnished by the issuer or obtained by Standard and Poor's from other sources it considers reliable. Standard and Poor's does not perform any audit in connection with any rating and may, on occasion, rely on unaudited financial information. The ratings may be changed, suspended or withdrawn as a result of changes in, availability of, such information, or for other circumstances.

The ratings are based, in varying degrees, on the following conditions:

- Likelihood of default-capacity and willingness of the obligator as to the timely payment of interest and the repayment of principal in accordance with the terms of the obligation.
- Nature of and provisions of the obligation.
- Protection afforded by and relative position of, the obligation in the event of bankruptcy, reorganization or other arranged under the laws of bankruptcy and other laws affecting creditors' rights.[1]"

In keeping with the above parameters, Standard and Poor's defines their corporate bond ratings as follows:

AAA	Debts rated AAA have the highest rating assigned by Standard and Poor's. The capacity to pay interest and repay principal is extremely strong.
AA	Debts rated AA have a very strong capacity to pay interest and repay principal and differs (only in small degree) from the higher-rated issues.
A	Debts rated A have a strong capacity to pay interest and repay principal although it is somewhat more susceptible to the adverse effects of changing circumstances and economic conditions than a higher-rated category.
BBB	Debts rated as BBB are regarded as having an adequate capacity to pay interest and repay principal. Although it normally exhibits adequate protection parameters, adverse economic conditions or changing circumstances would more than likely lead to a weakened capacity to pay interest and repay principal for debt.

[1]Standard and Poor's Corporation Bond Guide.

BB, B, CCC, CC, C	Debts rated BB, B,CCC, CC, and C are regarded on the whole as speculative with respect to capacity to pay interest and repay principal in accordance with the terms of the obligation. BB indicates the lowest degree of speculation and C is the highest degree of speculation. While such debt will likely have some quality and protective characteristics, these are outweighed by large uncertainties or major risk exposures to adverse conditions.
D	Bonds rated D are in default and payment of interest and/or repayment of principal is in arrears.

Each bond rating agency has their own method for assigning ratings. Some rating agencies use alphabetic characters while others use numerical characters. Below is a comparison of Moody's and Standard and Poor's:

Standard and Poor's	*Moody's*
AAA	Aaa
AA	Aa
A	A
BBB	Baa
BB	Ba
B	B
CCC	Caa
CC	Ca
C	C

Moody's ratings do not issue any ratings below C. Therefore, bonds rated Caa, Ca, and C by Moody's might be in default whereas Standard and Poor's usually gives bonds in default a D rating.

Standard and Poor's also adds plus and minus signs to its ratings from AA through CCC. Thus a bond might be rated as AA–, BBB+, CCC+, or CCC–. These plus and minus signs indicate credit standing within a category. For example, a bond rated as A+ is slightly better than a bond rated A but lower than a bond rated as AA–.

In 1982, Moody's decided to modify its ratings between Aa and B, just as Standard and Poor's did with plus and minus. Moody's used the numbers 1, 2, and 3 to indicate the relative strength of issues within the same rating. For example, a bond rated as Baa2 is stronger than one rated as Baa3, but slightly weaker than one rated as Baa1.

Not all bonds are rated, however. Companies have to pay a rating agency to receive this service, at a cost of $5,000 to $75,000, based upon the nature of the issue. There are hundreds of millions of dollars worth of bonds that are nonrated (NR) because companies either do not request the rating, or do not want to pay for it. As a matter of policy, however, Standard and Poor's rates practically all public corporate bond issues of $10 million or more, with or without a request from the issuer.

THE CRITICAL LEVEL

Using the Standard and Poor's (S&P) nomenclature, bonds rated BBB– or higher are considered as investment grade bonds and bonds rated BB+ or lower are considered speculative or junk bonds. The critical level, therefore, is BBB–.

Banks and financial institutions are legally bound to invest only in BBB– or better bonds. Consequently, companies are under pressure to influence the rating agencies for investment-grade ratings. There are two reasons for this. The company will pay lower interest rates for investment grade bonds than for junk bonds, and second, it might be easier to issue and place large offerings of bonds.

This by no means implies that junk bonds are really junk. The difficulty is to distinguish the real junk from the perceived junk. Simply because a bond is rated as a junk bond does not mean that the company is incapable of servicing its debt. These companies might simply be underrated. During the recession from 1980 to 1984, some junk bonds were outstanding investments, outperforming treasury bonds by a whopping 82 percent.

Understanding this critical level of bond rating can be beneficial. Financial institutions must adhere to government regulations. If a bond is downgraded from BBB to BB+, then the financial institution might have to liquidate their holdings in the bond. These types of bonds are often referred to as "fallen angels." In the next week or two following a bond downgrading, a much larger than normal volume of bonds will be traded, and a buyer can often get in at a good return. Fallen angels can still have good protective characteristics.

Likewise, if an investor feels that a bond might be upgraded, say from BB+ to BBB–, then there could be large, wholesale buying. The day following the Wall Street Journal's announcement that ASARCO was upgraded to investment grade, the volume of bonds traded was more than 20 times the daily average, and the bond rose in price by $20.

Most rating changes do not occur overnight, however. To assist investors, Standard and Poor's developed their "CreditWatch" report, which advises the general public that a bond is being considered for possible upgrading or downgrading. A bond might be on CreditWatch for months before any rating changes

CreditWatch

Issuer	Potential Credit Implications	Current Ratings: Senior Debt	Current Ratings: Sub. Debt	Current Ratings: Comm. Paper	CreditWatch Write-up: Issue	CreditWatch Write-up: Page
Industrials						
Lorimar Telepictures Corp.	Developing		B+		5/16/88	10u
Lubrizol Corp.	Negative	AA			9/12/88	8
Macmillan Inc.	Negative	A–	BBB+		9/19/88	11u
Malrite Communications Group Inc.	Developing		B		8/22/88	10
Mark IV Industries Inc.	Negative		B–		8/8/88	10
Matrix Corp.	Positive		B		9/19/88	11u
Metropolitan Broadcasting Corp.	Developing		CCC+		4/18/88	11
Muse Air Corp. (assumed by Continental Airlines Inc.)	Negative	B			7/4/88	9u
Nabisco Inc. (RJR Nabisco Inc. unit)	Negative	A			10/24/88	10
National Intergroup Inc.	Negative		B+		10/10/88	9
Northview Corp.	Negative		CCC		12/21/87	12
Pennwalt Corp.	Negative	BBB–	BB**		8/22/88	11u
Petrie Stores Corp.	Negative		BBB–		9/19/88	9
Philip Morris Inc. (Philip Morris Companies Inc. unit)	Negative	A		A-1	10/24/88	10
Philip Morris Companies Inc.‡	Negative	A		A-1	10/24/88	10
Phillips Alaska Pipeline Corp.	Positive	BB+			9/26/88	11
Phillips Petroleum Co.	Positive	BB+	BB–		9/26/88	11
Piggly Wiggly Southern Inc.	Positive		B–		4/11/88	11
Pillsbury Co.	Negative	A		A-1	10/10/88	9
Polaroid Corp.	Negative	A		A-1	7/25/88	10
Ramada Inns Inc.	Developing		B–		9/19/88	9
Resorts International Inc.	Negative		B–		6/6/88	12u
Reynolds Tobacco Inc. (RJR Nabisco Inc. unit)	Negative	A			10/24/88	10
R.J. Industries Inc.	Negative	A			10/24/88	10
RJR Nabisco Inc.‡	Negative	A	A**	A-1	10/24/88	10
Seaboard System Railroad§§	Negative	AA+/A+			9/26/88	12
Sea-Land Services Inc. (gtd. by CSX Corp.)	Negative	A			9/26/88	12
Service Merchandise Co. Inc.	Negative		B+		9/26/88	12
Servico Inc.	Negative		CCC		7/25/88	11
Sheller-Globe Corp. (Knoll International Holdings Inc. unit)	Developing		B–		7/25/88	9
Showboat Inc.	Negative		B–		8/29/88	10
Southern Pacific Co.	Negative	BBB			9/26/88	13u
Southmark California Inc.	Negative		CCC		9/12/88	8
Southmark Corp.	Negative	B–	CCC		9/12/88	8
Staley (A.E.) Manufacturing Co.	Negative	BBB+			4/18/88	11
Staley Continental Inc.	Negative	BBB+	BBB–**	A-2	4/18/88	11
Standard Brands Inc. (RJR Nabisco Inc. unit)	Negative	A			10/24/88	10
Stanley Interiors Corp.	Negative		B–		9/5/88	11
Sysco Corp.	Negative	A+			6/13/88	10
Texas Air Corp.	Negative	B	CCC+		7/4/88	9u
Texas International Airlines Inc. (assumed by Continental Airlines Inc.)	Negative		CCC+		7/4/88	9u

Source: Standard and Poor's *Bond Guide*, December 1988.

Fig. 4-1. *Bonds on Standard and Poor's* CreditWatch.

occur. It is also possible that no rating change will occur, just an affirming of the existing rating. Moody's has a similar process. They place the bond "under review." These reevaluation periods provide the investor with an early-warning system that a potential rating change is possible. See Figs. 4-1 and 4-2. Standard and Poor's *Bond Guide*[2] illustrate Standard and Poor's reporting system. Figure 4-1 lists the industrial bonds that were placed on CreditWatch. "Negative" indicates that the rating could be lowered during this period. "Positive" indicates that the rating could be raised. "Stable" is assigned to a bond when ratings are not likely to be changed, and should not be confused with expected stability of the company's financial performance. "Developing" is used for those unusual situations in which future events are so unclear that the rating might potentially be raised, lowered, or maintained. Each designation is followed by a discussion of the key factors supporting Standard and Poor's outlook. Figure 4-2 shows bonds that have undergone a rating change. Standard and Poor's maintains constant surveillance of corporate debt to assess the potential for a rating change. According to Standard and Poor's:[3]

[2]Standard and Poor's *Bond Guide*, November 1988.

[3]Standard and Poor's, *Debt Ratings Criteria: Industrial Overview*, 1986, pp. 11–12.

CHANGES IN DEBT RATINGS/DESIGNATIONS

Corporate:	Old	New
AMPAD Corp, Cv Sub Deb, 8s, 2010	BBB	BBB+
Alaska Housing Finance Corp, State Assisted Mtg Ser A, 16 1/4s, '99	A	Call
Allied Bancshares, Notes, 12s, '93	A+	A
Avon Capital, (Euro): Notes 6 3/4s, '91, 8 3/4s, '89, Bonds: 5 3/8s, '94, 6 1/4s, '98	BBB−	BB
Avon Int'l Finance NV, Notes, 10 1/4s, '92	BBB−	BB
Bank of Montreal, Flt'g Rt Sub (Euro) Deb: '91, '96, '98	AA−	A+
Bank of Montreal (Chicago Branch), Sub Notes, 10s, '98	AA−	A+
Bank of Nova Scotia, Flt'g Rt Sub (Euro) Deb: '94, 2000	AA−	A+
Bank of Nova Scotia (New York Agency), Sub Deb, 10 1/4s, '98	AA−	A+
Banks of Mid-America Inc, Install Notes, 10 3/4s	CCC−	D
Calton Inc, Sr Notes, 12 1/4s, '96	B−	B+
Castle & Cooke, SF Deb, 8 1/2s, '97	B+	BB+
Sub Notes, 12s, '91	B	B−
Centran Corp, Deb, 7.85s, '97	A	A+
Cenvill Investors, Sr Sub Notes, 9 1/4s, '93	BBB−	BB+
Citicorp, Notes, 12 1/2s, '93	AA	Call
Clabir Corp, Sub Deb, 14 1/2s, 2004	C	D
Clevite Industries, Sub Deb, 12 3/8s, 2001	B	CCC+
Commerce Bancshares, Notes, 12.35s, '90	A	Call
Commercial Alliance, Sub Notes, 15 1/8s, '92	A	NR
Commonwealth Edison, 1st Mtg: Ser 50, 12 1/4s, '91, Ser 51, 13 3/8s, 2013	BBB+	Call
Data-Design Labs, Cv Sub Deb, 12 1/4s, 2000	NR	Call
Dayton Hudson Corp, Sr Unsecured Debt, (Euro): Bonds: 7 1/2s, '92, 8 1/4s, '93, Notes, 10 5/8s, '95	AA−	A+
Duquesne Light, 1st Mtg, 13s, 2013	BBB	Call
EDO Corp, Cv Sub Deb, 7s, 2011	B+	B
El Paso Products, Sr Sub Ext'd Reset Notes (12 3/4s, '89), '95, Sub Notes, 13 3/4s, '98	B	BB−
Financial TrustCo Capital Ltd, Sub Deb, 15 7/8s, '99	B+	C
Sr Sub (Euro) Deb, 13.95s, 2001	BB−	C
First Boston, Sub Deb, 10 1/4s, '95	A	A−
First Interstate Bancorp, Sr Unsec Debt, (Euro) Notes: 12 5/8s, '89, Med-Term, '96	A+	A
Var Rt Sub Notes, '97, Sub Cap Notes, 8 5/8s, '99	A	A−
First Interstate Int'l Fin Ltd, Bonds, 6s, '92	A+	A
First Interstate Overseas Fin NV, Flt'g Rt Sub Notes, '95	A	A−

Corporate:	Old	New
Goodrich (B.F.) Co, SF Deb, 8 1/4s, '94, Var Rt Notes, '91	BBB−	BBB
Sub SF Deb, 7s, '97	BB+	BBB−
Guarantee Savings Federal S & L Assoc., Sub Cap Notes, 14 7/8s, '97	BB−	BB+
Healthcare USA, Sr Sub Deb, 10 7/8s, '98, Cv Sub Deb, 8 1/4s, 2003	CCC	D
Inco Ltd, Sr Unsec (Euro) Debt, SF Deb: 6.85s, '93, 12 3/8s, 2010	BBB	BBB−
Iowa Electric Light & Power, 1st Mtg 'T', 14 3/4s, '91	A	Call
MCorp Inc, Sr Unsec Debt	CCC	D
Flt'g Rt Sub (Euro) Notes, '97	CC	D
Maxicare Health Plans, Sr Sub Notes, 11 3/4s, '96, Cv Sub Deb, 7s, 2010	CCC	D
Mead Corp, SF Deb: 8 1/2s, '95, 9 7/8s, 2000, 9s, 2017, Notes, 15 7/8s, '92	BBB+	A−
Cv Sub Deb, 6 3/4s, 2012	BBB	BBB+
Mueller Co, Sr Notes, 12 1/8s, '96	B−	BBB−
Sr Sub Deb, 12 1/2s, 2001	CCC+	BB+
Panhandle Eastern Pipe Line, SF Deb: 7 1/4s, '89, 8 5/8s, '89, 8 5/8s, '90	BBB−	Call
Pennsylvania Power & Light, 1st Mtg, 13 1/8s, 2013	A−	Call
Perry Drug Stores, Cv Sub Deb, 8 1/2s, 2010	B	B−
Petrolane Inc, Notes, 14 7/8s, '91	NR	Call
Polycast Technology Corp, Sub Notes, 10 3/8s, '95	CCC−	NR
Resorts International, Sub SF Deb: 10s, '98, 10s, '99, 11 3/8s, 2013	B−	CCC+
Resorts International Financing, Sub Deb, 16 5/8s, 2004	B−	CCC+
Rio Grande Indus, Sr Sub Notes, 13 5/8s, '95, Sub Deb, 14 3/8s, 2005	BB+	B+
Sequa Corp, Sub SF Deb: 11 1/4s, '96, 11 1/2s, '96	BB−	Call
Society Corp, Notes: 12 1/2s, '92, 8 1/4s, '93, 8 7/8s, '96	A	A+
Southern Pacific Railroad, 1st Mtg 'F', 2 3/4s, '96	BBB	BB+
Southern Pacific Transportation, 1st & Ref Ser B, 8.2s, 2001	BBB	BB+
Southwestern Energy, Sr Cv Deb, 8 1/2s, 2010	BBB+	A−
St. Louis Southwestern Railway, 1st Mtg, 4s, '89	BBB	BB+
Tenneco Corp, SF Deb: 7s, '93, 5 1/8s, '90	BBB+	Call
Tennessee Gas Pipeline, 1st Mtg P.L. Bonds: 9s, '89, 8 1/4s, '91	BBB+	Call
Texas & New Orleans Railroad, 1st & Ref Ser C, 3 3/8s, '90	BBB	BB+
Toronto-Dominion Bank (New York Branch), Sub Notes, 10.2s, '98	AA+	AA
Union Camp, Sr Unsec Debt	AA−	A+
Wells Fargo & Co., Notes, 12.3s, '90	AA−	Call
Whirlpool Acceptance, (Euro) Notes, 7 1/8s, '91	AA	AA−
Whirlpool Corp, SF Deb: 9 5/8s, 2000, 9 1/8s, 2016, Deb, 9.1s, 2008	AA	AA−

Source: Standards and Poor's *Bond Guide*, December 1988.

Fig. 4-2. *Changes in debt ratings.*

"A Standard and Poor's rating evaluates default risk over the life of a debt issue, an assessment of all future events to the extent they are considered likely. But Standard and Poor's also recognizes the potential for future performance to differ from present expectations. The rating outlook addresses this possibility by focusing on the most probable alternate scenarios that could result in a rating change. The rating outlook does not address the rating impact of every possible deviation from expectations. Therefore, an actual future rating action may differ from the rating outlook designation.

The rating outlook covers approximately a three-year time horizon. Over the short-term, performance is not likely to diverge materially from expectations, and most ratings should be stable for at least a year or two. However, if a speculative-grade issuer faces an unusually high degree of near-term unpredictability, the rating outlook designation might address a time frame of less than three years.

When the rating outlook is affected by considerations beyond the typical three-year horizon they also are highlighted. For instance, upgrade potential for Conwood Corp., with subordinated debt rated 'B−,' is a function of increasing concern about the health risks of its smokeless tobacco products. Over the next few years, however, the health issue is not expected to have any adverse financial impact."

Not all issues are placed on CreditWatch before Standard and Poor's rules on a change. Companies generally appear on CreditWatch when a rating change is likely to occur, but significant information is lacking that prevents immediate action. In 1983, 75 percent of all the issues placed on CreditWatch had negative implications. By the end of the year, 92 issues were downgraded, 75 had ratings affirmed, and 31 were upgraded.

In 1988, Standard and Poor's had 450 ratings placed on CreditWatch. These 450 ratings were divided into the following categories: 188 were downgraded, 118 were upgraded, 106 were affirmed, and 38 were withdrawn. These numbers are substantial when you consider that in 1987 there were only 352 activities on CreditWatch with 118 downgrades, 65 upgrades, 136 affirmed, and 33 withdrawn.

Corporations view bond ratings as "financial protection." A good rating makes it easier to borrow money in the future. It is not uncommon for companies to approach the rating agencies for advice on what must be done to maintain the current rating or move up in the ratings.

WHAT A RATING MEANS

The majority of bond investors have a relatively poor understanding of what a bond rating really means. A good bond rating is *not* an ironclad guarantee against default or bankruptcy, nor does a poor rating imply financial dangers. Also, bond ratings are not protection against "acts of god," quality of management, and rapidly changing economic conditions. The major role of agencies such as Moody's and Standard and Poor's is to provide the general public with a *second opinion* of the investment as it relates to the probability that the current protective characteristics of the bond issue will change.

Ideally, each investor should determine the protective characteristics of each issues.This is seldom done because the average investor has neither the time nor access to the necessary financial data to accurately assess risk. Financial institutions and pension fund managers often perform their own analysis rather than simply seek out evaluations from rating agencies. Risk is a function of knowledge, and the question, of course, is who has more knowledge.

Ratings are, and probably always will be, "judgment calls" about the firm's ability to meet its debt obligations. Moody's Investors Service has this to say about ratings:

> "Since ratings involve a judgment about the future, on the one hand, and since they are used by investors as a means of protection, on the other, the effort is made when assigning ratings, to look at 'worst' potentialities in the 'visible' future rather than solely at past record and status of the present. Investors using the ratings should not, therefore, expect to find them a reflection of statistical factors above. They are not statistical ratings

[4]Moody's Public Utilities Manual (New York: Moody's Investors Service, 1967) p.v.

> but an appraisal of long-term risks, such appraisal giving recognition to many nonstatistical factors.[4]"

In order to use credit ratings properly, you need to first understand what a rating is and is not. A credit rating is not a recommendation to purchase, sell or hold a particular security. A rating performs the isolated function of credit risk evaluation, which is only one element of the entire investment decision-making process. A rating cannot constitute a recommendation because it does not consider other factors such as market price and the risk preference of the investor. A rating is not a general-purpose evaluation of an issuer. For example, an issuer with an AA rating on a particular obligation is not necessarily better than an issuer with a BBB rating because the AA rating might be based primarily on a specific security or third-party support underlying the obligation.

Although many questions are asked in other areas during Standard and Poor's rating process, the rating does not mean that Standard and Poor's has performed an audit. It also does not attest to the authenticity of the information provided by the issuer and upon which the rating might be based. Ratings can be changed, withdrawn, or placed on CreditWatch as a result of changes in, or unavailability of, information.

Ratings do not create a trustworthy relationship between Standard and Poor's and an investor who uses the ratings because there is no legal basis for the existence of such a relationship.

There are several parties involved in the sale and purchase of a debt issue. The actual structure of an issue is the function and responsibility of the issuer and its advisors. Standard and Poor's only uses the materials prepared by those in a position to attest to such materials' accuracy and completeness. Standard and Poor's will react to a proposed financing, will publish papers outlining its criteria for that type of issue, and will interpret and make evaluations for the benefit of an issuer, underwriter, bond counsel, financial advisor, etc., but it does not function as an investment banker or financial advisor. This would ultimately serve to impair the objectivity and credibility that are vital to Standard and Poor's continued performance as an independent rating agency.

It is commonplace for companies to structure financing transactions to reflect Standard and Poor's credit criteria so they can qualify for higher ratings. Standard and Poor's guidance is also sought with regard to credit-quality issues that might affect corporate creditworthiness. For example, companies solicit Standard and Poor's view of the sale of accounts receivable,the utilization of captive finance subsidiaries, or other innovative financing techniques before putting these into practice. It is not uncommon for debt issuers to undertake specific, and sometimes significant, actions for the sake of maintaining their ratings.

As an example, one large company faced a downgrade of its A-1 commercial paper rating because of a growing component of short-term, floating-rate debt.

It chose to restructure its debt and abide by Standard and Poor's view of what was prudent in order to keep its rating.

Many companies go one step further and incorporate specific rating objectives as corporate goals. Ironically, the choice of objective is often inconsistent with what Standard and Poor's believes would be in the company's ultimate best interests. Indeed, Standard and Poor's questions whether linking a company's long-term financial strategy to a specific rating category makes any sense at all.

Standard and Poor's does not encourage companies to manage themselves with an eye toward a specific rating. The more appropriate approach is to operate for the good of the business as management sees it, and to let the rating follow.

RATING CHANGES

Rating changes can occur several times over the life of a bond, and the change can be more than one level such as BBB to B–. In 1981, Standard and Poor's increased 136 ratings but decreased 167 ratings, including such giants as DuPont, Ford, General Motors, and RCA. In 1982, Standard and Poor's lowered the ratings of 246 corporations, and in 1985, a record 272 downgrades occurred. In 1985, Moody's changed the ratings on 277 issues, with 124 increases and 153 decreases.

Moody's 1985 Upgrades:

Financial Institutions:	16
Industrials:	35
Utilities:	46
Transportation:	7
	124

Moody's 1985 Downgrades:

Financial Institutions:	14
Industrials:	121
Utilities	15
Transportation:	3
	153

Table 4-1 shows the number of Standard and Poor's corporate rating changes between 1981 and 1988.

There are many reasons why bonds are upgraded or downgraded but for simplicity sake, they can be divided them into three categories:

- Financial flexibility
- Mergers, acquisitions, and divestitures
- Strategy and environment

TABLE 4-1
Standard and Poor's Corporate Rating Changes

*1981 to 1988**

	1981	*1982*	*1983*	*1984*	*1985*	*1986*	*1987*	*1988*
Upgrades	136	92	104	164	125	149	188	261
Downgrades	167	246	203	173	272	364	284	386

*The 1988 Corporate Rating Actions Summarized.***

	Upgrades Number of	Amount (Bil.$)
Industrials	129	87.9
Financial Institutions	65	17.9
Utilities	40	34.3
Transportation	8	1.3
International	19	16.6
Total	261	158.0

	Downgrades Number of	Amount (Bil.$)
Industrials	182	56.1
Financial Institutions	122	65.6
Utilities	38	35.0
Transportation	32	6.1
International	12	5.6
Total	386	168.4

The upgrades and downgrades affected every rating category from AAA to D. The changing composition to and from junk bonds in 1988 can be seen in Table 4-2.***

*Standard and Poor's *CreditReview*, February 6, 1989, p. 14

**Ibid. p. 15

***Ibid. p. 16

Financial flexibility is usually quantitative financial parameters such as cash flow, stock buyback, profitability and debt protection. The following examples illustrate financial flexibility changes that resulted in ratings changes.[5]

- Groliers, Inc.: Moody's Investor Services raised the senior debt ratings of this book publisher to Ba from B3, citing its improved profitability, thus reducing its financial leverage.

[5] The changes in this section were reported by Standard and Poor's *CreditWeek* and *The Wall Street Journal* between January 1987 and July 1988.

TABLE 4-2
Junk Bonds' Changing Composition

Into Speculative Grade

	Senior debt rating
American Standard Inc.	B+
Avon Capital Corp.	BB
Avon Products Inc.	BB
Bell & Howell Co.	B+
Bucyrus-Erie Co. (Becor Western Inc. unit)	CCC+
Builders Transport Inc.	B+Δ
Cenvill Investors Inc.	BB+
Eagle Picher Industries Inc.	B+
Federated Department Stores Inc.	B
Flexi-Van Leasing Inc.	B+
Fort Howard Corp.	BB−
Fort Howard Cup Corp. (formerly Maryland Cup Corp.)	B+
Gould Inc.	BB+
Insilco Corp.	B+
Interco Inc.	B
International Technology Corp.	CCC+
Maxus Energy Corp.	BB+
ONEOK Inc.	B
Pneumo Corp. (PA Holdings Corp. unit)	B+
Pulte Home Corp.	BB+
Quantum Chemical Corp. (formerly National Distillers & Chemicals Corp.)	BB−
Research-Cottrell Inc.	B
St. Louis Southwestern Railway Co.	BB+
Santa Fe Natural Resources Inc. (Santa Fe Southern Pacific Corp. unit)	BB+
Singer Co.	CCC+
Southern Pacific Co.	BB+
Southern Pacific Railroad Co.	BB+
Southern Pacific Transportation Co.	BB+
Stevens (J.P.) & Co.	BB+
Stop & Shop Companies	B
Texas & New Orleans Railroad Co.	BB+
United States Gypsum Co. (USG Corp. unit)	BB−
USG Corp.	BB−
Victoria Bankshares Inc.	BB+

Out of Speculative Grade

	Senior debt rating
Alumax Inc. (AMAX Inc. unit)	BBB−
AMAX Inc.	BBB−
AMAX International Finance Corp.	BBB−
Anitec Image Technology Corp. (International Paper Co. unit)	BBB+
Asarco Inc.	BBB−
Cain Chemical Inc. (Occidental Petroleum Corp. unit)	BBB−
Circus Circus Enterprises Inc.	BBB
Colorado National Bank Denver, CO	BBB−
Community Psychiatric Centers	BBB+
Community Psychiatric Centers N.V.	BBB+
CTI International Inc. (General Electric Capital Corp. unit)	AAA
DEKALB Corp.	BBB
Facet Enterprises Inc. (Pennzoil Co. unit)	BBB+
First City Bank of Houston	BBB−
Freeport McMoran Inc.	BBB−
GATX Corp.	BBB−Δ
Glendale Federal Savings & Loan Association	BBB−/A-3
Harnischfeger Corp.	BBB
Hudson Bay Oil & Gas Co.	BBB
Hutton (E.F.) Group Inc. (Shearson Lehman Hutton Holdings Inc. unit)	A
INCO Ltd.	BBB−
Inland Steel Co.	BBB−
Koger Properties Inc.	BBB
Lear Petroleum Corp. (British Petroleum Co. PLC unit)	AA
Loop Inc.	BBB+
Mitchell Energy & Development Corp.	BBB−
Missouri-Kansas-Texas Railroad Co.	AA
Mueller Co. (Tyco Laboratories Inc. unit)	BBB−
Navistar Financial Corp.	BBB−
Navistar International Transportation Corp.	BBB−
Noranda Aluminum Inc.	BBB
ONEOK Inc.	BBB
Pembroke Capital Co. Inc. (Texaco Inc. unit)	BBB+
Phelps Dodge Corp.	BBB
PNPP Funding Corp. (Ohio Edison Co. unit)	BBB−
Reserve Oil & Gas Co. (Texaco Inc. unit)	BBB+
SeaFirst Corp.	BBB−
Texaco Capital Inc.	BBB+
Texaco Convent Refining Inc.	BBB+
Texaco Inc.	BBB+
Tri-Star Pictures Inc. (now Columbia Pictures Entertainment Inc.)	BBB+
USLICO Corp.	BBB−

ΔSubordinated debt.

Source: Reprinted from Standard and Poor's *CreditReview*, Feb. 6, 1989, p. 16.

- GAF Corp.: Standard and Poor's upgraded subordinate debt from B to B+ citing the company's cost-cutting maneuvers and streamlining have helped earnings.
- Gencorp Inc.: Moody's downgraded Gencorp from Ba2 to Ba3 citing that the company's recapitalization program will cause a sizeable increase in debt and reduce its financial flexibility.
- National Steel: Standard and Poor's lowered the senior-secured debt from B+ to B citing that while National Steel had taken positive steps to strengthen its cost and market positions, it has yet to sustain even a modest level of profitability.
- Fluor Corporation: Standard and Poor's lowered the rating of this construction and natural resources management company from BBB+ to BB because of industry over capacity, weak pricing conditions, and the expectation that profitability and cash flow protection might not rebound in the foreseeable future.
- Harte-Hanks Communication: Moody's placed the company under review for possible upgrading because the company strengthened its balance sheet and improved its fixed-charge coverage as it pays off debt with proceeds from selected asset sales.
- Harnischfeger Industries: Standard and Poor's increased the ratings on the senior debt from BB to BBB and the subordinate debt from B+ to BBB− citing improved earnings and a stronger capital position.
- Chevron: Standard and Poor's increased the ratings from AA− to AA citing sustained financial flexibility in a time of decreasing oil prices.
- Westinghouse Electric: Standard and Poor's increased senior debt ratings from AA− to AA citing improved operating performance and better prospects after a series of restructurings.

Sometimes the accounting method that a company uses can have a bearing on its rating. Moody's placed Middle South Utilities bonds under review for possible downgrading because of the company's potential exposure to financial and regulatory risk as a result of new utility accounting standards.

During 1987 and 1988, financial institutions were plagued with high-risk loan portfolios where interest and principal payments from second- and third-world debtors were in question. As a result, many banks were downgraded by the rating agencies. One such financial institution, Mellon Bank Corporation, decided to establish an independent liquidation bank in which Mellon would transfer $1 billion of low-quality assets for write-downs, transfers, or sale at a reduced price. This resulted in Moody's placing Mellon under review for an increase in its rating because risk was reduced. At the same time, the stock price ''dropped'' because of a reduction in projected earnings. This example shows that stock prices and bond ratings can move in opposite directions especially if the company uses stockholder earnings to reduce debt.

The second reason for rating changes is mergers, acquisitions, and leveraged buy outs. Since the early 1980s, perhaps the greatest cause for rating changes has been leveraged buy outs (LBO's). LBO's can result in huge debt, destruction of debt protection, changes in corporate strategy and direction, changes in management, and surgical disection and divestiture of selected corporate assets.[6] The following are examples of rating changes due to mergers, acquisitions and LBO's:

- First Jersey National Corporation: Standard and Poor's placed this company on CreditWatch for possible upgrading of its senior debt, currently rated as BBB+ because of the company's agreement to be acquired by London-based National Westminster Bank LPC, which has a rating of AAA.
- Harcourt Brace Jovanovich, Inc.: Standard and Poor's placed this BB+-rated debt on CreditWatch with implications for downgrading because of a threat posed by a takeover bid from British Printing and Communications Corporation. Although the company rejected the bid, the offer could lead to defensive measures (through debt) that might strain the already heavily leveraged company.
- International Controls Corporation: Standard and Poor's downgraded the engineering and aerospace concern from B- to CCC+ citing the recent leveraged buy out by management. The rating company cited weak cash flow, which might not allow a significant reduction of debt.
- Circle K Corporation: Standard and Poor's placed this convenient stores operator's debt on CreditWatch for possible downgrading because of its announcement to buy 1,000 convenient stores from Southland Corporation and Charter Company, stating that the near-term impact on the company's leverage and profitability might not be favorable.
- Baker International and Hughes Tool: Because of the merger between these two companies, Moody's lowered the ratings of Baker's senior debt from A2 to Baa1 and raised the senior debt of Hughes from B2 to Baa1, thus placing both debts at the same level.
- Carlton, Inc.: Standard and Poor's placed the B- senior debt on CreditWatch for possible downgrading because of a proposed purchase by a New Jersey investor. If debt financing is used to pay for the acquisition, Carlton debt as a percentage of sales would jump from 55 percent to 75

[6]For a more detailed analysis of merger effects on bond ratings, see Appendix A.

percent. Defensive measures, such as management buy out or recapitalization, would also weaken credit.

- Gillette Company: Moody's lowered the rating of the company's long-term debt from Baa2 to Baa3 because of the significant increase in the debt level that would result from the company's buyback plan for 16 million shares of stock.
- American Motors Corporation: Standard and Poor's raised the ratings from CCC to BBB because of the recent purchase of American Motors by Chrysler Corporation.

The third reason credit ratings are changed is strategy and the environment. This category includes such items as the corporation's current and future strategy, environmental projections such as inflation rate effects, and asset valuation exposure perhaps because of changes in buyer habits or saturated/overpriced markets. Asset valuation can also occur as a result of organizational restructuring and accounting methods.

Another, often overlooked, reason for quality changes in bonds is exposure to risk caused by the actions of a third party. For example, as the real estate market began to lose its luster in 1987–88, corporations whose prime source of income was real estate development (and the financial institutions that provided funds) were downgraded by more than one level. Other corporations whose investment portfolios were heavily endowed with these bonds were also downgraded if the interest from these bonds were to be used as a prime source of debt reduction. Several examples of rate changes within this category are listed below:

- Texas American Bankshares: Moody's downgraded the senior debt of this bank holding company to B1 from Ba2 citing the company's exposure to troubled real estate markets and continued asset deterioration.
- Leisure & Technology, Inc.: Standard and Poor's raised the subordinate debt from CCC to CCC+ citing a more fully developed management of an orderly growth that resulted in improved company earnings.
- U.S. Shoe: Moody's placed the company under review for possible downgrading citing an uncertain fashion environment, lackluster sales, and increased promotional activity, all of which are hurting returns.
- Inco Ltd (Toronto): Moody's placed the company under review for upgrading prompted by extremely strong nickel prices that have improved the company's financial conditions. Although nickel prices might not increase, the company is using its strong cash flow to reduce debt and is well-positioned to weather lower nickel prices should they occur.
- Asarco Inc.: Standard and Poor's increased the senior debt rating from BB+ to BBB– citing strong conditions in the metals market, less vulner-

ability to a slide in metal prices, cost-cutting, and its plan to diversify through acquisitions. Furthermore, Asarco should be able to complete acquisitions without materially reversing the balance sheet.

- Southmark: Standard and Poor's lowered the senior debt rating from BB+ to B citing the real estate slump that hurt Southmark's ability to realize value through rapid turnover of real estate assets and impaired, high-debt levels that have reduced earnings and cash flow.
- W.W. Grainger: Standard and Poor's upgraded the revenue bonds from AA to AA+ citing excellent distribution skills, which have helped to offset the cyclical nature of the business. The earnings have been good despite economic slumps.
- Avon Products: Moody's downgraded the senior debt from A2 to Baa1 citing a gradual shift away from the core business which has led to greater use of financial leverage to reposition the company for improved profitability.
- Wendy's International: Standard and Poor's placed Wendy's on CreditWatch for possible downgrading due to intense competition and saturated markets.

EVENT RISK

Recently, Standard and Poor's has begun assessing the degree of protection provided in the bond indenture against a sudden and dramatic decline in credit quality resulting from takeovers, recapitalizations, or similar restructurings. The ranking system is based solely on Standard and Poor's analysis of bond indenture provisions, and no opinion of the likelihood or potential of such events occurring is implied. Event-risk covenant rankings supplement Standard and Poor's traditional debt ratings, which evaluate fundamental credit quality.[7]

A Standard and Poor's event-risk covenant ranking is an assessment of a corporate debt obligation's protection against event risk—the potential for a sudden and dramatic decline in credit quality resulting from a large stock repurchase or dividend payment by the obligor, the obligor's acquisition by another entity, or other restructurings that remove assets from or add liabilities to the obligor. See Table 4-3.

[7]The remainder of this section has been reprinted from Standard and Poor's *CreditWeek*, July 24, 1989.

TABLE 4-3
Event Risk Covenant Ranking

Issuer/Issue	*Covenant Ranking*	*Rating*
Becton, Dickinson & Co.		
9.95% nts 1999	E-3	A+
8 3/8% nts 1996	E-5	A+
9 1/4% sf debs 2016	E-5	A+
Cummins Engine Co.		
9 3/4% sf debs 2016	E-5	BBB
Eaton Corp.		
9% debs 2016	E-5	A
Enron Corp.		
9 1/2% crdt sens nts 2001	E-1	BBB–
Grumman Corp.		
10 3/8% nts 1999	E-4	BBB
Harris Corp.		
10 3/8% debs 2018	E-3	A–
Knight-Ridder Inc.		
9 7/8% debs 2009	E-3	AA–
Lyondell Petrochemical Co.		
9.95% nts 1996	E-3	BBB
10% nts 1999	E-3	BBB
Northwest Pipeline Corp.		
10.65% debs 2018	E-4	BBB
Super Valu Stores Inc.		
8 7/8% nts 1999	E-3	A+
Xtra Inc. (gtd: Xtra Corp.)		
md term nts ser A	E-4	BBB

The ranking assesses the obligation's provisions with respect to event risk and is based in varying degrees on the scope, perceived effectiveness, and benefits to holders of the protective provisions. Rankings are as follows:

E-1 Strong protection against event risk. Protection is provided against virtually all anticipated events and the effectiveness of protective provisions appears sound.

E-2 Significant protection against event risk. Protection is provided against most anticipated events. The effectiveness of protective provisions appears sound.

E-3 Some protection against event risk. Protection may not be provided against some anticipated events, or the effectiveness of protective provisions is questionable, or the benefits of protection are modest.

E-4 Weak protection against event risk. Protection is provided only against some anticipated events, or the effectiveness of protective provisions is questionable, or the benefits of protection are modest.

E-5 Insignificant or no protection against event risk.

Event-risk covenant rankings are relative, non-absolute assessments. Even for debt ranked E-1, protection is not guaranteed, and indenture covenants might not be enforceable. Rankings supplement Standard and Poor's traditional debt ratings and an obligor's creditworthiness to a specific obligation. Neither ratings nor rankings incorporate an assessment of the event-risk vulnerability of the obligor. Event-risk covenant rankings and debt ratings are not recommendations to purchase, sell, or hold a security, because they do not assess market price or suitability for a particular investor.

Bonds sold before 1975 often contained covenants restricting the issuer from paying dividends, buying back stock, or incurring new debt. These provisions can afford strong event-risk protection by preventing the issuer from engaging in these activities or requiring the issuer to redeem the bonds before forbidden transactions are executed. For most of these issues, only a small amount of debt is outstanding, and with the passage of time, retained earnings available for restricted payments have grown to levels that no longer provide significant limitations. Issuers of investment-grade bonds have been very reluctant to incorporate these features in more recent public offerings, although such issues could receive a favorable event-risk ranking.

During the past few years, bonds have been sold with provisions that permit the holder to redeem them (put) at face value, or require the issuer to raise the interest rate, if a credit-damaging event occurs. These provisions have been nicknamed ''poison puts'' because their original purpose was to deter a hostile takeover under the guise of bondholder protection. Becton, Dickinson Corp.'s 9¼ percent debentures, due 2016, are an example. Standard and Poor's ranks them E-5, indicating significant event-risk protection. The bonds can be put only if there is a corporate change of control that is not approved by the board of directors. This protection is flawed because most takeovers and leveraged buy outs (LBO) are ultimately approved by the board.

Since bondholders' angry reaction to RJR Nabisco Inc.'s announced LBO proposal last October, issuers have been experimenting with more substantial protective provisions. Bonds issued by Harris Corp. and Northwest Pipeline Inc. were among the first to provide such additional protection.

This type of protection can be triggered by large dividend payments and stock repurchases, as well as a change of control, whether or not the board approves. Nevertheless, these issues are assigned rankings of E-3 or E-4. In general, these provisions are weak because the trigger threshold is high. For example, an issuer might repurchase up to 30 percent of its stock without triggering the put, despite the significant, negative credit impact of such a move. The option to initiate a large, debt-financed acquisition without triggering the put is another, but lesser, shortcoming. Lower thresholds could yield higher rankings for deals of this type.

The value of the protection to the bondholder can also affect the ranking. Protection in the Harris and Northwest Pipeline deals evaporates if the issuer deteriorates to speculative grade before the designated event. A bondholder can suffer a large loss if a speculative grade issuer does an LBO and its bond rating plunges to "CCC+" from "BB+."

Enron Corp.'s 9.5 percent credit-sensitive notes, due 2001, are ranked E-1. They are the only obligation to-date to receive Standard and Poor's top ranking. The event-risk protection is simple. If the bond's rating is lowered, the required interest payments rise by a predetermined formula. The cause of the downgrade is irrelevant, and thus any conceivable event would be covered. The size of the rate increases is viewed as providing meaningful and sufficient compensation. Also, this formula approach avoids the subjectivity of the interest rate reset mechanics that impair Northwest Pipeline's and Xtra's bonds. Enron's interest rate step-up is largest because the rating crosses to speculative from investment grade. Its senior debt is now rated "BBB–."

Even an E-1 ranking does not mean there is guaranteed protection against all event-induced, bondholder losses. There is still some small or remote risks, such as the liquidity risk of resets, which blemish even Enron's protection. Although Enron's bonds provide very strong event-risk protection, an interest rate reset does not assure liquidity for the bonds. A bondholder that is not allowed to own bonds rated below a certain level is not assured that he can sell his bonds without taking a loss.

Event-risk rankings can be raised or lowered. Debt rating changes can affect some protective provisions. Therefore, rankings can change as a result of a rating change. For example, Northwest Pipeline's protected issue loses protection if the rating drifts below "BBB–" due to ordinary credit erosion. In that event, the ranking would be lowered to E-5 from the current E-4.

Changed interpretations of takeover laws or new legislation could have a profound and widespread impact, resulting in numerous ranking changes.

RATING VARIABLES

The variables used to determine a rating can be characterized as quantifiable ("hard") variables and qualifiable ("soft") variables. The quantitative variables are almost entirely financial ratios and include:

- Size of the firm
- Size of the debt
- Profitability
- Inflation rate
- Size of debt/total outstanding debt
- Cash flow/total debt

- Cash flow
- Financial leverage
- Current ratio
- Interest rate
- Times interest earned (interest coverage ratio)
- Operating income/sales
- Cash flow/interest
- Sinking fund
- Capitalization ratio
- Acid test
- Stabililty of Cash flow

Public studies have shown that statistical analysis of as little as six or seven of these variables can be used to predict investment-grade ratings to within one grade level at an accuracy of 60 to 80 percent.

Unfortunately, the historical financial data of the company does not provide a true indication of the potential risks. Qualitative data is also required and this includes such elements as:

- Company's market share and product mix
- Company's position within the industry
- Company's financial prospects
- Company's management
- Company's sensitivity to the economy
- Industry prospects
- Industry sensitivity
- Industry volatility
- Industry competitiveness
- Industry regulations

Obtaining the qualitative data is often more difficult for the rater. Even annual reports might not provide the rater with information such as unfunded pension liabilities,which might be a substantial future cash claim.

Bond raters must evaluate not only the statistical data, but the intangibles of judgment about such factors as quality of management and future changes in tastes and technologies that can influence long-term profit possibilities. The real uncertainties of these judgment calls far outweigh the statistical conclusions. In the past, there has been severe criticism of rating agencies, with such statements as:

- Raters never consider alternative financing methods.
- Raters don't consider the time horizon or future financial conditions.
- Raters look entirely upon past history.
- Although raters look at the right financial ratios, their weighings are subjective.

- Agencies stress new issue ratings rather than a continuous process to reevaluate older ratings.
- Raters look at firms on an individual basis, rather than within their environment.

Bond raters today are much more sophisticated and knowledgeable than in the past. Criticisms that frequently appeared in the trade literature seems to have disappeared. As stated by Danos, et al:[8]

"The senior bond raters we interviewed told us that ratee forecasts aid the rating process in a number of ways. They stated that the analysis of forecasts often provides insight into management's planning process, financing strategies, assumptions about the future, and response to expectations about the future. In addition, bond raters' ability to analyze and question management about actual performance for a period is thought to be enhanced when the actual performance can be compared to previously obtained projections for the period.

Specifically, our discussions with bond raters led us to expect that the impact of ratee forecasts on bond ratings varies but depends primarily on expected rating class, relationships between historical and projected financial information, management's track record of forecast accuracy, and interactions among these factors.

We found bond raters to be very knowledgeable about the history of and prospects for both specific industries and individual businesses. Ratee industry trends and forecasts and historical financial data are normally part of raters' general background knowledge. Therefore, initial impressions are formed before formal analysis of current financial information is begun. ....

Bond raters participate in an ongoing training and review process. This process includes presentations of their assigned rating cases to bond rating review committees and consideration of presentations made by others, as well as discussion within these rating committee meetings. Bond raters have the unique exposure to management forecasts; they have access to many forecasts, they evaluate many forecasts, the forecasts are summarized and reported in a highly structured format, and they are evaluated according to specific directives. We expected the bond raters' training and review process, coupled with their repeated exposure to forecasts, to foster the development of sharply defined schemata for ratee historical financial information, financial forecasts, and their relationship to each other."

Above all, the most important thing to look for in a credit analysis is not what the company is doing today, or what it has done in the past, but what decisions is the company making today that will enhance the value of the company tomorrow. These decisions are not quantifiable and, therefore, might result in a conflict of

[8]Paul Danos, Doris L. Holt, and Eugene A. Imhoff, Jr., "Bond Raters' Use of Management Financial Forecasts: Experiment in Expert Judgment," *The Accounting Review*, Vol. LIX, No. 4, 1984, pp. 291.

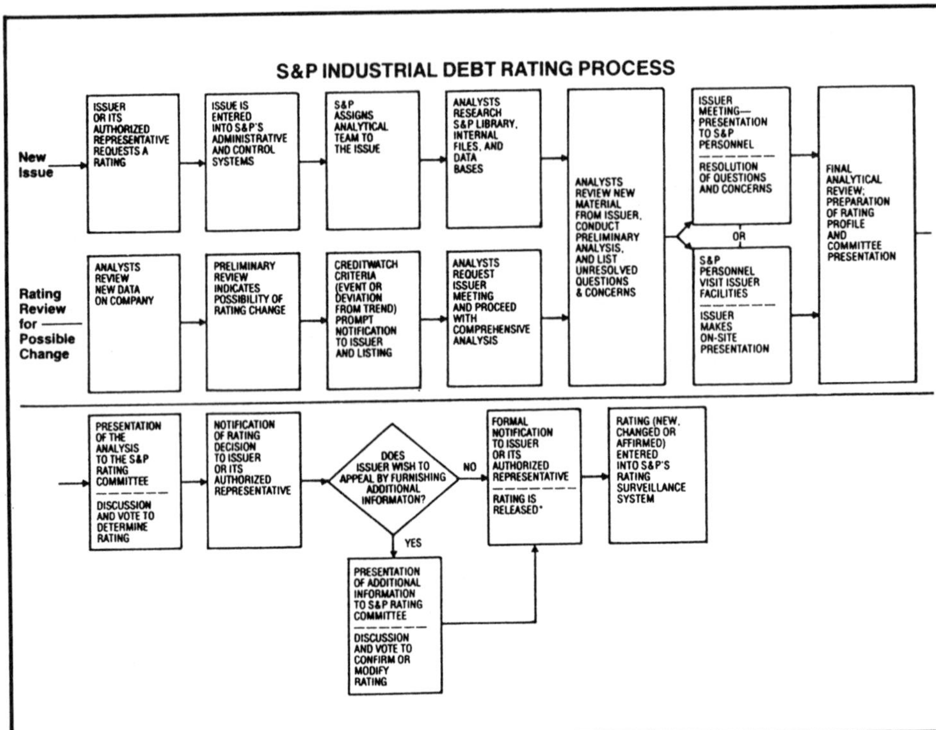

Source: Standard and Poor's *Debt Rating Criteria*, 1986, pg. 12.

Fig. 4-3. *Standard and Poor's industrial debt rating process.*

opinion between raters and rating agencies. These are honest differences of opinion and both positions can be defended.

Bond raters McCarthy, Crisanti, and Maffei appear to be tougher on the companies than other rating firms. They hold company management at a distance and work mainly from company published data and positioning in the industry. Their response to upgrading and downgrading issues generally runs ahead of the pack.

Unlike McCarthy, Crisanti, and Maffei, Standard and Poor's believes rather strongly that contact with the bond issuer's management should be an essential part of establishing bond ratings. This can be seen from Figure 4-3[9]. The following is a short synopsis of how Standard and Poor's forms a rating for an issuer:

Standard and Poor's first meets with the management of the issuing organization to review their key operating and financial plans in detail, as well as their management policies and any credit factors that will have an impact on their rating. A team of analysts, others who are familiar with the company or industry, and senior members of the staff are then assigned to them. Usually, the company is represented by its chief financial officer, although senior operating execu-

[9]Standard and Poor's *Debt Rating Criteria*, 1986, pp. 12–13.

tives also participate, and the chief executive officer usually deals with the strategic issues.

At the meeting the prospectus, or offering circular, annual and interim financial statements, and the company presentation is provided. The company presentation is particularly important because it represents management's view of the business and financial outlook. The company presentation is usually provided by the potential issuers before the meeting with the rating company, and includes:

1. A five-year projection, including income statements, balance sheets, and source and application of funds analysis, together with underlying assumptions.
2. Comparisons with competitors.
3. An analysis of capital spending plans.
4. Financing alternatives, if not apparent from the data presented.
5. Other key factors the issuer believes might have an impact on their rating. This could include business segment analysis and forecasts, reserve values, portfolio analysis, etc.

The role of financial projections in the rating process needs to be clarified. Standard and Poor's ratings are not based just on an issuer's financial projections but on a company's own assessment of the company's outlook. Nonetheless, management's financial projections are a valuable tool in the rating process because they are indicative of management's plans for the future, how it assesses the company's prospects, and how it plans to deal with its problems. Projections also illuminate the financial strategy of the company. Its anticipated reliance on internal cash flow or outside funds. The projected balance sheets provide the rating company with a company's objectives in terms of debt leverage, working capital needs, and the like.

After the issuer meeting, a rating committee meeting will usually meet. Once the rating is determined, the issuer is notified of the rating and the major considerations supporting it. There is usually a short time allowed for any new information to be considered or feedback from the issuer that would affect the rating before it is made public.

No matter how sophisticated the rating game becomes, many critical elements have gotten much harder to pin down. Compounding this problem are the new variable rate bonds, questionable economic conditions, industry instability, and the shortening of debt maturities.

For a more detailed analysis of the methodologies used to determine creditworthiness, see Appendix B.

TABLE 4-4
Bonds Maturing in the Year 2000

	Title	*Coupon%*		*Yield to Maturity%*
AA	American Telephone & Teleg.	6.		9.31
	" " "	8.75		9.62
	Baltimore Gas and Electric	8.625		9.66
	Carolina Telephone & Teleg.	9.125		9.67
	Chesp. Potomac T&T WVA	5.0		9.62
	Consolidated Edison	9.375		9.7
	General Telephone Illinois	8.5		9.61
	General Telephone Indiana	9.0		9.66
	General Telephone Michigan	9.0		9.97
	Great Northern Railroad	3.125		9.96
	Hawaiian Telephone	8.75		9.72
	Iowa-Illinois Gas & Electric	8.75		9.66
			Average	9.68
AA –	Duke Power	8.5		9.72
	GMAC	8.75		10.09
	General Telephone Northwest	9.25		9.97
	General Telephone Southwest	9.25		9.96
	Haliburton	9.25		9.92
			Average	9.93
A +	Atlantic City Electric	8.875		9.96
	Atlantic Richfield	8.625		9.81
	Atlantic Richfield	7.70		10.00
	Boston Edison	9.375		9.97
	Delmarva Power & Light	8.375		9.65
			Average	9.88
A	Alabama Power	9.0		10.01
	Ashland Oil	8.8		10.00
	Carolina Power & Light	8.75		10.00
	Central Power & Light	8.75		10.00
	Gulf Power	8.875		9.97
	Hawaiian Electric	9.0		10.01
			Average	10.00
A –	Beneficial Corporation	7.45		10.65
	Brown Group	9.875		10.22
	Central Louisiana Elec.	9.375		10.04
	" " "	9.5		10.06
	Dow Chemical	8.9		9.76
	International Paper	8.85		10.05
			Average	10.13
BBB +	Arizona Public Service	10.625		10.32
	Central Hudson Gas & Elec.	9.375		10.31
	Connecticut Light & Power	8.875		10.30

	Title	*Coupon%*		*Yield to Maturity%*
	Dallas Power and Light	9.375		10.07
	Dayton Power and Light	9.50		10.31
	Deere and Company	8.45		10.21
	Hartford Electric Light	9.25		10.32
	Indiana-Michigan Electric	8.875		10.31
	Jersey Central Power & Light	8.75		10.54
			Average	10.3
BBB	Cities Service	9.75		10.45
	Detroit Edison	9.15		10.71
	Duquesne Light	8.75		10.36
	Georgia Power	8.625		10.37
			Average	10.47
BBB–	Consumer Power	8.625		10.85
	Ohio Edison	9.25		10.41
			Average	10.63
BB+	Asarco	9.75		10.78
	Marathon Oil	8.50		11.24
			Average	11.01
BB	Amax	9.375		11.23
	Arkansas Power & Light	9.625		12.40
	Louisiana Power & Light	9.375		12.64
			Average	12.09
BB–	American Fructose	9.4		12.07
	Inland Steel	9.5		10.98
	Long Island Lighting	9.125		11.18
	Owens Corning	9.5		10.90
	Phillips Petroleum	8.875		10.92
			Average	11.21
B+	ARMCO	9.2		12.66
	Gulf States Utilities	7.875		10.42
	N. L. Industries	9.375		11.34
			Average	11.47

BOND RATINGS VERSUS YIELD TO MATURITY

The further a bond is from maturity, the greater the yield to maturity (see Tables 4-4 and 4-5). Table 4-4 identifies the 1987 year and yields to maturity for selected bonds maturing in 2000. Table 4-5 shows the yield to maturity for similar bonds maturing in 2004.

After comparison, the 2004 maturities are generally greater than the 2000 maturities. The reason why bonds with greater maturities have greater yields is

TABLE 4-5
Bonds Maturing in the Year 2004

Ratings	*Title*	*Coupon*		*Yield to Maturity*
AAA	AMOCO Oil	9.2		9.73
	Illinois Bell	8.0		9.61
			Average	9.67
AA+	Central Illinois Public Service	8.5		9.77
AA	Baltimore Gas & Electric	8.125		9.77
	Consolidated Edison	9.125		9.95
			Average	9.86
AA−	Chesapeake Potomac T&T MD	5.875		9.82
	Duke Power	9.75		9.82
	Florida Power & Light	8.50		9.79
	GMAC	9.4		10.12
			Average	9.89
A+	CIT Group	9.85		10.21
	General Telephone South	8.25		10.07
	Idaho Power	8.375		10.07
			Average	10.12
A	Alabama Power	9.75		10.11
	Carolina Power & Light	9.75		10.11
	Central Power and Light	9.385		10.11
			Average	10.11
A−	Appalachian Power	8.5		10.15
	Houston Power and Light	8.125		10.16
			Average	10.15
BBB+	Central Hudson	9.25		10.40
	Commonwealth Edison	9.375		10.64
	Connecticut Light and Power	8.75		10.41
	Hartford Electric Light	9.25		10.41
			Average	10.46
BBB	Cincinnati Gas and Electric	9.15		10.47
	Columbus and Southern Ohio Electric	9.9		10.46
	Detroit Edison	9.875		10.74
	Duquesne Light	8.625		10.46
	Firestone Tire and Rubber Co.	9.25		10.45
	Georgia Power	8.625		10.49
	Northern Indiana Public Serv.	8.9		10.46
			Average	10.50
BBB−	El Paso Electric	9.0		10.51
BB	NAVISTAR	9.0		12.55
B	Mississippi Power & Light	9.875		13.65
	New Orleans Public Service	10.0		13.40
			Average	13.52

because the greater the time span, the more likely it is that economic conditions can change, perhaps for the worst.

The next section discusses how Standard and Poor's decides on a bond rating and is taken from Standard and Poor's *Debt Rating Criteria*.

STANDARD AND POOR'S RATING METHODOLOGY[10]

The rating methodology profile (RAMP) is Standard and Poor's analytical framework; it is the format for all rating deliberations. By dividing the analytical task into several categories, each of which is scored, it provides the discipline to ensure that all salient issues are considered. The first categories are oriented to business, or competitive analysis; the remainder relate to financial analysis (see Fig. 4-4). However, there is no formula for combining these scores to arrive at a rating conclusion. Ultimately, there is no real way to separate the RAMP's variables because they are all interdependent.

It is important to understand that the rating process is not limited to examining various financial measures. Proper assessment of debt protection levels requires a broader framework. This involves a thorough review of business fundamentals, including judgments as to the company's competitive position and evaluation of management and its strategies. Clearly, such judgments are highly subjective. Yet, that is at the heart of every rating.

At times, a rating decision might be heavily influenced by financial measures. At other times, business risk factors might dominate. To the extent that a firm is strong in the one respect and weak in the other, the rating will balance the different factors. Viewed differently, the degree of a firm's business risk sets the expectations for the financial risk it can afford at any rating level. By first analyz-

Rating Methodology Profile

Business Risk *Industry Characteristics*	*Financial Risk* *Financial Characteristics*
Issuer Position	
e.g. *Technology*	Financial Policy
e.g. *Marketing*	Profitability
e.g. *Efficiency*	Capital Structure
e.g. *Management*	Cash Flow Protection
Composite: Competitive Position	Financial Flexibility

Source: Standard and Poor's *Debt Rating Criteria*, 1986, pg. 21.

Fig. 4-4. *Standard and Poor's rating methodology profile, which ensures that all aspects of the business are considered in a rating.*

[10]Standard and Poor's Debt Rating Criteria, 1986, pp. 21–30.

Food & beverage industry
Guidelines for debt leverage ratios*
Competitive Position vs. Peer Group

Rating Category	*Well Above Average*	*Above Average*	*Average*	*Industrial Medians*
BBB	60%	55%	50%	35%
A	50	45	40	30
AA	40	35	30	25
AAA	30	25	N.A.	15

*Debt leverage = total debt as % of capitalization

Source: Standard and Poor's *Debt Rating Criteria*, 1986, pg. 21.

Fig. 4-5. *Standard and Poor's reviews corporations according to how they measure up within their own industry.*

ing the industry characteristics and how a firm is positioned to succeed in that environment, Standard and Poor's establishes the financial benchmarks before proceeding to the quantitative part of the analysis. An example of leverage expectations, as they pertain to the packaged food industry, is shown in Fig. 4-5. (These measures are contrasted with the median levels for all industrials.)

INDUSTRY RISK

Each rating analysis begins with an assessment of the company's environment. To determine the degree of operating risk that faces a participant in a given business, Standard and Poor's analyzes the dynamics of that business. This analysis focuses on the strength of the industry prospects, as well as the competitive factors that affect that industry.

The many factors that are assessed include: Is the industry in a growth, stable, or declining phase? Does the business display cycles independent of the economy as, for example, agriculture? Or, if it moves with the economy in general, is it more or less volatile? Does it lead or lag economic trends or does it have contracyclical tendencies?

What is its vulnerability to technological change, labor unrest, or regulatory interference? Are assets typically concentrated in receivables and inventory, or is there a need for fixed plant of a specialized nature? The list goes on. The implications of increasing competition are obviously crucial. Standard and Poor's knowledge of the investment plans of the major players in an industry offers a unique vantage point from which to assess competitive prospects.

While any particular profile category can be *the* overriding consideration, it must be noted that the industry risk assessment will go a long way toward setting the upper limit on the rating to which any participant in the industry can aspire. Specifically, it would be very difficult to imagine Standard and Poor's assigning "AA" and "AAA" bond ratings of "A-1+" commercial paper ratings to companies with heavy participation in industries considered to be of above-average risk, regardless of how conservative a financial posture is maintained. Examples of some of the industries Standard and Poor's would so characterize are integrated steel makers, tire and rubber companies, homebuilders, and most of the mining sector.

Conversely, some industries are regarded favorably by Standard and Poor's. They are distinguished by such traits as steady demand growth, an ability to maintain margins without impairing future prospects, flexibility in the timing of capital outlays, and moderate capital intensity. Industries possessing one or more of these attributes include manufacturers of branded consumer products, drug firms, and publishing and broadcasting. Again, high marks in this category do not translate into high ratings for all industry participants, but it certainly doesn't hurt to have the cushion of strong industry fundamentals to fall back on.

Often a changed industry outlook will lead to rating changes for firms competing in that industry. Whether a specific company's rating is raised or lowered as a result of a changed industry outlook depends on that company's ability to achieve the attributes for success and avoid the pitfalls in that business. A change in an industry's outlook certainly prompts Standard and Poor's to closely examine its ratings in that area, but all participants may not be affected equally by the revised outlook. For example, decline of the aluminum industry fundamentals led to a review and subsequent downgrading of every industry participant with rated debt in the spring of 1985. However, Alumax Inc.—by virture of its more protected niche in fabricated aluminum for construction—was reduced less than the others.

KEYS TO SUCCESS

As part of the industry analysis, the key rating factors are identified—the keys to success and areas of vulnerability. The nature of competition is, obviously, different for different industries. Competition can be based on price, quality of product, distribution capabilities, image, product differentiation, service, or some other factor. Competition may be on a national basis, as is the case with major appliances. But in other industries competition is global—chemicals, for example, and in still others, such as cement, competition is strictly regional.

The basis for competition determines which factors are analyzed for a given company. The accompanying chart highlights the factors that are considered critical in the pulp and paper products business—and the specific considerations which determine a company's position in each. (See Fig. 4-6.) In addition, for any particular company, one or more factors can hold special significance, even if that factor is not common to the industry. For example, the fact that a company

Rating Factors for Pulp and Paper Industry

(The predominant product lines determine the weighted importance of these variables.)

Cost Position

Low-cost status
- Operating margins
- Return on assets
- Mill margins
- Mill cash cost/ton
- Mill cost/ton
- Man hours/ton

Modern efficient asset base
- Capital expenditures as a percent of net fixed assets over last 10 years
- Repair and maintenance expenditures as a percent of net fixed assets over last 10 years
- Ratio of capital expenditures to inflation-adjusted depreciation.
- Are facilities "built-out" or is there room for additions?
- Are facilities integrated (on-site pulping)?
- Are machines new, in good running order?
- Mill site configuration and layout
- Process control and computer utilization

Mill Location
- Closeness to growth markets
- Closeness to major metropolitan regions
- Closeness to deep seaports for export
- Freight advantages
- Harvest costs

Labor Relations
- Union vs. nonunion mills
- History of labor disruptions
- Advantageous wage rates and work-rule flexibility
- Union contract expiration schedules

Customer Satisfaction

Quality, Service, Customer Loyalty
- Brightness, opacity, strength, runability, printability
- Independent surveys
- Evaluations by commercial printers and publishers, and customers
- Capacity utilization (Although not a pure indicator of quality, service, or customer loyalty, it does provide some directional insight.)

Product Mix

Value-added vs. commodity grades
Sales revenue per product ton
Diversity of mix
Breadth of products: full line or one-product supplier?
Consumer vs. nonconsumer end markets
Relative pricing sensitivity in key grades

Self-Sufficiency

Fiber self-sufficiency and long-term adequacy
- Fiber sources: internal sources vs. long-term private cutting contracts vs. gov't. contracts vs. outside market purchases
- Fiber mix: softwood vs. hardwood vs. recycled paper
- Reforestation programs

Energy mix and self-sufficiency
- Fuel mix: internal sources vs. oil vs. coal vs. gas
- Co-generation hydropower
- Ability to quickly convert or change to alternative energy source

Marketing Prowess

Gain or loss of market share
Distribution channels

Ratio of advertising cost to sales
New product introductions
Degree of influence on pricing

Forward integration
- Percent of in-house paper used by converting facilities
- Wholesale and retail distribution centers

Standard and Poor's *Debt Rating Criteria*, 1986, pg. 23.

Fig. 4-6. *Companies that participate in more than one industry, need to weigh the importance of each item according to its importance in the overall scheme of the business.*

has only one major production facility should certainly be included as an area of vulnerability.

Diversification Factors

When a company participates in more than one business, each segment is analyzed separately. A composite is formed from these building blocks, weighting each element according to its importance to the overall organization. Then the potential benefits of diversification, which may not be apparent from the additive approach, are considered. General Electric Co., Allied Signal Inc, and Figgie International Inc. are cases where the balance of different businesses is a major supporting factor in their ratings.

Obviously, to be considered a diversified company, no single business segment can be dominant. General Motors Corp. has received much attention for diversifying into aerospace and computer software. But GM is not a diversified firm since its success is substantially determined by one line of business.

Limited credit will be given if the various lines of business react similarly to economic cycles. For example, Falconbridge Ltd.'s diversification from nickel into copper is not expected to stabilize its performance; similar risk factors are associated with both metals.

Most critical is a company's ability to manage diverse operations. Skills and practices needed to run a business differ greatly among industries, not to mention the challenge posed by participating in several different industries. For example, in the rush to diversify into financial services, a number of companies entered businesses that were unfamiliar and which they had difficulty managing. Initially, Armco Inc. was lauded for its diversification from steel into insurance. More recently, this business has suffered major write-offs, stemming in part from poor control over how the business was operated.

Some firms have adopted a portfolio approach to their diverse holdings. The business of buying and selling businesses is different than running operations, and is analyzed differently. The ever-changing character of the company's assets typically is viewed as a negative. On the other hand, there is often an offsetting advantage, namely, greater flexibility in raising funds when each line of business is a discrete unit that can be sold off.

Size Considerations

Standard and Poor's has no minimum size criteria for any given rating level. Size becomes a rating issue when it affects a company's ability to compete. Obviously, the need to have a broad product line or a national marketing structure are factors in many businesses. In this sense, sheer mass is not important; demonstrable market advantage is.

Market share analysis is often an important rating consideration. However, large shares are not always synonymous with market advantage or industry dominance. For instance, where an industry has a number of large but comparably-sized participants, none may have a particular advantage or disadvantage.

Conversely, where an industry is highly fragmented, even the large firms may lack pricing leadership potential. The textile industry is an example.

Small companies also can hold dominant market positions which lend them competitive benefits. Two examples are Jostens Inc. in school rings and Great Lakes Chemical Corp. in bromine chemicals.

Still, small companies by definition are more concentrated in terms of product, number of customers, or geography. In effect, they lack some elements of diversification that can benefit larger firms. To the extent that markets and regional economies change, there is protection inherent in a broader scope of business. This consideration is balanced against the performance and prospects of a given business.

MANAGEMENT EVALUATION

Management is assessed for its role in determining operational success, and also for its risk tolerance. The first aspect is incorporated in the competitive position analysis; the second is weighed as a financial policy factor.

Essentially, subjective judgments lead to Standard and Poor's conclusions regarding each aspect of its management evaluation. Opinions are formed during the meetings that take place with senior management on a regular basis. While management's track record may seem to offer an objective basis for evaluation, it often is difficult to determine how results should be attributed to management's skills. Standard and Poor's must decide to what extent they are the result of good management, devoid of management influence, or achieved despite management.

Management credibility is an important factor. Plans and policies have to be judged for their realism. Once earned, credibility can support continuity of a particular rating. When a company is faced with stress or a restructuring, Standard and Poor's often will rely on management to carry out plans for restoring creditworthiness. For companies with less credibility, Standard and Poor's view is that stated policies often will not be followed, and the ratings will reflect that skepticism.

Organizational Considerations

Standard and Poor's evaluation also is sensitive to potential organizational problems. These include situations where:

- There is significant organizational reliance on an individual chief executive or financial officer, especially one who may be close to retirement.

- The finance function and finance considerations do not receive high organizational recognition.
- The transition of management—to professional and organizational from entrepreneurial or family-bound—has not yet been accomplished.
- A relatively large number of changes occur in a short time.
- The relationship between organizational structure and management strategy is unclear.
- A substantial presence by one or a few shareholders exists, providing stability of ownership or constraints on management prerogatives. (Depending on circumstances, this could have either positive or negative implications.)

The organizational structure, first and foremost, needs to be understood in the context of the business environment, including past practices and future needs. Where appropriate, Standard and Poor's will discuss unresolved questions with management to develop this understanding. When valid issues and questions still remain, Standard and Poor's cautiously factors them into the rating evaluation.

MEASURING PERFORMANCE AND RISK

Having evaluated the issuer's competitive position and the environment in which it operates, the analysis proceeds to several financial categories. To reiterate: the company's business-risk profile determines the level of financial risk appropriate for any rating category. Financial risk is portrayed largely through quantitative means, particularly by using financial ratios. Medians for key ratios are to be found on page . Benchmarks vary greatly by industry, and several analytical adjustments typically are required to calculate the ratios for an individual company.

Accounting Quality

A rating is not an audit, and the rating process does not entail Standard and Poor's auditing a company's financial records. Ratings are based on audited data, generally for a five-year period. Analysis of the audited financials begins by reviewing the accounting quality. The purpose is to determine whether ratios and statistics derived from financial statements can be used accurately to measure a company's performance and position *relative* to both its competition and the larger universe of industrial companies. The rating process is very much one of comparisons, so it is important to have a common frame of reference.

Accounting policies reviewed include, among other things:

- Consolidation basis.

- Income recognition (for example, successful efforts versus full cost in the oil industry and percentage of completion versus completed contract in the construction industry).
- Depreciation methods and asset lives.
- Inventory pricing methods.
- Amortization of intangibles.
- Investment tax credit policy.
- Employee benefits.

Similarly, the impact of purchase accounting and varied off-balance-sheet liabilities is assessed. To the extent possible, analytical adjustments are made to better portray reality. Although it is not always possible to completely recast a company's financial statements, it is useful to have some notion of the extent to which performance is overstated or understated. At the very least, the choice of accounting alternatives can be characterized as generally conservative or liberal.

Financial Policies

Standard and Poor's emphasizes the importance of management's philosophies and policies involving financial risk. A surprising number of companies have not given this question serious thought, much less reached strong conclusions. For many firms, debt leverage (calculated without adjustment to reported figures) is the only focal point of such policy considerations. More sophisticated business managers have thoughtful policies that recognize cash-flow parameters and the interplay between business and financial risk.

Many firms that have set goals do not have the wherewithal, discipline or management commitment to achieve these objectives. A company's leverage goals, for example, need to be viewed in the context of its past record and the financial dynamics affecting the business. If a management states, as most do, that its goal is to operate at 35 percent debt-to-capital, Standard and Poor's factors that into its analysis only to the extent it appears plausible. For example, if a company has aggressive spending plans, that 35 percent goal would carry little weight, unless management has committed to a specific program of asset sales, equity sales or other actions which in a given time period would produce the desired results.

Standard and Poor's does not encourage companies to manage themselves with an eye toward a specific rating. The more appropriate approach is to operate for the good of the business as management sees it, and let the rating follow. Certainly, prudence and credit quality should be among the most important considerations, but financial policy should be consistent with the needs of the business rather than an arbitrary constraint.

In any event, pursuit of the highest rating attainable is *not* necessarily in the company's best interests. 'AAA' may be the highest rating but that does not suggest that it is the "best" rating. Typically, a company with virtually no financial risk is *not* optimal as far as meeting the needs of its various constituencies. A company has shareholders as well as bondholders. An underleveraged firm is not minimizing its cost of capital, thereby depriving its owners of potentially greater value for their investment.

If opportunities are foregone merely to avoid financial risk, the firm is making poor strategic decisions. In fact, it may be sacrificing long-term credit quality for the facade of low risk in the near term. A recent financial article describes a company that curtailed spending expressly "to become an 'A' rated company." As a result, ". . . the company's business responded poorly to an increase in market demand. Needless to say, the sought after 'A' rating continued to elude the company."

In this light, a corporate objective of having its debt rated 'AAA' or 'AA'—and maybe even 'A'—can be suspect. Whatever a company's financial track record, Standard and Poor's must be skeptical if corporate goals are implicitly irrational. Standard and Poor's seeks to understand how a firm's "conservative financial philosophy" is consistent with the firm's overall goals or needs or otherwise arises from the nature of its operations.

PROFITABILITY FACTORS

This category actually encompasses two analytical areas. First, a company's earning power is measured. In the long run, profit potential is the most important determinant of credit protection. Second, earnings are viewed in relation to a company's burden of fixed charges. Otherwise strong performance can be detrimentally affected by aggressive debt financing, and the opposite is also true. In both respects, Standard and Poor's appraises the financial health of the company from an operating viewpoint, inasmuch as a corporation is viewed as an ongoing enterprise rather than as one being liquidated.

The more significant measures of profitability that Standard and Poor's uses are:

- Return on capital
- Profit margins
- Earnings on assets/business segments
- Inflation-adjusted earnings/reported earnings

Pretax return on average invested capital and operating income as a percent of sales are ratios that indicate a company's financial health regardless of how it is capitalized. Obviously, all else being equal, a company that generates higher operating margins and returns on capital has a greater ability to generate equity capital internally, attract capital externally and withstand business adversity. Earnings power ultimately attests to the value of the firm's assets.

While the absolute levels of the ratios are important, it is equally important to focus on trends and to compare these ratios with those of competitors. Various industries follow different cycles and have different earnings characteristics. Therefore, what may be considered favorable for one business may be relatively poor for another. For example, the drug industry usually generates high operating margins and high returns on capital. Defense contractors generate low operating margins and high returns on capital. The pipeline industry has high operating margins and low returns on capital. Comparisons with a company's peers will influence Standard and Poor's perception of a firm's competitive strengths and price leadership flexibility.

There are several fixed-charge coverage ratios that Standard and Poor's evaluates, but the two primary ones are pretax interest coverage and pretax coverage of interest plus total rents. If preferred stock is outstanding and material, fixed charges are adjusted to include preferred dividends. To reflect more accurately the ongoing earnings available to pay fixed charges, the reported figures are typically adjusted. The effect of LIFO liquidations, foreign exchange gains and unremitted equity are excluded, as well as those of nonrecurring or extraordinary gains and losses. Similarly, Standard and Poor's is interested in coverage of interest payable, and adjustments are made where interest has been capitalized.

The analysis of earnings protection and the other financial categories covers both historical and projected performance. Because ratings are an assessment of the likelihood of timely payment of interest and future repayment of principal, the evaluation emphasizes future performance. The rating analysis does not attempt to forecast performance precisely or to pinpoint economic cycles. Rather, the forecast analysis considers the variability of expected future performance based on a range of economic and competitive scenarios.

Particularly important today are management plans for sources of future earnings growth. Standard and Poor's evaluates whether existing businesses can provide satisfactory growth, especially in a less inflationary environment, and to what extent acquisitions or divestitures may be necessary to achieve corporate goals. At first glance, a mature cash generating company offers a great deal of bondholder protection. But Standard and Poor's assumes a corporation's central focus is to augment shareholder values over the long run. In this context, a lack of indicated earnings growth potential is considered a weakness. By itself, this may hinder a company's ability to attract financial and human resources. Moreover, limited internal earnings growth opportunities may lead management to pursue growth externally, implying greater business and financial risks.

LEVERAGE AND ASSET PROTECTION

Financial leverage, simply put, is the extent to which a firm uses someone else's funds or capital to finance itself. The more leveraged a company is, the less able it is to pay off its borrowed funds. It is less able to withstand diminution in asset values or cash flows than a company with lower leverage. In this sense, the notion of leverage is used to indicate the burden of fixed charges a company must service.

In another vein, the concept of asset protection refers to measurement of the relative amount of equity supporting the asset base. A variation on this theme is asset protection relative to outstanding debt. Here, the focus tends more toward viewing the company on a liquidating basis rather than as an ongoing concern. Since ratings primarily address the risk of default, and only secondarily whether a creditor ultimately will be paid, Standard and Poor's views leverage as being chiefly a proxy for the level of fixed charges that must be serviced rather than as a measure of asset protection. Nonetheless, the nature of the assets is a critical determinant of the appropriate leverage for a given level of risk. Assets with stable cash flow or market values justify greater use of debt financing than those with clouded marketability. In this context, receivables, grain and tobacco inventory, and even standalone business entities would be viewed positively—compared to assets that might be concentrated in, say, fixed plant and equipment.

Balance Sheet Ratios

Several ratios are employed by Standard and Poor's to capture the degree of leverage utilized by a company. They include:

- Long-term debt/long-term debt + equity
- Total debt/total debt + equity
- Total debt + off-balance sheet liabilities/total debt + off-balance sheet liabilities + equity

The traditional measure of long-term debt/capitalization has lost its significance as a measure of *permanent* debt leverage, since companies rely increasingly on short-term borrowings. It is now commonplace to find permanent layers of short-term debt, which finance not only seasonal working capital but an ongoing portion of the asset base. Management reluctance to refinance during periods of high interest rates has contributed to this phenomenon in recent years.

Off-balance sheet items that are factored into the leverage analysis include:

- Operating leases
- Pension obligations

- Debt of joint ventures and unconsolidated subsidiaries
- Guarantees
- Take-or-pay contracts and obligations under Throughput and Deficiency agreements
- Receivables that have been factored or transferred
- Potential legal judgments or settlements of lawsuits

Standard and Poor's uses various methodologies to determine the proper capitalized value for each of the off-balance sheet items. In general, the relevance of the activity financed to mainstream business and the likelihood of its need for financial support are key considerations. Thus, debt of joint ventures which are sound, standalone credits may be viewed as a much less onerous liability than capitalized operating rents and require their own methodology for apportioning debt between a parent's industrial operation and its captive finance activity (whether done at a subsidiary or at the parent level).

Knowing the true values to assign a company's assets is key to knowing its equity base. Yet, Standard and Poor's does not purport to perform asset appraisals as the basis for its ratings. Standard and Poor's analysis of asset protection attempts to highlight materially undervalued or overvalued assets relative to book value so that leverage can be viewed in an alternate light. When intangible assets are material, Standard and Poor's assesses whether earnings support the value of this goodwill before determining whether to regard it at full value. In fact, the value of all corporate assets is ultimately measured by their long-term earnings power.

Financial statements of merged and acquired companies pose a special analytical challenge. Current accounting standards allow the acquired company's assets and equity to be written up to reflect the acquisition price. Suddenly its equity has grown, its debt ratio has dropped and management wants to add debt to bring the debt ratio back to pre-acquisition levels. Unfortunately, the company has the same earning power as before. It really cannot support more debt and still justify its credit rating. In this example the answer at present is clear, but down the road it becomes muddied, as the ability to relate to pre-acquisition financial statements is lost.

The broad question of "true" values of debt and equity in an environment of changing prices is one of the reasons that greater emphasis is being placed on other rating criteria, as traditional leverage guidelines diminish in importance.

Creative Financing

As financing techniques become more innovative, ratio analysis becomes more complicated—and probably more tenuous as well. Standard and Poor's distinguishes between different and hybrid debt securities based on their respective features.

In the case of convertible securities at conversion, Standard and Poor's will consider them as equity. Otherwise they are debt, albeit at a reasonable capital cost. Many well-intentioned companies project conversion within a short time but fail to accomplish it. Conversion is subject to enough variables beyond management's control that a prediction of when it might occur becomes a presumptuous exercise. An exception to this approach is adjustable rate convertible notes, such as those issued by Mapco Inc. Borg-Warner Corp. and Hercules Inc. The strong disincentive for the investor to opt for cash payment—which would be only about half the face amount—accords these issues quasi-equity treatment.

In evaluating a current popular hybrid product, convertible exchangeable preferred stock, Standard and Poor's would not give credit for its convertibility into common. However, Standard and Poor's generally will not be overly concerned that the issue might be exchanged for debt securities. This is because such an exchange would likely coincide with a change to tax-paying status, indicating improved profitability and offsetting the increase in debt on the balance sheet.

Issues sold at original issue discounts, such as zero coupon debt, for purpose of capital structure analysis are valued net of unamortized discount, which is the amount of legal liability. However, Standard and Poor's knows that the borrowings will grow larger with time. The full face value is thus taken into account in cash flow analysis. In any event, the "bullet" refinancing requirement has negative implications for financial flexibility. The need to refinance a very large amount at one time can become a challenge.

Liquid yield option notes (LYONS) have even more negative potential, unless the issuer carefully manages the repayment risk. LYONS are zeros with two twists—a stock-conversion option and a put feature allowing holders to sell the notes back to the company. Generally, the put dates begin at the start of the third year after the issue is sold and can be exercised annually thereafter. The LYONS' conversion option has scant credit quality impact, even less than with other convertible debt issues. The potential for conversion diminishes as time goes on, in contrast to typical convertibles, since the value of the debt rises while the conversion ratio is held constant. The put feature, however, makes it hard for a company to plan an orderly refinancing of the large amount that such an issue can eventually reach. The potential exercise of the put would likely come at a time of high interest rates (the put protects investors from declines in value if interest rates rise); this implies that an even more challenging scenario could develop. It is, therefore, critical that the issuer take advantage of the redemption provision, and periodically replace some of its new LYONS debt. Standard and Poor's intends to monitor the redemption of LYONS debt, so that the amount potentially inflicting repayment shock on the issuer doesn't reach inordinate dimensions.

CASH FLOW ADEQUACY

Earnings may be the best long-term determinant of creditworthiness, but when an interest or principal payment date arrives, earnings are not what matters. The obligation can't be serviced out of earnings, which is just an accounting concept; the payment has to be made with cash. Although there is usually a strong relationship between cash flow and reported earnings, many transactions and accounting entries affect one and not the other. Analysis of cash flow patterns can reveal a level of debt-servicing capability that is either stronger or weaker than might be apparent from earnings.

Cash flow analysis is critical in all credit rating decisions. Lately, it has taken on added importance as the debt market has been increasingly populated by speculative grade issues. Companies with investment grade ratings generally have ready access to external cash to cover temporary shortfalls. Junk bond issuers lack this degree of flexibility and have fewer alternatives to internally generated cash for servicing debt.

Cash Flow Ratios

Discussions about "cash flow" often suffer from lack of uniform definitions of terms. The table (right) presents terminology with respect to specific cash flow concepts.

Ratios show the relationship of cash flow to debt and debt service, and also to the firm's needs. Since there are calls on cash other than repaying debt, it is important to know the extent to which those requirements will allow cash to be used for debt service—or, alternatively, lead to greater need for borrowing.

Some of the specific ratios that are considered are:

- Funds from operation/total debt
- Total debt/discretionary cash flow = debt payback period
- Funds from operation + interest/interest
- Free operating cash flow + interest/interest
- Free operating cash flow + interest/interest + average annual principal repayment obligation = debt service coverage
- Funds from operation/capital spending requirements
- Capital expenditures/capital maintenance

Interpretation of the ratios is not simple: higher values often can be indicative of problems rather than strength. A company serving a low-growth or declining market may exhibit relatively strong cash flow owing to minimal fixed and working capital needs. Growth companies, in comparison, often exhibit thin or even negative cash flow because investment is needed to support growth. For the low-growth company, credit analysis weighs the positives of strong current cash flow against the danger that this high level of protection might not be sustainable. For the high-growth company, the problem is just the opposite: weighing the negatives of a current cash deficit against prospects of enhanced protection once current investment begins yielding cash benefits.

How cash flow data are interpreted depends on a company's asset mix, growth rate, strategic policies, and other factors. There is no simple correlation between creditworthiness and the level of current cash flow.

Focusing on coverage and free cash flow becomes more critical when analyzing a weaker company. Speculative grade issuers typically face near-term vulnerabilities, which are better measured by such a focus. Where long-term viability is more assured—that is, higher in the rating spectrum—there can be greater emphasis on the level of funds from operations and its relation to the total debt burden. These measures clearly differentiate between levels of protection over time.

Measuring Cash Flow

Standard and Poor's uses its own format for measuring cash flow. Financial disclosure guidelines governing cash flow reporting are too broad to force a clear presentation of the data. The statement of changes in financial position, or "funds flow" statement, addresses the cash flow issue, but is an awkward tool. Not only do companies use a variety of conflicting formats, but many reports reconcile to working capital rather than cash. Nonetheless, by examining this statement and the balance sheet, it is possible to construct an approximation of the major elements of a company's cash flow picture that also facilitates comparative analysis among companies.

The Table 4-6 illustrates Standard and Poor's format using Palm Beach Inc. At the top is the item from the funds flow statement usually labeled *"funds from operations"* or *"working capital from operations."* This quantity is net income adjusted for depreciation and other noncash debits and credits that have been factored into it. Subtract the net increase in working capital investment to arrive at *"operating cash flow."*

Next, capital expenditures and cash dividends, respectively, are backed out to arrive at *"free operating cash flow"* and *"discretionary cash flow."* Finally, the cost of acquisitions is subtracted from the running total, proceeds from asset disposals added, and other miscellaneous sources and uses of cash netted together. *"Prefinancing cash flow"* is the end result of these computations, which represents the extent to which the company's cash flow from all internal sources has been sufficient to cover all of its internal needs.

The bottom part of the table reconciles prefinancing cash flow to the various categories of external financing and to changes in the company's own cash balance. In the example, Palm Beach experienced a $14.7 million cash shortfall in 1984, which had to be met with a combination of additional borrowings and a drawdown of its own cash.

TABLE 4-6
Cash Flow Summary: Palm Beach Inc.

($Mil.)	***1984***	***1983***	***1982***	***1981***	***1980***
Working capital from oper. (FFO)	18.58	22.34	16.78	21.68	19.10
Dec. (inc.) in noncash current assets	(33.12)	1.05	25.13	(23.07)	(41.68)
Inc. (dec.) in nondebt current liab	15.07	(12.61)	(10.49)	4.12	11.13
Net dec. (inc.) in working capital	(18.06)	(11.56)	14.64	(18.95)	(30.55)
Oper. cash flow	0.52	10.78	31.42	2.73	(11.45)
(Capital expenditures)	(11.06)	(9.74)	(6.18)	(7.41)	(8.58)
Free oper. cash flow	(10.53)	1.04	25.24	(4.69)	(20.03)
(Cash dividends)	(4.45)	(5.14)	(5.56)	(5.56)	(5.56)
Discretionary cash flow	(14.98)	(4.09)	19.68	(10.24)	(25.59)
(Acquisitions)	0.00	0.00	0.00	0.00	0.00
Asset disposals	0.73	0.23	0.00	0.00	0.00
Net other sources (uses) of cash	(0.44)	(0.09)	1.11	0.62	0.88
Prefinancing cash flow	(14.70)	(3.95)	20.79	(9.62)	(24.70)
Inc. (dec.) in short-term debt	3.00	0.00	(44.00)	14.60	25.40
Inc. (dec.) in long-term debt	6.12	13.02	31.05	(1.13)	(0.82)
Net sale (repurchase) of equity	0.32	(7.07)	(5.52)	0.00	0.00
Dec. (inc. in cash and securities	5.25	(2.00)	(2.32)	(3.86)	0.13

The Need for Capital

The analysis of cash flow in relation to capital requirements begins with an examination of a company's capital needs, including both working and fixed capital. While this analysis is performed for all debt issuers, it is critically important for fixed capital-intensive firms and for rapidly growing working capital-intensive firms. Companies with predominant needs for working capital benefit by being able to finance a significant portion of their current assets through trade credit. However, rapidly growing companies must place greater reliance on nontrade credit. Examples include many of the small and medium-sized computer manufacturers. Despite strong profitability, the dynamic growth of these companies typically involves a buildup in receivables and inventories that cannot be financed internally or through trade credit.

The key to determining the working capital requirements of a company is to first establish a projected growth rate and a turnover rate for inventory and receivables. In the last few years, improved working-capital management techniques have greatly reduced the investment that might otherwise have been required. This makes it difficult to base expectations on recent trends. In any event, improved turnover experience would not be a reason to project continuation of such a trend to yet better levels.

Because Standard and Poor's sees companies as ongoing enterprises, it expects they will provide funds continually to maintain capital investments as modern, efficient assets. Cash flow adequacy is viewed from the standpoint of a company's ability to internally finance capital-maintenance requirements, as well as its ability to finance capital additions. It is not always easy to quantify the requirements for capital maintenance. In the absence of a better figure (which can be derived only from a detailed analysis provided by the company), Standard and Poor's uses the current cost depreciation expense as a rough approximation.

An important dimension of cash flow adequacy is the extent to which a company has the flexibility to alter the timing of its capital requirements. Expansions are typically discretionary. However, large plants with long lead times usually involve, somewhere along the way, a commitment to completion of the project.

For many firms, capital spending needs must also include funds for acquisitions. There are companies, with cash flow adequate to the needs of the existing business but which are known to be acquisition-minded. Their choice of acquisition as an avenue for growth means that this activity must also involve a need for capital.

Management's stated acquisition goals and past takeover bids that were not consummated provide a basis for judging the prospects for future acquisitions. Moreover, for some companies, the need for acquisitions is not a luxury. For example, Freeport-McMoran Inc., faces the depletion of its sulfur reserves, its main generator of cash and profits. Clearly, it can be expected to be very active in attempting to at least replace those revenues.

FINANCIAL FLEXIBILITY

A number of analytical tasks are performed under this category. First, the previous assessment of financial factors (profitability, asset protection, cash flow) are combined to arrive at an overall view of financial health. Next, sundry considerations that do not fit in other categories are examined. These might include serious legal problems, lack of insurance coverage, or restrictive covenants which place the firm at the mercy of its bankers.

Then, Standard and Poor's evaluates the company's options under stress. In this vein, the potential impact of various alternatives to expectations is considered, along with a firm's contingency plans. Access to various capital markets, affiliations with other entities, and ability to sell assets are important factors.

Flexibility can be jeopardized when a firm accumulates bank borrowings and commercial paper with the hope of funding out when market conditions improve. Reliance on short-term money or interest-sensitive, longer maturity funds creates obvious risks. An unusually short maturity schedule for long-term debt and limited-life preferred stock is also a negative. Of course, there is no problem if maturing obligations can be financed with internally generated funds. But a growing business typically refunds maturing debt and preferred stock with new debt.

A firm's access to various capital markets can become an important factor in financial flexibility. A company's experience with different financial instruments and capital markets gives management alternatives if conditions in a particular financial market suddenly sour. The size of a company and its financing needs can play a role in whether it can raise funds in the public debt markets. Similarly, a firm's role in the national economy—and this is particularly true outside the U.S.—can determine its access to bank and public funds.

Access to the common stock market is primarily a question of management's willingness to accept dilution of earnings per share, rather than whether funds are available. When a new common stock offering is projected as part of a company's financing plan, Standard and Poor's tries to measure management's commitment to this financing vehicle, even at unattractive prices.

All firms are viewed as going concerns and Standard and Poor's does not normally expect a company to repay debt by liquidating operations. Clearly, there is little benefit in selling natural resource properties or manufacturing facilities if these must be replaced in few years. Nonetheless, a company's ability to generate cash through asset disposals may enhance its financial flexibility. Potential asset disposals will be considered as providing added flexibility only if Standard and Poor's believes they can be accomplished under terms acceptable to the company. Management's stated intention to sell certain assets is not enough. Standard and Poor's must be mindful of market conditions as well.

Pension obligations and serious legal problems are two prominent and slippery analytical areas. Apart from the question of how to value unfunded pension obligations, there are other implications. A large pension burden can hinder a company's ability to sell assets because a potential buyer is reluctant to assume the liability. This off-balance sheet item also has played a pivotal role in discouraging some managements from closing excess, inefficient and costly manufacturing facilities. Such a closing might require the immediate recognition of future pension obligations and result in a substantial charge to equity. The firm's financial flexibility is thus impaired.

When there is a major lawsuit against the firm, the analyst may use a range of estimated costs to reflect the uncertainty inherent in all litigation. Moreover, there often are intangible costs which are reflected qualitatively in Standard and Poor's assessment of a firm's prospects. Disputes with suppliers or customers can have a long-term effect on a company's competitive position. A well-publicized product failure may cost a company far more in lost sales than the payment to any injured individual. A potential liability so large that it seems to threaten a firm's solvency—such as recently faced by Texaco—often will limit the company's access to capital, at least temporarily.

5

Bond Classifications

THERE IS NO UNIFORMLY AGREED UPON METHODOLOGY FOR CLASSIFYING bonds. There are, however, three commonly used approaches. Each approach is based upon the needs of the investor.

CLASSIFICATION BY AN ISSUING AGENCY

When bonds are classified by an issuing agency, they can be broken down into government or nongovernment categories, but more frequently used categories are:

- Public utilities
- Financial institutions
- Transportation
- Industrial

In each case, further subdivisions are possible. For example, transportation can be broken down as airline, railroad, and trucking. Public utilities can be broken down into gas, electric, gas and electric, nuclear, and water.

Sophisticated bond investors use these subdivisions to identify industry trends. Is this bond selling above or below the industry average? Why? What economic factors could affect this company, either positively or negatively? How about the industry as a whole? Table 5-1 shows the bond classification codes as they appear in the Standard and Poor's Bond Guide. The classifications are broken down by industry.

TABLE 5-1
Industry Code of Classifications

- 0-Not specific
- 1-**Abrasives**
- 2-**Aerospace**
  - a-Major Contractor
  - b-Subsystems/comp.
  - c-Research/develop.
- 3-**Aircraft mfg./comp.**
  - a-Services
- 4-**Air Transport.**
  - a-Cargo/charter
- 5-**Aluminum/prod.**
- 6-**Arms/Ammunition**
- 7-**Auto rental/serv.**
- 8-**Auto parts/equip.**
- 9-**Auto/Truck mfrs.**
  - a-Trucks, trailers
  - b-Motor homes
- 10-**Banking**
  - a-Bank holding
  - b-Savings & Loan
- 11-**Beverages**
  - a-Beer & Ale
  - b-Distillers
  - c-Wines & Liquors
  - d-Distributors
  - e-Soft drink syrup
  - f-Bottlers
- 12-**Broadcasting**
  - a-CATV
  - b-Radio
  - c-TV
  - d-Equipment
- 13-**Building**
  - a-Brick, cement
  - b-Climate controls
  - c-Contracting, engr. construction
  - d-Forest products
  - e-Hardware/hand tool
  - g-Plumbing
  - h-Roofing, Wallbd.
- 14-**Chemicals**
  - a-Fertilizers, agric.
  - b-Industrial gases
  - c-Sulphur
- 15-**Coatings, paint, var.**
- 16-**Containers**
  - a-Glass
  - b-Metal
  - c-Paper
  - d-Plastic
- 17-**Conglomerate/div.**
  - a-Diversified
- 18-**Cosmetics/Toilet**
- 19-**Cosm.-Toil.-Drugs**
- 20-**Data Processing**
  - a-Service/leasing
  - b-Components
- 21-**Drugs**
  - a-Ethical
  - b-Proprietary
  - c-Research
- 22-**Ecological sv./eq.**
- 23-**Education**
- 24-**Electronics/Electric**
  - a-Industry leaders
  - b-Component, controls
  - c-Motors
  - d-Hsehld. appliances
  - e-Infor. sv., communic. sy.
  - f-Radio, TV, tape
- 25-**Equip. lease/rental**
- 26-**Finance**
  - a-Small loan
  - b-Agency
  - c-Factoring
  - d-Leasing
  - e-Receivables
  - f-Services
  - g-S.B.I.C.
- 27-**Food**
  - a-Bakery, mill, sugar
  - b-Canned
  - c-Corn refiners
  - d-Dairy prod.
  - e-Meat/poultry
  - f-Pkgd./snacks
  - g-Distributors
  - h-Candy, gum
  - i-Seafood
  - j-Frozen
- 28-**Food serving**
  - a-Food servicing
  - b-Fast foods
  - c-Restaurants
  - d-Vending
- 29-**Glass/products**
- 30-**Graphic Arts**
  - a-Printing
  - b-Supply, equip.
- 31-**Health Care Ctrs.**
- 32-**Home Furnishings**
  - a-Carpets, floor cov.
  - b-Furniture
  - c-Cooking ranges
- 33-**Hotels/Motels/Inns**
- 34-**Housewares**
- 35-**Insurance**
  - a-Life
  - b-Broker/agency
- 36-**Investment**
- 37-**Jewelry, silverware, time pieces, china**
- 38-**Land dev./Rl. Estate**
- 39-**Leather/Shoes**
  - a-Shoe producer
  - b-Shoe mfr./dstr.
  - c-Shoe dstr.
  - d-Leather
- 40-**Leisure/Amusement**
  - a-Boating
  - b-Bowl./billiard
  - c-Musical instr.
  - d-Photo eq./finishing
  - e-Records/tape
  - f-Sports/Outdoor eq.
  - g-Tourism/resorts
  - h-Toys, games
- 41-**Machinery**
  - a-Agriculture
  - b-Construction mtl. handling
  - c-Industrial
  - d-Machine tools
  - e-Specialties
  - f-Steam gener.
- 42-**Manufacturing/Distr**
  - a-Consumer
  - b-Industrial
- 43-**Medic. eq./supply**
  - a-Lab./research
- 44-**Metal**
  - a-Precious fab.
  - b-Copper fab.
  - c-Lead, zinc fab.
  - d-Other fabric'tg
- 45-**Mining**
  - a-Canadian
  - b-Coal
  - c-Copper
  - d-Lead, zinc
  - e-Uranium
  - f-Gold, silver
- 46-**Mobile/Modular Hms.**
  - a-Components
- 47-**Motion Pictures**
  - a-Producer
  - b-Distributor
  - c-Theatres
- 48-**Office Equipment**
  - a-Bus. machines
  - b-Furniture
  - c-Forms, supplies
  - d-Service
- 49-**Oil & Gas**
  - a-Crude producer
  - b-Domestic
  - c-International
  - d-Retailer
  - e-Well supply, sv., drilling
  - f-Canadian
- 50-**Paper/Products**
- 51-**Pet & Supplies**
- 52-**Plastic/Products**
- 53-**Publishing**
  - a-Books
  - b-Periodicals
  - c-Newspapers
  - d-Textbooks
- 54-**Railroads Class 1**
  - a-Switching & terminal cos
  - b-Other
- 55-**Rail Equipment**
  - a-Car builders
  - b-Car leasing
  - c-Parts, access.
- 56-**R.E. Invest. Trust**
- 57-**Rendering**
- 58-**Retail Stores**
  - a-Apparel
  - b-Convenience fds.
  - c-Food supermkts.
  - d-Variety
  - e-Drugs
  - f-Department
  - g-Discount
  - h-Mail ord./gen. ch.
  - i-Showrm./catalog
  - j-Furniture
  - k-Fabric
- 59-**Retail mdse'r**
- 60-**Rubber**
  - a-Fabricating
- 61-**Securities**
- 62-**Services**
- 63-**Shipping/bldg.**
- 64-**Soaps/vegetable oil**
- 65-**Specialty instr.**
- 66-**Steel-Iron**
  - a-Major integrated
  - b-Other integrated
  - c-Stainless
  - d-Other specialties
  - e-Ore producer
  - f-Refractories
  - g-Steel mill mach.
  - h-Coal
- 67-**Telecommunications**
  - a-Local
  - b-Long Distance
  - c-Independent
  - d-Telegraph
  - e-Satellite
  - f-Equip./science
- 68-**Textiles**
  - a-Producer
  - b-Synthetic fibers
  - c-Apparel mfr.
- 69-**Tobacco**
  - a-Cigarettes
  - b-Cigars
  - c-Leaf/snuff
- 70-**Transportation**
  - a-Bus
  - b-Freight forwarding
- 71-**Trucking**
- 72-**Utilities-Electric**
  - a-Operating
  - b-Holding
- 73-**Utilities-Gas**
  - a-Pipeline cos.
  - b-Distributors
  - c-Producer, gath.
  - d-LP gas
- 74-**Utilities-Water**
- 75-**Util.-Diversified**
- 76-**Vending**

Source Standard and Poor's *Bond Guide*, December 1988.

CLASSIFICATION BY METHOD OF INTEREST PAYMENT

There are three types of bonds classified under method of interest payment: bearer bonds, registered bonds, and income bonds. Bearer bonds are the oldest form of bonds, dating back to the turn of the century. Each bond had "coupons" attached to it. On the interest payment date, the bondholder would clip off the coupon and either mail it into the company for payment, or take it to the bank for payment. The owner's name did not appear on the bonds nor did the company issuing the bearer bonds have any knowledge of who the bondholder was. Just as the name implied, the current "bearer" of the bonds had the right to clip the coupons on the interest payment dates. The bondholder endured grief if the bonds were lost, stolen, or damaged because the title was virtually traceless.

There are still "bearer" bonds in circulation today, although most companies have given the bondholder the right to "register" his bonds. Even though the semiannual payments reflect interest payments, we still use the word "coupon" as a remembrance of days gone by.

With registered bonds, the name of the bondholder appears on the bond and the issuing company keeps records of ownership. Changes of ownership take place only through endorsement by the owner. When you open a bond account with a brokerage house, it is often easier to allow your broker's corporation to hold the bonds for you than to store them in a safety deposit vault. When this happens, the bonds are registered in the name of the brokerage house. Your monthly statement indicates that ownership is yours through the brokerage house. Interest payments are made to the brokerage house who then deposit the payments to your account, usually the following day.

Registered bonds can be fully or partially registered. A fully registered bond has principal and interest payments made to the registered owners only. Partially registered bonds might be registered for principal repayment only, but the coupons are "bearer" coupons and must be clipped and returned for payment as with bearer bonds.

The third type of bond is the income bond. When a corporation issues a bond, the bondholder is promised full interest payment on predetermined dates. Failure to pay in full is a breach of contract and might result in default, reorganization, or bankruptcy. Income bonds promise to pay interest, but the amount of interest depends on corporate income. A corporation issuing a 12 percent income bond might pay only a 5 percent, 8 percent, or 10 percent coupon based on income. The board of directors determines the amount of interest to pay.

Income bonds were initially the product of railroads that had just come out of bankruptcy. Because of this relationship with bankrupt companies, investors treated income bonds as being highly speculative. During the 1950s, corporations issued more and more income bonds (rather than stock) because the coupon paid is an *interest expense* and treated as fully deductible before taxes. Common and preferred stock dividends, on the other hand, are after-tax payouts. Unfortunately, today's investors still consider income bonds as speculative regardless of the quality rating of the company, thus creating much less of a demand than before.

CLASSIFICATION BY METHOD OF SECURITY

In order to entice investors, corporations can issue various pledges of real or personal property as security for bonds. This security, or absence thereof, is above and beyond the general credit rating of the issue.

TYPES OF BONDS

There are perhaps 20 or more different classification of bonds, depending upon the risk, security, and payments. Some bonds are relatively simple to understand while others are so complex that you would need a financial attorney to explain the terms and conditions identified in the prospectus.

First-Mortgage Bonds

These bonds are the highest security that a corporation can offer the bondholders by granting them a first-mortgage lien on virtually all of its properties. If the corporation defaults on its payments, the first-mortgage bondholders have the right to foreclose on the mortgage and sell the property to satisfy unpaid obligations. This seldom happens because corporations in default generally undergo financial reorganization to satisfy creditors.

Purchasing a first-mortgage bond offers the bondholder some degree of protection. The bondholder, however, must be willing to accept a lower interest rate than if the bonds were unsecured. This difference is usually no more than a half of a percentage point.

As corporations grow and acquire assets, there is a continuous need for more capital. Corporations then issue a series of bonds as shown in Figs. 5-1 and 5-2. If you buy a series first-mortgage bond, you know that other first-mortgage bonds will be issued later. To further protect bondholders, the issuing corporation might declare in the prospectus that no further first-mortgage bonds can be issued unless a certain percentage of the debt of principal is paid off. This is referred to as an "after-acquired clause" and states that all subsequent issues are restricted by the terms and conditions of the preceding issues.

It is not uncommon for a corporation to retire part of a series earlier than its scheduled maturity date so as to meet the terms and conditions for issuing a new series. As an example, you might wonder why a corporation is redeeming a bond with an 8.5 percent coupon when it could be redeeming bonds with a 10.25 percent coupon. The reason is that the restrictions imposed by the 8.5 percent bond have a greater impact on future financing than the 10.25 percent bond does.

This announcement is neither an offer to sell nor a solicitation of offers to buy any of these securities. The offering is made only by the Prospectus and the related Prospectus Supplement.

NEW ISSUE

June 24, 1988

$125,000,000

Pennsylvania Power & Light Company

First Mortgage Bonds, 9⅝% Series due 1998

Price 99.338%

plus accrued interest from June 1, 1988 to date of delivery

Copies of the Prospectus and the related Prospectus Supplement may be obtained in any State in which this announcement is circulated only from such of the undersigned as may legally offer these securities in such State.

The First Boston Corporation

Morgan Stanley & Co.
Incorporated

Drexel Burnham Lambert
Incorporated

Salomon Brothers Inc

Source: *Wall Street Journal*, June 24, 1988.

Fig. 5-1. *A Pennsylvania Power and Light tombstone ad.*

Companies are reluctant to issue bonds with the words "second mortgage" in the description because the word connotes weakness. To get around this, companies use the words "general and refunding" or "first and refunding" as shown in Fig. 5-3. This implies that some portion of the assets have a first mortgage lien while other assets have a second or third mortgage lien.

Collateral Trust Bonds

Not all corporations have physical assets that can be used as collateral for first-mortgage bonds. An example might be a holding company that owns no assets outright. In this case, the issuing corporation will pledge securities, such as

This announcement is neither an offer to sell nor a solicitation of offers to buy any of these securities. The offering is made only by the Prospectus and the related Prospectus Supplement.

NEW ISSUE

June 24, 1988

$75,000,000

Illinois Power Company

First Mortgage Bonds, 10% Series due 1998

Price 99.44%

plus accrued interest, if any, from June 30, 1988

Copies of the Prospectus and the related Prospectus Supplement may be obtained in any State in which this announcement is circulated only from such of the undersigned as may legally offer these securities in such State.

The First Boston Corporation

Goldman, Sachs & Co.

Kidder, Peabody & Co.
Incorporated

Source: *Wall Street Journal*, June 24, 1988.

Fig. 5-2. *An Illinois Power Company tombstone ad.*

stock, as collateral. Usually, the market value of the pledged securities exceeds the value of the bonds. If the market value of the securities decrease, then the issuing corporation must provide additional security.

The pledged securities are held by the bond's trustee. If stock is pledged, then the issuing company still retains the voting rights. If the issuing company defaults on the bond's interest payment, then the bond's trustee retains the voting right and could liquidate the stock to protect the bondholders.

Equipment Trust Certificates

When a company wants to raise capital, it must specify how the capital will be used. If the capital will be used to purchase equipment such as planes or railroad

This announcement is neither an offer to sell nor a solicitation of an offer to buy these securities.
The offer is made only by the Prospectus.

New Issue / June 2, 1988

$100,000,000

Connecticut Yankee Atomic Power Company

12% General and Refunding Mortgage Bonds, Series A, due June 1, 2000

Price 100% and accrued interest, if any, from June 8, 1988

Copies of the Prospectus may be obtained in any State in which this announcement is circulated only from the undersigned or others as may legally offer these securities in such State.

Salomon Brothers Inc

One New York Plaza, New York, New York 10004
Atlanta, Boston, Chicago, Dallas, Los Angeles, San Francisco, Zurich.
Affiliates: Frankfurt, London, Tokyo.
Member of Major Securities and Commodities Exchanges.

Source: *Wall Street Journal*, June 2, 1988.

Fig. 5-3. *A Connecticut Yankee tombstone ad.*

cars, then this equipment can be used as collateral for the bondholder. In actuality, the company might not actually own the property until the bonds are paid off or substitute property of equal or greater market value exists.

Figure 5-4 is an example of equipment trust certificates for aircraft purchases. Equipment trust certificates are similar to first-mortgage bonds and can be issued in series form as shown in Fig. 5-4. It is not uncommon for a company to use equipment trust certificates to raise only a percentage of the capital needed, say 60 to 70 percent. The balance might come from on-hand cash, stocks, or from the sale of other assets. The equipment purchased and used as collateral, however, might be worth 30 to 40 percent more than the outstanding bonds.

This announcement is under no circumstances to be construed as an offer to sell or as a solicitation of an offer to buy any of these securities. The offering is made only by the Prospectus.

NEW ISSUE

May 25, 1988

$166,400,000

USAIR

1988 Equipment Trusts E through L
1988 Equipment Trust Certificates, Series E through L

These Certificates, which are being offered at par, will mature serially in the principal amounts and on the dates set forth below, with interest payable thereon on each January 1 and July 1, commencing January 1, 1989.

Maturity Date for Each Series	Principal Amount for Each Series of Certificates	Interest Rate for Each Series
January 1, 1992	$1,667,000	9.35%
January 1, 1993	1,762,000	9.60
January 1, 1994	361,000	9.75
January 1, 1995	1,484,000	9.95
January 1, 1997	662,000	10.25
January 1, 1998	689,000	10.35
January 1, 1999	596,000	10.50
January 1, 2000	633,000	10.55
January 1, 2001	966,000	10.60
January 1, 2002	421,000	10.70
January 1, 2003	1,092,000	10.70
January 1, 2004	830,000	10.75
January 1, 2005	882,000	10.80
January 1, 2006	1,446,000	10.85
January 1, 2007	1,838,000	10.85
January 1, 2008	2,049,000	10.90
January 1, 2009	2,285,000	10.90
January 1, 2010	1,137,000	10.90

(Plus accrued interest, if any, from the date of issuance for each series of Certificates.)

Copies of the Prospectus may be obtained in any State in which this announcement is circulated from the undersigned or other dealers or brokers as may lawfully offer these securities in such State.

Merrill Lynch Capital Markets

Fig. 5-4. *A US Air tombstone ad.*

When a company is highly leveraged or of low quality, the company might have to use collateral for bonds in order to obtain funds. Today, companies like TWA are securing notes with everything from light bulbs, spare parts, and warehouse items, to landing rights at airports. This extra collateral is needed to satisfy potential bond purchasers.

In the past, aircrafts and aircraft engines were primarily used as collateral. Today, however, traditional inventory financing has evolved to include minor spare parts for short-term notes. These bonds are often called "light bulb" bonds. Some people question how bondholders would obtain the collateral, and its worth, should the company default or go into bankruptcy.

Debentures

Unsecured bonds are called debentures. These bonds are not backed by collateral or pledges, and therefore, must attract investors by offering higher interest rates than secured bonds. Debenture bondholders are treated as general creditors of the issuing corporation. This means that debenture bondholders have claims to those properties not pledged to other bonds. Debenture bondholders can have claims to pledged property if the value of the pledged property exceeds the debt against which it was pledged. Figure 5-5 identifies sinking fund debentures.

Subordinated Debentures

Some companies issue subordinated debenture bonds that are lower in rank than regular debentures. In case of default, the subordinated debenture bondholders would stand behind the secured bondholders, debenture bondholders, and perhaps, even general creditors. To attract investors, companies issuing subordinated debenture bonds must offer high coupon rates. There even exists senior subordinated debentures such as the one shown in Fig. 5-6.

Because high coupon rates could alter a company's cash flow, companies have come up with "convertible subordinated debentures" such as the one shown in Fig. 5-6. With convertible debentures, the issuing corporation will offer the buyer a trade-off of a lower coupon rate for the right to convert the bonds into shares of stock at a predetermined conversion rate. If the buyer feels that the company's stock could increase, then the convertible subordinate debenture bonds could provide large capital gains in addition to interest.

Guaranteed Bonds

Sometimes, the bonds of one corporation can be guaranteed by a second corporation. These bonds are referred to as guaranteed bonds. For example, the Flexi-Van Leasing, Inc. debentures shown in Fig. 5-7 are guaranteed bonds,

$100,000,000

Westvaco Corporation

10¼% Sinking Fund Debentures due July 1, 2018

Price 100%

Plus accrued interest, if any, from June 29, 1988

Upon request, a copy of the Prospectus Supplement and the related Prospectus describing these securities and the business of the Company may be obtained within any State from any Underwriter who may legally distribute it within such State. The securities are offered only by means of the Prospectus Supplement and the related Prospectus, and this announcement is neither an offer to sell nor a solicitation of any offer to buy.

Goldman, Sachs & Co. **Merrill Lynch Capital Markets**

The First Boston Corporation **Morgan Stanley & Co.** Incorporated

Salomon Brothers Inc **Shearson Lehman Hutton Inc.**

June 24, 1988

Source: *Wall Street Journal*, June 24, 1988.

Fig. 5-5. *A Westvaco tombstone ad.*

because Flexi-Van Corporation (the second corporation) has unconditionally guaranteed the payment of principal and interest. In most cases, the bond rating will be based on the quality of the guarantor rather than the issuing corporation. Some bonds are guaranteed by more than one company. For example, the bonds issued by DCS Capital Corporation are guaranteed by Dow Chemical Corporation, Union Carbide, and Shell Canada.

BONDS WITH SPECIAL CHARACTERISTICS

There are several types of bonds with special characteristics. Each has their own advantages as well as disadvantages.

This announcement is neither an offer to sell nor a solicitation of offers to buy any of these securities. The offering is made only by the Prospectus.

NEW ISSUE May 31, 1988

$50,000,000

AST
RESEARCH INC.

8½% Convertible Subordinated Debentures Due 2013

The Debentures are convertible at any time prior to maturity, unless previously redeemed, into shares of Common Stock of the Company at a conversion price of $15.50 per share, subject to adjustment under certain conditions.

Price 100%
plus accrued interest, if any, from June 6, 1988

Copies of the Prospectus may be obtained in any State in which this announcement is circulated only from such of the undersigned as may legally offer these securities in such State.

The First Boston Corporation Bear, Stearns & Co. Inc.

Source: *Wall Street Journal*, May 31, 1988.

Fig. 5-6. *An AST tombstone ad.*

Participating Bonds

Participating bonds have the characteristics of both stocks and bonds because they share in the firm's earnings. These bonds usually have a guaranteed minimum coupon, but the actual payout can be much greater based on earnings. The additional coupon payments look somewhat like dividends. These bonds are unpopular with stockholders, who prefer to keep all earnings for themselves.

Zero Coupon Bonds

Zero coupon bonds pay no interest prior to maturity and are issued at a substantial discount from par, perhaps $200 to $300. For example, XYZ Corporation issues a zero coupon bond in 1986 for $200 with a maturity date of 2006. At maturity, XYZ Corporation agrees to pay you $1,000. There are, however, no

Source: *Wall Street Journal*, June 2, 1988.

Fig. 5-7. *A Flexi-Van tombstone ad.*

coupon payments with maturity. Should you purchase this bond and hold it until maturity, your compounded yield to maturity would be 8.4 percent.

On December 15, 1988, Merrill Lynch's zero coupon bond with a maturity date of 2006 was trading at $250. Had you purchased this bond, your return on investment would be approximately 8.5 percent irrespective of the current market interest rates. On the same day, Allied Corporation had their zero coupon bond maturing in 1996 and trading at $533.75. Holding this bond to maturity will yield 9.4 percent.

The main advantage of this bond is that the investor does not have to worry about reinvesting interest payments during periods of unfavorable interest rates.

The disadvantage is that the Internal Revenue Service taxes the price appreciation each year as though the price gain payments were made in cash.

Put Bonds

Put bonds were first issued in the United States in 1974 by Citicorp. All put bonds have early redemption provisions that allow the bondholder to put, or sell, the bond back to the issuer before the maturity date at a predetermined buyback price called the strike price. Investors who purchase this bond have a "floor," in which the bond cannot fall below in price.

Deferred Interest Bonds (DIBs)

Deferred interest bonds are bonds issued substantially below par. The issuing corporation promises to pay $1,000 at maturity, but no interest for five years or more. When interest payments begin, however, the coupon rate is fairly high (see Table 5-2). As time progresses toward the date when interest payments begin, the selling price of the bond is expected to increase toward par. The risk is that the company might not be able to make the interest payments.

Pay-In-Kind Bonds

Although pay-in-kind bonds have coupons, the exact amount of interest paid depends on the company's financial position. Pay-in-kind bonds might not make any interest payments, whereas participating bonds have a minimum interest payment that must be met. These interest payments might be in the form of additional debt, however, rather than cash interest payments.

Non-Cash Payment Bonds

There is a special class of bonds called non-cash payment bonds where the interest is paid in stock. An example would be Tiger International Bonds, 11.5 percent, maturing in 1995. At the interest payment dates, the coupon payment is made in common stock.

CONVERTIBLE BONDS

Convertible bonds are a special type of corporate bond that provides investors with a financial instrument that is similar to both stocks and bonds. Convertible bonds not only have a face value of $1,000 and a coupon, but they also allow the investor to exchange the bonds into a predetermined number of common stock shares. Convertible bonds, therefore, are part bond and part stock.

Convertible bonds have the features of regular corporate bonds, coupons, maturity dates of 10 to 20 years, credit ratings, and call provisions. The daily

TABLE 5-2
Deferred Interest Bonds

Index Yield Data by Period

	Period
Past 12 Months Return	9.64%
Past 9 Months Return	18.94%
Past 6 Months Return	17.10%
Past 3 Months Return	6.89%
Recent 1 Month Return	4.18%

Weighted Average Price Index[1]

Issues Comprising Index

Description	*Type of Issue*	*Coupon*	*Maturity*	*Rating*	*Issue Size ($Mill)*	*First Coupon*	*Market Value 6/30/87*
Borg-Warner	Sr.Sub.Dis.Deb.	0/14.00	07/15/99	B3/B –	400.0	01/15/93	247.0
Burlington	Jr.Sub.Dis.Deb.	0/16.00	10/01/03	B3/B –	470.0	04/01/94	232.7
Eckerd	Sub. Dis. Deb.	0/13.00	05/01/06	B2/B –	345.0	11/01/91	240.6
Harcourt Brace	Sub. Deb.	0/14.75	09/15/02	B3/CCC	507.5	03/15/93	304.5
Macy Merger	Jr.Sub.Dis.Deb.	0/16.50	11/15/06	B3/CCC +	910.0	11/15/93	466.4
National Gypsum	Sub. Dis. Deb.	0/15.50	06/30/04	B2/B –	1003.0	12/31/91	704.6
Multimedia	Sub. Dis. Deb.	0/16.00	06/30/05	NR/NR	400.0	12/31/90	350.0
Owens-Corning	Sub. Dis. Deb.	0/15.00	12/01/06	B3/NR	1000.0	06/01/92	710.0
Owens-Illinois	Jr.Sub.Dis.Deb.	0/15.00	06/01/03	B3/B –	400.0	12/01/93	212.5
Sheller-Globe	Sr. Sub. Nts.	0/13.00	06/15/00	B3/NR	220.0	12/15/88	145.2
Supermkts Gen.	Jr.Sub.Dis.Deb.	0/13.125	06/01/01	B3/NR	164.0	12/01/91	89.4
VIACOM(Arsenal)	Sr.Sub.Dis.Deb.	0/14.75	06/15/02	B1/B –	399.0	12/15/91	293.3
					$6,218.5		3,996.2

Monthly Performance

	Jun/87	*Jul/87*	*Aug/87*	*Sep/87*	*Oct/87*	*Nov/87*	*Dec/87*	*Jan/88*
Index Price	61.38	60.43	61.36	56.58	51.85	54.95	57.46	60.35
[2]Stand. Dev.	3.71	3.39	3.29	2.74	2.12	2.19	2.10	2.47

	Jan/88	*Feb/88*	*Mar/88*	*Apr/88*	*May/88*	*Jun/88*
Index Price	60.35	63.80	62.96	64.36	64.59	67.29
[2]Stand. Dev.	2.47	2.63	2.61	2.81	2.93	3.10
Stand. Dev. of Index	4.17					

[1]Weighted by market value

[2]Standarad deviation calculation applies only to Eckerd, Macy, and National Gypsum.

Source: Merrill Lynch *High-Yield Securities Midyear Review/Forecast*, July 1988, p. 14.

trading history of convertible bonds are listed along with regular corporate bonds in most newspapers (see Fig. 2-2). Convertible bonds fluctuate in price because of rating changes as well as changes in stock prices.

To illustrate how corporate bonds work, consider Alpha Corporation's need to raise $100 million, and Alpha has decided to accomplish this by issuing either stock or bonds. Issuing stock will dilute the equity of existing stockholders. Furthermore, the dividends to stockholders are paid with *after tax* dollars. The choice is now narrowed down to regular corporate bonds or convertible bonds. Based upon Alpha's current credit rating, Alpha would have to offer a 12 percent coupon for regular corporate bonds. However, should Alpha issue a convertible bond, Alpha might be able to sell the convertible bonds with a coupon of 8 percent. Bond interest is paid for with *pretax* dollars.

Why should an investor purchase Alpha's convertible bonds with an 8 percent coupon when other bonds have 12 percent coupons? The answer lies in the nature of a convertible bond. Assume that the terms and conditions for Alpha's 8 percent coupon convertible bond state that the bond can be exchanged for 40 shares of common stock. The number of shares that a bond can be exchanged for is referred to as the bond's "conversion ratio," and the value of the exchangers called the "conversion value." If the stock is selling at $20 per share at the time of issuance of the convertible bond, then the conversion value is $800. If the stock increases in price, to say $30 per share, then the conversion value would be $1,200. The investor finds that his bond has appreciated by $400 (assuming he paid $800 initially) in addition to receiving an 8 percent coupon. This would be very attractive for the average investor.

In general, convertible bonds sell above their conversion value. The difference between the conversion value and the current market price of the bond is referred to as the bond's "conversion premium." In the above example, if the stock were selling at $20/share and the bond is selling at $900, then the conversion premium would be $100.

Simply put, when you invest in convertible bonds, you are betting that the value of the stock will increase. You should *not* invest in convertible bonds unless you are prepared to become a stockholder in that company. In other words, you are willing to accept a lower coupon for the privilege of exchanging your bond (at a later time) into common (or perhaps preferred) stock to realize capital appreciation.

The relationship between the bond's selling price and the stock price is nonlinear. If the stock increases by 25 percent, then the bond might simply increase by 10 percent. Likewise, if the stock decreases by 50 percent, the bond might decrease by only 15 percent because the bond still pays its coupon. Because the convertible bond is related to the stock price, brokerage houses will lend you 50 percent of the value of the convertible bond but up to 70 percent of the cash value of non-convertible bonds. There are several reasons why the convertible bond market is attractive to corporations:

- Corporation might have difficulty borrowing funds any other way.
- Coupons are less than on regular bonds.
- Coupons are paid for with pretax dollars.
- Companies can "force" conversion such that debt is paid off with equity rather than cash.
- Companies do not want to issue additional stock at the current stock price.
- Convertible bonds do not contain as many restrictions as do regular bonds.

There are several reasons why convertible bonds are attractive to investors:

- Opportunity for capital appreciation.
- More security than purchasing stock outright (i.e., creditor rather than owner).
- Coupon interest fixed.

Convertible bonds are not for every investor, however, because there are downside risks:

- For financial planning, it is better to invest in regular bonds with higher coupons. This provides better financial planning although you might miss the opportunity for capital gains.
- The fate of a convertible bond is closely tied to the value of the stock. If the company faulters and the stock drastically erodes in price, the value of the convertible bond will be low and you might not get your money back until maturity.
- Convertible bonds with large conversion premiums offer little protection should the stock price erode. In this case, the conversion premium would degrade such that the selling price approaches conversion value.
- Know the call features of a bond. Some bonds have sliding scale call features where the conversion ratio (i.e., number of shares) *decreases* as the bond approaches maturity.
- Should the company's stock not be paying any dividends and the company executes the call provisions, you sacrifice all of interest accrued from the last interest payment date.

Finally, keep in mind that convertible bonds suffer from the risk of default, perhaps more so than regular bonds. Very few convertible bonds are rated BBB or greater. Table 5-3 shows typical convertible bonds and their significant data.

TABLE 5-3
Convertible Bonds

CONVERTIBLE BONDS: Issue, Rate, Interest Dates and Maturity	S&P Debt Rating	Bond Form	Outstdg. Mil.-$	Conv. Ex-pires	Shares per $1,000 Bond	Price per Share	Div. Income per Bond	1988 RANGE Hi	1988 RANGE Lo	Curr Bid Sale(s) Ask(A)	Curr. Return	Yield to Mat	Stock Value of Bond	Conv. Parity	STOCK DATA Curr. Price	STOCK DATA P/E Ratio	Earnings Per Share Yr. End	1987	1988	Last 12 Mos	1987 Dil-u't'n
• Avnet, Inc ....8s [1]jj 2013	A+	R	100	2013	19.23	52.00	9.62	96	80	s80¼	9.97	10.2	37½	41¾	•19½	13	Je	0.64	1.46	[9]1.45	n/r
• AVX Corp 8¼s Mn15 2012	B+	R	70.1	2012	45.45	22.00	10.91	108	85½	96	8.59	8.65	73¼	21⅛	•16⅛	8	Dc	1.20	E2.00	[9]1.86	n/r
Axiom Systems ....10s fA 1998	NR	R	3.00	1998	800.00	1.25	....	100	60	60	16.6	19.2	70	¾	⅞	d	Mr	d0.70	....	d0.70	n/r
• Baker Hughes[2] 9½s jD15 2006	BBB+	R	99.1	2006	16.98	58.91	7.81	99	88½	s90	10.5	10.7	21⅞	53	•12⅞	29	Sp	d2.22	P*0.45	0.45	n/r
• Bally Mfg 6s mS15 1998	B+	R	32.6	1998	34.49	28.99	8.28	96	72	s91¼	6.58	7.26	72	26½	•20⅞	15	Dc	1.62	E1.40	[9]1.06	n/r
• Bally Mfg 10s jD15 2006	B+	R	100	2006	30.60	32.68	7.34	99	85¼	s98¾	10.1	10.1	63⅞	32¼	•20⅞	15	Dc	1.62	E1.40	[9]1.06	n/r
Baltimore Bancorp ...6¾s Ao 2011	BBB	R	29.4	2011	38.27	26.13	19.14	91½	77	83½	8.08	8.39	48⅜	21⅞	•12⅝	90	Dc	△1.77	....	[9]0.14	n/r
Bank of Boston.......7¾s Jd15 2011	A+	R	95.3	2011	42.70	23.42	52.95	128⅛	101⅜	106⅛	7.30	7.19	100⅞	24⅞	•23⅝	5	Dc	0.10	E4.65	[7]2.77	n/r
• Bank of New York.......8¼s jJ 2010	A-	R	150	2010	27.53	36.33	52.86	109	93⅞	s106	7.78	7.67	96¾	38½	•35⅛	6	Dc	▲2.97	E6.00	[9]5.87	2.81
Barris Indus(Sr)........6¾s Ms 2012	B+	R	60.0	2012	44.94	22.25	....	59½	48	48	14.0	14.6	27½	10⅝	6⅛	d	My	1.73	0.11	[8]d0.98	n/r
• BASIX[3]Corp[4] ....8¾s § 2005	NR	R	29.5	2005	88.73	11.27	....	46½	26	37½	....	Flat	2¼	4¼	•¼	d	Dc	d4.46	....	[6]d3.98	n/r
• [5]Baxter Travenol Lab........4⅛s mN 1991	BBB	R	2.00	1991	105.26	9.50	52.63	260	260	181⅝	2.41	....	181⅝	17¼	•17¼	13	Dc	1.14	E1.32	[9]1.25	1.12
• [5]Baxter Travenol Lab..4¾s Jj 2001	BBB	R	15.0	2001	85.32	11.72	42.66	208½	150⅝	147⅛	3.23	....	147⅛	17¼	•17¼	13	Dc	1.14	E1.32	[9]1.25	1.12
BayBanks Inc[6]........5s Jj15 1994	NR	R	1.46	1994	72.73	13.75	116.37	349⅛	260	330⅞	1.51	....	330⅞	45½	45½	9	Dc	△4.58	....	[9]5.28	4.37
BB&T Financial[7] 8¾s QMr15 2005	A-	R	34.5	2005	56.34	17.75	40.56	115½	99	106½	8.22	8.02	97⅛	18⅞	17¼	9	Dc	▲1.79	....	[9]1.92	1.71
Ben & Jerry's Homemade ...9½s jD 2007	NR	R	6.00	2007	[8]64.52	15.50	....	127½	98	104	9.13	9.05	101⅜	16⅛	15¾	24	Dc	0.56	....	[9]0.67	n/r
◆Bergen Brunswig........7⅜s jJ 2010	BBB-	R	135	2010	[9]41.10	24.33	13.15	109	85½	s102	7.48	7.43	90⅞	24⅞	◆22⅛	12	Au	0.87	P1.89	1.89	*1.71
◆[10]Bergen Brunswig .....6⅞s jJ 2011	BBB-	R	43.0	2011	[10]67.20	14.88	....	103	59	s65	10.5	11.1	26⅞	9⅝	◆4	11	Au	0.25	P0.37	0.37	n/r
• Beverly Enterprises 7⅝s Ms15 2003	CCC+	R	68.0	2003	48.85	20.47	....	63	49	s54	14.1	15.8	26¼	11	•5⅜	27	Dc	△d0.58	E0.20	[9]d0.66	n/r
• Beverly Enterpr(Zero)[11] ....0s [12] 2003	NR	R	[13]30.4	2003	13.32	....	....	29¼	25¾	s27½	....	....	7⅛	20⅝	•5⅜	27	Dc	△d0.58	E0.20	[9]d0.66	n/r
Bindley Western Ind 8⅜s Ao 2010	B	R	55.0	2010	68.31	14.64	....	90	76	82	10.5	10.7	46⅛	12	6¾	25	Dc	□0.30	....	[9]0.27	n/r
Bio-Response...........8½s mS 2001	CC	R	22.2	2001	263.16	3.80	....	26⅛	10	10	....	....	6⅝	⅜	¼	d	Dc	d1.13	....	[3]d1.18	n/r
Bio-Technology Gen'l[14] 7½s Ao15 1997	CC	R	20.0	1997	95.24	10.50	....	67⅞	40	45	16.6	22.2	28⅝	4¾	3	d	Dc	d1.00	....	[6]d1.12	n/r
Bio-Technology Gen'l.........11s Ms 2006	CC	R	10.2	2006	114.29	8.75	....	89	44	49½	22.2	22.7	34¼	4⅜	3	d	Dc	d1.00	....	[6]d1.12	n/r
BioTechnica Int'l..8¾s aO15 1996	NR	R	23.0	1996	208.33	4.80	....	95	60	82	10.6	12.3	57¼	3⅞	2¾	d	Dc	d1.88	....	d1.88	n/r
• Boise Cascade.............7s Mn 2016	BBB	R	97.9	2016	22.83	43.80	31.96	118	100	s102½	6.83	6.79	91⅛	44⅞	•40	7	Dc	3.70	E5.95	[9]5.84	n/r
• Bolt Beranek/Newman ....6s Ao 2012	B	R	84.7	2012	33.33	30.00	2.00	82	58½	s61	9.84	10.5	40	18¼	•12	14	Je	d0.46	0.96	[9]0.86	n/r
◆Bowmar Instrument......13½s jD15 1995	NR	R	10.1	1995	129.87	7.70	....	76	66	73½	18.3	20.8	13	5⅝	◆1	d	Sp	d0.47	....	[6]d0.61	n/r
• BRE Properties[15] ......9½s Jd 2008	A-	R	50.0	2008	[9]32.26	31.00	77.42	108½	96	s100¾	9.43	9.41	97⅛	31¼	•30⅛	15	Jl	▲2.52	1.87	[10]1.99	n/r
BRIntec Corp ....7½s Mn 2011	B	R	50.0	2011	40.00	25.00	....	61	51	57¾	12.9	13.5	20½	14½	5⅛	d	Dc	d0.10	....	[9]d0.20	n/r
• Brown & Sharpe Mfg.......9¼s jD15 2005	NR	R	19.0	2005	38.10	26.25	12.19	100	83	92	10.0	10.2	53⅜	24⅛	•14	..	Dc	d0.25	....	[9]0.13	n/r
Brown(Robert C.)& Co ...7½s Jd15 2011	NR	R	11.9	2011	75.47	13.25	....	68	50½	58	12.9	13.4	42½	7⅝	5⅝	d	Dc	△0.06	....	[9]d0.31	n/r
• Browning-Ferris Ind.......6¼s fA15 2012	A	R	345	2012	24.39	41.00	11.71	96	82¼	s89½	6.98	7.17	64	36¾	•26¼	17	Sp	1.15	P1.51	1.51	n/r
◆BSN Corp.............7¾s Ao15 2001	CCC	R	28.8	2001	64.10	15.60	....	82	60	66	11.7	13.4	38½	10¼	◆6	d	Dc	△0.21	....	[9]d0.06	n/r
Builders Transport....8s fA15 2005	B+	R	28.8	2005	40.98	24.40	....	80	71	71½	11.1	11.9	47⅝	17½	11⅝	20	Dc	△1.04	....	[9]0.58	n/r
Builders Transport...6½s Mn 2011	B+	R	38.0	2011	26.49	37.75	....	66	53	56	11.6	12.3	30¾	21⅛	11⅝	20	Dc	△1.04	....	[9]0.58	n/r
• Bulova Watch[16] ....6s Fa 1990	NR	R	4.38	1990	26.20	38.17	....	94	88	94	6.38	11.6	21	35⅞	8	5	Dc	*1.75	....	[3]1.48	n/r
◆Burnham Pacific Prop 8½s jJ15 2012	NR	R	21.2	2012	57.14	17.50	75.42	108	66	107⅞	7.88	7.76	107⅞	18⅞	◆18⅞	36	Dc	[17]0.43	....	[9]0.52	n/r
Burnup & Sims.......12s mN15 2000	NR	R	35.0	2000	51.95	19.25	....	106½	80	102⅝	11.6	11.5	98	19¾	18⅞	27	Ap	0.50	0.52	[10]0.69	n/r
• Businessland, Inc.......8s Fa15 2006	B-	R	40.3	2006	91.95	10.875	....	131	90	118⅜	6.76	6.24	118⅜	12⅞	•12⅞	15	Je	0.34	P0.74	[9]0.87	*0.71
• Businessland, Inc .....5½s Ms 2007	B-	R	50.0	2007	48.78	20.50	....	83	60	s78	7.05	7.77	62¾	16	•12⅞	15	Je	0.34	P0.74	[9]0.87	*0.71
Cadnetix Corp[18]......6¾s Mn 2012	CCC+	R	24.9	2012	56.50	17.70	....	70	52	52	12.9	13.5	46⅝	9¼	8¼	31	Je	0.46	*0.38	[9]0.27	n/r
◆Canandaigua Wine..........7s jJ 2011	B-	R	60.0	2011	[19]24.39	41.00	....	65	53	53	13.2	13.8	18⅝	21¾	◆7⅝	d	Au	d2.03	Pd0.85	d0.85	n/r
Cannon Group 8⅞s Ao15 2001	NR	R	80.5	2001	20.00	50.00	....	70	24	70	12.6	14.0	9	35	•4½	d	Dc	d11.1	....	[9]d6.50	n/r
Cardinal Distribution......8¼s Jd15 2010	B-	R	39.9	2010	63.37	15.78	5.07	117¼	79	111	7.43	7.23	108½	17½	17⅛	8	Mr	1.21	....	[9]2.20	1.06

Uniform Footnote Explanations—See Page XVI. Other: [1]Due Oct 1. [2]Was Hughes Tool. [3]File bankruptcy Chapt 11. [4]Default 6-1-88 int. [5]Now Baxter Int'l. [6]Was Baystate Corp. [7]Was Branch Corp. [8]Into Cl A com. [9]Cl A. [10]Cv into & data of Commtron Corp Cl'A'. [11](HRO)On ea Sep 30. [12]Due 7-16-2003. [13]Incl disc. [14](HRO)On 4-15-92 at 109.175. [15]Was BankAmer Rlty Inv. [16]Contr by Loews Corp. [17]12 Mo Dec'87. [18]Daisy Sys offers$6.50 cash & $3 debs to Dec 13. [19]Into Cl'A'.

Source: Standard and Poor's *Bond Guide*, December 1988.

Convertible bonds are a science in themselves. While regular bonds can be purchased and put into a safety deposit box for 20 years or more, convertible bonds require constant vigilance. Stock price fluctuations and call provisions make convertible bonds attractive to risk-lovers who have the time for constant portfolio analysis. Since this book is written more for financial planning for the average investor, only regular bonds are considered for the remainder of the book.

6

Junk Bonds

THERE HAS BEEN VERY LITTLE CHANGE IN THE INVESTMENT WORLD OVER the past 10 years that can match the explosion of the junk bond market. Junk bonds are subinvestment grade securities. They are rated either BB+ or less by Standard and Poor's or Baa or below by Moody's. Junk bonds have made it possible for small firms to buy out larger ones with high yield, low quality bonds. Most junk bonds are essentially unsecured and offer yields of 5 percent or more over investment grade securities.

THE MARKET EXPLOSION

Ten years ago, the junk bond market was virtually nonexistent except for fallen angels (i.e., once quality firms that have been downgraded because of bad economical times) and railroads. Today, the junk bond market contains corporate representation from virtually every industry. Table 6-1 shows how the amount of straight public debt has increased in the junk bond market over the interval from 1970 to 1985. At the beginning of 1986, there were more than 1,100 junk bonds issued by more than 500 different companies (to select from).

Pioneered by Drexel Burnham Lambert, Inc., the junk bond market is now approaching total offerings in excess of $2 billion. Junk bonds are potent tools in the hands of corporate raiders such as T. Boone Pickens, Carl Icahn, and Sir James Goldsmith, who have become experts at highly leveraged buy outs.

For many years, pension fund managers have restricted themselves to the top levels of investment-grade securities, but with the high differential in profitability between investment and noninvestment-grade bonds, their nervousness over failures and defaults has subsided. Although it is true that some junk bonds

TABLE 6-1
Outstanding Public Straight Debt 1970 to 1985 ($MM)*

		Low Rated Debt[a]			
Year	*Par Value Public Straight Debt Outstanding Over Year*[b]	*Straight Public Debt*[c]	*Percent of Public Straight Debt*	*Amount Outstanding Per Issuer*	*Amount Outstanding Per Issue*
1985	$395,500(est.)	$59,078	14.9	$135	$55
1984	363,300	41,700	11.5	125	49
1983	339,850	28,223	8.3	93	39
1982	320,850	18,536	5.8	69	33
1981	303,800	17,362	5.7	62	32
1980	282,000	15,125	5.4	59	31
1979	260,600	10,675	4.1	47	30
1978	245,000	9,401	3.8	49	30
1977	228,500	8,479	3.7	46	27
1976	209,900	8,015	3.8	41	27
1975	187,900	7,720	4.1	41	27
1974	167,000	11,101[d]	6.6	59	35
1973	154,800[e]	8,082	5.2	45	29
1972	145,700	7,106	4.9	45	29
1971	132,500	6,643	5.0	45	29
1970	116,200	6,996	6.0	48	32

[a]Source: Standard and Poor's *Bond Guide* and Moody's *Bond Record*, July issues of each year. Defaulted railroads excluded. Also includes nonrated debt equivalent to rated debt for low-rated firms.

[b]Average of beginning and ending years' figures (1975–1985).

[c]Includes high-yield exchange debt.

[d]Includes $2.7 billion in Con Edison debt.

[e]Estimates for 1973 and earlier based on linear regression of this column versus the Federal Reserve's Corporate Bonds Outstanding figures (*Federal Reserve Bulletin.*)

* Source: Altman, E.I. and Nammacher, S.A., *Investing in Junk Bonds*, John Wiley, New York, 1987, p. 20.

default each year, the overall risk can be minimized by establishing a well-diversified portfolio.

Junk bond enthusiasts argue that the current strong appeal of junk bonds is because the bond market is not as ultraconservative as it once was. Even conservative investment counselors are beginning to advocate using junk bonds in IRA's and corporate retirement accounts, as well as for investment opportunities. Critics acknowledge that if the economy's growth rate was steady rather than cyclical, this fast-growing sector of the marketplace would be considered a worthwhile risk. The true test of junk bonds will be how they withstand downturns in the economy.

UNDERSTANDING JUNK BONDS

Every language has its obscenities and none is more displeasing to bond dealers than the words "junk bonds." In more pleasant terms, junk bonds are referred to as high-yield, high-risk bonds or even deep-discounted bonds.[1] Yet the words "junk bonds" have become common usage probably because of the lack of general acceptance by the investors of the terminology.

Who in their right mind would invest a large percentage of their savings into junk? Hundreds of thousands of investors have already done this because the underlying fact is that junk bonds are still and foremost bonds. In case of default, bondholders stand well ahead of stockholders. Consider corporate bankruptcies such as W.T. Grant and Braniff. In both cases, the stockholders saw their equity vanish but the bondholders did fairly well. In the case of W.T. Grant, their 6 percent coupon bond was selling for $400 six months before they filed for bankruptcy. After bankruptcy, the bond was trading on the over-the-counter market for $630, yielding more than a 50 percent profit to the bondholders in less than six months.

Junk bonds can be issued using collateral just as with investment grade securities, perhaps with aircraft equipment or real estate. Unfortunately, if a company comes out of bankruptcy, the junk bonds might still be selling substantially below par and you are still in a losing position even though the bond is collateralized. For the most part, however, junk bonds are unsecured.

The main concern of the junk bond manager is risk, not interest rates. If interest rates increase, the bond price will fall, perhaps more than with investment-grade bonds. As long as the company does not default, however, the annual interest is still paid. The only loss that the investor will face should the investor decide to sell at the lower price is a capital loss. Junk bond investors can lose money if they overreact without sufficient justification. The problem is that the uninformed investor overreacts to bad news and is anxious to liquidate. If an investor does not become anxious, then he might not sustain any loss. Patience is the key to successful junk bond investments. Some market gurus who claim to be experts in junk bonds have made fortunes just by taking chances on junk bonds that were selling so low that the general trading public classified them as throwaways.

Junk bonds might not be very well known, they might not be right for every investor, but there should be no doubt that the junk bond market is beginning to flourish. Anise Wallace[2] said:

"Behind the superior performance of these junk bonds is what portfolio

---

[1]Actually, deep discounted bonds are ones that come to market with a discount of 15 percent or more. Most dealers, however refer to them as junk bonds rather than deep discounted bonds.

[2]Anise Wallace, *Junk Bonds: Performance Plus Stability, The New York Times*, August 2, 1987, Section F, p. 14.

managers call an attractive supply and demand equation. Until this year, the value of new issues had doubled every year. In fact, the $140 billion junk market now represents almost 20 percent of the total fixed-income markets. But this year, the pace is slowing and is slightly behind last year's record $40 billion. Early in the year, in fact, there was a relative shortage of such junk bonds after the new tax law temporarily slowed the pace of takeovers.

At the same time, demand has exploded. Institutional investors such as savings and loans, insurance companies and pension funds are pouring billions of dollars into high-yielding issues. Individuals are also snapping them up. The number of mutual funds that invest in junk bonds has increased to 67 from 37 in 1984. And assets of these funds totaled $30 billion at the end of June, up from $7 billion three years ago.

As in the equity market, institutional investors are buying the issues of the largest offerings—those resulting from mergers, recapitalizations and other corporate restructurings. This emphasis on big names is a result of two forces. In the first place, junk bond investors want to be able to unload securities of lower-rated companies at the mere whiff of trouble. A greater number of investment bankers are willing to make markets in issues of large deals, thus investors aren't tied to the fortunes or misfortunes of the underwriter. Consequently some of the most popular issues with these managers are the bonds of Borg-Warner, Owens-Illinois, Holiday, Beatrice and Colt Industries.

Second, the influx of cash flow from income and new investors has swelled many of these funds, almost forcing them to buy the issues of the largest companies. For instance the I.D.S. Extra Income Fund has grown to $1.1 billion from $500 million last year. As a result, fund manager John A. Utter rarely considers the bonds of offerings valued at less than $100 million. 'It has to be a larger and larger issue,'' he said.

The true test in the junk bond market is its ability to perform during a downturn in the economy, such as during a recession. As a result, many investors are avoiding junk bonds whose income is closely tied to the economy. Even a modest downturn in the economy could result in massive defaults in weak industries such as steel, restaurants, and construction.

THE TYPICAL, NEW HIGH-YIELD BOND ISSUE[3]

Table 6-2 summarizes the characteristics of new, straight-debt issues in 1985 and the comparable figures for 1983 to 1985 and 1978 to 1979. In 1985, the average new issue was just under $60 million. There were at least 210 new issues, including exchange debt offers, with 188 of the straight debt variety. At the same time, the average return on assets went up to 2.8 percent from 1.9 percent in 1984. The median return on assets also rose from 2.7 percent in 1984

[3] This section has been adapted from Altman E.I., and Nammacher, S.A., *Investing in Junk Bonds*, John Wiley, New York, 1987, pp. 40-47.

TABLE 6-2
Profile of New, High-Yield, Straight-Debt Issues and Issuers (1978-1985)

	Average					*Median*					*Standard Deviation*				
	1978	*1979*	*1983*	*1984*	*1985*	*1978*	*1979*	*1983*	*1984*	*1985*	*1978*	*1979*	*1983*	*1984*	*1985*
							Issue Characteristics								
Size of issue ($MM)	28.7	29.0	86.2	120.6	78.0	25.0	20.0	60.0	77.5	60.0	19.6	21.3	123.7	150.6	150.6
Coupon rate (percent)	—	12.3	12.0	13.3	12.9	—	12.3	11.8	14.5	13.9	1.0	1.1	1.8	3.9	3.4
Yield to maturity (percent)	—	12.6	14.0	15.2	14.9	—	12.6	13.8	15.4	14.7	1.1	1.2	1.3	1.4	1.3
S&P rating	B/B+	B/B+	B/B+	B/B+	B/B+	B/B+	B/B+	B/B+	B/B+	B/B+	—	—	—	—	—
Number of issues	52	41	86	124	188										
							Firm Characteristics								
Age of firm (years)	22.8	26.0	28.2	31.1	36.0	18.0	20.0	20.1	26.0	26.0	14.7	19.6	22.4	23.1	30.5
Asset size ($MM)	176	285	1,074	1,588	1,108	107	127	322	735	410	187	487	1,776	2,435	2,154
Return on assets (percent)	—	—	1.5	1.9	2.8	—	—	2.7	2.7	3.5	—	—	7.8	8.2	9.8
Number of firms	**50**	**40**	**68**	**99**	**135**										

to 3.5 percent in 1985. Despite this higher average return, the overall credit quality of new, 1985 issues actually appears to have gone down.

The typical (median) new issuer in 1985 was 26 years old with $410 million in assets. The $60 million median-issue size was equal to 1983s median but below the record year of 1984 when the median size was $77.5 million. The expected yield to maturity was 14.7 percent with a 13.9 percent coupon rate. The average coupon rate was lower than the median because of the number of discount and zero coupon bonds issued and falling interest rates.

Tables 6-3, 6-4, and 6-5 detail the frequency distributions found in Table 6-2 of the age, issue, size, and assets of the firms studied. The distributions show the following:

- In 1985, 24 percent of the firms were relatively young (less than 15 years in business) while another 25 percent were in business for 15 to 24 years (Table 6-3). A rather large proportion (more than 51 percent) of 1984 and 1985 new issuers were seasoned firms, in business more than 25 years. This compares to 43 percent new issuers for 1978 to 1979 and 41 percent

TABLE 6-3
Age of Firm Distribution[a] (1983 to 1985 New Issuers)

Age of Issuer (years)	*Number of Firms*			*Percent of Firms*		
	1983	*1984*	*1985*	*1983*	*1984*	*1985*
0–4	8	11	7	10.4%	10.2%	6.3%
5–14	23	17	20	29.9	15.7	17.9
15–24	15	24	28	19.4	22.2	25.0
25–34	5	21	9	6.5	19.4	8.0
35–44	4	5	14	5.2	4.6	12.5
45–54	5	4	9	6.5	3.7	8.0
55–64	11	14	9	14.3	13.0	8.0
65–74	5	8	7	6.5	7.4	6.3
>75	11	4	9	1.3	3.7	3.0
Total sample	77	108	112	100.0	100.0	100.0
Average (yrs)	28	31	35	—	—	—
Median (yrs)	20	26	26	—	—	—

[a]Includes exchange debt issuers. Data not available on all firms.

TABLE 6-4
Issue Size Distribution (1983 to 1985 New Issuers)

Size of Issue ($MM)	*Number of Issues*			*Percent of Total Issues*		
	1983	*1984*	*1985*	*1983*	*1984*	*1985*
0–20	7	6	7	8.1%	4.8%	3.7%
21–40	25	27	57	29.1	21.8	30.3
41–60	12	18	41	13.9	14.5	21.8
61–80	15	13	18	17.4	10.6	9.6
81–100	10	19	20	11.6	15.3	10.6
101–150	10	15	21	11.6	12.1	11.2
151–200	1	14	8	1.2	11.3	4.3
201–300	4	3	12	4.7	2.4	6.4
301–500	1	5	2	1.2	4.0	1.1
501–1000	—	3	1	0	2.4	0.5
> 1001	1	1	1	1.2	0.8	0.5
Total sample	86	124	188	100.0	100.0	100.0
Average size	$86.2	$120.6	$77.0	—	—	
Median size	$60.0	$ 77.5	$60.0	—	—	

in 1983. The difference might be the result of more aggressive underwriting efforts and buy outs, as well as a robust market. Surprisingly, the median age of new issuers from 1983 to 1985 is only slightly above the 1978 to 1979 median—24 vs. 19.

- Table 6-4 lists the distribution by size of issue. The very small issue, under 20 million, proportion dropped again in 1985 to less than 4 percent,

TABLE 6-5
Size of Firm (Total Assets) Distribution
(1983 to 1985 New Issuers)

Size of Firm's Assets ($MM)	*Number of Firms*			*Percent of Firms*		
	1983	*1984*	*1985*	*1983*	*1984*	*1985*
0–100	14	12	24	20.3%	14.6%	21.6%
101–200	14	12	10	20.3	14.6	9.0
201–300	7	10	12	10.2	12.2	10.8
301–400	7	9	7	10.2	11.0	6.3
401–500	4	3	10	5.8	3.7	9.0
501–600	2	0	7	2.9	0.0	6.3
601–700	0	2	5	0.0	2.4	4.5
701–800	2	2	5	2.9	2.4	4.5
801–900	2	2	2	2.9	2.4	1.8
901–1000	2	1	3	2.9	1.2	2.7
1001–2000	5	12	12	7.2	14.6	10.8
2001–3000	6	6	1	8.7	7.3	0.9
3001–4000	0	1	6	0.0	1.2	5.4
4001–5000	1	4	1	1.4	4.9	0.9
5001–10000	3	5	5	4.3	6.2	4.5
> 10001	0	1	1	0.0	1.2	0.9
Total sample	69	82	111	100.0	100.0	100.0
Average size	$1,075	$1,588	$1,108	—	—	—
Median size	322	735	415	—	—	—

but the moderate size categories ($21 to $60 million) increased to about 50 percent of all new issues versus 36 percent in 1984 and 44 percent in 1983. Larger issues dropped back to 1983 levels.

- Firm size was impressive with over 23 percent (1985), 26 percent (1984), and 21 percent (1983) of the firms having assets over $1 billion (see Table 6-5). As expected, median total assets of new issuers in 1983 to 1985 was considerably higher than the earlier 1978 to 1979 medians. The new issue market is no longer the primary province of the small, unseasoned company. Takeover issues had a very small impact on these statistics because there were relatively few issues of that type.

UNDERWRITERS[4]

Drexel Burnham Lambert has been the leading underwriter (and driving force) in the high-yield market for a number of years. Through 1985, it was responsible for at least 287 issues and about 57 percent of the almost $46 billion in new issue dollars since 1978. According to Securities Data Corp., Drexel, once a relatively small firm in its field, became the second largest corporate bond underwriter in

[4]Ibid, pp. 45–47.

TABLE 6-6
New, High-Yield Public Debt Issues (1978 – 1985[a]) Full Credit to Lead Manager ($000)[b]

Underwriter	*1985*		*1984*		*1983*	
	Amount	*Number*	*Amount*	*Number*	*Amount*	*Number*
Drexel Burnham Lambert	7,238,515	83	10,358,000	67	4,346,151	46
Salomon Brothers	1,464,311	13	865,000	9	422,538	4
Morgan Stanley	1,050,000	13	319,000	5	80,000	1
Lehman/Loeb	707,653	8	718,000	8	230,000	1
Merrill Lynch	665,776	9	530,000	4	427,000	5
First Boston	640,000	9	390,000	5	325,000	3
Goldman Sachs	615,000	5	100,000	1	125,000	1
Bear, Stearns	456,100	7	360,000	4	380,000	5
Prudential-Bache	435,000	8	950,000	13	275,000	6
E.F. Hutton	230,000	2	145,000	3	190,000	2
Blyth Eastman/Paine W.	206,044	2	65,000	1	235,000	3
Others	804,025	29	151,969	4	381,500	9
Total	14,670,424	188	14,951,969	124	7,417,189	86

Underwriter	*1982*		*1981*		*1980*		*1979*		*1978*	
	Amount	*Number*	*Amount*	*Number*	*Amount*	*Number*	*Amount*	*Number*	*Amount*	*Number*
Drexel Burnham Lambert	1,543,800	28	935,667	19	498,000	15	408,000	14	464,500	15
Salomon Brothers	—	—	60,000	1	115,000	2	—	—	—	—
Morgan Stanley	—	—	—	—	40,000	1	—	—	—	—
Lehman/Loeb	25,000	1	225,000	2	222,500	5	75,000	2	75,000	2
Merrill Lynch	699,000	7	240,000	4	50,000	1	75,000	1	157,875	3
First Boston	—	—	—	—	—	—	171,000	1	68,750	3
Goldman Sachs	—	—	—	—	—	—	—	—	—	—
Bear, Stearns	35,000	1	30,000	1	105,000	4	235,000	7	120,775	6
Prudential-Bache	40,000	1	—	—	—	—	30,000	2	20,000	1
E.F. Hutton	82,542	2	25,000	1	89,125	2	68,000	4	90,000	3
Blyth Eastman/Paine W.	225,000	1	—	—	52,000	1	173,000	4	155,000	3
Others	147,311	7	132,500	4	270,000	12	72,000	10	341,000	16
Total	2,797,653	48	1,648,167	32	1,441,625	43	1,307,000	45	1,492,900	52

[a]Bonds rated BB, Ba or lower, and high yield non-rated bonds. Includes utilities, excludes convertibles and exchange offers.

[b]In cases of consolidation, credit goes to surviving firm.

the United States securities industry in 1984 behind Salomon Brothers, primarily because of its specialization in this new, high-yield debt area. Table 6-6 and Fig. 6-1 provide details on new issues and ratings by the underwriter.

In 1985, and even more so in 1986, Drexel Burnham Lambert faced more competition from a host of other investment banks. What was once an area to be eschewed by prestigious bankers, is now perceived by many banks as a high profit, almost glamorous area. Indeed, underwriting fees have averaged about 3 percent of new issue dollars and trading, and commission profits from secondary market activities have added handsome returns to underwriters and market makers.

The two firms that appear to have made the largest gains in this market in 1984 and 1985 are Salomon Brothers and Morgan Stanley. In 1985, both were the lead underwriter in more than $1 billion in new debt involving 13 issues each.

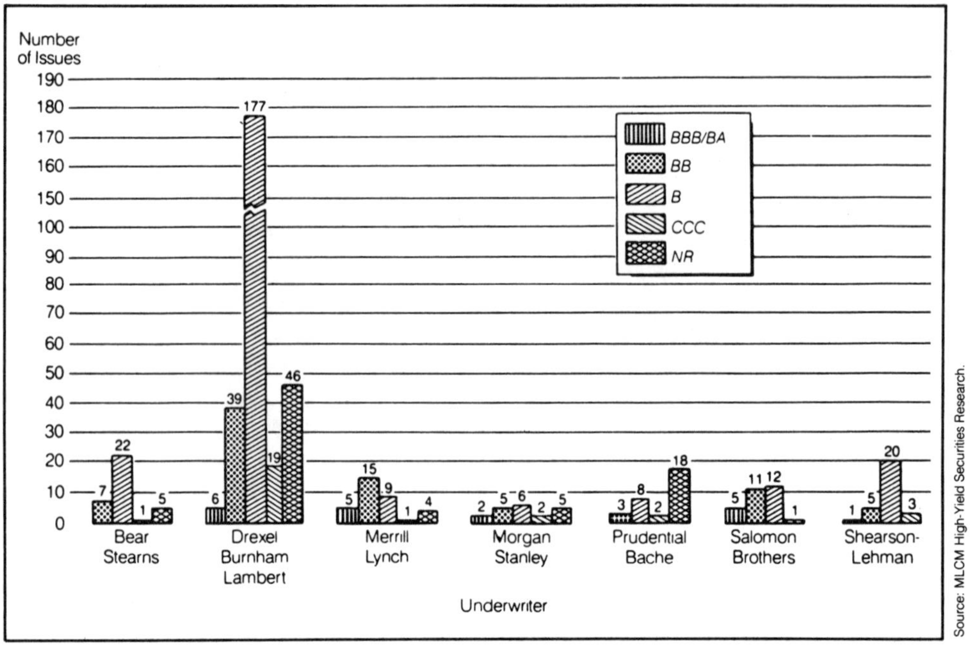

Fig. 6-1. New, high-yield debt issues—underwriter by Standard and Poor's bond rating 1987–1985.

Drexel Burnham Lambert's market share "dropped" to about 50 percent of the straight-debt new issue market in 1985. Salomon Brothers and Morgan Stanley followed with shares of 10 percent and 7 percent respectively. Drexel Burnham Lambert's market share would have been substantially larger if all types of high-yield debt issues were included (i.e., exchange, secondary, and best effort offerings, etc.).

In early 1986, Drexel Burnham Lambert was still the leading underwriter, but firms such as Merrill Lynch, First Boston, Salomon Brothers, Goldman Sachs, Kidder Peabody, Morgan Stanley, and Shearson Lehman are capturing an increasing share of the market, especially in the nonrated sector. It is expected that this reduced market share for the "industry" leader will continue as competition heats up.

UNDERWRITER'S DEFAULT EXPERIENCE[5]

In September 1986, *The Wall Street Journal* highlighted recent default records of the top 15 junk bond underwriters. The article tabulated results on all $99.49 billion in junk bonds that were sold publicly between January 1, 1980 and September 11, 1986. The record of defaults varied substantially, ranging from 0 percent to 17 percent. Four firms in the study had no bonds defaulting: Shearson

[5]This section is from Jane Tripp Holde, Junk Bonds, Probus Publisher, Chicago, Illinois, 1988, pp. 38–42.

TABLE 6-7
Default Rate of Junk Underwriters ($millions)[1]

Lead Manager	*Junk Bonds Sold between 1/1/80 and 9/11/86*	*Amount Defaulted*	*Amount Defaulted*
Drexel Burnham	$44,927	$ 845	1.9
Merrill Lynch	8,964	896	10.0
Salomon Brothers	4,652	25	0.5
Shearson Lehman	4,450	0	0.0
First Boston	3,875	290	7.5
Goldman Sachs	3,301	0	0.0
Morgan Stanley	3,089	25	0.8
Bear Stearns	2,945	169	5.7
E.F. Hutton	2,343	84	3.6
Prudential-Bache	2,308	230	10.0
Kidder Peabody	1,791	0	0.0
L.F. Rothschild	1,456	150	9.2
Smith Barney	1,220	53	4.3
Paine Webber	1,364	0	0.0
Donaldson Lufkin	958	160	17.0
	$86,043	$2,927	3.4

[1]Bonds included in the study are all publicly issued bonds with a rating below BBB–. Convertible bonds were included. Full credit was given to the lead manager.

Sources: IDD Information Services, Edward Altman, New York University, and *The Wall Street Journal*, September 29, 1986, pp. 21 and 43.

Lehman, Goldman Sachs, Kidder Peabody, and Paine Webber. Donaldson Lufkin had the misfortune of realizing a 17.0 percent default rate on the junk bonds it underwrote during this period (see Table 6-7).

A quick look at the tabulated default experiences reveals three dominant facts. First, the default experience of some underwriters has been exceedingly high. Second, the default experience varies considerably among the underwriters. Third, the overall default rate has been reasonable, 3.4 percent. After looking at these figures, you might decide that care should be taken in selecting an underwriter from whom to buy your junk bonds. Care should *always* be taken in every aspect of investment management. However, the care should be your own analysis. Buying bonds from an underwriter who has had few (or no) defaults to date does not relieve you from this responsibility. More important, the numbers can be very misleading unless you understand how they were calculated and the story behind each of the numbers.

Several underwriters complained about the methodology of the study. These complaints centered around three issues: the definition of default, the definition of the universe, and the assignment of ''credit'' for the issues.

First Boston objected to the study's defining default as issues that have been rated D by Standard and Poor's during any time since 1980. Under this definition, Castle & Cooke was included in First Boston's defaults. In 1985, Castle & Cooke missed some interest payments and was downgraded to D. In fact, the interest payments were paid within a grace period specified by the bond covenant and therefore the issue was never technically in default. Drexel Burnham does not have the same objection to the definition of default. This might be because Drexel is adept at "helping" clients whose results are shaky. It can do this by restructuring the debt or by arranging to have another client assume the debt. The restructuring can consist of an exchange of the original debt for equity, or for new debt with reduced terms. Although a loss of principal is often involved, no "default" is tallied according to the definition of *default*.

Several firms objected to the study's definition of the *universe* as all publicly issued speculative-grade bonds, because this includes convertibles but excludes private placements. The inclusion of convertibles increased the default rate at four of the surveyed firms: Donaldson Lufkin, First Boston, Bear Stearns, and Salomon Brothers. If convertibles had been excluded, these firms' default rates would have been shown in Table 6-8.

Donaldson Lufkin also objected to the exclusion of private placements. This is understandable. Donaldson's high rate of default reflects the default of four oil and gas issues that defaulted in 1980 and 1981. The group that was responsible for this effort was disbanded. Donaldson has since been acquired by the Equitable Life Assurance Society of the United States. Under the new structure, Donaldson has resumed underwriting junk bonds. However, its recent effort in this area has been primarily in private placements. In fact, the firm has issued more than $1 billion of private placement junk bonds. Because this new effort is not reflected in the study, Donaldson feels that its participation in junk underwriting is unfairly presented.

Merrill Lynch objects to the study assigning full credit of a default to the lead manager. This calculation particularly hurt the firm when Merrill Lynch was accorded full blame for $375 million of defaulted LTV bonds for which it was lead manager. Also, First Boston and Shearson Lehman were not credited with any of this issue, although they were comanagers.

TABLE 6-8

Comparison of Default Rates When Convertibles are Excluded

Firm	*Default Rate Including Convertibles*	*Default Rate Excluding Convertibles*
Donaldson Lufkin	17.0%	11.0%
First Boston	0.0	7.5
Bear Stearns	4.2	5.7
Salomon Brothers	0.0	0.5

Source: IDD Information Services, Edward Altman, New York University, and *The Wall Street Journal*, September 29, 1986, pp. 21, 43.

Given the difficulty of calculating default rates and the concerns expressed by some of the surveyed underwriters, *The Wall Street Journal* study should not be considered in isolation but rather in the overall context of junk analysis. It points out the risks inherent in the market: pockets of defaults. It also points out the rewards: issues that continue to survive and pay above market rates.

A close look at the issues that make up defaulted bonds reveals a concentration in steel and energy issues. It is no wonder then that sound analysis and diversification are essential, even in a market that more than likely offers above-average returns. Only time will tell whether defaults will increase to the point where the yield advantage of high-yield bonds is nullified, and the predictions of some of the doomsayers come true.

Even if you think that the junk market offers great rewards and do not believe that these rewards will be diminished in the near future, you might still be unnerved by the thought that actual defaults could occur in your own portfolio and decimate performance. Such thoughts are reinforced by the news media who give front-page coverage to companies going bankrupt, such as LTV and Frontier Airlines. No doubt, this concern is at the heart of investing in high-yield securities. While there is no guaranteed way of avoiding defaults in a personal portfolio, there are proven ways of substantially reducing the risk.

One way of reducing the risk is to analyze your investments thoroughly before you buy them and to continue to review them as long as they are held. This analysis is necessary whether you are investing in individual securities or buying shares in a mutual fund that specializes in high-yield securities. It is just as important when investments are made in high-grade securities. High-grade investments can default, too! Penn Central's commercial paper was rated prime when the railroad filed for bankruptcy.

The second way of reducing the risk of high-yield securities is by diversifying your portfolio. Diversification should reflect terms of maturity, type of security, and industry concentration, as well as the number of issuers. The benefits of diversification have long been accepted doctrine of common stock investing. Diversification increases the total expected rate of return per unit of risk. With the increased acceptance of bond index funds, diversification is also being accepted as doctrine in fixed-income investing.

JUNK BOND CLASSIFICATIONS

Not all high-yield bonds are junk. Some bonds carry high-yields but with increasing quality and asset growth. Others were once quality bonds that were downgraded because of leveraged buy outs. According to Robert Levine, junk bonds can be classified as:[6]

- Gyrojunk Bonds

[6]Ben Weberman, "The Real and the Junk," *Forbes*, July 28, 1986, p. 224.

- Geriatric Bonds
- Juvenile Bonds
- LBO Bonds
- Blind Trust Bonds

Gyrobonds are investments that are well protected by good assets one day, and the next day, find themselves naked.[7]

The best example is Metro-Goldwyn-Mayer, once owned by Kirk Kerkorian. He split MGM into two companies: MGM Grand, the gaming company, and MGM/UA, with the filmmaking business and film library. In 1980, the film company was distributed to the stockholders, with Kerkorian being the majority holder. Bondholders of the original MGM no longer had a stable cash flow provided by the film library. Their debt was bumped down from the lower end of the investment category to the truly junk.

The second category is the geriatric bonds. These are the once-proud smokestack industries, such as steel, that have lost their competitiveness because of antiquated facilities. These companies have the opportunity to turn themselves around but with an extremely heavy capital investment program. Many are also called "fallen angels" because their AA ratings have deteriorated to B. Borderline geriatric bonds can be rejuvenated. Such was the case with Navistar and Harnischfeger, whose junk bond ratings have been upgraded to investment grade. Geriatric bonds can sometimes provide investors with excellent opportunities for profits and returns. This is especially true when rating agencies haven't yet recognized that a turn-around has occurred.

The third bond category is juvenile bonds. These are usually young companies with a poor balance sheet and little cash flow because of heavy startup costs. These issuing companies can sometimes have low ratings because they are too young to have a long history of debt payment during bad times.

The fourth category is leverage buy out bonds. The bond ratings of these companies have been either upgraded, or more commonly, downgraded because of the debt effect on the balance sheet as a result of the buy out.

The final category is blind trust bonds. These bonds are controlled by highly ambitious corporate raiders whose next move is uncertain. These bonds are almost impossible to analyze.

Every investor has his own methodology for classifying investments. Worthy classifies junk bonds as:[8]

- Atomics. While these junk bonds are the shakiest, they aren't all going into default. Some will scrape by, perhaps with the sort of exchange offer Drexel Burnham has pioneered for clients. Table 6-9 is an example of Atomic Bonds. (Total debt includes bank debt.)

[7]Ibid.

[8]Ford S. Worthy, *The Coming Defaults in Junk Bonds, Fortune*, March 16, 1987, pp. 26–34.

TABLE 6-9
"Atomic" Junk Bonds

ATOMICS

COMPANY	PRIMARY UNDERWRITER	DEBT/ EQUITY RATIO	TOTAL JUNK BONDS in millions	TOTAL DEBT in millions
Allegheny Beverage	Smith Barney	5.9	$192	$381
American Healthcare Management	Drexel Burnham	12.8	$80	$435
Cannon Group	Drexel Burnham	7.8	$243	$596
Care Enterprises	Drexel Burnham	4.2	$68	$179
Compact Video	Drexel Burnham	3.9	$80	$174
Consolidated Oil & Gas	None	14.8	$42	$104
Consul Restaurant	Piper Jaffray	3.7	$21	$26
Lifestyle Restaurant	L.F. Rothschild	2.9	$12	$16
Michigan General	Drexel Burnham	5.6	$110	$146
Pay 'N Save	Drexel Burnham	3.5	$295	$343
Pennsylvania Engineering	None	10.9	$12	$86
Penril	Drexel Burnham	3.2	$18	$35
Po Folks	Kidder Peabody	4.4	$16	$75
Pope Evans & Robbins	Bear Stearns	2.8	$35	$39
Preway	Drexel Burnham	10.3	$56	$60
Quanex	Drexel Burnham	2.5	$103	$112
Reading & Bates	Smith Barney	5.1	$60	$486
Spendthrift Farm	Prudential-Bache	3.7	$30	$44
Texas International	Drexel Burnham	2.8	$190	$298
Thousand Trails	Prudential-Bache	6.9	$57	$188
Wean United	None	3.6	$27	$37
Western Union	Salomon Brothers	3.9	$526	$924
Westworld Community Healthcare	Drexel Burnham	15.2	$65	$123
Winners	Prudential-Bache	3.5	$25	$49

TABLE 6-10
"Subatomic" Junk Bonds

SUBATOMICS				
COMPANY	PRIMARY UNDERWRITER	DEBT/ EQUITY RATIO	TOTAL BONDS OUTSTANDING in millions	TOTAL DEBT in millions
Arrow Electronics	Bear Stearns	2.2	$110	$164
Ducommun	Donaldson Lufkin	2.8	$35	$160
Kaneb Services	Smith Barney	2.0	$55	$185
Kay	Bear Stearns	3.1	$10	$165
Lear Petroleum	Drexel Burnham	6.5	$196	$266
MCO Holdings	Drexel Burnham	4.5	$81	$327
Price Communications	Morgan Stanley	3.4	$375	$447
Radice	E.F. Hutton	3.3	$34	$168
Service Merchandise	Merrill Lynch	3.6	$300	$904
Texstyrene	Drexel Burnham	2.3	$50	$82
Universal Health Services	Morgan Stanley	3.0	$85	$333
Valero Energy	Shearson Lehman	3.4	$277	$897

- Subatomics. These bonds must be handled with care. A little less risky than atomics, the subatomic bonds of these companies still need to be approached with caution. Like the atomics, they are vulnerable but not necessarily doomed. (See Table 6-10.)
- Quality Junk. These bonds are considered the top of the junk heap. More like investment grade outfits than junk, these companies have low leverage, low stock-price volatility, and a lot of equity. These companies may be upgraded to investment grade. (See Table 6-11.)

Beauty is in the eyes of the beholder, and what some consider to be junk, others see as beauty.

CREATING JUNK BONDS THROUGH LEVERAGED BUY OUTS

In recent years, junk bond financing has been heavily relied on for highly-popular leveraged buy outs (LBO). This popularity for LBO's can be seen in Table 6-12.

TABLE 6-11
"Quality" Junk Bonds

QUALITY JUNK

COMPANY	PRIMARY UNDERWRITER	DEBT/ EQUITY RATIO	TOTAL JUNK BONDS in millions	TOTAL DEBT in millions
Caesars World	Drexel Burnham	0.8	$233	$495
Castle & Cooke	Goldman Sachs	0.4	$173	$455
Circus Circus	Drexel Burnham	0.2	$75	$180
Federal Paper Board	First Boston	0.6	$144	$472
Fuqua Industries	Shearson Lehman	0.5	$159	$311
GAF	Drexel Burnham	0.3	$486	$486
GenCorp	Kidder Peabody	0.1	$103	$208
B.F. Goodrich	Goldman Sachs	0.4	$92	$489
Rorer Group	First Boston	0.5	$326	$452
Tele-Communications	Drexel Burnham	0.8	$505	$2,163
Telex	Drexel Burnham	0.1	$21	$106
Texaco	Salomon Brothers	1.0	$6,722	$9,394
United Brands	Drexel Burnham	0.2	$96	$135
Whittaker	Dominick & Dominick	1.0	$44	$268

There are two types of LBO's. First, there is Company A, which wants to acquire Company B. Company A then assumes a large debt, whether it is through loans, junk bonds, or both to acquire Company B. After the acquisition, the debt must be supported by the assets of both firms. Company A then begins to liquidate several Company A and Company B assets to reduce the debt to manageable levels.

The second type of LBO is when a company is made private by a LBO that is initiated by the company's own management and is often referred to as a management buy out. This might be the result of avoiding acquisition or a hostile takeover by another firm. As with the first type of LBO, once the deal is finalized, assets are usually sold to reduce the debt.

TABLE 6-12
Leveraged Buy Out Transactions (1978–1986)

	Aggregate Value ($000)	*Number of Transactions*	*Average Size ($000)*
	Completed Transactions of $35MM or More		
1978	—	—	—
1979	$ 471,293	2	$235,647
1980	721,953	3	240,651
1981	3,136,298	17	184,488
1982	3,365,175	20	167,809
1983	3,807,671	29	131,299
1984	14,202,457	48	295,885
1985	11,299,446	34	332,337
1986 through (2/28/86)	19,370,418	33	586,982
Total	$56,365,711	186	$303,041

Source: Morgan Stanley & Co., Incorporated and Altman, D.I., and Nammacher, S.A., *Investing in Junk Bonds*, John Wiley, New York, 1987, pp. 172.

During mergers, acquisitions, and LBO's, stockholders often receive premiums of up to 50 percent or more for their stock. Bondholders, however, might suffer as the acquiror leverages up for acquisition. Not all acquisitions and LBO's result in bond-quality downgrading but, as a general observation, the larger the acquisition, the greater the probability of downgrading. This can be seen in Table 6-13, which shows 22 domestic deals of more than $1 billion completed in 1985.

Perhaps the best example of bondholder reaction to the RJR Nabisco leveraged buy out[9] is by looking at Fig. 6-2. The corporate bond market remained in disarray as worried investors shunned investment-grade industrial issues in the wake of RJR Nabisco Inc.'s massive proposed leveraged buy out.

Prices of RJR Nabisco bonds and many other corporate bonds tumbled. As buyers disappeared for many industrial issues, underwriters led by First Boston Corp. struggled to find buyers for a $300 million issue by Eastman Kodak Co.

On the other hand, bonds issued by utilities, banks, and foreign companies—with little chance of being affected by a leveraged buy out—sold briskly.

Bond investors were frightened by the prospect that other, huge industrial companies could become buy out targets. These deals are frequently disastrous for bond investors because they can involve massive new debt that causes the value of existing bonds to plunge.

Investor's fears increased borrowing costs for many companies. "There's a lot of concern at the moment," said James R. Messing, a vice president at First Boston. Industrial companies that attempt to auction their bond issues to the

[9]Winkler, M., and Herman, T., Adapted from "Takeover Fears Rack Corporate Bonds," *The Wall Street Journal*, Tuesday, October 25, 1988, pp. c1, c21.

TABLE 6-13
U.S. Industry Merger and Acquisitions Completed in 1985 (over $1 billion)

Acquiror	*S&P Ratings Before*	*S&P Ratings After*	*Transaction Size ($ Billions)*	*Acquired*	*S&P Ratings Before*	*S&P Ratings After*
Philip Morris	A+	A	5.70	General Foods	AA	A
Allied Corp.	A	A	5.00	Signal Comp.	A+	A
General Motors	AA+	AA+	5.00	Hughes Aircraft	—	—
R. J. Reynolds	AA	A	4.91	Nabisco	AA	A
Baxter Travenol	AA−	BBB+	3.80	American Hospital Supply	AA	BBB+
Capital Cities	AA−	A	3.50	American Broadcasting	AA−	A−
Monsanto	A	A−	2.73	G. D. Searle	AA−	A−
Coastal Corp.	**BB−**	**B−**	**2.50**	**American Natural Resources**	**A−**	**A−**
Kohlberg, Kravis, Roberts	**NR[a]**	**NR**	**2.50**	**Storer Communications**	**BB−**	**CCC**
Inter North	A	BBB	2.27	Houston National Gas	BBB+	BBB
Cox Enterprises	NR[b]	NR	2.10[c]	Cox Communications	NR	NR
Pantry Pride	**—**	**CCC**	**1.83**	**Revlon**	**A+**	**B**
Kholberg, Kravis, Roberts	**NR[a]**	**NR**	**1.70**	**Union Texas Petrol (50%)**	**—**	**BB−**
Rockwell International	AA	AA	1.65	Allen Bradley	—	—
Cooper Industries	A	A−	1.50	McGraw Edison	A−	A−
HHF	**NR[a]**	**NR**	**1.45**	**Levi-Strauss**	**A**	**B+**
Farley Metals	**NR[a]**	**NR**	**1.40**	**Northwest Industries**	**BBB**	**B**
Textron	AA−	BBB+	1.40	AVCO	BB+	BBB+
Chesebrough-Ponds	AA−	BBB	1.30	Stauffer Chemical	A	BBB
Procter & Gamble	AAA	AAA	1.24	Richardson Vicks	A	A
MidCon Corporation	BBB	BBB	1.14	United Energy Res.	BBB	BBB+
Wickes	**CCC**	**CCC**	**1.09**	**Consumer/Ind. Prods. Div. of G&W**	**—**	**—**

[a]For LBO's that resulted in noninvestment grade ratings, acquiring companies were classified as noninvestment grade even though they had no formal rating.

[b]Classifieds investment grade on basis of P-2/A-2 commercial paper ratings.

[c]Includes holdings already owned by Cox Enterprises.

Sources: Morgan Stanley & Co., Incorporated and Securities Data Corp.

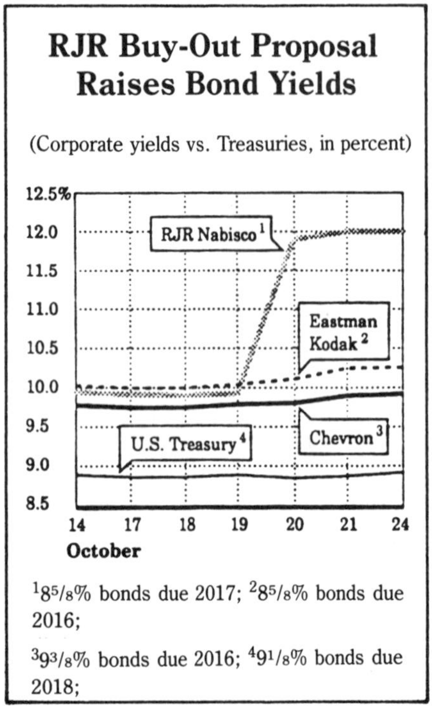

Source: Merrill Lynch Fixed Income Research.

Fig. 6-2. Merrill Lynch High-Yield 175 Index.

highest bidder right now are ''making a big mistake,'' he said. ''The bids aren't there.''

Once plans to take the company private for $17.6 billion were announced, yields on many highly rated industrial bonds have increased as much as 0.25 percent in relation to benchmark government issues. The casualties included bonds of such highly rated companies as Kodak, Chevron Corp., Atlantic Richfield Co., Unisys Corp., and Coca-Cola Co., whose yields suddenly diverged from treasurys.

The prospect of RJR creating a mountain of debt to fund its buy out and transform its bonds into high-yield, high-risk junk bonds paralyzed investors and shocked traders, said John Griff, a managing director in charge of corporate bond syndication at Merrill Lynch Capital Markets. Reflecting the apparent lack of buyers in the market, he said there were ''only dealer quotes'' for yields because ''there are no customer purchases.''

The RJR buy out plan inflicted heavy losses on RJR bondholders. Some RJR long-term bonds fell nearly four points, or almost $40 for each $1,000 face amount. That brought the total loss on one RJR issue since the buy out plan was announced last week to more than 16 points, or more than $160 for each $1,000 face amount, while its yield soared to about 12 1/4 percent from just over 10 percent late last Wednesday.

John Lonski, a senior economist at Moody's Investors Service Inc., said that anxiety created by the RJR proposal "is going to raise yields on industrial bonds relative to other corporate issues" in the current climate. "Investors are demanding extra compensation now," he added.

Mr. Messing of First Boston said an industrial company might easily be forced to pay as much as $27.50 more per $1,000 bond to borrow long-term as a result of the RJR proposal.

Some investors already are shunning industrial bond issues. "I'm avoiding them like the plague," said William H. Gross, a managing director of Pacific Investment Management Co., Newport Beach, Calif., which manages a $17.5 billion bond portfolio. "There's very little that's really safe to own out there right now except pure Treasury debt," he said.

Some traders think that investors may overreact to the news and dump their corporate bond holdings at first sale prices. If so, they say that could create tremendous bargains in many corporate issues. So far, though, there has been little selling pressure. Several traders said they received inquiries from large institutions about the market, but few orders to sell or buy.

"We have been across-the-board interest by corporate bond buyers in the utility sector, instead of industrials," said Eunice Reich, a first vice president at Merrill Lynch Capital Markets. Added William H. James, director of corporate bond trading at First Boston, "We have seen an improved demand for utilities and Yankee bonds, and, to a lesser degree, bank and finance paper," he said. Yankee bonds are dollar-denominated bonds issued in the U.S. by foreign institutions.

Traders said the spread on some Yankee bonds and utility company debt has narrowed significantly compared with Treasurys.

For example, Tokyo 10-year debt was trading at about 50 basis points above U.S. Treasurys last Wednesday. It traded yesterday at 38 basis points over Treasurys. World Bank paper was trading around 45 basis points over U.S. Treasurys last week and is now about 37 basis points above Treasurys.

Some traders had expected investors to rush to buy bonds of the nation's very biggest companies that are viewed as least vulnerable to takeovers or restructurings. So far, though, that hasn't happened. "No, you haven't seen a wholesale run for higher-quality industrials, like the IBMs and Exxons of the world," said Mr. James of First Boston. One possible explanation is that investors can earn nearly the same returns on treasuries as on IBM issues.

The trouble in the corporate market hurt sales of the $300 million issue of Kodak debentures due in 16 years. Details of the new issue were announced Friday, less than 24 hours after the RJR news broke. Only a third of the issues was sold as of yesterday, the underwriters said.

The market's disarray caught many experts by surprise. Even though bond investors have been stung many times in recent years by takeovers and restructurings, traders say the gargantuan size of the proposed RJR buy out made people realize that few companies are too large to be affected.

"This isn't new, but now it's hitting the big time," said Andrew Morse, a senior vice president at Drexel Burnham Lambert Inc. "This was an accident looking for a place to happen."

It will also force investors to pay closer attention to the fine print of the bonds they own. "Anybody who owns an industrial bond that isn't protected against something like this is sitting on a credit toxic waste site," Mr. Morse said.

One beneficiary of the upheaval has been utility bonds. Some investors view utilities as safer than industrials on the theory that regulators wouldn't permit utilities to create massive amounts of new debt.

A test of this theory is likely to come today. Florida Power & Light Co. is expected to offer about $125 million of new bonds through underwriters led by Salomon Brothers Inc.

Late yesterday, some traders were guessing that the yield on the issue would be about 0.85 to .90 of a percentage point over comparable Treasury issues. Syndicate officials said that if this issue had been priced last week, the bonds would have yielded closer to 0.90 to 0.95 of a percentage point over Treasurys.

Some shocked bond-fund managers are taking steps to stem any future damage from industrial bond issues.

At Vanguard Group's $59 million Bond Market Fund senior vice president Ian MacKinnon said he'll hold onto the fund's small RJR holding, which makes up less than 1 percent of the portfolio. "We were a little bit appalled at what's happened to the price," he said. "But the damage has been done."

But Mr. MacKinnon said he is looking to substitute Canadian corporate and government issues, among others, for U.S. corporate bonds. Such issues are "usually province-related or fairly non-leverageable kinds of operations," he said. Vanguard's bond funds also are likely in the future to include more agency issues, such as Fannie Maes or Freddie Macs, or utility issue, Mr. MacKinnon said.

Other fund managers are sitting tight. At Dreyfus Corp., Barbara Kenworthy, senior portfolio manager for taxable fixed-income funds, said she sold the funds RJR bonds about a year ago. The funds currently are overweighted in utilities and bank issues, among others, that are less likely to be affected by takeovers and restructurings.

And although Ms. Kenworthy sees attractive prices for some corporate bonds, she won't bite just yet. "If my read of the market is correct, I could go out there with some really lowball bids," she said. "But it's still a little early to do anything."

Meantime, some fund managers worry whether other bond issues they hold will be hurt by future takeovers. Edward Taber III, head of T. Rowe Price Associates Inc.'s fixed-income area, said that recent corporate-credit analysis by the firm suggests that the "industrial area will be an extremely perilous place to play in the future."

POISON PILL BONDS

For years, bondholders felt that large corporations with investment grade ratings were the safest possible investments. The reason for this is, with few exceptions, leveraged buy outs, which generate bond downgrading occur with small- and medium-sized firms. On October 20, 1988, however, RJR Nabisco announced a $17.6 billion buy out. The old debt, rated A, fell by as much as $200 per bond because of the huge billion dollar debt that would be needed for the buy out. The RJR Nabisco situation made it clear that even giants as IBM, General Motors, and General Electric could be a target for LBO's.

Bondholders, who previously would simply sit on the sidelines, are now becoming aggressive. ITT's Hartford Insurance Group purchased $25 million of a new RJR Nabisco $300 million offering. The RJR Nabisco leveraged buy out reduced the value of the bonds by $1.4 million virtually overnight. ITT is now filing suit against RJR Nabisco citing that the prospectus failed to disclose that RJR's senior management were considering fundamental and major changes that would jeopardize the bond's ratings and decrease their market price. Likewise, Metropolitan Life is suing RJR Nabisco for their $40 million paper loss as a result of the LBO.

In the past, some new offerings of bonds have included covenants for "poison puts" (i.e., like poison pills) that allow bondholders to "put" their bonds back to the issuing company at a par value of $1,000 should certain conditions exist. These earlier poison puts were expected to allow bondholders to get all of their money back in case of a hostile takeover. This defense proved impotent because almost every "hostile" takeover eventually becomes "friendly." These poison puts also failed to protect bondholders from a company's voluntary recapitalization to avoid a takeover by loading on huge debt in order to pay a one-time dividend or to buy back some of its own stock. As expected, this move generally downgraded the bond rating.

Recently, there have appeared on the marketplace new "super poison puts," which give the bondholders greater investment safeguards. Examples of this would be Harris and Williams Companies:[10]

"In what could be the first of a flurry of new bond issues with greater investor safeguards, two corporations have filed to sell bonds carrying a new super "poison put" aimed at curbing highly leveraged corporate deals.

The new poison puts would enable bondholders to get back their initial investment in the event of a takeover, merger, or recapitalization of the company

[10]Mathew Winkler, "Harris, William Cos. Units are First to Offer Super Poison Puts," *Wall Street Journal*, Wednesday, November 16, 1988, pp. 5. c1, c20.

that issued the bonds. Harris Corp. and Williams Cos.'s Northwest Pipeline unit will offer a total of $250 million of bonds with the new protection as early as this week.

In the wake of RJR Nabisco Inc.'s announcement of a $17.7 billion buy out last month, the corporate bond market has fallen in disarray. Prices of many industrial corporate bonds have plunged because investors fear that a huge boom in leveraged buy outs will load up many companies with excessive debt.

RJR's single-A-rated bonds have been transformed into high-yield, high-risk junk bonds. Prices of some RJR long-term bonds lunged 20 points, or $200 per $1,000 face amount. Buyers of corporate bonds have been demanding new safeguards to protect against a debasement of their bonds by highly leveraged deals.

The new poison puts "offer the investor significantly more protection than any previously employed in the high grade market," said Steven R. Bragg, a vice president at Salomon Brothers, Inc., lead underwriter of Harris's $150 million issue of 30-year debentures.

Investment bankers at Salomon and First Boston Corp., which is managing a $100 million, 30-year debenture issue for Northwest Pipeline, said both companies will significantly reduce their borrowing costs as a result of the new investor safeguards. The offerings were registered with the Securities and Exchange Commission earlier this week.

The new covenants attached to the bonds protect investors from more than half a dozen situations of corporate restructuring typically resulting in credit downgradings. The downgradings cause prices of these securities to lose a substantial portion of their initial value. The two investment banks, working independently, devised similar investor safeguards for the two issues.

Older style poison puts have been attached to many new bonds offering since 1986, when the leveraged buy out trend took off. But in virtually all cases, these covenants ultimately proved useless to investors. The reason is that they allowed bondholders "put" their bonds back to the issuer at par value (the issue price) in the event of an unfriendly takeover. That made the put worthless, since almost all takeovers ultimately become agreed-upon.

Existing poison puts also failed to protect bondholders from a company's voluntary recapitalization, in which a company loads up on debt to pay a big, one-time dividend to shareholders or buy back its stock. Such a move results in the downgrading of the company's bonds.

The Harris and Northwest Pipeline offerings differ markedly from previous such offerings because they guarantee investors won't suffer the consequences of any restructuring, regardless of whether it's friendly or not.

The poison put in the Harris and Northwest issues is only good for 10 years, on one-third of the bonds' maturity. "Obviously, not every loophole is closed," said Mr. Bragg of Salomon. "But this 10-year protection is significantly longer than anything we've had in the past."

According to the prospectuses filed with the SEC, the issues protect investors against the following ''designated events'' if combined with a credit-rating downgrade to below investment grade.

—The bond issuer, in order to defend itself, merges into another company.
—An outsider purchases more than 20 percent or 30 percent of the common stock of the issuer or its parent.
—The issuer, its parent or any related entity buys more than 30 percent of their stock.
—The issuer issues a major dividend or makes a major stock purchase totaling more than 30 percent of another company.

For Northwest Pipeline holders, Northwest Pipeline must do one of two things in the event the bonds are trading below par after the designated event occurs: redeem the bonds at par or adjust the coupon upward so that the bonds would trade at par.

The Harris issue differs only in that the option rests with the investor. The investor has the right to put his bonds to Harris at par.

''It's too early to say whether stronger safeguards are here to stay,'' said Curt Welling, a managing director and co-head of capital markets at First Boston. ''This is a high-profile subject. I would expect many investment-grade issuers are having a conversation right now about what the savings might be to have tighter investor protection covenants in their bond offerings.''

Enron Corporation recently developed an innovative technique to finance its BBB– new offering. If the bonds are downgraded, then the 9.5 percent coupon will jump to 12 percent. If the quality increases to A–, then the coupon decreases to 9.4 percent. This is a partial ''poison pill'' protection measure should anyone try to buy out Enron where the restructuring causes a downgrading of quality.

1985 RATING CHANGES[11]

In terms of rating changes, 1985 was a particularly bad year for existing debt holders involved in mergers, acquisitions, stock repurchases, and leveraged buy outs. Standard and Poor's (1986) lowered ratings on 272 corporate issues (industrial, financial, utility, transportation, and foreign), well above 1984s more normal level of 173. Only 125 issues were upgraded, versus 164 in 1984. The credit quality of ''industrial'' firms took a sharp turn for the worse in 1985, with rating decreases outnumbering increases by nearly four to one (187 vs. 49). Acquisitions, divestitures, leveraged buy outs, and stock repurchases accounted for 28 percent of all industrial debt rating changes and a full 31 percent of the

[11]This section has been adapted from Altman, D.I., and Nammacher, S.A., *Investing in Junk Bonds*, John Wiley, New York, 1987, pp. 174–179.

downgrades. In effect, these restructurings accounted for approximately 58 downgrades and only eight upgrades!

On the other hand, Moody's (1986) raised ratings on 124 issues and lowered 153 in 1985. Fifty-one of the downgrades were caused by restructurings (acquisitions, divestitures, leveraged buy outs or share repurchases). Forty-eight of them were in the "industrial" sector alone. This is opposed to 35 downgrades for the same reasons in 1984.

Table 6-14 highlights Moody's downgrades in more detail. Thirty-three percent of all of the downgrades caused by restructuring affected 38 percent of the debt involved in all downgrades. In the industrial sector, the numbers are more lopsided. The 48 issues downgraded because of restructuring represented 40 percent of the industrial rate reductions, but they involved 53 percent of the total long-term, debt dollars, whose ratings were lowered.

These statistics present a rather bleak view of the debt-holders' position, because they concentrate only on rating changes. Fortunately, a fair percentage of deals (generally where the acquirer is much larger than the target or where debt plays a smaller role) result in a reconfirmation of existing ratings. One recently compiled set of statistics helps to get a better, although limited, view of the bondholders' situation.

Standard and Poor's (1985) analyzed a sample of companies in order to assess the impact acquisitions and divestitures had on their ratings. The results show a somewhat brighter picture of the effects acquisitions have on existing bondholders (see Table 6-15). It should be noted, however, that the numbers include only those companies whose deals caused them to be placed on Standard and Poor's CreditWatch list (comprised of companies whose ratings are under review) and might be a biased sample. Many, perhaps a sizable majority, of the transactions are between businesses (or involve subsidiaries) with either no Standard and Poor's or Moody's rating or that have no publicly traded debt outstanding.

TABLE 6-14
Reasons Behind Moody's Downgrades (1985)

	Companies			*Long-Term Debt ($Billions)*		
	Restructuring	*Fundamental*	*Total*	*Restructuring*	*Fundamental*	*Total*
Industrial	48	73	121	$37.1	$33.4	$ 70.4
Utilities	2	13	15	2.7	22.7	25.4
Transportation	1	2	3	1.0	0.1	1.1
Bank and finance	0	14	14	0.0	10.5	10.5
Total	51	102	153	$40.8	$66.7	$107.5
Percent of total	33%	67%		38%	62%	

Source: Forsyth, R., "Bad Grades—Takeovers Teach a Costly Lesson to Bondholders," *Barron's*, February 24, 1986.

TABLE 6-15
Rating Impact of Acquisitions and Divestitures
(for 12 months ending July 31)

	Acquiring/Divesting Companies					*Acquired/Divested Companies*					*Combined Total*	
	1983	*1984*	*1985*	*Total*	*Percent*	*1983*	*1984*	*1985*	*Total*	*Percent*	*Total*	*Percent*
Upgrade	3	2	6[a]	11	12%	7	8	3	18	18%	29	15%
Downgrade	6	19	18	43	47	10	12	23	45	46	88	46
Maintained	9	15	7	31	34	6	7	8	21	21	52	27
Other[b]	1	2	1	4	4	1	8	3	12	12	16	8
Under review	—	—	2	2	2	—	—	3	3	3	5	3
Total	19	38	34	91		24	35	40	99		190	

[a]Four of these issuers had same parent company (Occidental Petroleum).

[b]Rating withdrawn, issue called, and so on.

Source: Standard and Poor's *CreditWatch*, 1985.

Of the 91 issues of acquiring/divesting companies put on CreditWatch from July 31, 1982 to July 31, 1985, 45 percent were downgraded. Those deals where ratings were maintained represented 34 percent, while only 12 percent were upgraded, and most of these were because of divestitures or spinoffs that improved cash positions. Of the 99 acquired/divested companies listed, 46 percent were downgraded, 21 percent were unchanged, and 18 percent were upgraded. In all, 46 percent of the 190 issuers included were downgraded, and 42 percent remained unchanged or were upgraded. While the investor stands a much stronger chance of a downgrade over an upgrade, there is also a fair chance of having the current rating reaffirmed.

If one keys in on deals where the issuer was rated below investment grade by Standard and Poor's prior to the deal, a marginally better picture emerges, with ratings being maintained or upgraded on 49 percent of the transactions and downgraded on 33 percent. Unfortunately, the sample size is far too small to draw any formal conclusions from, but the numbers in Table 6-16 might still be of some interest to you.

If one looks at companies crossing the line between junk and investment grades, issuers falling from investment grade into the high-yield debt category outnumbered those that rose from junk to investment grade by almost 4 to 1 (see Table 6-17). The crossover of investment grades into junk can cause real dollar losses (as opposed to paper losses) to institutional investors governed by policies that force the immediate sale of securities falling below investment grade. Investors with the option to hold high-yield debt stand a better chance of weathering what might be a short-term rating downgrade because of a major, debt-oriented deal and subsequently recouping their paper losses as the balance sheet improves and before ratings are restored (or exceeded).

TABLE 6-16
Companies with Noninvestment-Grade Ratings Prior to Deal (for 12 months ending July 31)

	Acquiring/Divesting Companies					*Acquired/Divested Companies*					*Combined*	
	1983	*1984*	*1985*	*Total*	*Percent*	*1983*	*1984*	*1985*	*Total*	*Percent*	*Total*	*Percent*
Upgraded	—	—	2	2	11%	—	5	2	7	33%	9	23%
Downgraded	1	4	2	7	39	—	2	4	6	29	13	33
Maintained	—	3	3	6	33	1	1	2	4	19	10	26
Other	1	—	—	1	6	—	2	—	2	9	3	8
Under review	—	—	2	2	11	—	—	2	2	9	4	10
Total	2	7	9	18		1	10	10	21		39	

Source: Standard and Poor's, *CreditWatch*, 1982-1985.

TABLE 6-17
Acquisition and Divestiture—Related Movement between Investment and Noninvestment Grades

Direction	1983	1984	1985	Total
From investment grade to noninvestment grade	4	5	10	19
From noninvestment grade to investment grade	0	3	2	5

Source: Standard and Poor's *CreditWatch*, 1985. For 12 months ending July 31.

JUNK BOND PROFITABILITY

Between 1974 to 1984, the default rate of junk bonds averages 1.52 percent with substantial year-to-year variations.[12] Yet, the actual losses from defaults are much lower than the default rate indicates because defaulted bonds traded at an average of 41 percent or par shortly after default occurred.

Because the actual default rate of low quality-high yield bonds is only about 1 percent, underwriters have been quick to show investors that these bonds will provide returns that exceed treasury securities and high-yield bonds, even after this low default rate. For example, assume you buy 100 different junk bonds at par of $1,000 each and the average portfolio yield is 13.5 percent, one of two things could happen:

CASE I: One percent of the bonds default before the first interest payment and the defaulted bond is trading "flat" (i.e., without inter-

[12]Altman, E.I., and Nammacher, S.A., "The Default Rate Experience on High-Yield Corporate Debt, *Financial Analysts Journal*, July-August 1985, pp. 25–41.

est) at \$500/bond. At the end of year 1,

Interest paid: 99 bonds × \$135 =	\$13,365
Capital loss of \$500	−500
	\$12,865

With one percent of the bonds defaulting, your return on investment is still 12.865 percent.

CASE II: Five percent of the bonds default before the first interest payment and the bonds are trading flat at \$500/bond. At the end of year 1,

Interest paid: 95 bonds × \$135 =	\$12,825
Loss of \$2,500 on 5 bonds	−2,500
	\$10,325

With a five percent default rate, your return on investment is 10.325 percent.

It should be obvious that, if the default rate holds near 1 percent (or even up to 5 percent), junk bonds can provide a much greater return on investment than higher-grade securities.

JUNK BONDHOLDERS

If the junk bond market does, in fact, exceed \$200 billion, then it should be no surprise to anyone that institutional investors must be very active in the market. According to *Pension and Investment Age* (January 20, 1986), three of the six largest pension funds with combined 1985 assets of over \$80 billion, invest in high-yield bonds.

Table 6-18 indicates portfolio fund investment in high-yield debt, categorized by industry. Table 6-19 shows the most popular high-yield debt held by mutual funds. Tables 6-20 and 6-21 identify the breakdown of high-yield debt of entertainment and airline industries held by mutual funds.

SOURCES OF INFORMATION

For the fixed-income securities investor, there are four primary sources of information for both quality and junk bonds:

- *The Wall Street Journal*
- *Barron's Market Week*
- Rating agency newsletters/periodicals
- Investment house newsletters/periodicals

TABLE 6-18
Portfolio Fund Investments in High-Yield Debt by Industry (Number of Issues)[a]

Industry	*Number of Issues in Each Industry*	*Percent by Industry (Total Invested by Mutual Funds)*	*Percent by Industry (Total Available Securities)*
Manufacturing	204	35.9%	40.5%
Entertainment	42	11.1	8.3
Finance	73	8.9	14.5
Oil and gas	45	8.6	8.9
Communication	24	7.9	4.8
Medical	24	6.3	4.8
Utility	18	6.2	3.6
Retail	23	6.0	4.6
Airline	22	5.2	4.4
Transportation	18	2.8	3.6
Conglomerates	11	1.1	2.2
	504	100.0%	100.0%

Source: Altman, E.I. and Nammacher, S.A., *Investing in Junk Bonds*, John Wiley, New York, 1987, p. 81.
Portfolio breakdowns provided by individual funds to the authors.

[a]Each mutual fund's contribution is measured as of their last available portfolio release. Most funds are as of mid to late 1985. Sample consists of 33 mutual funds.

The Wall Street Journal (WSJ) is perhaps the most commonly used source of information for the average investor. In addition to the bond transaction listing shown in Fig. 2-2, the WSJ also has the Market Diary as shown in Table 6-22 and the Bond Market Data Bank shown in Table 6-23. The main advantage of the *Wall Street Journal* is that it comes out Monday through Friday and might provide you with the opportunity to buy or sell your bonds at the best available price. In addition, the WSJ contains articles that provide additional insight on a company's operations and future prospects.

Barron's Market Week is well suited for "weekend warrior" investors, who, when it comes to portfolio management, simply can't devote daily time. Because *Barron's* comes out weekly, it provides an accurate analysis of the week's transactions. In addition to bond listings, *Barron's* identifies the weekly and yearly high's and low's while the WSJ lists only the last transaction.

In addition to weekly transactions, *Barron's* contains a "Market Laboratory/Bonds" section, which includes the information shown in Table 6-24.[13] *Barron's* also contains articles on current thinking in the stock and bond markets.

Rating agencies such as Standard and Poor's publish the monthly *Bond Guide* and *CreditWeek*. The *Bond Guide* is easily affordable by the average investor, but the periodical *CreditWeek* is usually purchased by institutions and pension fund managers. Many local libraries subscribe to both the *Bond Guide* and *CreditWeek*. For the average investor, the advantage of reading *CreditWeek* would

[13]*Barron's*, December 12, 1988, p. 139.

TABLE 6-19
The Most Popular High-Yield Debt Issuers[a] Held by Mutual Funds

Issuer	*Industry*	*Number of Funds Holding Issuer*	*Percent of Total Funds (33)*
Consumers Power Co.	Utility	24	72.7%
Middle South Energy	Utility	24	72.7
Long Island Lighting	Utility	23	69.7
Minstar	Manufacturing	20	60.6
International Harvester	Manufacturing	19	57.6
People Express	Airline	19	57.6
Harnischfeger	Manufacturing	17	51.5
Pantry Pride	Retail	17	51.5
Republic Health	Medical	17	51.5
Mattel	Entertainment	17	51.5
Wickes Companies	Retail	17	51.5
Texas Air Corp.	Airline	17	51.5
Swan Brewing	Manufacturing	16	48.5
MCI Communications	Communication	16	48.5
Resorts International Inc.	Entertainment	16	48.5
Turner Broadcasting System	Communication	16	48.5
MacAndrews & Forbes Group	Manufacturing	16	48.5
LTV Corp.	Manufacturing	16	48.5
Nortek	Manufacturing	16	48.5
I.C.H. Corp.	Finance	15	45.5
Price Communications	Communication	15	45.5
Jones Intercable	Entertainment	15	45.5
ACF Industries	Manufacturing	15	45.5
Conair Acquisition	Finance	15	45.5
United Cable Television	Communication	15	45.5
Coast Savings & Loan Assoc.	Finance	14	42.4
Triangle Industries	Manufacturing	14	42.4
Grolier Inc.	Entertainment	14	42.4
Eastern Air Lines	Airline	14	42.4
Nu-Med	Medical	14	42.4
Chicago & Northwestern Railway	Transportation	13	39.4
Coleco Industries	Manufacturing	13	39.4
Woodward & Lothrop	Retail	13	39.4
Gelco Corp.	Finance	13	39.4
Oak Industries	Communication	13	39.4
Petro-Lewis Corp.	Oil	13	39.4
Pan American World Airways	Airline	13	39.4
McLean Industries	Manufacturing	12	36.4
General Defense Corp.	Manufacturing	12	36.4
Public Service Co. of New Hampshire	Utility	12	36.4
Republic Airlines	Airline	12	36.4
United Merchants & Manufacturers	Manufacturing	12	36.4
Resorts International Financing	Entertainment	12	36.4
ARA Holdings	Finance	12	36.4
Crystal Oil	Oil	12	36.4
Republic Steel Corp.	Manufacturing	11	33.3
AMAX Inc.	Manufacturing	11	33.3
McCrory Corp.	Retail	11	33.3
Health Resources Corp. of America	Medical	11	33.3
Beverly Enterprises	Medical	11	33.3
Public Service Co. of Indiana	Utility	11	33.3
Global Marine	Oil	11	33.3
Arrow Electronics	Manufacturing	11	33.3
Metromedia	Communication	11	33.3

[a] Those held by over 33% of funds.

TABLE 6-20
Entertainment High-Yield Debt Issuers Held by Mutual Funds

Issuer	*Number of Funds Holding Issuer*	*Percent of Total Funds*
Mattel	17	51.5%
Resorts International Inc.	16	48.5
Jones Intercable	15	45.5
Grolier Inc.	14	42.4
Resorts International Fin.	12	36.4
Plitt Theater Holdings	10	30.3
Six Flags	10	30.3
Elsinore Corp.	10	30.3
Cannon Group	9	27.3
Circus Circus Enterprises	9	27.3
Cablevision System Dev.	8	24.2
Bally's Park Place Funding	8	24.2
Golden Nugget Inc.	8	24.2
Thousand Trails	7	21.2
MGM Grand Hotels	7	21.2
Orion Pictures	6	18.2
Caesars World Fin.	5	15.2
Tri-Star Pictures	5	15.2
Plitt Theater	5	15.2
Showboat Inc.	5	15.2
Mickleberry Corp.	4	12.1
Shaughnessy Dev. Corp.	4	12.1
Vagabond Hotel	4	12.1
Caesars World Inc.	4	12.1
Golden Nugget Financial Corp.	4	12.1
Elsinore Finance Corp.	4	12.1
Lorimar Productions	3	9.1
Days Inn of America	3	9.1
New World Picture	3	9.1
Spendthrift Farms	3	9.1
Trump's Castle Funding	3	9.1
GNAC	2	6.1
Twentieth Century-Fox Film	2	6.1
MGM/UA Entertainment	1	3.0
Sahara Resorts	1	3.0
Horn & Hardart Co.	1	3.0
Ramada Inns	1	3.0
Pizza Time Theater	1	3.0

Source: Altman, E.I., and Nammacher, S.A., *Investing in Junk Bonds*, John Wiley, New York, 1987, pp. 86-87.

TABLE 6-21
Airline High-Yield Debt Issuers Held by Mutual Funds

Issuer	*Number of Funds Holding Issuer*	*Percent of Total Funds*
People Express	19	57.6%
Texas Air Corp.	17	51.5
Eastern Air Lines	14	42.4
Pan American World Airways	13	39.4
Republic Airlines	12	36.4
Western Air Lines	7	21.2
Muse Air Corp.	7	21.2
World Airways	6	18.2
Trans World Airlines	4	12.1
Texas International Airlines	2	6.1
US Air	1	3.0
Frontier Holdings	1	3.0
American West Airline	1	3.0
Midway Airline	1	3.0
US Air Financial N.V.	1	3.0
US Group	1	3.0
Frontier Airlines	1	3.0

Source: Altman, E.I., and Nammacher, S.A., *Investing in Junk Bonds*, John Wiley, New York, 1987, pp. 93–94.

be the rationale used by Standard and Poor's to assess the creditworthiness of a bond. Table 6-25 shows a typical company synopsis from *CreditWeek*.[14]

Almost all rating agencies provide this type of newsletter. Tables 6-26, 6-27, and 6-28 show high-yield credit comments as published by McCarthy, Crisanti and Maffei.[15] Merrill Lynch publishes a quarterly and semiannual *High Yield Securities Review*. This periodical contains high-yield market analysis, such as that shown in Fig. 6-3 and industry analysis and investment opportunities for such industries as:

- Airline
- Automotive
- Broadcast/Cable
- Building Materials
- Casinos
- Chemical
- Oil and Gas
- Retail
- Steel
- Textile/Apparel

[14]*CreditWeek*, Standard and Poor's Creditweek, March 23, 1987, p. 18.

[15]*Credit Comments*, McCarthy, Crisanti and Maffei, Inc., New York, August 12, 1988.

TABLE 6-22
Wall Street Journal Market Diary

MARKETS DIARY 10/24/88

STOCKS Dow Jones Industrial Average — 2170.34 -13.16

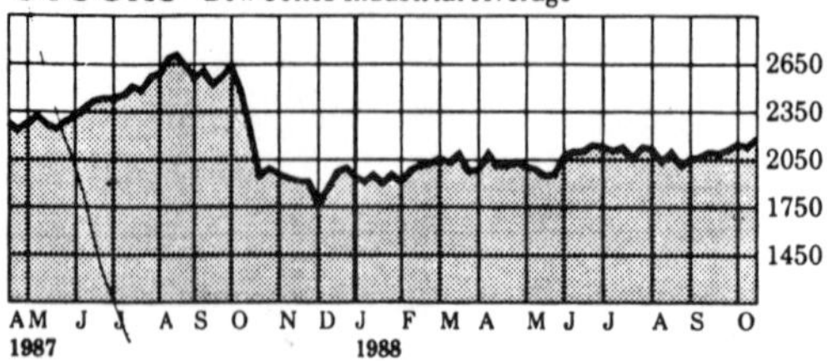

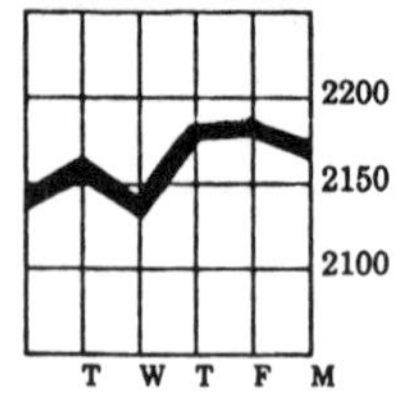

INDEX	CLOSE	NET CHNG	PCT CHNG	12-MO HIGH	12-MO LOW	12-MO CHNG	PCT	FROM 12/31	PCT
DJIA	2170.34	– 13.16	– 0.60	2183.50	1766.74	+ 376.41	+20.98	+ 231.51	+11.94
DJ Equity	265.27	– 0.86	– 0.32	266.13	209.24	+ 52.44	+24.64	+ 34.77	+15.08
S&P 500	282.28	– 1.38	– 0.49	283.66	223.92	+ 54.61	+23.99	+ 35.20	+14.25
Nasdaq Comp.	387.23	– 1.36	– 0.35	396.11	291.88	+ 88.33	+29.55	+ 56.76	+17.18
London (FT 30)	1499.4	– 9.9	– 0.66	1514.7	1232.0	+ 192.3	+14.71	+ 126.1	+ 9.18
Tokyo (Nikkei)	27281.54	– 57.03	– 0.21	28423.38	21036.76	+ 5078.98	+22.88	+ 5717.54	+26.51

BONDS Shearson Lehman Hutton T-Bond Index — 1251.81 -2.39

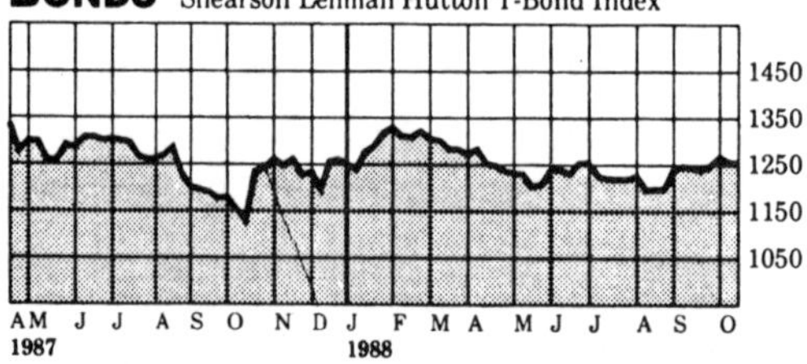

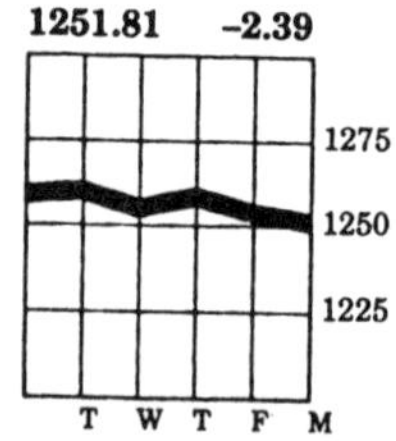

INDEX	MON	MON YIELD	FRI	FRI YIELD	YR AGO	12-MO HIGH	12-MO LOW
Shearson Lehman Hutton treas.	1251.81	9.09%	1254.20	9.07%	1257.03	1329.29	1194.42
DJ 10 Industrials	89.89	9.42	90.06	9.58	85.36	90.64	84.76
DJ 10 Utilities	90.11	9.91	90.00	9.93	84.49	91.88	84.28
Bond Buyer municipal	91-23	7.74	91-22	7.75	83-20	99	82-13
Merrill Lynch corporate	93.81	9.85	93.98	9.83	91.23	96.50	90.73

INTEREST Federal Funds (N.Y. Fed, Fulton Prebon) — 8.31% +0.03

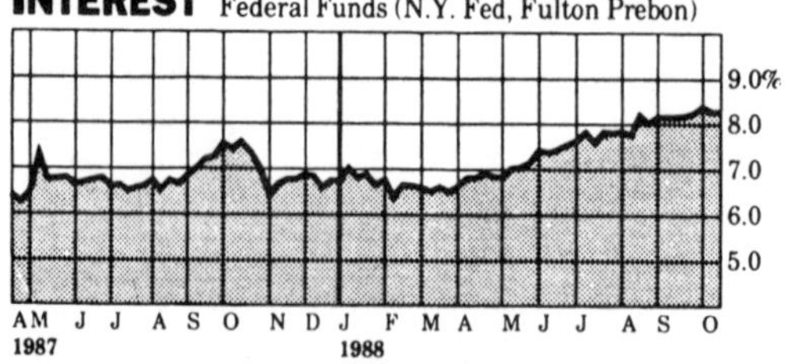

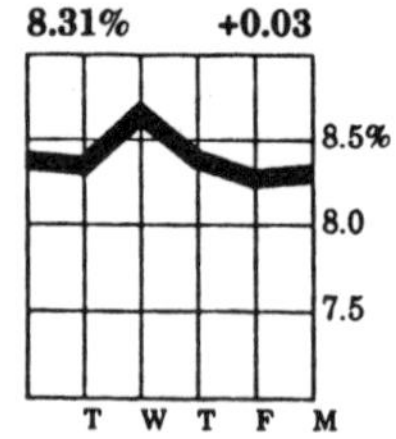

ISSUE	CLOSE	FRI	YEAR AGO	12-MO HIGH	12-MO LOW
3-month T-bill	7.51%	7.44%	5.22%	7.51%	5.03%
3-month CD (new)	7.93	7.93	6.63	7.99	6.18
Dealer Comm. Paper (90 days)	8.25	8.25	7.25	8.43	6.35
3-month Eurodollar deposit	8.69	8.69	7.69	8.81	6.68

Source: The *Wall Street Journal*, October 24, 1988.

TABLE 6-23

Wall Street Journal

BOND MARKET DATA BANK 12/9/88

MAJOR INDEXES

HIGH	LOW (12 MOS)		CLOSE	NET CHG	% CHG	12-MO CHG	% CHG	FROM 12/31	% CHG
U.S. TREASURY SECURITIES (Shearson Lehman Hutton indexes)									
1152.47	1099.80	Intermediate	1101.12	− 2.01	− 0.18	− 14.04	− 1.26	− 25.03	− 2.22
1329.29	1194.42	Long-term	1250.27	+ 0.29	+ 0.02	+ 53.60	+ 4.48	+ 0.03	− 0.00
1193.37	1122.99	Composite	1135.57	− 1.45	− 0.13	+ 1.51	+ 0.13	− 19.31	− 1.67
U.S. CORPORATE DEBT ISSUES (Merrill Lynch: Dec. 31, 1986 = 100)									
96.50	90.73	Corporate Master	93.11	− 0.08	− 0.09	+ 2.38	+ 2.62	+ 0.45	+ 0.49
97.31	93.34	1-10 Yr Maturities	93.91	− 0.08	− 0.09	+ 0.57	+ 0.61	− 0.73	− 0.77
96.01	88.66	10+ Yr Maturities	92.80	− 0.09	− 0.10	+ 4.12	+ 4.65	+ 1.58	+ 1.73
95.93	91.77	High Yield	93.79	− 0.03	− 0.03	+ 2.00	+ 2.18	+ 1.04	+ 1.12
96.38	90.58	Yankee Bonds	92.51	− 0.07	− 0.08	+ 1.94	+ 2.14	+ 0.27	+ 0.29
TAX-EXEMPT SECURITIES (Bond Buyer; Merrill Lynch: Dec. 31, 1986 = 100)									
92-14	82-13	Bond Buyer Municipal	90	+ -7	+ 0.24	+ 5-12	+ 6.35	+ 2-10	+ 2.67
95.33	89.97	New 10-yr G.O. (AA)	90.91	− 0.32	− 0.35	+ 0.88	+ 0.98	− 2.38	− 2.55
93.42	86.12	New 20-yr G.O. (AA)	89.59	unch		+ 3.47	+ 4.03	+ 0.85	+ 0.96
98.46	85.79	New 30-yr revenue (A)	94.57	− 0.54	− 0.57	+ 8.78	+ 10.23	+ 5.54	+ 6.22
MORTGAGE-BACKED SECURITIES (current coupon; Merrill Lynch: Dec. 31, 1986 = 100)									
97.17	90.98	Ginnie Mae (GNMA)	92.48	− 0.17	− 0.18	+ 1.78	+ 1.96	− 0.21	− 0.23
96.14	90.07	Fannie Mae (FNMA)	91.36	− 0.23	− 0.25	− 0.74	− 0.80	− 2.30	− 2.46
97.33	90.17	Freddie Mac (FHLMC)	91.69	− 0.23	− 0.25	+ 1.63	+ 1.81	+ 0.11	+ 0.12
CONVERTIBLE BONDS (Merrill Lynch: Dec. 31, 1986 = 100)									
93.95	85.90	Investment Grade	91.53	− 0.10	− 0.11	+ 5.55	+ 6.45	+ 3.63	+ 4.13
91.29	78.44	High Yield	87.00	unch		+ 8.58	+ 10.94	+ 5.62	+ 6.91

CORPORATE BONDS

Quotes of representative taxable issues at mid-afternoon New York time, provided by First Boston/CSFB Ltd.

ISSUE (RATING: MOODY'S/S&P)	COUPON	MATURITY	PRICE	CHANGE	YIELD	CHANGE
FINANCIAL						
Citicorp (A2/AA−)	9.000	04/15/99	93.894	− 0.305	9.955	0.050
Ford Credit Co (Aa2/AA)	8.875	05/15/94	97.280	− 0.205	9.525	0.050
GMAC (Aa3/AA−)	8.000	10/15/93	93.799	− 0.180	9.625	0.050
GMAC (Aa3/AA−)	7.875	03/01/97	89.145	− 0.256	9.825	0.050
Household Fin (A1/AA−)	7.750	10/01/99	85.311	unch	10.000	unch
IBM Credit (Aaa/AAA)	8.000	08/15/90	98.094	− 0.034	9.235	0.025
UTILITY						
Commonwlth Ed (Baa1/BBB+)	11.125	05/01/18	103.993	− 0.001	10.675	unch
Pacific G&E (A1/A)	8.125	01/01/97	91.060	− 0.384	9.750	0.075
Sou Bell Tel (Aaa/AAA)	8.625	09/01/26	89.311	0.225	9.688	− 0.025
Sou Cal Ed (Aa2/AA)	9.375	02/15/17	94.345	− 0.223	9.975	0.025
Sowest Bell Tel (Aa3/AA−)	11.875	10/18/21	110.991	− 0.248	10.660	0.025
INDUSTRIAL						
Amoco (Aaa/AAA)	8.625	12/15/16	89.476	0.217	9.725	− 0.025
Capital Cities (A1/A+)	8.750	03/15/16	88.347	unch	10.000	unch
Du Pont & Co (Aa1/AA)	6.000	12/01/01	73.595	unch	9.600	unch
Exxon Shipping (Aaa/AAA)	Zero	09/01/12	13.128	unch	8.742	unch
East Kodak (A2/A−)	9.125	03/01/98	95.065	− 0.288	9.950	0.050
Mobil (Aa2/AA)	8.625	07/01/94	95.656	− 0.204	9.650	0.050
FOREIGN						
Australia (Aa1/AA+)	7.625	09/15/97	88.713	unch	9.550	unch
Hydro-Quebec (Aa3/AA−)	8.250	04/15/26	87.053	unch	9.520	unch
Int Bk Recon Dev (Aaa/AAA)	9.875	10/01/97	102.646	unch	9.422	unch
Sweden (Aaa/AAA)	8.125	11/01/96	92.204	unch	9.550	unch

Source: The *Wall Street Journal*, December 9, 1988.

TABLE 6-24
Barron's Bond Summary

Weekly Bond Statistics

	Last Week	Prev. Week	Yr-Ago Week
New Offerings, (mil $) (v)			
Corporate	1,035	2,000	4,013
Municipal	1,419	1,477	1,045
Best Grade Bonds-y (Barron's index of 10 high-grade corporate bonds.)	9.48	9.52	9.67
Interm-Grade Bonds-y (Barron's index of 10 medium-grade corporate bonds.)	9.97	9.96	10.32
Confidence Index (High-grade index divided by intermediate-grade index; decline in latter vs. former generally indicates rising confidence, pointing to higher stocks.)	95.1	95.6	93.7
Other Confidence Indicators:			
T-Bill/Euro$ Futures (TED) Spread (Difference between nearby contracts; lower spread indicates higher confidence in financial system.)	N/A	+1.33	+2.26
Salomon Govt/Corp. Yield Spread (Difference in yield between medium-grade seasoned 10% coupon long-term industrial and long-term Treasury, calculated by Salomon Brothers; lower spread indicates higher confidence in corporate finances.)	+2.14	+2.18	+2.51
Shearson Lehman Hutton T-Bond Index (Index of prices of long-term government bonds. Dec. 31, 1980 = 1000.)	1250.27	1227.73	1196.67
Ryan Index (Index of total return from active Treasury notes and bonds. Dec. 31, 1979 = 100.)	272.94	270.94	252.00
Bond Buyer 20 Bond Index (Index of yields of 20 general obligation municipal bonds.)	7.68	7.66	8.10
Bond Buyer Municipal Bond Index (Index of 40 actively-traded tax-exempt bonds; component issues are changed regularly to keep the index a current picture of the market. The municipal bond futures contract traded on the Chicago Board of Trade is based on this index.)	7.92	7.95	8.65
Stock/Bond Yield Gap-s (Difference between yield on highest-grade corporate bonds and yield on stocks on the DJIA.)	−5.77	−5.73	−5.98
Yield on Dow Jones Bond Averages:			
20 Bonds, (y)	9.90	9.89	10.30
10 Utils, (y)	9.92	9.91	10.38
10 Inds, (y)	9.87	9.87	10.21

v-Week ended Thursday. y-Yield to maturity, week ended Thursday.

Bond Volume

	Last week	Prev. week	Yr-Ago week
Sales NYSE, th $	144,647	150,438	170,340
Sales AMEX, th $	13,400	10,590	18,360

Daily	Dec. 5	6	7	8	9
NYSE, th $	26,300	34,090	28,640	28,690	26,930
AMEX, th $	2,160	3,240	2,880	2,640	2,480

Bond Indexes

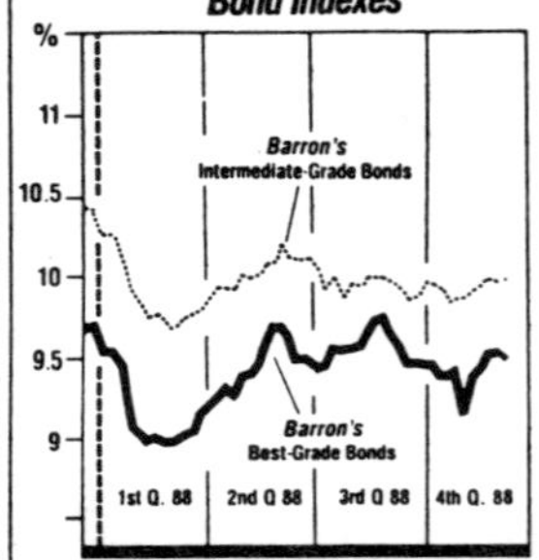

Treasury-Junk Yield Spread

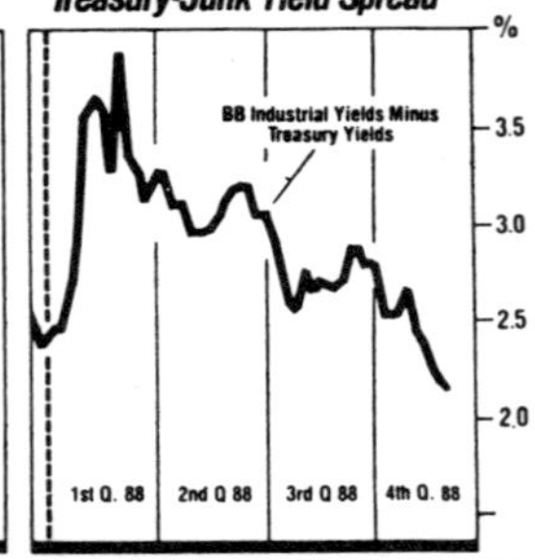

Dow Jones Bond Averages

Daily	Dec. 5	6	7	8	9
20 Bonds	89.02	89.30	89.41	89.34	89.31
10 Util	88.85	89.13	89.45	89.38	89.30
10 Ind	89.19	89.48	89.38	89.31	89.33

Dow Jones Weekly Bond Averages

	First	High	Low	Last	Chg.
20 Bonds	89.02	89.41	89.02	89.31	+ 0.33
10 Util	88.85	89.45	88.85	89.30	+ 0.57
10 Ind	89.19	89.48	89.19	89.33	+ 0.10

Dow Jones Bond Averages For 1988

	First	High	Low	Last	Chg	%
20 Bds	86.92	91.25	86.92	89.31 +	2.64 +	3.05
10 Util	86.65	91.88	86.05	89.30 +	2.66 +	3.07
10 Ind	87.19	90.64	86.96	89.33 +	2.60 +	3.00

New York Exchange Bond Diary

Daily	Dec. 5	6	7	8	9
Total	695	745	668	653	641
Advances	242	337	302	252	242
Declines	279	239	222	241	248
Unchanged	174	169	144	160	151
New Highs	10	13	8	9	10
New Lows	12	15	15	16	12
Sales th $	26,300	34,090	28,640	28,690	26,930

American Exchange Bond Diary

Daily	Dec. 5	6	7	8	9
Total	92	94	83	86	76
Advances	28	35	35	35	29
Declines	46	33	29	31	27
Unchanged	18	26	19	20	20
New Highs	0	0	1	2	1
New Lows	4	5	6	5	1
Sales th $	2,160	3,240	2,880	2,640	2,480

Yearly Highs and Low of Dow Jones Bond Averages

The table below lists the yearly high and low range based upon the closing average for each day during the year.

	INDUSTRIAL BOND AVERAGE				UTILITY BOND AVERAGE			
Year	High	Date	Low	Date	High	Date	Low	Date
1988	90.64	Mar. 4	86.96	Jan. 13	91.88	Mar. 3	86.05	May 26
1987	93.10	Feb. 9	83.00	Oct. 19	98.23	Jan. 22	79.51	Oct. 19
1986	91.64	Dec. 19	84.82	Jan. 27	95.79	Dec. 17	81.85	Jan. 14
1985	84.58	Dec. 30	75.61	Mar. 7	82.88	Dec. 30	68.62	Jan. 4
1984	76.22	Dec. 27	69.61	May 25	70.31	Nov. 26	59.43	May 14
1983	77.13	May 6	71.51	Feb. 16	78.88	May 11	65.76	Dec. 15
1982	71.23	Dec. 30	57.36	Feb. 16	72.71	Nov. 12	53.80	Feb. 11
1981	66.15	Jan. 21	56.32	Oct. 27	66.18	Jan. 7	53.61	Oct. 1
1980	74.92	Jan. 4	61.55	Dec. 18	78.63	June 20	59.40	Dec. 16
1979	84.28	July 9	74.25	Dec. 26	88.60	Feb. 2	72.40	Dec. 31
1978	86.79	Jan. 3	82.78	Dec. 28	95.00	Jan. 4	86.27	Dec. 29
1977	89.18	Sept. 19	85.31	Mar. 7	99.10	Jan. 7	94.98	Dec. 29
1976	87.85	Dec. 31	78.58	Jan. 2	98.58	Dec. 30	87.46	Jan. 2
1975	79.05	Nov. 20	74.51	Jan. 3	88.05	Feb. 25	81.03	Jan. 2
1974	80.82	Jan. 8	70.81	Oct. 4	91.70	Feb. 15	78.52	Oct. 4
1973	85.90	Jan. 11	77.55	Aug. 15	92.00	Jan. 19	88.85	Aug. 7
1972	86.06	Dec. 5	84.05	Apr. 20	91.97	Dec. 19	89.55	Apr. 25
1971	84.96	Dec. 31	80.22	June 30	89.80	Dec. 30	85.45	Jan. 5
1970	80.86	Dec. 11	73.95	June 12	85.67	Dec. 22	77.03	Jan. 2
1969	82.37	Feb. 4	75.81	Dec. 23	80.33	Jan. 20	75.68	Dec. 24
1968	84.81	Aug. 23	80.72	Dec. 24	82.13	Aug. 13	79.02	Dec. 23
1967	89.46	Jan. 30	81.86	Dec. 14	85.67	Jan. 31	78.72	Dec. 5

Bond Rating Changes

	FROM	TO
Moody's		
UPGRADE	FROM	TO
Northern Indiana Public Service		
1st mrtg	Baa2	Baa1
pref stk	baa3	baa2
Union Carbide Corp		
notes & debs	Ba2	Ba1
DOWNGRADE	FROM	TO
Mesa Capital Corp		
sub debt	Ba1	Ba3
Pennwalt Corp		
sink fd deb	Baa1	Baa3
com pp	2	3
Duff & Phelps		
UPGRADE	FROM	TO
AMAX		
sen debt	12	10
sub debt	13	11
Minnesota Power & Light Company		
1st mrtg bd	7	6
pfd stk	8	7
DOWNGRADE	FROM	TO
Philip Morris Companies, Inc		
com pp	1+	1
Public Service Company of New Mexico		
1st mrtg bds	7	9
pref stk	8	10
Fitch		
UPGRADE	FROM	TO
Kentucky Power Co		
1st mrtg bd	BBB	BBB+
comm pp	3	2
Tampa Electric Co.		
1st mrtg bd	AA	AA+
DOWNGRADE	FROM	TO
Boston Edison Co		
1st mrtg bd	A+	BBB+
pfd stk	A−	BBB
Standard & Poor's		
UPGRADE	FROM	TO
Greyhound Financial Corp		
16⅛% nt, 03/01/92	BBB−	BBB
13⅞% nt 04/01/94	BBB−	BBB
$250 mil sr debt	BBB−	BBB
$75 mil sr med−term nt	BBB−	BBB
DOWNGRADE	FROM	TO
CSX Corp		
$250 mil 9½% deb, 07/01/16	A	BBB+
$200 mil 8.4% nt, 08/01/96	A	BBB+
General Signal Corp		
8⅞% sf deb, 05/01/99	AA−	A
Sara Lee Corp		
7⅜% sf deb, 11/01/96	AA	AA−
$150 mil 8¾% sf deb, 05/15/16	AA	AA−
$205 mil sr debt	AA	AA−

Ryan Index©

The Ryan Index is an unweighted average of total return on active Treasury notes and bonds with maturities of two years to 30 years.

Dec.		
	05	271.78
	06	274.21
	07	273.78
	08	273.34
	09	272.94

Source: ©1987, Refco Partners.

Source: *Barron's* December 12, 1988, p. 139.

TABLE 6-25
Consolidated Edison Debt Review

Income analysis	—Year ended Dec. 31—				
(Mil. $)	1986	1985	1984	1983	1982
Revenues	5,197.7	5,497.9	5,728.8	5,515.6	5,067.4
Pretax oper. income	1,700.7	1,107.9	1,155.7	1,118.8	897.8
Interest expense	198.6	188.1	184.4	181.7	185.6
Income taxes	438.4	411.6	404.8	390.0	260.2
AFDC	10.1	10.3	22.4	14.7	18.5
Net income	546.4	563.7	620.0	575.8	492.6
Preferred dividends	38.1	38.4	38.7	39.0	39.6
Pretax interest coverage (x)	5.96	6.18	6.56	6.32	5.06
Excluding AFDC (x)	5.91	6.13	6.44	6.24	4.96
Pfd. dividend coverage (x)	4.40	4.49	4.72	4.52	3.62
Excluding AFDC (x)	4.36	4.45	4.64	4.46	3.55
Pretax return on capital (%)	16.10	16.12	17.21	16.99	14.31
Excluding AFDC (%)	15.96	15.98	16.89	16.77	14.03
Return on equity (%)	12.72	13.19	15.07	15.15	13.93
Excluding AFDC (%)	12.47	12.93	14.49	14.74	13.37
Pretax oper. ratio (%)	67.3	79.8	79.8	79.7	82.3
Income tax rate (%)	44.5	42.2	39.5	40.4	34.6
AFDC/common earnings (%)	2.0	2.0	3.9	2.7	4.1
Payout ratio (%)	62.9	56.5	47.3	45.2	47.3

Financial statistics	—Year ended Dec. 31—				
(Mil. $)	1986	1985	1984	1983	1982
Gross cash flow	893.2	985.7	989.0	942.6	787.0
Net cash flow	535.4	650.4	675.1	661.0	533.0
Capital outlays	489.8	523.3	455.4	405.7	427.7
Net plant	7,057.7	6,883.9	6,591.5	6,313.4	6,223.5
CWIP	260.6	217.7	276.1	310.5	253.3
Total assets	9,111.2	8,944.9	8,688.1	8,246.9	7,872.1
Total capital (mil. $)	7,428.4	7,273.7	7,160.6	6,888.1	6,623.2
Long-term debt (%)	36.9	36.6	34.7	36.7	38.8
Preferred stock (%)	8.8	9.0	9.3	9.6	10.1
Common equity (%)	54.3	54.3	56.0	53.8	51.1
Cash flow/debt (%)	33.0	38.3	39.5	37.0	29.9
Cash flow/capital (%)	12.2	13.7	14.1	14.0	12.0
Net cash flow/capital (%)	7.3	9.0	9.6	9.8	8.1
Net cash flow/capital outlays (%)	109.3	124.3	148.2	162.9	124.6
Capital outlays/capital (%)	6.7	7.3	6.5	6.0	6.5
Current ratio (x)	1.67	1.94	2.01	2.01	1.77
Net plant/capital (%)	95.0	94.6	92.1	91.7	94.0
Net plant/debt (%)	257.6	258.3	265.3	250.0	242.1
CWIP/common equity (%)	6.5	5.5	6.9	8.4	7.5

Figures 6-4 through 6-8 and Tables 6-29 and 6-30 identify typical material in Merrill Lynch's periodical. Figure 6-4 shows the net amount of downgraded dollars from investment to noninvestment grade securities. Figure 6-5 shows the high-yield bonds within the retail industry broken down by sectors. Figures 6-6, 6-7, and 6-8 show typical returns for various kinds of bonds. Table 6-29 identifies the best/worst junk bond performances for a six month period (December 87–June 88), and Table 6-30 identifies performance of the high-yield energy issues.

TABLE 6-26
Best Products Debt Review

Company	*Analyst*	*Default Risk 1 (Lowest) – 7 (Highest)*
BEST PRODUCTS CO., INC.	Thomas P. Razukas	2 Years: 2 5 Years: 4

The Prospect Group Inc. has acquired a 9.9% interest in Best and may seek total control. Prospect is a holding company that conducts its major operations principally through subsidiaries acquired in leveraged transactions. Prospect's major operating subsidiary, Murray Bakery Products, was recently sold. Other operations include Forschner Group, a sole U.S. distributor of Swiss Army Knives, and venture capital investments. Prospect has spent roughly $33 MM to acquire its stock in Best. We estimate the company still has substantial funds to continue to acquire Best's common, as cash balances totaled $43 MM on 3/31/88, and roughly $100 MM was received from the sale of Murray.

We are not changing our default risk profile at this time, because Best has performed as anticipated. However, further investment by Prospect, or potential defensive maneuvers by Best, add considerable uncertainty. At a price of 101 (YTC 12.35%), Best's 12⁵/₈% senior subordinated notes are providing appropriate value for its current risk profile, but event risk has risen considerably. Thus, the downside risk outweighs any upside potential at this time, and we recommend investors *lessen their holdings*.

TABLE 6-27
Stone Container Debt Review

Company	*Analyst*	*Default Risk 1 (lowest) – 7 (highest)*
STONE CONTAINER CORP.	Brian E. Bogart	2 Years: 1 5 Years: 3

Earnings continued to be strong in the second quarter of 1988, at $78.1 MM versus $32.5 MM in the 1987 second quarter. First-half net was $143.4 MM, compared with $58.7 MM. Results were aided by higher prices, high operating rates, and lower tax rates. For the full year, we expect EBIT coverage of about 5.4X and EBDIT coverage of around 6.6X. Even in the event of a slower economy in 1989, net income should remain relatively healthy. Debt reduction is continuing, and, aided by rising equity, should result in a debt ratio well below 50% by year-end 1988. The company recently negotiated new unsecured bank credit facilities that carry lower interest rates.

At some point we expect an increase in debt leverage. The company's improving financial strength could make it attractive to potential acquirers, although Stone family interests control about 24% of the stock. Management has denied rumors of a recapitalization or LBO. We believe the company is most likely to continue its history of growth through acquisitions, but note that favorable industry conditions have pushed prices of many potential targets to high levels.

We are maintaining our *hold* recommendation on the Stone $13^5/_8$% subordinated notes of 6/1/95 (price $107^1/_2$ for an 11.13% yield to first par call @ 6/1/92). These notes are nonrefundable prior to 6/1/90, but currently callable at 107.8. The Southwest Forest $12^1/_8$% subordinated debentures of 9/15/01 (price 102 for an 11.70% yield to first par call @ 9/15/95) are also a *hold*.

TABLE 6-28
Mattel Debt Review

Company	*Analyst*	*Default Risk 1 (Lowest) – 7 (Highest)*
MATTEL, INC.	Anne K. Lorsung	2 Years: 3 5 Years: 4

Mattel, Inc. has reported its results for the quarter ended June 30. Sales dropped from $256.4 MM to $207.1 MM and pretax income (before extraordinary items) fell from $7.2 MM to $5.4 MM. The sales drop was somewhat worse than expected as a result of poor demand for some declining product lines. However, EBIT coverage of interest and preferred dividends remained at about 1.4 times, reflecting last year's balance sheet and operational restructuring. In addition, inventories were about one-third lower than last year, which should enable the company to avoid major writeoffs. We are maintaining Mattel's 3-4 default risk rankings, and we recommend that investors *hold* the 11 5/8s of '03 and 14 3/4s of '00 at current prices of 90 and 104, respectively.

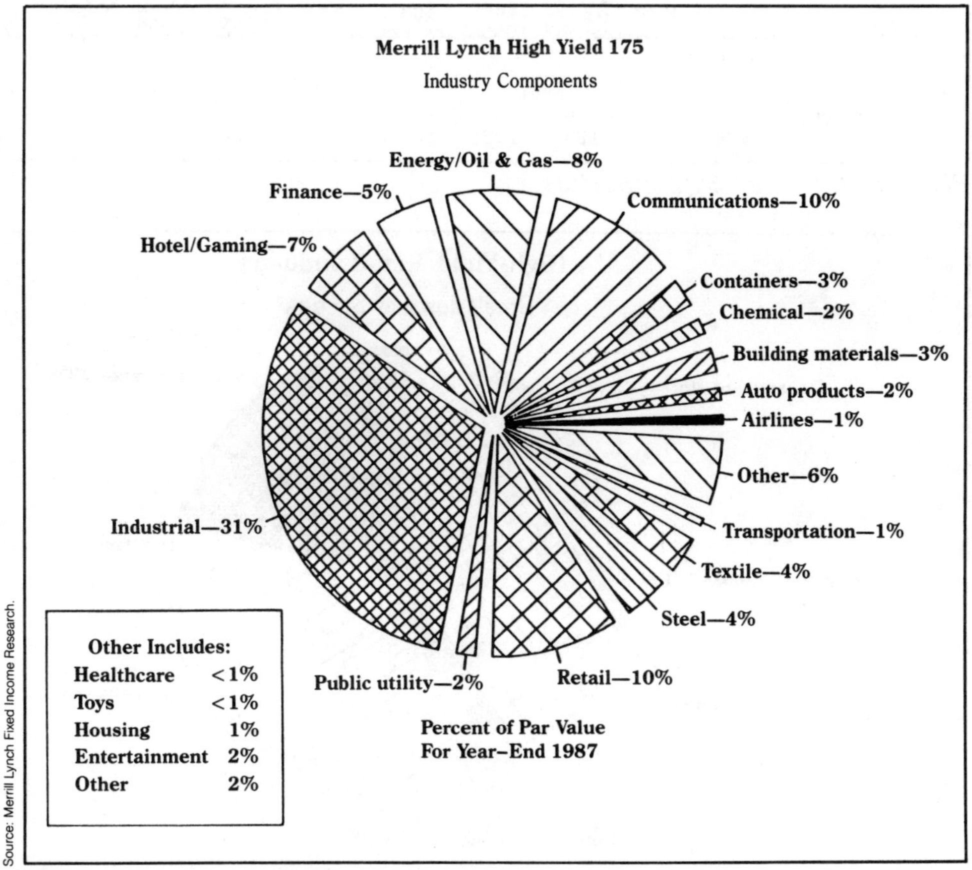

Fig. 6-3. Merrill Lynch High-Yield 175 Index.

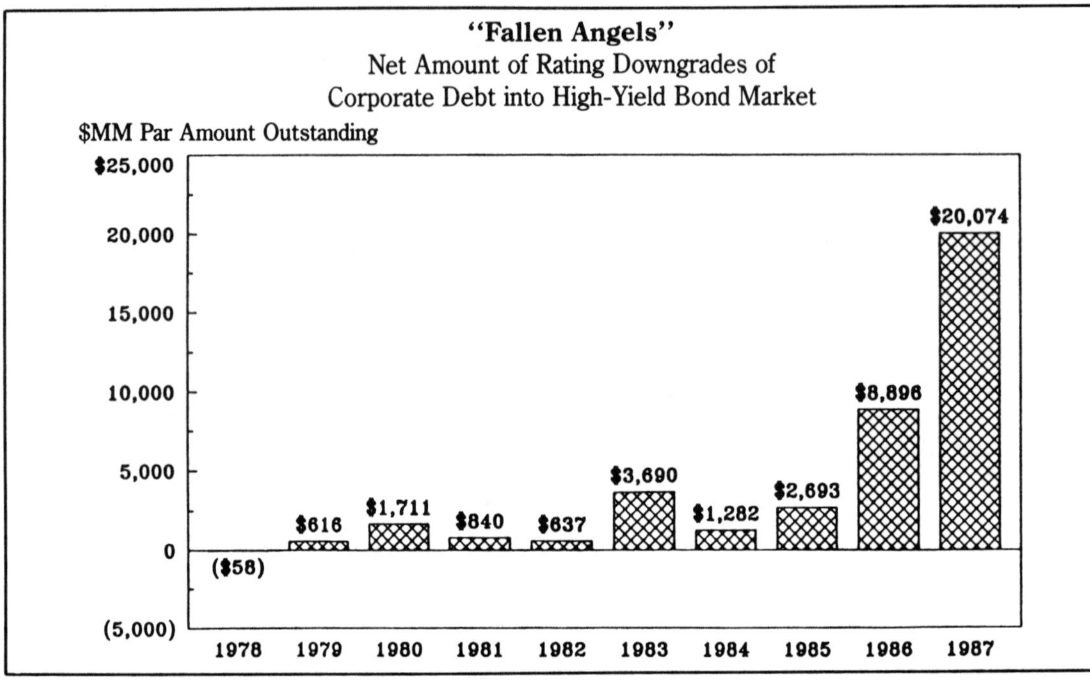

Source: Moody's Bond Survey.

Fig. 6-4. High-yield "fallen angels."

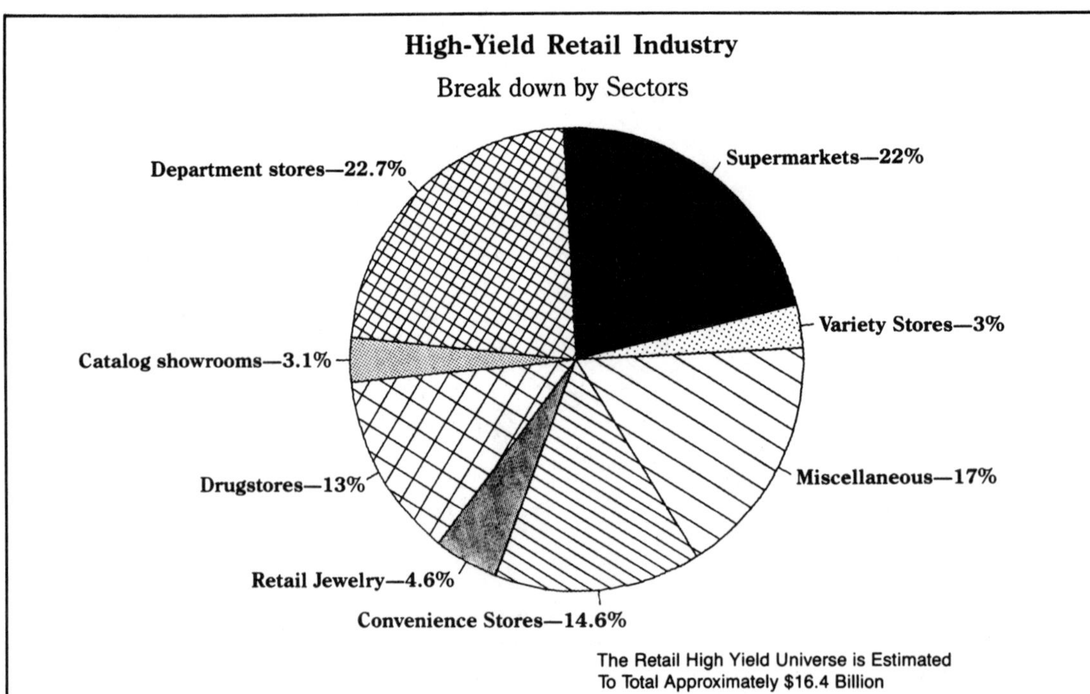

Source: MLCM High-Yield Research.

Fig. 6-5. High-yield retail industry.

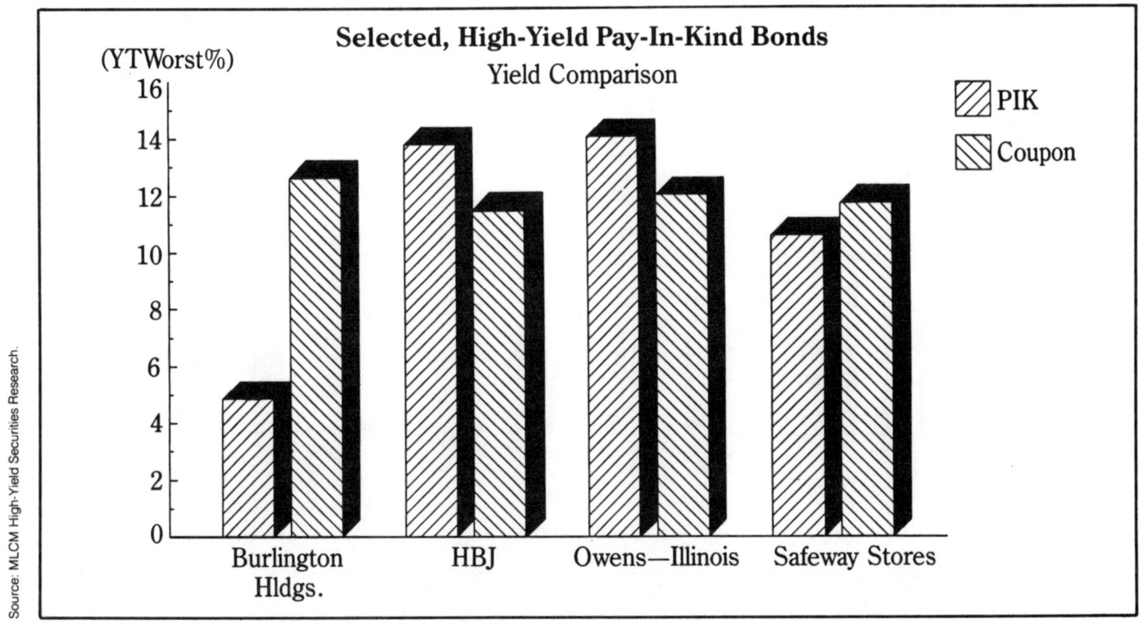

Fig. 6-6. *Selected high-yield pay-in-kind bonds.*

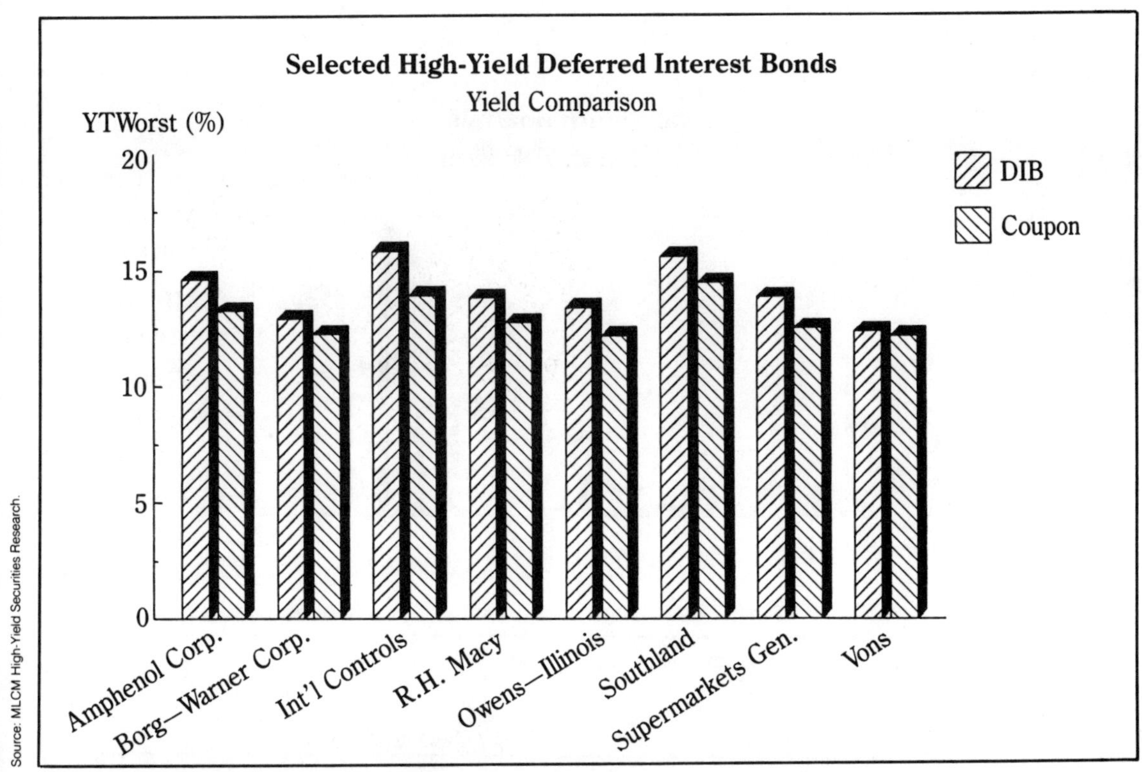

Fig. 6-7. *Selected, high-yield deferred interest bonds.*

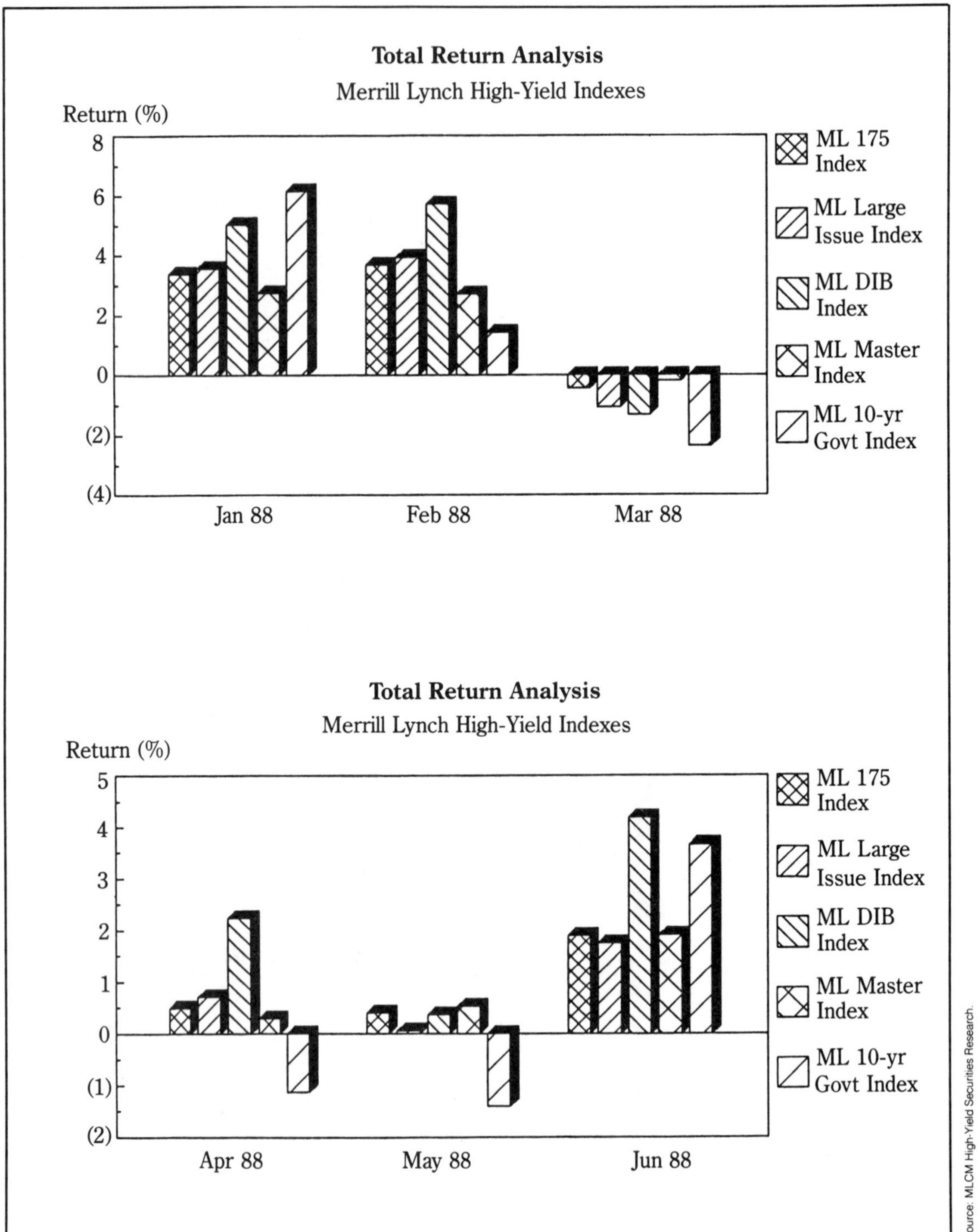

Fig. 6-8. *Total return analysis.*

TABLE 6-29
Performance of Selected, High-Yield Issues
(Best/Worst Total Returns from Dec. '87 – June '88)

Company	*Coupon*	*Maturity*	*Price Dec-87*	*Price Jun-88*	*High 1988*	*Low 1988*	*Price Change*	*Total Return*
BORG WARNER	0.000%	15-Jul-99	39.000	61.375	61.375	39.000	22.375	57.37%
RESORTS INTL	16.625%	01-Sep-2004	83.000	104.125	104.875	80.000	21.125	35.47%
SERVICE MERCHANDISE	11.750%	15-Dec-96	73.500	92.500	92.500	82.750	19	33.84%
HOME SHOPPING	11.750%	15-Oct-96	68.000	85.000	85.000	66.625	17	33.64%
NATIONAL GYPSUM	0.000%	30-Jun-2004	53.250	69.625	69.625	59.500	16.375	30.75%
BORG WARNER	12.750%	15-Jul-97	83.500	102.000	102.000	91.500	18.5	29.79%
FRUEHAUF CORP	13.500%	15-Dec-96	67.000	79.000	81.000	70.000	12	27.99%
BURLINGTON CORP	0.000%	01-Oct-2003	39.500	49.250	49.250	42.750	9.75	24.68%
CALTON INC	12.250%	15-Jun-96	77.500	90.000	90.000	77.500	12.5	24.03%
OWENS CORNING	0.000%	01-Dec-2006	57.000	70.500	70.500	57.250	13.5	23.68%
AMPHENOL CORP	0.000%	15-Oct-2002	61.250	75.500	75.500	61.250	14.25	23.27%
FRUEHAUF CORP	13.750%	15-Dec-2001	67.000	75.500	79.500	69.250	8.5	22.95%
NUTRI-SYSTEM INC	12.000%	15-Aug-96	92.500	107.500	107.500	98.500	15	22.70%
DAYTON WALTHER	14.000%	15-Jul-97	87.000	98.250	98.250	87.500	11.25	20.98%
HARCOURT BRACE	0.000%	15-Sep-2002	49.000	59.250	59.250	54.500	10.25	20.92%
BURLINGTON INDS	14.250%	01-Oct-99	94.750	106.375	107.000	99.250	11.625	19.79%
NATIONAL GYPSUM	14.500%	29-Apr-2001	93.500	104.000	104.250	96.500	10.5	18.98%
NATIONAL GYPSUM	11.375%	31-Mar-97	80.750	90.125	90.125	85.250	9.375	18.65%
ECKERD (JACK) CORP	0.000%	01-May-2006	58.500	69.000	69.000	64.250	10.5	17.95%
CLINTON MILLS	12.000%	01-Apr-99	88.250	97.500	98.000	92.125	9.25	17.28%
CONTINENTAL AIR	11.375%	15-Mar-99	70.000	76.250	76.250	70.375	6.25	17.05%
AMPHENOL CORP	15.000%	15-Sep-97	99.000	108.000	108.000	99.000	9	16.67%
BURLINGTON INDS	13.875%	01-Oct-96	95.500	104.375	107.000	100.500	8.875	16.56%
CAIN CHEMICAL	12.875%	30-Jun-2002	100.500	110.625	110.625	103.875	10.125	16.48%
CHEVY CHASE SVGS	13.500%	15-Jul-2002	92.250	100.500	100.500	92.250	8.25	16.26%
SOUTHLAND CORP	16.750%	15-Dec-2002	100.500	108.000	106.000	102.500	7.5	15.80%
McCRORY CORP	15.750%	15-Jul-91	89.600	95.500	95.000	89.750	5.9	15.37%
CAIN CHEMICAL	12.625%	30-Jun-97	100.500	109.625	109.625	103.625	9.125	15.36%
MCI COMMUNICATION	10.000%	01-Apr-2011	85.750	93.000	93.000	89.500	7.25	14.29%
PIGGLY WIGGLY	11.750%	15-Apr-97	98.250	105.500	108.500	98.250	7.25	13.36%
SOUTHLAND CORP	15.750%	15-Dec-97	100.500	105.875	105.875	102.375	5.375	13.18%
MAYFLOWER CORP	12.625%	15-Dec-96	89.000	94.375	94.375	90.000	5.375	13.13%
GENERAL DEVELOPMENT	12.625%	01-Sep-2005	83.500	88.000	94.750	88.000	4.5	12.95%
TRUMP PLAZA	12.875%	15-Jun-99	96.500	102.250	102.250	96.875	5.75	12.63%
WICKES CORP	11.875%	01-Jun-2001	89.750	95.000	96.375	92.250	5.25	12.47%
AMSTAR CORP	11.375%	15-Feb-97	90.250	95.500	95.500	90.250	5.25	12.12%

TABLE 6-29 continued

Company	Coupon	Maturity	Price Dec-87	Price Jun-88	High 1988	Low 1988	Price Change	Total Return
STATER BROTHERS	14.250%	01-Nov-95	104.500	110.000	110.750	105.500	5.5	12.08%
WICKES CORP	15.000%	01-May-95	104.250	109.250	109.250	107.000	5	11.99%
LEISURE & TECH	15.750%	15-Oct-99	97.250	101.000	101.000	95.000	3.75	11.95%
UNION TEXAS PETE	13.000%	01-Jul-95	101.000	106.500	108.000	105.000	5.5	11.88%
ECKERD (JACK) CORP	11.125%	01-May-2001	88.500	93.375	96.750	91.000	4.875	11.79%
GRAPHIC CONTROLS	13.500%	15-Jul-99	94.000	98.000	98.000	96.250	4	11.44%
SOUTHLAND CORP	0.000%	15-Dec-97	61.500	68.500	68.500	61.375	7	11.38%
TRUMP CASTLE	7.000%	15-Jun-99	62.000	65.500	66.000	61.625	3.5	11.29%
FIRST BRANDS	12.500%	01-Sep-98	96.000	100.500	104.250	98.125	4.5	11.20%
PHILLIPS PETE	14.750%	15-Mar-2000	110.500	115.250	115.500	112.375	4.75	10.97%
MACY R.H.	0.000%	15-Nov-2006	46.000	51.000	52.000	47.500	5	10.87%
DART GROUP	14.000%	15-Sep-95	98.500	102.000	102.000	99.500	3.5	10.66%
OWENS CORNING	11.750%	15-Nov-2001	97.750	102.125	103.625	100.500	4.375	10.49%
HARCOURT BRACE	13.750%	15-Sep-99	103.250	107.125	108.000	104.375	3.875	10.41%
PHILLIPS PETE	13.875%	15-Mar-97	109.000	113.375	114.000	110.750	4.375	10.38%
TYLER CORP	11.000%	15-Jul-97	95.625	100.000	101.000	99.000	4.375	10.33%
COASTAL CORP	11.750%	15-Jun-2006	97.000	101.125	102.500	99.500	4.125	10.31%
SUPERMARKETS GENERAL	14.500%	15-Sep-97	105.500	109.000	109.000	107.250	3.5	10.19%
TRIANGLE PACIFIC	12.500%	01-Jul-98	93.500	96.750	96.750	94.750	3.25	10.16%
VIACOM INTL	0.000%	15-Jun-2002	65.000	71.500	72.250	68.250	6.5	10.00%
MCI COMMUNICATION	9.500%	01-Aug-93	94.000	98.625	98.750	97.000	4.625	9.97%
SOUTHLAND CORP	0.000%	15-Dec-2007	42.375	46.375	46.375	41.250	4	9.44%
LASALLE ENERGY	11.750%	01-Jul-99	87.500	89.750	93.250	89.750	2.25	9.29%
MUELLER CORP	12.125%	15-Jul-96	84.250	86.000	86.000	82.000	1.75	9.27%
GUARDIAN SVGS	12.625%	15-Jan-2002	77.750	78.625	81.000	78.000	0.875	9.24%
OWENS ILLINOIS	12.750%	01-Jun-99	100.750	103.375	106.250	101.500	2.625	8.93%
CONTAINER CORP	0.000%	30-Sep-2006	67.000	72.750	72.750	69.375	5.75	8.58%
MACY (R.H.)	14.500%	15-Oct-98	106.500	108.375	111.250	103.500	1.875	8.57%
OWENS ILLINOIS	12.250%	01-Jun-96	100.250	102.375	104.750	99.500	2.125	8.23%
BCI HOLDINGS	11.000%	15-Apr-96	100.500	103.125	103.125	102.000	2.625	8.08%
PEOPLES EXPRESS	11.750%	15-Jun-95	80.000	80.250	80.250	75.375	0.25	7.66%
HERTZ PENSKE	11.500%	15-Jul-97	101.250	103.000	103.000	100.500	1.75	7.41%
HOLIDAY INNS	10.500%	01-Apr-94	96.500	98.375	99.000	97.250	1.875	7.38%
STONE CONTAINER	13.625%	01-Jun-95	107.000	108.000	109.125	107.375	1	7.30%
MACY (R.H.)	14.500%	15-Nov-2001	105.750	106.125	109.000	101.000	0.375	7.21%
OWENS ILLINOIS	0.000%	01-Jun-2003	49.250	52.750	52.750	50.000	3.5	7.11%

TABLE 6-29 continued

Company	*Coupon*	*Maturity*	*Price Dec-87*	*Price Jun-88*	*High 1988*	*Low 1988*	*Price Change*	*Total Return*
SAFEWAY STORES	11.750%	15-Nov-96	99.500	100.500	102.250	98.125	1	6.91%
UNION CARBIDE	9.750%	15-Apr-94	95.375	96.875	98.750	96.375	1.5	6.68%
LEISURE & TECH	13.625%	01-Sep-96	88.625	87.500	88.250	82.000	-1.125	6.42%
SAFEWAY STORES	12.000%	15-Nov-98	100.500	100.875	103.000	98.625	0.375	6.34%
CONTAINER CORP	12.375%	30-Sep-98	104.750	105.125	107.500	103.000	0.375	6.26%
FMC CORP	12.500%	01-Jun-2001	104.500	104.750	107.625	101.625	0.25	6.22%
BCI HOLDINGS	12.750%	15-Apr-2001	105.250	105.250	108.000	104.375	0	6.06%
BCI HOLDINGS	12.500%	15-Apr-98	104.375	104.375	107.250	103.375	0	5.99%
HOLIDAY INNS	11.000%	01-Apr-99	94.375	94.500	98.625	93.125	0.125	5.96%
FMC CORP	12.250%	01-Jun-98	103.500	103.500	107.375	101.250	0	5.92%
FORSTMANN FABRICS	11.750%	01-Apr-98	98.250	98.125	101.500	97.000	-0.125	5.85%
ALLIED STORES	10.500%	15-Mar-92	95.250	95.500	100.250	95.500	0.25	5.77%
COLT INDUSTRIES	12.500%	15-Oct-2001	104.250	104.000	107.500	100.000	-0.25	5.76%
ALLIED STORES	11.500%	15-Mar-97	88.000	86.000	95.000	86.000	-2	4.26%
ENVIRODYNE INDS	12.000%	15-Jun-96	102.000	98.000	104.500	98.000	-4	1.96%
PST HOLDINGS	12.750%	01-Jun-92	90.500	85.750	90.500	85.750	-4.75	1.80%
PAY & SAVE (PNS)	12.125%	15-Jul-96	75.000	70.000	75.250	55.000	-5	1.42%
MUELLER CORP	12.500%	15-Jul-2001	84.500	79.000	83.500	79.000	-5.5	0.89%
RAPID AMERICAN	14.500%	01-Mar-94	93.000	86.500	93.000	86.000	-6.5	0.81%
EII HOLDINGS	12.850%	01-Mar-97	94.250	87.500	108.250	87.500	-6.75	-0.34%
EII HOLDINGS	13.050%	01-Mar-99	94.500	87.000	108.250	87.000	-7.5	-1.03%
U.S. HOME	12.375%	01-Jun-96	90.000	82.250	90.000	82.000	-7.75	-1.74%
ALPINE GROUP	13.500%	01-Oct-96	92.000	83.000	92.000	83.000	-9	-2.45%
PST HOLDINGS	13.125%	01-Jun-97	87.000	78.000	83.625	76.000	-9	-2.80%
SYNTHETIC INDS	11.500%	01-Apr-99	67.250	57.000	71.500	55.000	-10.25	-6.69%
MDC CORP	11.250%	15-May-96	76.000	63.000	76.250	63.000	-13	-9.70%
REVCO CORP	13.125%	15-Dec-94	90.500	53.000	88.000	50.000	-37.5	-34.19%
GENERAL HOME	12.750%	01-May-98	44.000	20.500	45.000	20.500	-23.5	-38.92%
MAXICARE HEALTH	11.750%	01-Oct-96	80.000	34.000	75.000	34.000	-46	-50.16%
REVCO CORP	13.300%	15-Dec-96	90.000	36.000	85.500	35.000	-54	-52.61%
ITEL CORP	12.625%	15-Jan-93	N/A	102.875	102.875	101.625		
GRAND UNION	13.000%	02-Mar-98	N/A	102.500	102.500	96.492		

TABLE 6-30
High-Yield Energy Industry

Company	Outstanding ($MM)	Maturity	Ratings MY/S&P	Nearest Date	Call Price	Sinking Fund Date	Sinking Fund Amt($MM)	Retired	Issue Date
COASTAL CORP.									
8.48% SUB. FXD RT NTS	600.0	11/15/91	BA3/B+	ANYTIME	108.00	--	--	--	11/12/86
11.125% SR. SUB. NTS.	200.0	3/01/98	BA2/BB-	2/15/95	100.00	--	--	--	2/24/88
11.25% SR. DEBS.	500.0	6/15/96	BA1/BB-	6/15/93	100.00	--	--	--	6/24/86
11.75% SENIOR NOTES	400.0	6/15/06	BA1/BB-	6/15/96	103.92	6/15/96	30.00	90%	6/26/86
ENRON									
7% SR. SUB. DEBS. (VAR)	700.0	2/15/99	BA3/BB+	2/15/92	104.00	6/15/96	175.00	75%	2/06/87
FREEPORT-MCMORAN									
10.875% SUB DEB	150.0	5/15/01	BA3/BB-	5/15/96	100.00	5/15/96	22.50	75%	5/8/86
LASALLE ENERGY									
11.75% SR BONDS	230.0	7/01/99	NR/NR	7/01/92	100.00	7/01/96	46.00	60%	7/07/87
MCDERMOTT									
12.25% SUB DEBS	200.0	6/15/98	BA1/BB+	6/1/93	104.59	6/1/96	50.00	50%	6/13/88
MESA CAPITAL									
12% SUB. DEB.	300.0	8/01/96	BAA3/BB+	ANYTIME	111.00	--	--	--	7/25/84
MITCHELL ENERGY									
11.25% SR. NTS.	250.0	1/15/97	BA2/BB	1/15/92	103.21	1/15/95	62.50	25%	1/27/87
OCCIDENTAL PETE									
8.95% SUB. NTS.	700.0	4/15/94	BA1/BBB-	ANYTIME	100.00	4/15/90	70.00	30%	4/17/85
9.65% SR. SUB. NTS,	1200.0	10/15/94	BAA3/BBB-	ANYTIME	100.00	4/15/90	120.00	51%	10/23/84
PHILLIPS PETROLEUM									
FLT. RT. NTS.	1973.0	3/15/95	BA1/BB-	ANYTIME	100.00	--	--	--	3/4/85
12.875% NTS.	187.0	9/01/92	BA1/BB-	9/1/89	100.00	--	--	--	8/24/82
13..875% SR. NTS.	1306.0	3/15/97	BA1/BB-	3/15/92	103.00	3/15/93	261.00	60%	3/28/85
14.75% SUB. DEBS.	1088.7	3/15/00	BA3/B	3/15/92	103.00	3/15/96	218.00	60%	3/28/85
ROWAN									
13.75% SR. NTS.	125.0	7/15/96	BA1/BB	7/15/89	105.00	--	--	--	7/16/86
SMITH INTERNATIONAL									
13.00% NOTES	90.0	12/31/94	B1/B+	CURRENTLY	100.00	--	--	--	12/31/87
TESORO PETE.									
12.75% SUB DEB	120.0	3/15/01	B2/B	CURRENTLY	107.76	3/15/93	11.25	75%	3/8/83
TOSCO									
12.50% 1ST MTG. BONDS	150.0	12/15/91	B3/B+	12/15/90	104.00	12/15/89	8.34	--	12/23/86
USX									
(MARATHON) 9.5% GTD. NTS.	1200.0	3/01/94	NR/BB+	--	--	--	--	--	1/29/87
9% INTRM. NTS.	400.0	1/15/92	BA1/BB+	--	--	--	--	--	6/26/86
UNION TEXAS									
13% SUB. NTS.	310.0	7/01/95	B1/BB+	7/01/91	104.00	7/01/93	7.75	--	11/08/85

EVALUATING INFORMATION

Managing a junk bond portfolio requires active involvement, perhaps on a daily basis. Both bad and good news can cause major shifts in the selling price of junk bonds. A bondholder must be able to evaluate the information quickly and evaluate alternatives.

On January 23, 1989, GAF Corporation offered to purchase their 11 3/8 percent Senior Subordinated Notes, due on 1995 for $995 each. At the time of the solicitation, the offering of $995 per bond was equal to the current market price. Therefore, there was no incentive for the bondholder to sell other than to liquidate a bond rated as B+. On February 15, 1989, GAF increased the solicitation price to $1,032.50 for each $1,000 principal amount. On the surface, this deal looks better than the initial offer of $995, but there is another alternative. GAF obviously has capital or funding available to repurchase the bonds. Financially, they should be reasonably able to make their 11 3/8 percent coupon payments. And because 11 3/8 percent is greater than the prevailing money market rates, it might be better to hold the bonds knowing that the amount outstanding has been reduced by those who accepted the tender offer. On July 31, 1989, these GAF bonds were trading at 108 3/4.

A similar situation occurred with the Best Products Company 12 5/8 percent Senior Subordinated Notes due July 1, 1996. The covenant on the bond mandated that if the company's Consolidated Tangible Net Worth drops below $250 million, then the company must purchase $20 million of these notes on August 14, 1989. On May 5, 1989, Best Products offered to increase the coupon from 12 5/8 percent to 13 3/8 percent if the bondholders agreed to remove the covenant on Tangible Net Worth. At that time, the bonds were rated as B by Standard and Poor's and selling for $920 per bond. On May 5, approximately $133,495,000 of the notes were outstanding.

Should you agree to lift the covenant in exchange for an increase in coupon? If you agree to the exchange, you will receive an additional $7.50 per bond in coupon payments each year. The selling price of the bond will almost assuredly drop, however, because of the increased debt. If you do not agree to the exchange, the selling price of the bonds will probably increase and you have a 14.8 percent chance of having your bonds purchased at par on August 14. That would give you $80 per bond more than the current selling price.

On July 6, 1989, Best Products offered to purchase all outstanding bonds at $1,036 per bond. The selling price of the bonds quickly increased to more than $1,020 per bond. Now the question is whether or not to accept the purchase at $1,036 per bond. If you accept the purchase, you probably have made a very good profit and eliminated some junk bonds from your portfolio. On the other hand, all of those people that accept the offer will reduce the amount of outstanding principal, thus making it easier for the company to meet its 12 5/8 percent coupon payments. Second, 12 5/8 percent coupons are substantially higher than the prevailing rates and, with the bond now selling over par, holding the bonds might be a better alternative.

Sometimes, a newspaper story can entice an investor to buy or sell junk bonds. During the bankruptcy proceedings of Eastern Airlines, Texas Air announced plans to purchase $2.8 billion worth of aircraft to modernize its fleet. Since the company must have financing available, and since the actual purchase would not occur until the mid-1990s, purchasing the 15¾ percent bonds maturing in 1992 seems like a very acceptable risk, even though the bond rating is B.

7

Margin Buying for Corporate Bonds

SINCE THE TAX LAWS HAVE BEEN REVAMPED, INVESTMENTS IN THE CORporate bonds market will become increasingly popular as investors try to maintain the same dollar or percent return before the tax law revision. Corporate bonds have long been considered primarily suited to conservative investors, such as pension/profit sharing funds, IRA accounts, and retirees who require a known or fixed return on their investments. For the non-conservative investor, purchasing corporate bonds on margin (i.e., through borrowed funds) offers the opportunity for a 15 to 20 percent or more annual return on investment. There are four critical factors to consider before selecting corporate bonds:

- Margin Borrowing Rate
- Bond Ratings
- Call Provisions
- Liquidity

MARGIN BORROWING RATE

Margin buying of corporate bonds is purchasing bonds using partially borrowed funds. The borrowed funds are provided by the brokerage house. Most brokerage houses allow you to borrow up to 70 percent of the current selling price of the bond *provided that the bond is listed on, and actively traded on, the New York Stock Exchange* of the *American Stock Exchange*. Some brokerage houses have exceptions to this, however.

The critical factor in margin buying is the interest rate, that you must pay on the borrowed funds. The interest rate that the borrower must pay will be between .5 to 2 percent above the "call money" rate, which is the broker's charge based on stock exchange collateral. The call money rate is most often less than the prime lending rate. The call money rate is listed in the *Wall Street Journal* and can change daily. Therefore, your interest rate can change daily.

The interest rate to the borrower will be between .5 to 2 percent *above* the call money rate, based on how much money is borrowed. The table below illustrates a call money rate of 8 percent:

Broker Call Money Rate, %	*Amount Borrowed, $*	*Points Over Call Rate, %*	*Total Borrowing Rate, %*
8.0	0–2,000	2.0	10.0
8.0	2,000–10,000	1.50	9.5
8.0	10,000–30,000	1.25	9.25
8.0	30,000–50,000	1.0	9.0
8.0	over 50,000	0.5	8.5

Using this table as an example, it is economically advantageous to borrow more than $50,000 because you will get the lowest borrowing rate. Remember, however, that the investor must have at least $25,000 of his own money invested in order to borrow $50,000 (i.e., 30/70 leveraged ratio).

For example, assume you want to buy a bond that sells for $1,000 and has a 12 percent coupon. (Note that the calculations that follow assume a 1/3 / 2/3 margin leverage; you put up 1/3 and borrow 2/3). If you pay $1,000 and do not borrow any funds, your return will be 12 percent. If you pay $1,000 and buy three bonds, assuming that you could borrow at 8.5 percent interest, your return would be: 12% + 2 (12% – 8.5%) = 19% return. (Here, you earn 12 percent on the $1,000 you put up, and 7 percent on the $2,000 borrowed. Simply put, you are making money on borrowed funds.) If you pay $1,000 and buy two bonds, assuming that you could borrow at 8.5 percent interest, your return would be: 12% + 1(12% – 8.5%) = 15.5% return.

If you pay $1,000 and buy two bonds, assuming that you borrow at 10 percent, your return would be: (12% + 1(12% – 10%) = 14% return. If you pay $1,000 and buy three bonds, assuming that you must borrow at 10 percent, your return would be: 12% + 2(12% – 10%) = 16% return.

Generally, there is a four to five percentage point difference between investment grade and speculative grade bonds. Therefore, if investment-grade bonds are paying 10 percent, then speculative bonds might pay 14 percent. Using maximum leverage and a borrowing rate of 9 percent, margin-buying of investment-grade bonds will pay 12 percent, whereas speculative bonds might pay a 24 percent return on investment.

Consequently, the four parameters to consider in analyzing the margin borrowing rate are the amount of money you want to borrow, the broker call rate, your leverage position, and the quality of the bonds. Margin buying offers investors the opportunity to make larger-than-normal profits, provided they are willing to endure economic risks.

BOND RATINGS

Bond ratings indicate how well a corporation will be able to meet its current and long-term financial obligations. The higher the bond rating, the better the quality of the bond and, thus, the lower the return (i.e., coupon value). Lower-rated bonds incur higher risks and must pay a larger coupon to attract investors.

Bonds rated as BB, B, CCC, and CC are considered speculative. Buying lower-rated bonds on margin can yield very high returns, perhaps 30 to 40 percent, but if the bonds default, the loss can be equally as large.

Most margin accounts have either all, or a large percentage, of junk bonds because of the high returns. Buying top-quality bonds on margin is a losing proposition if the interest rates increase. Even if the interest rates remain the same, the investor is risking a lot of money to make an additional 1 to 2 percent on his investment.

Assume you have a margin account that allows you to borrow at the best leveraged position and you want to purchase 10 more bonds on margin. You select PAN AM's B-rated bond which matures in 2004 with a coupon of 15 percent. In October 1988 the bond was trading at $660 for a current yield of 22.7 percent, and the margin borrowing rate was 10 percent. You then purchase 10 of these bonds on margin. The closing date for the transaction is 30, October 1988 (Interest payment date is 15 October).

Purchase Price:	$6,600.00
Prepaid Interest (6.25/bond × 10)	62.50
Commission (10/bond × 10)	100.00
	$6,762.50

Most margin accounts allow you to borrow up to 70 percent of the purchase price. Therefore, you could borrow up to $4,620. You would have to pay:

Purchase Price (30% × $6,600)	$1,980.00
Prepaid Interest	62.50
Commission	100.00
	$2,142.50

Prepaid interest and commission cannot be on margin.

If the margin rate of 10 percent does not change, the selling price of the bond remains the same and the company makes the required interest payment. Your return on investment would be approximately:

$$22.7\% + 2(22.7 - 10)\% = 48.1\%$$

If the bond defaults, however, your loss could be great. Assume that on February 15, 1989 PAN AM files for bankruptcy and the bonds are trading at $200/bond. If you sell now, your loss would be:

Sale: [$600 − 200] × 10 bond	$4,600.00
Buying Commission	100.00
Selling Commission	100.00
Prepaid Interest	62.50
Margin Interest ($4,620 @ 10% for 120 days)	154.00
	$5,016.50

When the default occurs, or when the selling price drops, you could receive a "margin maintenance call" from your broker, which indicates money is due. Brokerage houses offer 30/70 financing leverage based on the ***daily price*** of the bonds. If your account balance drops below this ratio, you must come up with the additional funding or liquidate bonds to cover the shortage. To make matters even worse, bonds that are in default cannot be margined at all. Three facts should be obvious from this example.

- The lower the quality, the greater the margin return on investment and the greater the downside risk.
- If you buy at the maximum leverage, you must be prepared to receive "maintenance calls" due to bond price fluctuations.
- If the rating of the bonds are lowered, then the selling price will decrease and a maintenance call could result.

CALL PROVISIONS

Some bonds are issued with special provisions that let the issuer call the bond for redemption before the issued date of maturity. This is particularly true with high-coupon bonds and is used to protect the issuer should more favorable opportunities arise (such as refinancing at lower interest rates or a high cash-flow position).

Call provisions are generally five years or longer and might reduce the value of the bond to the issuer because the period of time that the bond will be outstanding might be uncertain. Therefore, many bonds identify "call protection," which is the amount of time (or calendar date), after a bond is issued so that the bond issuer cannot call the bond in for redemption.

As inducement for the investor, the issuer might offer the investor a "call premium," which is an extra payment over and above the par value of the bond in the event that the bond is called in. Another inducement might be a higher initial coupon for the privilege to call a bond in early. For example, in October 1985, Texas Air issued a bond selling at par ($1,000) with a coupon of 14.375 percent and a 1990 maturity date. The call date is October 15, 1988 at a call price of $1,060. Bonds with high coupons have call premiums over par. Bonds with low coupons or high risks might be issued substantially below par, in which case the call provision will be at par. For example, consider Wickes Companies, which issued an 11.375 percent coupon bond in April 1985 with a maturity date of 1997. The call provision is at par, $1,000, after May 1, 1995.

Table 7-1 identifies nine bonds in which the call provision was executed. Compare the last two columns. Notice that, by buying the bonds on margin, you can get a much greater return on investment.

Two of the bonds require further comment. The Beverly bond was purchased *over par* with a call provision at par. Obviously, a risk existed when buying the bond. Buying a B-rated Beverly bond outright (i.e., not on margin), yielded a negative return of .71 percent, but on margin, the loss was 8.12 percent over five months. The ATT bond in Table 7-1 is similar to the Beverly bond. The ATT bond was rated as "AA," which means that ATT will most certainly refinance these bonds at lower interest rates and exercise the call provision. There are several conclusions you can draw from Table 7-1:

- When buying bonds that sell over par, there is a risk that the bonds will be called in early, especially if there is a high coupon.
- Quality bonds will almost assuredly be called in and refinanced at a lower interest rate.
- Speculative bonds selling over par are also at risk of being called in early.
- When buying above-par bonds on margin, be sure that the call features of the bond provide some degree of protection.
- Buying bonds that sell below par eliminates the risk of early redemption.
- Buying below-par bonds on margin can generate substantial profits if the bonds are called in early.

Sometimes, corporations try to call in bonds earlier than identified in the call provision. Such was the case of the BB-rated Union Carbide bond in Table 7-1. Although the call date was 1990, Union Carbide *offered* the bondholders a premium of $150 per bond to allow the bonds to be called in early. The selling price of the bond would then approach the call price of the bond. For some bondholders it was attractive to exercise this option and make other investments.

There are also special offers made by corporations who are "locked into" high-yield bonds with long-term call provisions. LTV and Clabir tried to per-

TABLE 7-1
Typical Bonds with Call Dates Executed

Bond			*Purchase*	*Purchase*	*Call*	*Call*	*Non-Margin*	*Margin*
Title	*Coupon%*	*Maturity*	*Date*	*Price,$*	*Date*	*Price,$*	*ROI,%*	*ROI,%*
Enstar	12.75	1999	11/4/85	937.50	6/15/86	1038.25	18.68	24.0
Groliers	13	2002	8/7/85	928.75	6/27/86	1010.00	20.41	32.73
Beverly	15	2002	9/23/85	1057.50	2/5/86	1000.00	0.71	8.12
ATT	13.25	1991	7/9/85	1047.50	3/15/86	1015.00	5.33	3.99
Integ. Resources	12.875	1999	11/4/85	960.00	5/28/86	1032.14	12.13	18.6
Kaufman Broad	12.25	1999	12/17/85	980.00	10/15/86	1000.00	12.45	18.2
Realty Refund	12	1998	12/17/85	928.75	10/15/86	1000.00	18.43	25.0
Nortek	12.5	1999	12/12/85	972.50	6/16/86	1041.70	13.54	17.39
Union Carbide	13.25	1993	1/27/85	977.50	11/8/86	1136.25	26.4	38.9

Margin borrowing rate is averaged at 9.0% for the period of performance and the leverage is 33.33% cash and 66.67% borrowed.

suade bondholders to exchange the high-yield bonds for stock. Corporate raiders often offer bondholders incentives during buy out attempts, especially if bondholder approval is needed during mergers, acquisitions, or divestitures. Turner Broadcasting offered bondholders a 10 percent incentive to exchange MGM United Artist bonds for Turner Broadcasting Bonds. Bally offered to increase the coupon from 12 percent to 13 percent during its acquisition of the MGM Grand Hotel.

LIQUIDITY

Bonds that are listed and traded on the New York Stock Exchange have a high degree of liquidity. In other words, the bonds can be sold prior to maturity based on the prime interest rate and bond rating. Liquidity is an important factor because, if a major change takes place in your portfolio, such as a margin call by the brokerage house, the bonds might have to be sold to cover liabilities. American and New York Stock Exchange bonds are highly liquid, but perhaps not at the price you would like.

RISK ANALYSIS

Buying bonds on margin has the potential of a return on investment at least double that of money market rates, but there are risks that have to be considered:

- Increases in the broker call rate.

- Lowering of bond rating or inability to pay interest.
- Corporate buy outs.
- Delisting.

Broker call rates follow the prime lending rate. Increases in the broker call rate causes double jeopardy. First, the interest that you must pay on borrowed money will increase, and second, the selling price of the bond will decrease. For example, consider a bond with the following conditions:

Coupon:	12%
Maturity:	2000
Cost/Selling Price:	$1,000
Broker Call Rate:	9%
Margin Rate:	30/70%

If you were to buy 10 of these bonds, your cash outlay would be $3,000, and the brokerage house would lend you the remaining $7,000, assuming that you want to borrow at maximum leverage. The interest on the $7,000 borrowed would be $630. Now, assume that the broker call rate increases to 10 percent because the fed interest rate increases and the bond is selling for $900. Since the brokerage house will lend money based upon the *current* selling price, the maximum you can now borrow is $6,300. You will therefore receive a maintenance call for $700.

There are several ways to offset this risk. First, instead of borrowing at maximum leverage consider a 50/50 margin rate, which could be better. The profit percentage would be less and so would the need for additional out-of-pocket cash. Second, higher-quality bonds have smaller price deviations with changes in the broker lending rate. Third, bonds with a near-term maturity date, say five years or less, also have a narrower response to broker lending-rate changes.

The second risk is the lowering of the bond rating or the inability to pay interest. If a bond goes into default, the selling price will decrease, perhaps drastically, and a maintenance call will result. Likewise, if the rating of the bond is lowered, the selling price will be lower, and again, a maintenance call can result. Defaulted bonds might not be marginable.

Investment institutions often have bond investment funds that stipulate the ***minimum*** acceptable bond quality. If the quality drops below this minimum, the bond must be sold. Therefore, it is not uncommon for a large drop in selling price to occur if a bonds quality is lowered because of wholesale selling. This could generate an immediate margin call if you are already highly leveraged.

The third risk is the corporate buy out where Corporation A will propose a leveraged buy out of Corporation B by floating "junk" bonds. Such was the case when Pantry Pride bought out Revlon. The Revlon bonds, which were rated as "A," were downgraded to "CCC" as a result of the buy out and drastically dropped in price. This situation also occurs when a company issues junk bonds (in order to deter a corporate raider from buying them out) in order to buy back some of their own stock.

The fourth and worst scenario occurs when the bonds are no longer listed on the New York or American Stock Exchanges. This occurs when either the corporation no longer meets the exchange requirements (i.e., APL Corporation or Southeast Public Service), or when the firm is bought out by a company that is not listed on the exchanges. In either event, bonds that might have been quality bonds at one time or another are no longer available for margin.

ASSESSING RISK THROUGH STOCK PRICES

Not all high-yield, high-risk bonds are equal in risk. By proper analysis and selection, some of the risks can be minimized. Consider the 54 bonds shown in Table 7-2, all of which were rated from BB– to CCC at the end of 1986. Although most of these bonds are considered to be junk bonds, some have tremendous promise for growth and upgrading. By plotting available earnings coverage versus stock price as in Fig. 7-1 the better high-risk bonds can be identified.[1]

As shown in Fig. 7-2, the degree of risk can be identified. Bonds in the "divest" category are the highest possible risk if on margin. Figure 7-3 provides an explanation of the risks in each quadrant. The "Stars," "Blue Chips," and "Go-Go's" in Fig. 7-3 could cause a slow decay in price because of unfavorable economic conditions, giving you sufficient time to react. It must always be remembered, however, that regardless of what quadrant you are in, there still exists a great deal of risk. For example, in the first half of 1986, Wedtech reported a profit of $4.7 million on revenue of $72.2 million with $110.6 in receivables as assets. On August 22, 1986 Wedtech issued $75 million in "junk bonds." On December 15, 1986 Wedtech filed for bankruptcy. This example clearly indicates the high risks that exist and, simply because the bond is a new issue, there is no guarantee that as little as *one* coupon payment will be made.

It might seem strange to assess the risk of a bond by looking at the price of the stock as is shown in Fig. 7-1. The reason for this is that firms generally do not file for bankruptcy when selling over $10 per share. Therefore, the bondholder might be able to use the stock price as an indicator that he should consider liquidating the bonds. Obviously, there are many more stockholders than bondholders, and stocks respond quicker to bad news than do bonds. Knowing when the risks are too great is the key to purchasing or holding junk bonds.

---

[1]Available earnings coverage is the number of times that pretax earnings will cover fixed charges of funded debt, interest, and expenses.

TABLE 7-2
High-Yield, High-Risk Bonds Issue Description

Bond Number	*Title*	*Rating*	*Coupon, %*	*Maturity Year*
1	Allegheny	CCC	10.4	2002
2	Allis Chalmers	NR*	12.0	1990
3	Angeles	B+	12.5	1995
4	Armco	B+	8.7	1995
5	Arrow	B–	12.0	1998
6	Best Prod.	B+	12.625	1996
7	Care Ent.	CCC	16.0	1994
8	CDC	B+	12.750	1991
9	Chemetron	CCC	9.0	1994
10	Chris Craft	B–	15.0	1999
11	Clabir	CCC	14.5	2004
12	Coastal	B+	11.25	1996
13	Coleco	B–	14.375	2002
14	Collins Food	BB–	12.0	2008
15	Crane	BB–	10.5	1994
16	Essex Chem.	B	11.375	1998
17	Fin. Cp. Amer.	B–	11.875	1998
18	Flow General	NR*	14.3	2004
19	Gelco	BB–	14.625	1999
20	General Homes	B–	15.5	1995
21	Genesco	B–	15.25	1994
22	Gold Nug. Fin.	BB–	13.25	1995
23	Groliers	B	13.625	2003
24	ICN Pharm.	B–	12.875	1998
25	Interfirst	B+	9.75	1999
26	Intermark	B–	11.875	1999
27	Iroquois Bds.	B–	12.0	1999
28	Kay	B–	13.5	1998
29	Long Is. Light	B	12.625	1992
30	Mattel	B	11.625	2003
31	MGM Grand	B+	12.0	1996
32	Mickelberry	B–	11.5	1998
33	Navistar Fin.	CCC	11.95	1995
34	Orion Pictures	B	10.0	1999
35	Pan AM	B–	15.0	2004
36	Pier 1	B	11.5	2003
37	PS Group	B+	14.0	1993
38	Pub. Sv. NH.	CCC	15.75	1988
39	Quanex	B+	15.25	1999
40	Ramada	B–	10.0	1993
41	Revlon	CCC	11.75	1995
42	Showboat	B–	13.0	2004
43	Stand. Pac.	B–	12.75	1999
44	Steego	B	14.75	2001
45	Stone Cont.	B	13.625	1995
46	Tesoro	B	12.75	2001

(Table 7-2. continued.)

Bond Number	*Title*	*Rating*	*Coupon, %*	*Maturity Year*
47	Texas Air	B	15.75	1992
48	Todd Ship	B–	14.0	1996
49	Triton En.	B–	13.5	1994
50	United Brds.	B–	10.25	2005
51	U.S. Homes	B	13.25	1994
52	Valero	B	16.25	2001
53	Wickes	B	12.0	1994
54	West. Union	CCC	16.0	1991

*Non-rated bonds

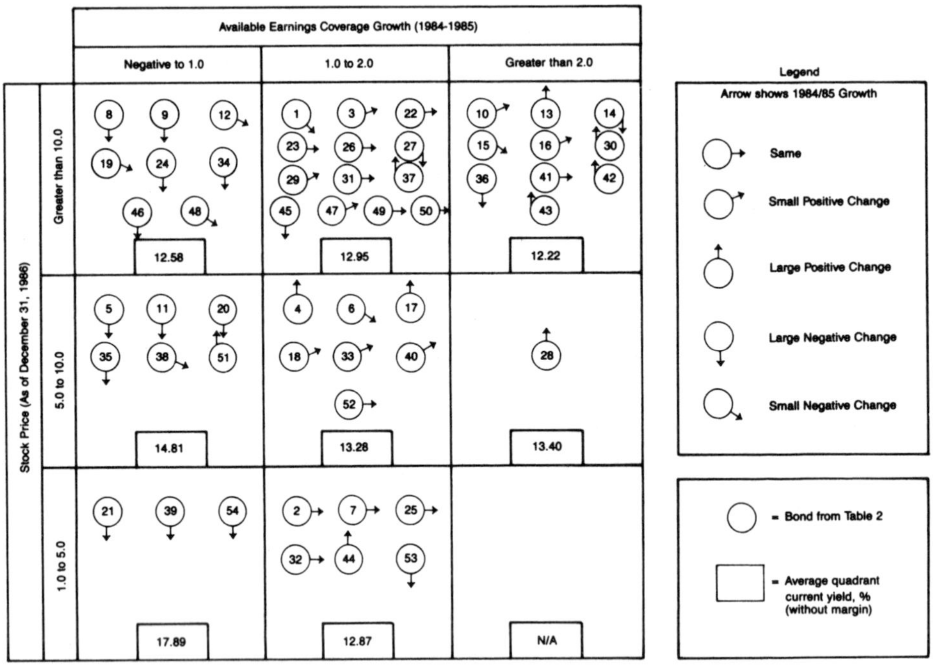

***Fig. 7-1.** Risk analysis for high-yield, high-risk bonds.*

From January through December 1988 the following bonds either defaulted on interest payments or filed for bankruptcy protection under Chapter 11:

Industrial Bonds	**Amount (Mil. $)**
Allegheny International	400
Anglo Energy	82
Basix	50

Cannon Group	206
Care Enterprises	70
Clabir Corporation	20
Coleco Industries	332
Delaurentiis Entertainment	65
General Defense	170
General Homes	140
Geothermal Resources	60
Medicare Health Plans	300
Nelson Entertainment	58
Pope, Evans and Robbins	35
Revco	175
Robert Bruce Industries	15
Texas International	155
Wessex Corporation	22
	$2355

Financial Institutions	**Amount (Mil. $)**
Bank of Mid-America	35
Financial Corp. of America	75
First RepublicBank Corp.	562
MCorp.	688
PHM Credit Group	82
Texas America Bancshares	75
	$1521

Utilities	**Amount (Mil. $)**
ALC Communications	60
Public Service of New Hampshire	1500
	$1560

In most cases, the stock was identified in the "divest" category prior to default. Even bonds like Coleco, which were shown in the "invest" category in Fig. 7-2 had their stock price drop to the "divest" category before default. The prudent investor could have divested at $700/bond.

The stock market often reacts quicker to bad news than the bond market does. Consider the LTV bond with a 14 percent coupon and maturing in the year 2004. From May to July 1986 the stock had a 50 percent decrease from 9 to 4.5. At the same time, the bond decreased by 10 percent from $960 to $850. The

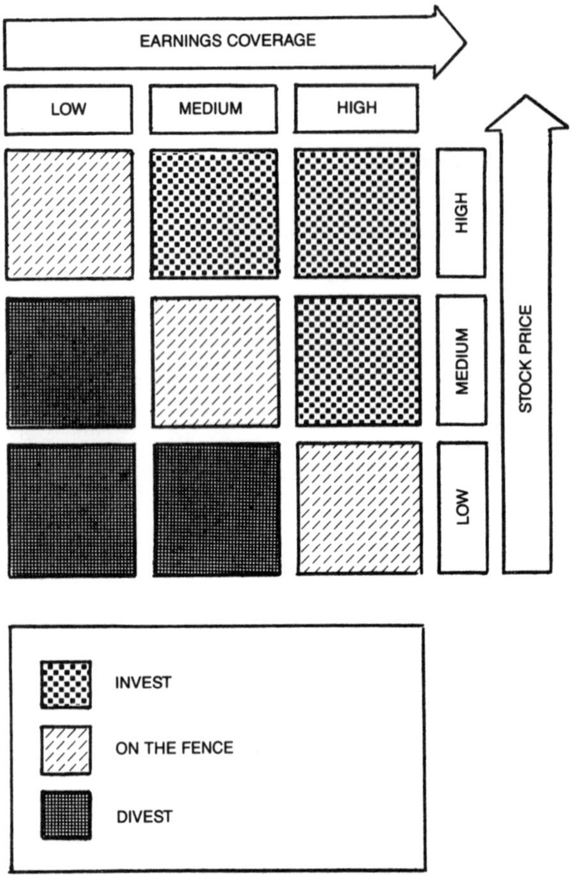

Fig. 7-2. An example of a risk analysis.

bond was selling for $850 the day before LTV filed for bankruptcy protection under Chapter 11.

Combining Figs. 7-1 and 7-3, the investor can decide upon how much risk he wants to take. For example, assuming you could borrow money at a call rate of 9 percent and with maximum leverage, investment in "Stars" will yield a return of 19.85 percent, but "Gamblers" will produce a yield of 26.41 percent. Is it worth the added risk to earn an additional 6.56 percent when 19.85 percent is substantially higher than current market rates? This technique is just one of the ways that the average investor can assess risks. Other factors that must be considered include:

- Industry Characteristics
- Total, Long-Term Outstanding Debt
- Price Range of Stock/Bond
- Current Yield
- Yield to Maturity

Earnings Coverage →

Stock Price ↑

Wildcatters • Excellent stock market acceptance • Companies with increasing debt • Restructuring companies • Marginal risk of possible downgrading	**Stars** • Excellent stock market acceptance • Potential for increased earnings • Downgraded investment–grade bonds • Favorable environmental conditions	**Blue Chips** • Best of the "Junk Bonds" • Prime for quality upgrading to investment–grade • Rapid downgrading less likely due to environmental changes • Can withstand some degree of lower earnings
Gamblers • Marginal stock market acceptance • Extremely sensitive to environmental conditions • Possible downgrading by more than one grade level	**Dark Horses** • Post-restructuring companies • Candidates for fractional upgrading (i.e., B+) • Good companies in a poor industry	**Go-Go's** • Good debt coverage over past two years • Stock market in a waiting game • Good industry to be in
Losers • Candidates for bankruptcy • High risks in short-term	**Plodders** • High, long-term risks • Low growth companies • Debt coverage marginable • Extremely sensitive to changes within industry	**Strugglers** • Stock market has poor expectations of company despite good debt coverage • Highly competitive industry with strong sensitivity to environmental changes

Fig. 7-3. *Quadrant risks.*

- Current Assets
- Current Liabilities

It could be argued that all of these variables have already been considered by Moody's and Standard and Poor's in determining their bond rating.

DISCOUNTED BONDS

Discounted and deep-discounted bonds offer an investor two sources of income: the coupon return and the capital gain as the bond approaches par (maturity). Discounted bonds are often less riskier than deep-discounted bonds because the time to maturity is shorter. Discounted bonds are somewhat less riskier than bonds selling over par because special call provisions usually do not exist.

In times of decreasing broker lending rates, discounted corporate bonds could appreciate to par very quickly. If a substantial capital gain is achieved, then the two questions that need to be answered are:

- Should I take my profit?
- If yes, where should I place the profits?

There are three common reasons for taking profit. First, the money is needed to pay taxes on the interest received. Second, the bond has appreciated to the point where the current yield is lower than what you can earn with other

TABLE 7-3
Typical Appreciation

Title	Bond Coupon,%	Year	Purchase Date	Purchase Price,$	Price Dec, 1986,$	Current Yield
Gold Nugget Fin.	13.25	1995	10/21/85	988.75	1080	12.25
Stone Container	13.625	1995	12/12/85	1008.75	1100	12.38
Union Carbide	13.25	1993	1/29/86	977.50	1140	11.62

investments. Third, the bonds may depreciate if kept. Consider the three bonds listed in Table 7-3. Each of these bonds could have been purchased initially for the coupon interest. But with the good appreciation, should the bonds be sold? If the bonds are close to the call date or if special call provisions exist, it is usually best to take the substantial profit and reinvest it elsewhere.

Assume you have a bond portfolio containing 10 of each bond shown in Table 7-4. You purchased the bonds in the last quarter of 1985 and by December 1986 your portfolio increased in value by $14,987.50 because of capital appreciation. If you sell the bonds, you would have $98,500 of which $14,987.50 is taxable. Assuming a 40 percent total tax bracket, after taxes you would have $92,505 for investing. If you have a margin account, however, then the capital gain can be used as collateral for purchasing more bonds.

To illustrate it differently, consider only the $14,987.50 capital gain. If you pay the 40 percent tax, you would have $8,992.50 for investment. This would allow you to purchase approximately $30,000 worth of bonds on margin. If you

TABLE 7-4
Total Appreciation Gains/Losses

Title	Bond Coupon%	Year	Purchase Date	Purchase Price,$	Price, Dec,86	Capital Gain/Bond	Current Yield
20th Century Fox	13.25	2000	9/23/85	935.00	1040	105.00	12.74
Tesoro	12.75	2001	9/27/85	820.00	950	130.00	13.42
Comdisco	9.65	2002	10/21/85	740.00	900	160.00	10.72
Harnishfegler	12.00	2004	10/21/85	875.00	1010	135.00	11.76
Resorts Intl.	11.875	2013	10/21/85	790.00	950	160.00	12.50
Showboat	13.00	2004	11/15/85	920.00	1030	110.00	12.62
AMR	10.25	2006	11/05/85	850.00	1020	170.00	10.05
Kay Corp.	13.50	1998	11/19/85	928.75	1020	91.25	13.25
Warner Comm.	11.50	2013	12/13/85	860.00	1030	170.00	11.16
Farley	7.50	1994	12/16/85	632.50	900	267.50	8.33
					TOTAL	1498.75	

do *not* sell the bonds and have a margin account, however, then you can purchase an *additional* $50,000 worth of bonds.

As a general rule, it is wise to sell a bond if the proceeds of the sale can be reinvested at high returns. For example, you pay $700 for a bond with an 8 percent coupon. Each year you receive $80. Now assume that the bond is selling for $900. If you sell the bond and purchase a 9 percent bond for $900 (neglecting commissions), your annual return is $90. With a margin account, however, the capital appreciation can be reinvested without paying tax on it until the asset is sold.

MARGIN DECISIONS

Perhaps the worst news you can get from your broker, other than an interest default disclosure, is an unexpected margin maintenance call. Margin maintenance calls most frequently occur during periods of increasing broker call rates, which increase your borrowing costs while decreasing your market value. There are two ways to handle maintenance calls. You can either provide additional capital to your account or you can liquidate assets to cover your obligations. Generally, if you enjoy living dangerously with maximum margin leverage, then you should maintain sufficient cash reserves should market or economic conditions change for the worst.

Liquidating assets, on the other hand, might not be as easy a decision as it sounds. Consider a situation in which you receive a maintenance call because the broker call rate and broker interest increased to 10.25 percent. Which bonds should you sell? The easiest situation is to sell bonds that are deteriorating because they will more than likely deteriorate further because of prime lending rate increases. It is generally better to liquidate these bonds and buy them back later when it appears that the firm's prospects have changed for the better.

The difficulty of selling bonds is establishing criteria for which bonds to dispose of. Consider the seven bonds shown in Table 7-5, all of which are investment-grade bonds that have appreciated in value. If you must sell one bond, which one will it be? There are several criteria that must be considered:

- Two of the bonds are selling over par. If the interest rates continue to increase, then the bonds might drop below par.
- Bonds selling at or over par are in danger of being called in for redemption. If the interest rates decrease in the near term, then the risk of redemption will increase far above par bonds.
- Five out of the seven bonds have current yields that are *below* the margin interest rate. In other words, you are *losing* money by having these bonds on margin.
- If the broker call rate increases further, then the current yield of all seven bonds will be less than the margin interest rate.

- If you have a diversified portfolio where the *total* portfolio return is say, 11.5 percent (because of lower-grade high-yield bonds), then you might want to hold bonds such as Manufacturer's Hanover, which still has $180 of appreciation remaining.
- If you feel that the prime rate will decrease in the near term, then you might want to retain these bonds for their additional appreciation, as long as the overall portfolio return is still adequate at present.
- If a bond is subject to quality downgrading such as Toledo Edison, then you might want to sell this bond and repurchase it later, after downgrading. Here, you would expect the selling price to drop appreciably.

Needless to say, from the above example, you could justify either holding or selling any of the bonds in Table 7-5. Some people use the simple strategy of saying, "If you have made a profit on the bond, and the current yield is less than the broker call rate, sell the bond!" This strategy is not always the correct choice, however.

The real critical issue is whether you believe that the broker call rate will increase further. To illustrate the importance of predicting interest rates, consider a portfolio that has a current yield of 10.25 percent and the broker call rate is 10.25 percent. Furthermore, assume a one-third, two-thirds margin rate (i.e., for each bond you own outright, you have two bonds on margin).

If the current yield is 10.25 percent and the broker call rate is also 10.25 percent, then you are earning 10.25 percent on the bond you own outright, but the two bonds on margin are at the break-even point (i.e., return = interest due). If the broker call rate increases to 11.25 percent, and the current yield of the bonds in the portfolio is 10.25 percent, then your total portfolio return is 8.25 percent (i.e., 10.25 percent + 2× [10.25% 11.25%] = 8.25%). In this case, it would benefit you to sell *all* of the bonds whose current yield is below

TABLE 7-5
Margin Selling Conditions

Bond Title	*Coupon,%*	*Maturity*	*Current Yield at Purchase*	*Current Cost,$*	*Current Yield,%*	*Average Profit,$*
Arizona Public Serv.	10.625	2000	10.44	1025.00	10.37	7.50
Commonwealth Ed.	9.125	2008	10.35	925.00	9.86	43.75
Duquesne Lt.	9.0	2006	10.62	912.50	9.88	64.04
Man. Hanover	8.125	2007	10.04	817.50	9.94	8.50
Mellon	8.6	2009	10.34	862.50	9.97	30.55
Niagara Mohawk	10.2	2005	10.86	1010.50	10.05	75.42
Toledo Edison*	9.65	2006	10.66	935.00	10.32	30.00

*On Standard and Poor's *CreditWatch* for possible downgrading below BBB – .

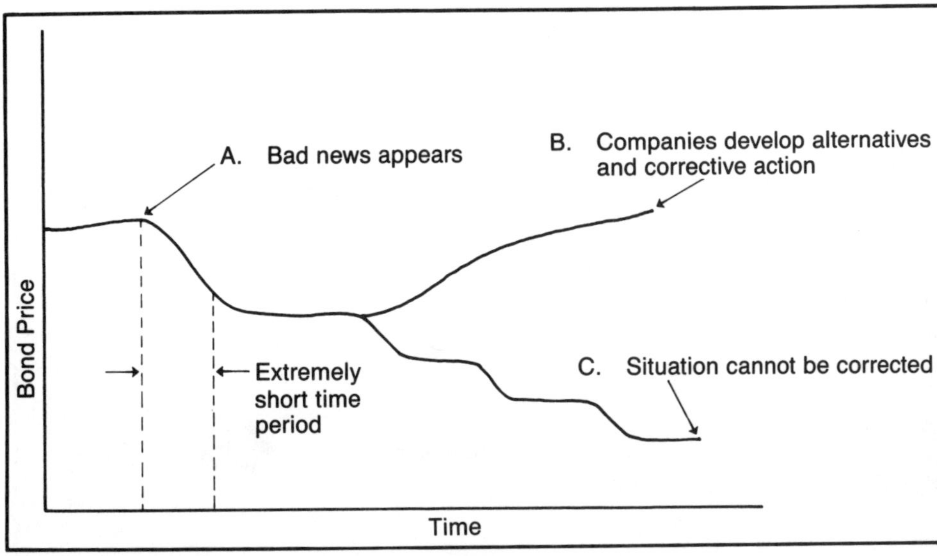

Fig. 7-4. Bond prices in reaction to bad news.

the 11.25 percent margin rate. If you sell all of these bonds, your portfolio yield will increase from 8.25 percent to more than 10.25 percent. Of course, if you feel that the prime rate will decrease such that the broker call rate will *decrease* to 9.25 percent, then you might want to hold onto them knowing that the portfolio yield will increase to 12.25 percent.

Therefore, perhaps the most critical decision for the investor is the prediction or gut-feeling of what will happen with interest rates.

To operate at maximum or near maximum leverage, and at the same time protect your portfolio against margin calls due to interest rate changes, requires a diverse portfolio, which includes a heavy percentage of high-yield, high-risk bonds. This might provide interest rate protection but increases your exposure to defaults or bankruptcies.

Both stocks and bonds react unfavorably to bad news. Noninvestment-grade bonds appear to have greater fluctuations than do investment grade bonds. The threat of a leveraged buy out can cause not only a decrease in the price of a bond, but also a change in rating. The RJR-Nabisco bonds, rated A by Standard and Poor's, lost as much as 20 percent of the bond's value for fear of being downgraded to noninvestment grade, and immediately appeared on Credit-Watch.

Noninvestment grade bonds can lose as much as 20 percent in one day as a reaction to bad news. Figure 7-5 shows the decline of Freuhauf's 12.5 percent bond due 1996 and rated CCC+, and Southmark's 11.5 percent 1991 bond rated B–. On December 21, the Southmark bond dropped 5⁵/₈ points, and on December 22 Fruehauf dropped 7³/₄ points followed by 3³/₄ points on December 23.

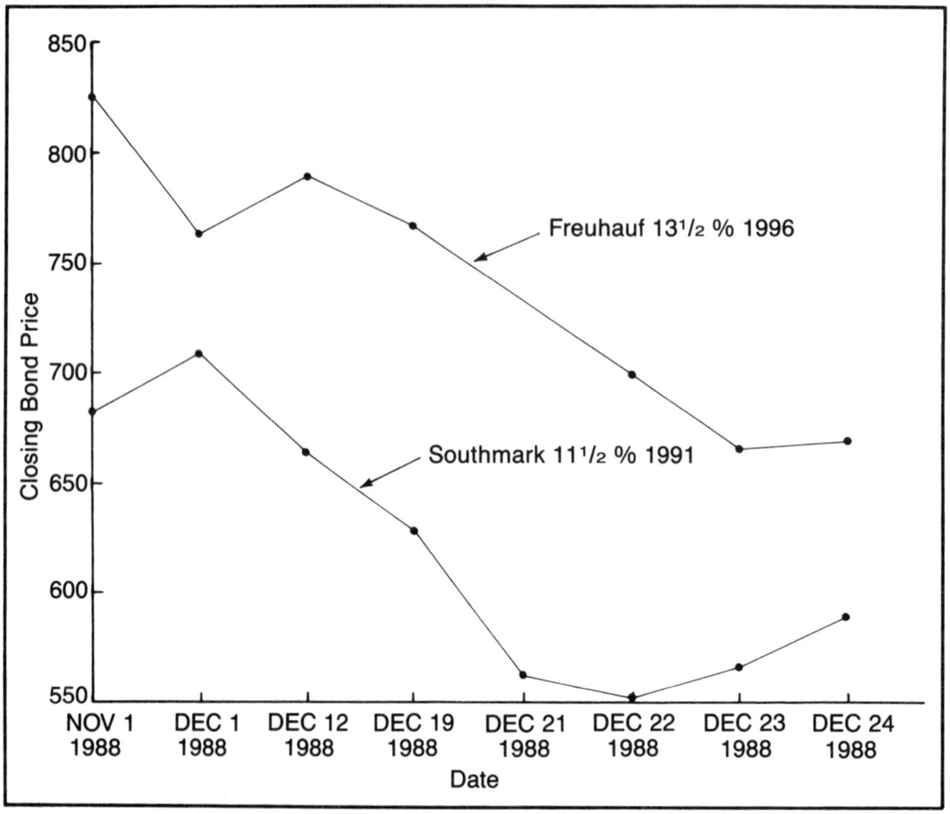

Fig. 7-5. *Market reaction of bond price to bad news.*

Institutional investors and brokerage houses subscribe to wire services and can react the same day the bad news appears. The average investor must wait until the information appears in the newspapers, and therefore might be better off waiting to see if the bonds rise in price. Simply put, Southmark and Freuhauf had their bonds downgraded within 48 hours of the bad news. By the time this information gets to the average investor, the bond's selling price has been discounted for the bad news.

UNDERSTANDING FAILURE

For most bond investors, a bond rating of BBB or better is interpreted as "put it in a safety deposit box and draw interest for 20 to 30 years." With junk bonds, however, downturns in the economy can be disasterous. Therefore, when investing in junk bonds, especially in margin accounts, it is imperative that the investor keep current in the high-risk bonds market rather than expecting his broker to do so. Section B of the *Wall Street Journal* lists all of the companies discussed in the journal. This is an excellent source of information on company status and economic conditions. Even industry economic conditions provide data on potential bad news.

Low-quality bonds have larger fluctuations than quality bonds when bad news appears. Consider the curves in Fig. 7-4. When the bad news appears in the newspapers, the bond price drops. The scared investor usually sells later only to find that he overreacted because the company corrected the situation. Often after the correction, the bond might be selling at a higher price than when the bad news appeared (i.e., Freuhauf Corporation).

As shown in Fig. 7-4, if the bad news cannot be corrected, then the bond price will continue to drop. Usually this type of decline is done in plateaus and the investor should bail out. These plateaus are critical because the bonds might still be paying interest and the investor can bail out at a reasonable price.

Sometimes, the investor is under a false illusion that simply because the bond has not defaulted on interest, the bond is a "good buy." Consider De Laurentiis Entertainment bonds with a 12.5 percent coupon, maturing in 2001 and paying interest on June and December 1. In March of 1988, the bond was selling at $220 and was not technically in default. The return on investment was 56.8 percent. Being a shrewd investor, you decide to purchase the bond. You are thoroughly convinced that the company will go into default at the next interest payment date of June 1, and you intend to sell the bonds in May of 1988 and collect the interest.

When you try to sell the bonds, you find that the buyers are offering only $100 per bond. If you sell the bond, you will collect the interest (from March to May) of $20, but your bond has depreciated by $120, giving you a loss of 54.5 percent. Had the bonds been purchased on margin, your loss would have been even larger. And had De Laurentiis announced in May that they would not make the interest payment in June, your total loss (without margin) would be:

Depreciation ($220 – $100)	$120
Prepaid interest (Dec – March)	40
Commission ($10 to buy/sell)	20
	180

Therefore, your loss would be $180/220, or 81.8 percent. It is true that some investors make fortunes investing in junk bonds that are on the verge of bankruptcy, but this should be done only by the experienced bond investor. At the low plateau levels, default is almost always imminent.

Dun and Bradstreet compile records of why businesses fail. Table 7-6 shows the reasons for the 16,794 businesses that failed during the recession in 1981. Table 7-7 shows the cause of failure broken down by industry. In the 1986 – 1987

TABLE 7-6
1981 Business Failures

Reason	*Percentage*
Inadequate line experience	11.1
Inadequate managerial experience	12.5
Unbalanced experience	19.2
Incompetence	45.6
Other	1.5
Unknown	10.1

Source: *The 1981 Dun & Bradstreet Business Failure Record*, used with permission.

TABLE 7-7
Causes of Business Failures

Cause	*Manufacturing*	*Wholesale*	*Retail*	*Construction*	*Commercial Services*
Inadequate Sales	58	59	61	64	50
Heavy operating expense	33	26	22	22	30
Receivables difficulties	12	12	2	9	5
Inventory difficulties	5	11	12	1	1
Excess fixed assets	5	2	3	2	6
Poor location	1	1	4	1	2
Competitive weakness	15	17	18	15	16

Note: Totals may exceed 100 percent because some failures are due to several causes.

Source: *The 1981 Dun & Bradstreet Business Failure Record*, used with permission.

Dun and Bradstreet report, categories for failure causes were listed as follows:[2]

Neglect Causes
Bad habits
Business conflicts
Family problems
Lack of interest
Marital problems
Occupational conflicts
Poor health

Experience Causes
Incompetence
Lack of line experience
Lack of managerial experience
Unbalanced experience

Sales Causes
Competitively weak

[2] *The 1987 Dun and Bradstreet Failure Record*, used with permission.

Disaster Causes
Act of God
Burglary
Employee fraud
Fire
Death of owner
Strike

Fraud Causes
Embezzlement
False agreement
False statement
Irregular disposal of assets
Misleading name
Premeditated overbuy

Economic Factors Causes
Insufficient profits
High interest rates
Loss of market
No consumer spending
No future

Economic decline
Inadequate sales
Inventory difficulties
Poor location

Expenses Causes
Burdensome institutional debt
Heavy operating expenses

Customer Causes
Receivables difficulties
Too few customers

Assets Causes
Excessive fixed assets
Overexpansion

Capital Causes
Burdensome contracts
Excessive withdrawals
Inadequate start capacity

THE ROUTE AWAY FROM FAILURE[3]

When a company becomes a financial failure, a remedy must be found to keep creditors at bay, otherwise creditors will file in the bankruptcy courts an involuntary petition of bankruptcy. Technically insolvent firms attempt either to extend or compose their debt. Extension delays interest and principal payments to give the firm time to overcome its short-term difficulties. Extension requests are sometimes made by companies not yet insolvent but anticipating such an eventuality. Lenders are more likely to respond favorably to a request for an extension made in advance because it demonstrates that financial matters are not out of control. Normally, all debt is extended for an equal period of time. Thus, all creditors contribute equally to the revitalization scheme. It is possible, however, that a disproportionately small lender might be able to exact continued interest and principal payments with the acquiescence of other lenders who prefer to extend their debt for a short period of time rather than push the firm into formal and costly bankruptcy proceedings.

---

[3]Harlan D. Platt, *Why Companies Fail*, Lexington Books, Lexington, Massachusetts, 1985, pp. 9–12.

A situation akin to this developed when International Harvester proposed a debt restructuring plan to its lenders. Several small banks, with relatively insignificant proportions of International Harvester's debt adopted a squeaky wheel policy, refusing to give in to the company's demands.

Debt composition involves lenders' voluntarily reducing the principal amount of the debt. The objective of composition is to permanently lower the firm's annual interest or fixed-charge requirements. Composition is designed to spawn a new environment in which costs are easier to cover because there is less interest to pay and profits are more easily earned. Lenders do not compose debt gratuitously. In exchange for composing debt, lenders often receive shares of stock or warrants to purchase shares at reduced prices. For example, in the International Harvester debt restructuring plan proposed December 15, 1983, $1 billion in debt would be converted into 70 million common stock shares, controlling about 63 percent of the company. In effect, composition converts debt into ownership. Composition is not an advantageous way to sell stock. Like a fire sale, damaged goods are being sold by composition. Consequently, the firm must discount the price of its stock below what it would sell for if there were no difficulties.

Frequently, composition and extension occurs simultaneously. For example, when a firm fails to make an interest payment or to cover a preferred stock dividend, it has begun to extend its debt. Immediately creditors are contacted, meetings are arranged, and a composition plan is proposed. All the while extension is occurring. Finally, a plan of composition is agreed on and debt repayment begins, or else the firm moves to the next step and enters the bankruptcy court either voluntarily or involuntarily.

The bankrupt firm, one whose real net worth is exceeded by its accumulated liabilities, has two choices: liquidate or reorganize.

When a firm is liquidated its assets are sold to the highest bidder, and the proceeds are distributed to creditors according to a specific plan. When a firm is reorganized, the creditors, shareholders, and representatives of the court come together and perform the miracle of rebirth. A company that has died is refashioned with improved financial and product characteristics and is reincarnated. The objective is to convert the dinosaur into an eagle. Of course, given the material with which they have to work, eagles often cannot be created. Something less, possibly a condor or a tortoise, is likely to rise from the ashes.

It is possible to create an eagle out of a dinosaur, though. Take the case of Toys-R-Us. After being refashioned by the courts and the committees of creditors and owners, the firm emerged as the dominant seller of toys in the Western world, selling almost 10 percent of all toys. Investors who paid $1 per share for Toys-R-Us immediately after it emerged from bankruptcy, today have stock worth in excess of $50 per share. Success stories like this one are typical. Many reorganized companies fail the second time. For example, HRT Industries, which is now in Chapter 11 bankruptcy proceedings, had been in Chapter 11 just nine years ago.

A general comparison of key aspects of each route out of failure is given in Table 7-8. Probably the most important difference among the four methods is that only in liquidation does the firm cease to exist. After extension, composition, and reorganization, the firm reemerges as a solvent enterprise. The longevity of this enterprise is, however, another matter. Liquidation is a solution of last resort because the firm's assets are often sold for less than their true worth in a liquidation sale. It is also true, however, that in an attempt to raise capital and lower debts, assets might be sold at deep discounts whenever a firm is in financial trouble.

Issuing new common shares is a common part of any company plan to emerge from financial difficulties. In some cases, (to create more equity capital and to reduce fixed-charge obligations) the shares are exchanged for debt. In other situations, new common-stock warrants (long-term stock options) might be sold to investors. Even when debt instruments are sold by a troubled company, conversion rights are frequently attached to the debt to allow the new lenders to convert the debt into stock and thereby participate fully in the company's recovery.

Creditors are not viewed as equals when a firm fails. Senior creditors are compensated before subordinated creditors, who are compensated before stockholders. Table 7-9 provides a simplified listing of the priority schedule for bank-

TABLE 7-8
Key Aspects of Failure

	Extension	***Composition***	***Liquidation***	***Reorganization***
Does the firm survive?	*Yes*	*Yes*	*No*	*Yes*
Do debt levels get reduced?	*No*	*Yes*	*Yes*	*Yes*
Do repayment delays occur?	*Yes*	*No*	*No*	*Yes*
Do all creditors suffer equally?	*Yes*	*No*	*No*	*No*
Do brankruptcy courts participate?	*No*	*No*	*Yes*	*Yes*
Do more common shares frequently get issued	*No*	*No*	*Yes*	*No*
Do the firm's assets often sell at less then true value?	*No*	*No*	*Yes*	*No*
Do parts of the company get sold to raise money	*Yes*	*Yes*	*No*	*Yes*

TABLE 7-9
Priority of Bankruptcy Claims

1. Costs associated with the bankruptcy, such as legal fees
2. Certain wages owed employees
3. Taxes owed
4. Secured creditors
5. Unsecured creditors
6. Preferred stockholders
7. Common stockholders

ruptcy claims. Because common stockholders are last on the list, their claims might not be repaid.

THE SWAP OFFERING

Companies with huge debt often look for alternatives in order to avoid bankruptcy or default. One alternative is to exchange the bonds for new securities or even cash. It is not uncommon for these new securities to be bonds or stocks. With an exchange for new bonds, the interest rate will probably be substantially below the existing rate. With stocks, the investor incurs an equity position rather than being a creditor. In either event, the investor could lose a large percentage of his original investment but might be able to recover somewhat. Of course, if the company's financial position continues to deteriorate, the investor could end up losing his entire investment.

An exchange offer often indicates that a company is in distress. It is also viewed as a sign of weakness. If the economy deteriorates to a recession or inflation, even marginally operational companies might be forced into making exchange offers in order to survive. If the economy continues to deteriorate after the swap, the investor's financial condition might be worse.

Based on the covenants on the bond, as much as 75 percent or more of the bondholders might have to approve the swap offering. Recently, the bondholders of Revco and Coleco turned down an exchange offer and forced the firms into bankruptcy, expecting to see better opportunities for financial recovery.

THE EXCHANGE OFFERING

Bankruptcy filings are an extreme nightmare for both the stock/bondholders as well as the corporation itself. Companies often exhaust all other possibilities before filing for bankruptcy or bankruptcy protection. The most common avoidance of bankruptcy is when either debt is swapped for equity (i.e., bonds are surrendered for shares of stock, which may or may not be paying dividends) or when the bonds are exchanged for other bonds.

Consider the exchange offer shown in Table 7-10. Neglecting the class B

OFFERING CIRCULAR

DE LAURENTIIS ENTERTAINMENT GROUP INC.

Offer to Exchange

$100 Principal Amount of
17½% Senior Notes due June 1, 1993
and 65 Shares of Class B Common Stock
for each
$1,000 Principal Amount of
12½% Senior Subordinated Notes due June 1, 2001
($65,000,000 principal amount outstanding)

THE SECURITIES OFFERED IN THIS OFFERING CIRCULAR INVOLVE A HIGH DEGREE OF RISK. SEE "RISK FACTORS AND OTHER CONSIDERATIONS."

THE EXCHANGE OFFER WILL EXPIRE AT 5:00 P.M., DALLAS, TEXAS TIME, ON MONDAY, JUNE 27, 1988, UNLESS EXTENDED (the "EXPIRATION DATE").

De Laurentiis Entertainment Group Inc. (the "Company") hereby offers upon the terms and subject to the conditions set forth in this Offering Circular (the "Offering Circular") and in the accompanying Letter of Transmittal (the "Letter of Transmittal", the Letter of Transmittal together with the Offering Circular constitute the "Exchange Offer"), to exchange $100 principal amount of a new issue of 17½% Senior Notes due June 1, 1993 of the Company ("New Notes") and 65 shares of a new class of common stock of the Company to be authorized as Class B Common Stock, par value $.01 (the "Class B Common") or if the Class B Common is not authorized within 90 days of the Expiration Date, 65 shares of the Company's $.01 par value Common Stock ("Common Stock") for each $1000 principal amount of the Company's 12½% Senior Subordinated Notes due June 1, 2001 ("Old Notes") validly tendered prior to the Expiration Date. See "The Exchange Offer — Terms of the Exchange Offer." *(Continued on following page)*

NEITHER THIS TRANSACTION NOR THE SECURITIES OFFERED HEREBY HAVE BEEN APPROVED OR DISAPPROVED BY THE SECURITIES AND EXCHANGE COMMISSION, NOR HAS THE COMMISSION PASSED UPON THE FAIRNESS OR MERITS OF THIS TRANSACTION OR UPON THE ACCURACY OR ADEQUACY OF THE INFORMATION CONTAINED IN THIS DOCUMENT. ANY REPRESENTATION TO THE CONTRARY IS UNLAWFUL.

The Board of Directors of the Company has unanimously approved the making of the Exchange Offer. However, neither the Company nor its Board of Directors is making any recommendation to any holder of Old Notes to tender Old Notes pursuant to the Exchange Offer. Each holder of Old Notes should make his own decision whether to tender his Old Notes after reading this Offering Circular.

The date of this Offering Circular is June 1, 1988.

Fig. 7-6. *An exchange prospectus.*

shares of common stock, the De Laurentiis Group is offering to provide the holders of each 12.5 percent bond with a new bond that pays 17.5 percent and matures in 1993. Unfortunately, for each $1,000 principal of the old bonds, you will receive $100 principal of new bonds, but at a higher interest rate. In effect, if the bondholders accept this offer, then De Laurentiis will be reducing its outstanding debt from $65 million to $6.5 million, a 90 percent reduction. Likewise, the annual interest paid is reduced from $8,125,000 to $1,137,500.

In the past, bondholders would accept the offer without question. Today, bondholders seem more willing to let companies go into bankruptcy hoping that they can do better. In the case of De Laurentiis, a minimum of 75 percent of the principal of the outstanding bonds (i.e., $48,750,000) was needed for approval. The 75 percent minimum was never met.

At Revco, the situation was somewhat different. Revco hired Drexel Burnham Lambert to offer an exchange of $703 million in junk bonds for equity (i.e., stock) in the company. The exchange offer never took place.

The bondholders pressed for accelerated payments of the overdue interest as well as for the face amount of the bonds. This forced Revco to file for bankruptcy. Perhaps the best example of bondholder pressure occurred with American Brands:[4]

"While well-regarded in some circles, Meshulam Riklis, former registered representative, promoter and businessman extraordinary, has never rated very high around here. On the contrary, a quarter-century ago, *Barron's*, on several occasions, chose to criticize the freewheeling executive's tendency to make extravagant projections of sales and earnings, use excessive leverage to gain his ends and generally engage in what a less debased day-and-age tended to frown on as frenzied finance. Our modest journalistic efforts, by the way, earned us at least a footnote to U.S. corporate history. In *The Magic of Mergers—The Saga of Meshulam Riklis*, published in the late sixties, a wide-eyed biographer credited us with (or blamed us for) nearly bringing down Riklis's Rapid American McCrory house of cards. Little did we realize that the man was simply ahead of his time.

Long before anyone ever heard of Mike Milken or Drexel Burnham, in short, Meshulam Riklis was showing the cockeyed world of finance a thing or two about the possibilities of high-risk, low-quality credit. So it's no more than right that he should be playing a major role, albeit an unwontedly low-profile one, in the hot new controversy that has erupted in the fast-growing market for junk bonds. Early last month, American Brands Inc. announced the sale of its recently acquired subsidiary, E-II Holdings, to an affiliate of privately owned Riklis Family Corp. Thereby it also triggered a lawsuit—Forstmann Leff Associates Inc., Columbia Savings & Loan Association, Prudential Insurance Co. of American and CNA Insurance Co., Plaintiffs, vs. American Brands Inc., AMBR Holdings Inc. and E-II Holdings Inc., Defendants—that promises to have sweeping implications for all buyers and sellers of stocks and bonds.

---

[4]The remainder of this section has been reprinted from Robert M. Bleiberg, "Bondholders Unite," *Barron's* July 4, 1988, p. 9.

Plaintiffs—which all told, apparently owned nearly half a billion dollars worth of senior subordinated notes and subordinated debentures of E-II Holdings—allege that the transaction caused them grievous financial harm. Specifically, by substituting the less-desirable credit standing of Riklis Family Group for that of American Brands, it swiftly let to a sharp markdown, exceeding $50 million, in the marketplace. Plaintiffs further claim that despite official assurances by American Brands in January that it planned to establish and operate E-II Holdings as ''core businesses,'' the parent company six months later turned around and made the deal with Riklis, thereby committing several violations of the securities laws that require prompt judicial relief.

Defendants counter that by acquiring E-II Holdings last winter, they didn't assume responsibility for the $1.5 billion in junk bonds that it had floated. Moreover, they point out that in January, they made a bona fide offer, at prices a few points above par, to redeem all of E-II's outstanding fixed-income obligations and were turned down. At a hearing in federal court last week, the judge ruled in their favor and denied plaintiffs' motion for a temporary restraining order against the sale. The legal action is scheduled to resume next week.

Connoisseures of fine irony have already had a field day. They gleefully observe that the $1.5 billion in subordinated debentures and notes were issued by E-II to help finance its proposed takeover of American Brands, an effort that came to an abrupt and perhaps inglorious (but high lucrative) end when the target, in what has come to be known as the PAC-Man defense, snapped up the predator instead.

They chortle over the fact that the institutions bringing the lawsuit—Forstmann Leff, Columbia Savings & Loan, Prudential Insurance and CNA—happen to be huge investors in junk bonds. As such, if anything, they should have been more keenly aware than most of the high risk, including what is known in the trade as event risk, which the purchase of such high-yield securities is bond to entail. ''My gums bleed for these people,'' said James Grant, who has made a career out of chronicling the ups and downs of the junk-bond market, in an uncharacteristically caustic comment.

Well, yes and no. While it may be hard to work up much sympathy for ''crybabies,'' as a leading business daily said they were being called, what they're crying about—or decrying—should be a source of some concern. As we pointed out many months ago (''Bondholders, Unite!—Issuers Are Getting Away With Highway Robbery,'' *Barron's*, Nov. 24, 1986), the wave of acquisitions and mergers, while usually (even unusually) profitable for stockholders, all too often has wound up costing holders of senior securities dear. As it happens, 1986 ranks as the worst year on this score in financial history, with nearly $200 billion worth of bonds suffering downgrades. After a short-lived improvement last year, the grim trend—Eastman Kodak, Federated Department Stores and Fort Howard come to mind—has resumed. One can't—or shouldn't—keep robbing Peter to pay Paul.

As the sums involved in the pending litigation suggest, we aren't talking peanuts here. On the nearly $500 million of E-II securities that they hold, plaintiffs allege a heavy market loss to date. "Following the announcement of the sale of E-II to Riklis, the price of the notes precipitously dropped from 101.5 percent of par . . . to 88 percent of par on June 24. Similarly, the price of the debentures plummeted from 102⅝ percent of par to 89 percent of par over the same time frame." Estimated loss: More than $60 million.

To make matters worse, so plaintiffs plaintively cry: "There's no way to estimate the impact upon the market value of the Notes and Debentures if the proposed transaction involving E-II is consummated. Nor can plaintiffs fix their damages by selling their Notes and Debentures because the effect on the market price of these securities by unloading a large principal amount (about one third of the $1.5 billion debt offering) held by Plaintiffs is incapable of being ascertained. Such a forced sale would trigger a downward price spiral . . ."

In their misery, however, E-II's hapless holders have plenty of company. Our editorial in November 1986 spoke of "highway robbery"; it should have added the word "interstate." In 1986, Moody's Investors Service Inc. downgraded $191.3 billion worth of securities, issued by 246 companies, far and away outstripping the previous year's peak.

Last year, as noted, corporate credit quality took a temporary turn for the better. Specifically, as Standard and Poor's reports, it lowered ratings on $188 billion of debt (down from $217 billion in 1986—the two services evidently don't always see eye to eye). That casualty list was partly offset by the $85 billion in securities that won higher ratings.

Moreover, January 1, this ugly trend has forcefully reasserted itself. In the first three months of 1988, Standard and Poor's says that "downgrades swamped upgrades by more than two-to-one," with a net $46 billion worth of corporate debt adversely affected. "The largest industrial downgrade involved Eastman Kodak's $3.6 billion of debt. Kodak's credit rating dropped to A– from AA after the company acquired Sterling Drug Inc. for $5.1 billion. In turn, Sterling Drug's rating fell to A– from AAA." A clutch of bank holding company credit ratings also suffered. As to the June quarter, it includes such noteworthy casualties as Federated Department Stores and Fort Howard, among many others.

On the merits of the pending litigation, we have no strong views. Ironies abound, nor was plaintiffs' case helped very much by the "ringleader of the lawsuit," who last week was quoted as saying, "I'm the underdog here," and adding, "I don't know if we're going to win, but we're right." True, in documents filed with the SEC, defendants' management clearly disclosed that it planned to operate, rather than liquidate, E-II's subsidiaries, an aim that it reiterated as late as early May. Things change, of course, but usually not this fast. On the other hand, it's indisputable that last January, as part of its takeover bid, American Brands offered to buy all the outstanding notes at 103 percent of their principal value plus accrued interest and the debentures at 104 percent. However, sniffing a windfall—while not what it used to be, the credit rating of American Brands is far superior to that of E-II—investors pushed up quotations to 108-9 percent, respectively, and the deal fell through. As Jim Grant perhaps inelegantly put it, one's heart doesn't bleed.

Save that for the luckless folk who thought they were buying a quality credit risk, only to wake up to harsh reality. In a takeover, they may easily turn into part of the capital structure of a successful suitor with a lower credit rating. By the same token, a rejected deal that leads to a corporate restructuring, typically involving the buyback of outstanding common shares at a handsome premium, sale of assets and the issuance of a huge amount of new debt, undercuts existing bondholders' protection and diminishes their claim. Perhaps by coincidence, last week also saw the formation of the Institutional Bondholders Rights Association, a group designed to help institutions that hold corporate debt to protect their interests in situations such as leveraged buy outs that threaten the value of their investments. It has its work cut out."

STOCKHOLDERS VS. BONDHOLDERS

Bondholders and stockholders can be on different sides of the fence when a company files for bankruptcy protection or simply tries to avoid bankruptcy through drastic measures. The most common drastic measure is when a company tries to reduce debt by exchanging debt for equity (i.e., stock). Bondholders receive the benefit of at least receiving some value whereas stockholders find their equity position drastically diluted by perhaps as much as 90 percent.

Raising capital creates problems for existing stockholders. It is not uncommon for a company to come out of bankruptcy by issuing a large bond offering to finance its reorganization. Since bondholder interest payments must be made before stockholder dividends, stockholders suffer.

Another example of conflicting interests between stockholders and bondholders occurred in December 1988 when Long Island Lighting Company (LILCO) was found guilty by a jury of lying to the state utility regulatory agency to fraudulently obtain a rate increase. Before the verdict, LILCO had consummated a deal with New York State to shut down the Shoreham Nuclear Power Plant in exchange for sizeable rate increases and other financial incentives.

LILCO then planned to begin paying common and preferred stock dividends as long as LILCO could obtain investment grade ratings from Standard and Poor's. The existing bonds, with double-digit coupons and a rating of B, would then be refinanced at a lower coupon rate with part of the difference going to stockholders.

For current bonds, such as holders of the 12 5/8 percent, 1992 bonds, you can be sure that the bonds would be redeemed. The guilty verdict, however, might kill LILCO's chances for an investment grade bond rating, thus annoying stockholders. Bondholders would then still enjoy the high coupons as long as LILCO remains solvent.

8

Portfolio Management

MANAGING A PORTFOLIO IS NOT A SINGLE-STEP PROCESS. INSTEAD, IT IS A series of integrated activities designed to give you the most for your money with the least risk. For the managers of large pension funds, portfolio management includes a staff of full-time security analysts who are supported by sophisticated computer-based information systems. For the average investor, however, the risks are greater and the sophistication of information is much less, perhaps simply restricted to a newspaper such as *The Wall Street Journal* or Standard and Poor's *Bond Guide*.

SETTING OBJECTIVES

The portfolio management process is a series of four steps. These four steps hold true regardless of the size of the portfolio and include:

- Objective-setting
- Strategy Selection/Reevaluation
- Portfolio Analysis
- Corrective Action

The first step is objective-setting. The most common objective is to accumulate funds for a liability that will exist in the future, such as retirement, a new home, or college deduction for the children. Selecting the objective is critical because it becomes the basis for the ultimate strategy that is selected. Unfortunately, few people have really well-defined objectives when first starting out with bond investments.

If the objective is retirement income, then you might prefer a "safe" strategy of quality bonds. You must further decide whether you plan to live off of the interest or whether you might "dip" into the principal. If your bond portfolio is to supplement another retirement plan, then you might want to maximize your cash flow and use a given percentage of the portfolio for "mad money"—investments into speculative bonds. If the entire bond account is supplemental income for investments, then you might want to develop a diversified margin portfolio. In any event, it should be obvious as to how important it is to know your objective before you begin the portfolio management process.

Objectives can and do change over one's lifetime. A promotion, an increase in salary, an inheritance, and a change in retirement tax laws can cause your objectives to change. Therefore, it must be understood that portfolio management is an iteration process. Even changes in the cost of living or consumer price index can cause a shift in planning.

ACTIVE MANAGEMENT STRATEGY

Once you set an objective, the next step is to identify the appropriate strategy. There are two commonly used management strategies: active and passive. With an active management strategy, one always seeks to maximize the return on investment for a given level of risk. In other words, the investor recognizes that bond prices are *not* in equilibrium and tend to fluctuate over time. To benefit from these temporary price disequilibriums, the investor must be able to recognize situations where switching from one bond to another will achieve either a larger price appreciation or increase in yield. For example, assume your level of acceptable risk is in bonds rated BB or higher. You invest in a bond rated BB, with a coupon of 11 percent, and your purchasing cost is $800. This gives you a current yield of 13.75 percent.

Suppose that the bond is now selling for $960 thus giving you a current yield of 11.46 percent. At the same time, a new bond offering occurs with a BB rating, a coupon of 14.5 percent, and selling for $960. If you switch from the old bond to the new one, your current yield will increase from 12.46 percent to 15.1 percent. In other words, instead of receiving $110 per year in interest payments, you now receive $145 per year.

The second type of active management strategy focuses on changes in the marketplace. If you feel that interest rates will drop, purchase longer maturity bonds so you can maximize capital appreciation. If interest rates are projected to increase, you should purchase short-term bonds that are much less sensitive to interest rate fluctuations. Unfortunately, few people can accurately predict interest rate movement.

Another consideration in the marketplace is industry or sector analysis. For example, when LTV filed for bankruptcy protection, the bond prices for *all* steel products dropped sharply reflecting "sympathy" pains. A shrewd investor realizes what's happening and tries to take advantage of these temporarily deflated prices.

The difficulty with active management strategies is that it takes a lot of time. The investor must be current on bond prices and market conditions in order to benefit from opportunities. Sometimes, the opportunity window might be less than a day or two.

PASSIVE MANAGEMENT STRATEGIES

Active management strategies maximize yields by controlling or manipulating the level of risk. With passive management strategies, the minimum acceptable return is identified and the investor selects the highest-quality levels to achieve this minimum return. For example, John has $150,000 that he wants to invest in bonds. John plans on retiring in five years and would like to withdraw $22,000 in interest, without touching the principal. Let us assume the following yields are available:

Bond Quality	*Yields %*
AA	9.3
A	9.6
BBB	10.3

If John invests in BBB-rated bonds, and reinvests the semiannual interest payments in the same bonds yielding 10.3 percent, then in five years the annual interest payment would be $25,223. This obviously satisfies John's requirement of $22,000. If John upgrades to A-rated bonds, however, then in five years his annual interest would be $22,772. Using a passive management strategy, John might prefer the latter because his minimum expectation is met and his quality rating would be A rather than BBB. Should John find that his financial requirements are less, then he might upgrade to AA-rated bonds for an annual return of $21,760.

There are two types of passive strategies. The first type, and the simplest, is the buy-and-hold strategy. As the title implies, the bonds are purchased and held to maturity, regardless of whether or not the bonds could be swapped or upgraded for better results. Consequently, passive strategies have the disadvantage of missing opportunities as a result of interest rate changes or better yields to maturity. Also, it is assumed that the investor lacks the time or desire to maintain an active strategy.

The second type of passive strategy is indexing or index-fund strategy. Companies as Salamon Brothers, Shearson-Lehman, Merrill Lynch, and *Barron's* have bond index funds that are usually composed of high-grade quality bonds. Tables 8-1 and 8-2 shows the Barron's Index. Figure 6-1 shows the breakdown by sector of the Merrill Lynch *High-Yield Bond Index*. If the investor

TABLE 8-1
Barron's Confidence Index—Best Grade

Barron's Confidence Index is the ratio of the average yield to maturity on best grade corporate bonds to the intermediate grade corporate bonds average yield to maturity. A list of the bonds on which the confidence index is based follows:

Best Grade Bonds

Name	Coupon	Age
AT&T	8¾%	2000
Anheuser-Busch	8⅝%	2016
Balt G&E	8⅜%	2006
DuPont	8½%	2006
Exxon Pipeline	8¼%	2001
Gen. Elec.	8½%	2004
GMAC	8¼%	2006
IBM	9⅜%	2004
Ill. Bell T	7⅝%	2006
Proc. & G.	8¼%	2005

Source: *Barron's*, December 12, 1988, p. 139.

TABLE 8-2
Barron's Confidence Index—Intermediate Grade

Barron's Confidence Index is the ratio of the average yield to maturity on best grade corporate bonds to the intermediate grade corporate bonds average yield to maturity. A list of the bonds on which the confidence index is based follows:

Intermediate Grade Bonds

Name	Coupon	Age
Ala Power	9¾%	2004
Beneficial	9%	2005
Cater Trac	8%	2001
Comwlth Ed	9⅛%	2008
Crown Zell	9¼%	2005
Firestone	9¼%	2004
GTE	9⅜%	1999
Union Carbide	8½%	2005
USX Corp	7¾%	2001
Woolworth	9%	1999

Source: *Barron's*, December 12, 1988, p. 139.

believes that these index bonds represent the best for the money/risk, then the investor would purchase similar bonds reflecting the same portfolio characteristics as the index, thus assuming that a favorable risk/return trade-off would be achieved. The assumption here is that the investor would be hard-pressed to develop a similar portfolio that would out-perform the index for the same levels of risk/returns.

IMMUNIZATION STRATEGIES

Children receive immunization shots to prevent them from disease. The same principle applies to bonds. A bond portfolio can be immunized to prevent the disease of fluctuating interest rates. Immunization is used to minimize the *reinvestment* risk over a specific time period or horizon. If you purchase a bond with a 10 percent coupon, you have $100 to reinvest each year. When it comes time to reinvest the $100, current yields might be higher or lower than the 10 percent target based on current interest rates. Therefore, immunization strategies have characteristics of both active and passive strategies.

Immunizing a portfolio to fund a predetermined schedule of liabilities is difficult and might require computer solution. The process is somewhat easier when you consider immunizing a single bond. To illustrate the process, consider an investor who purchases a 9 percent coupon bond for $1,000. The bond has 10 years remaining to maturity and the investor wants a total return of 9 percent:[1]

ILLUSTRATION: IMMUNIZATION OF A SINGLE BOND

Table 8-3 shows the total dollar return and realized compound yield for this bond from all three sources of return for six different holding periods and four possible changes in the interest rate immediately following the purchase of this bond. The target yield is 9 percent, which is the yield on the hypothetical bond. As can be seen from Table 8-3, if interest rates remain at 9 percent, then, regardless of the holding period, the total return will produce a yield equal to the target yield of 9 percent. However, if interest rates decrease below 9 percent, for example, to 5 or 7 percent, the total return and realized compound yield will be less than the target yield of 9 percent if the bond is held to maturity. The target yield is not achieved since the interest-on-interest component is less than the amount necessary to produce a 9 percent yield ($495). This, of course, is due to the reinvestment of the coupon payments at a lower rate. In fact, even if the bond is held for 9 years instead of 10, the capital gain realized is insufficient to offset the required interest-on-interest needed to produce the target yield. The opposite results if the bond is held for 1, 3 or 5 years. Although the interest-on-interest component is adversely affected by the lower reinvestment rate, the capital gain is large enough to produce a yield greater than the target yield. However, if the holding period is 6.79 years, which is equal to the duration of our hypothetical bond, the capital gain realized will exactly offset the lower interest-on-interest income due to the lower reinvestment rate, leaving the investor with the target yield of 9 percent.

If interest rates rise above the target yield, for example, to 11 percent as shown in Table 8-3, the opposite of what occurs if interest rates fall is true for holding periods above and below 6.79 years. That is, if a bond is held for more than 6.79 years, the interest-on-interest component more than compensates for the capital loss, resulting in a yield greater than the target yield. The capital loss

---

[1]Fong, H.G., and Fabozzi, F.J., *Fixed Income Portfolio Management*, Dow Jones Irwin, 1985, pp. 117–119.

TABLE 8-3
Holding Period Analysis

Income Source	*Interest Rate at Time of Reinvestment*	*Holding Period in Years* 1	3	5	6.79*	9	10
Coupon income	5%	$ 90	$270	$450	$611	$ 810	$ 900
Capital gain or loss		287	234	175	100	39	–0–
Interest on interest		1	17	54	105	191	241
Total return		$378	$521	$679	$816	$1,040	$1,141
(Total yield)		(37.0%)	(15.0%)	(11.0%)	(9.0%)	(8.5%)	(8.2%)
Coupon income	7%	$ 90	$270	$450	$611	$ 810	$ 900
Capital gain or loss		132	109	83	56	19	–0–
Interest on interest		2	25	78	149	279	355
Total return		$224	$404	$611	$816	$1,108	$1,255
(Total yield)		(22.0%)	(12.0%)	(10.0%)	(9.0%)	(8.6%)	(8.5%)
Coupon income	9%	$ 90	$270	$450	$611	$ 810	$ 900
Capital gain or loss		–0–	–0–	–0–	–0–	–0–	–0–
Interest on interest		2	32	103	205	387	495
Total return		$ 92	$302	$553	$816	$1,197	$1,395
(Total yield)		(9.0%)	(9.0%)	(9.0%)	(9.0%)	(9.0%)	(9.0%)
Coupon income	11%	$ 90	$270	$450	$611	$ 810	$ 900
Capital gain or loss		−112	−95	−75	−56	−18	–0–
Interest on interest		2	40	129	261	502	647
Total return		$ 20	$215	$504	$816	$1,294	$1,547
(Total yield)		(2.0%)	(6.7%)	(8.5%)	(9.0%)	(9.7%)	(9.8%)

* Duration of a 9 percent bond bought at par and due in 10 years.

dominates the higher interest-on-interest income from reinvesting at a higher rate producing a yield lower than the target yield for holding periods less than 6.79 years. Again, for a holding period of 6.79 years, the target yield is achieved, because the lower interest-on-interest income exactly offsets the capital loss from an increase in interest rates.

As can be seen from this illustration, to immunize a bond from a change in interest rates over a given investment horizon, a bond should be purchased for its duration, not its maturity. Therefore, if an investor has a 10-year investment horizon, a bond with a duration of 10 years, not a maturity of 10 years, should be purchased to immunize against a change in interest rates.

Immunization is said to exist if the total value of a portfolio at the end of some specific planning horizon is equal to the value expected when the portfolio was purchased. If the portfolio is fully immunized, the return will equal or exceed the promised returns. Keep in mind, however, that immunizing a portfolio eliminates the portfolio's interest rate risk. Immunization does *not* attempt to reduce any other risk other than interest rate risk.

REASSESSING YOUR STRATEGY

Some people are lucky in that they can maintain the same objectives and strategy for their bond portfolio over its lifetime. But for the rest of us, life's uncertainties often cause us to readjust our thinking. The most common reasons for changing strategies include:

- Interest rates increase to the point where the current yields of the portfolio bonds will not satisfy your future financial needs/liabilities. In this case, you might want to go to an active strategy that maximizes returns or to a passive, immunized strategy.
- Finding more free time to analyze your portfolio and make your own investments rather than using a broker. In this case, you would go from a passive to an active strategy.
- Finding that you have extra income and want to "dabble" in the bond market. In this case, you would go from passive to an active strategy.
- Accepting a new job that imposes severe demands on your time. Active strategies work best if you allocate solid blocks of time each date to analyze your portfolio as well as current market conditions and selling prices. Since your time is limited, you might want to develop a passive strategy.
- Finding that your financial picture has worsened to the point where you cannot justify the riskiness of certain bonds in your portfolio. To maintain a portfolio that includes high-risk or junk bonds usually requires an active strategy since bad news can cause the bonds to plunge lower in price. In this case, you might want to sell off the low-quality bonds and adopt a pas-

sive strategy at least for the time being. Passive strategies are well-suited for low-risk investors.

In each of the previous examples, it is obvious that your objectives and strategies must be in sync. If your objective changes, you should reevaluate your present strategy. Likewise, should you change strategies, you should reconsider whether you have the proper objective.

PORTFOLIO ANALYSIS

Portfolio analysis takes time and effort. The average investor believes that he does not have sufficient time to effectively manage his own portfolio when, in fact he does. There are software packages that can be used to assist the investor such as the portfolio management software that is used in this chapter and is offered in the back of the book. Using a portfolio software package, you can easily keep track of interest payments and dates, calculate the current account cash value, calculate the compound profit percent for your accounts, calculate your semiannual interest and accrued interest and much, much more. You can also print out helpful tables, including:

- Bond data information
- Semimonthly coupon payments
- Payoff through to maturity date of the last bond
- Bonds that will mature each year
- Annual appreciation/depreciation as bonds mature

Other capabilities include:

- A credit list
- Updated bond costs
- Call dates and call prices
- Current yields, yield to call date, and margin yield to maturity
- Borrowed interest rate

Portfolio management software can make managing your own financial needs simple and more efficient, and I recommend you use one, even if you'll be using a broker. Broker's can't be expected to analyze all of the new bond issues offered or the market to determine if they are advantageous to you. Everyone should take some responsibility for their own investments.

Portfolio analysis requires two inputs; first, the investor must know the current selling price for the bonds and second, the investor must know any recent rating changes. Bond prices can be obtained from Sunday newspapers, *Barron's*, and *The Wall Street Journal*. Rating changes are listed in *Barron's* on a weekly basis and Standard and Poor's *Bond Guide* on a monthly basis. *Barron's* indicates rating changes only, but Standard and Poor's *Bond Guide* also includes those bonds removed from CreditWatch or placed on CreditWatch.

The best way to explore portfolio analysis is with an example. John Smith is 48 years old. He would like to retire at age 60. In June 1988 Mr. Smith invested all of his savings into a bond account. He purchased 136 bonds for $125,797.50 plus accrued interest. His portfolio has a return of 10.60 percent. Table 8-4 identifies the content of Mr. Smith's portfolio.

TABLE 8-4
Mr. Smith's Portfolio

Bond Title	*Quality*	*Coupon*	*Maturity*	*Quantity*	*Month*	*Day*	*Coupon*
Amer Medical	BB+	11.000	1998	2	Apr-Oct	1	220.00
Asarco	BBB	9.750	2000	7	May-Nov	1	682.50
Ashland Oil	A−	11.100	2004	2	Jun-Dec	15	222.00
Athlone	CCC+	11.000	1993	2	May-Nov	15	220.00
Balfour	NR	13.500	1988	2	Jun-Dec	1	270.00
Bank America	BBB−	8.875	2005	2	Feb-Aug	15	177.50
Bank America	BBB−	8.350	2007	2	May-Nov	15	167.00
Beth Steel	B	8.450	2005	5	Mar-Sep	1	422.50
BPNA	AA	10.000	2000	1	Feb-Aug	15	100.00
CEI	BBB−	9.850	2010	5	May-Nov	1	492.50
CEI	BBB−	9.250	2009	5	May-Nov	1	462.50
Citicorp	AA	8.125	2007	2	Jan-Jul	1	162.50
Comdisco	BBB−	9.650	2002	3	May-Nov	1	289.50
Comm Edison	BBB+	8.250	2007	1	June-Dec	1	82.50
Comm Edison	BBB+	12.125	2013	2	May-Nov	1	242.50
Cons Power	BBB−	9.750	2006	2	Jan-Jul	1	195.00
Detroit Ed	BBB	9.875	2004	8	May-Nov	1	790.00
Duquesne Lt	BBB	10.125	2009	3	Feb-Aug	1	303.75
Fairchild	B+	9.750	1998	3	Apr-Oct	1	292.50
Fireman Fund	AA−	9.625	2016	1	Apr-Oct	15	96.25
Fuqua	B	9.875	1997	1	Mar-Sep	15	98.75
Georgia Pwr	BBB	9.875	2006	1	Jan-Jul	1	98.75
Georgia Pwr	BBB	10.500	2009	3	Feb-Aug	1	315.00
Georgia Pwr	BBB	11.000	2009	1	Apr-Oct	1	110.00
GMAC	AA−	9.750	2003	2	May-Nov	1	195.00
Inland Steel	BB−	7.900	2007	4	Jan-Jul	15	316.00
Integr Res	BBB−	10.750	1996	4	Apr-Oct	15	430.00
Jersey Power	BBB+	9.000	2008	1	Feb-Aug	1	90.00
Manu Hanover	BBB	8.125	2004	3	Mar-Sep	1	243.75
Manu Hanover	BBB	8.125	2007	6	Feb-Aug	15	487.50
Marathon Oil	BB+	8.500	2006	2	May-Nov	1	170.00
Mattel	CCC+	11.625	2003	3	Apr-Oct	15	348.75
McDermott	BB+	10.000	2003	7	Apr-Oct	1	700.00
Mellon	A−	8.600	2009	3	Jun-Dec	15	258.00
Nat Medical	BBB+	12.000	2000	1	Feb-Aug	15	120.00
Niag Mohawk	BBB+	10.200	2005	3	Mar-Sep	1	306.00

(Table 8-4. continued.)

Bond Title	*Quality*	*Coupon*	*Maturity*	*Quantity*	*Month*	*Day*	*Coupon*
Occidental	BBB	10.000	1991	5	Mar-Sep	15	500.00
Ohio Edison	BBB	11.875	2010	2	Jun-Dec	15	237.50
Oppenheimer	NR	12.750	2002	2	Jun-Dec	15	255.00
Pac Gas/Elec	A+	9.125	2006	1	Jun-Dec	1	91.25
Phil Electr.	BBB−	11.000	2011	2	Apr-Oct	1	220.00
Phil Electr.	BBB−	9.625	2002	2	Feb-Aug	1	192.50
Pier One	B	11.500	2003	2	Jan-Jul	15	230.00
Ramada	B−	10.000	1993	2	Mar-Sep	1	200.00
Rochester Gas	BBB+	8.375	2007	1	Mar-Sep	15	83.75
Shearson	A	10.750	2003	3	Mar-Sep	1	322.50
So. Pacific	BBB	10.350	1994	1	Jan-Jul	1	103.50
St. Regis	BBB	10.625	2010	1	Jun-Dec	15	106.25
Toledo Edisn	BBB−	9.625	2008	2	Apr-Oct	1	192.50
Union Carbid	BB+	8.500	2005	5	Jan-Jul	15	425.00
					Total Annual Coupon Value		$13338.25

Total Cost of Bonds	$125797.50
Total Maturity Value of Bonds	$136000
Current ROI	10.60 percent

Mr. Smith's first concern during portfolio analysis is to verify that the proper interest payments are being made. Table 8-5 shows the coupon payments that should be credited to his account on the 1st and 15th of each month. Brokerage houses are not infallible. Mistakes do occur, although rarely. This table allows Mr. Smith to identify discrepancies.

Table 8-5 can also show Mr. Smith his incoming cash flow. For example, on August 1, Mr. Smith will be credited with $450.63 in his account. If he wanted to purchase another bond for his account, say at $800, he must deposit another $400 to his account. If he waits until August 15 when $442.50 in interest will be received, however, he can purchase the $800 bond entirely with coupon interest rather than using additional capital. Therefore, using Table 8-5, Mr. Smith can project those dates when additional bonds can be purchased such that there will be a minimum of non-interest bearing cash in his account at any time.

Table 8-6 shows Mr. Smith the cash value of his account at the end of each year and his retirement income. There are four assumptions made in the generation of this table:

- The "cash value" column does not account for appreciation or depreciation in the bonds. It is simply his initial cost plus the coupon payments received through year end.
- It is assumed that all coupons are reinvested in bonds whose average return is the same as that of the portfolio (i.e., 10.60 percent).

- The "retirement" column indicates how much money Mr. Smith can withdraw each year end *without* touching the principal.
- No defaults or redemptions are considered.

Since Mr. Smith wants to retire at age 60, he will be able to withdraw $47,000 per year beginning in 2000. If he wants a retirement income of $55,000 per year, he must either postpone his retirement for another 1.5 years, or provide additional funds to his account between now and the year 2000 to meet his target retirement income. The "retirement" column is independent of the purchase price or current selling price, and depends entirely upon interest received.

Table 8-7 identifies all of the bonds in Mr. Smith's portfolio including the current yield, total profit/loss, and weekly profit/loss. The current yield column can be used as a measure of whether or not to sell a bond. For example, the Pacific Gas and Electric bond has increased in price to the point where the current yield is 9.61 percent. Mr. Smith could sell the bond and use the proceeds to purchase an Oppenheimer bond with a yield of 13.42 percent. Mr. Smith would make a higher return but would have to lower his quality level.

The "total profit/loss" column and the "weekly profit/loss" column are used to spot a bond trend and whether or not to sell. For bonds that have appreciated greatly, as the Bethlehem Steel bonds, Mr. Smith must decide *when* to

TABLE 8-5
Mr. Smith's Monthly Income

Month	*Day*	*Coupon$*
Jan	1	279.88
Jan	15	485.50
Feb	1	450.63
Feb	15	442.50
Mar	1	747.38
Mar	15	341.25
Apr	1	867.50
Apr	15	437.50
May	1	1662.25
May	15	193.50
Jun	1	221.88
Jun	15	539.38
Jul	1	279.88
Jul	15	485.50
Aug	1	450.63
Aug	15	442.50
Sep	1	747.38
Sep	15	341.25
Oct	1	867.50
Oct	15	437.50
Nov	1	1662.25
Nov	15	193.50
Dec	1	221.88
Dec	15	539.38

TABLE 8-6
Mr. Smith's Retirement Income

Year	*Cash Value*	*Retirement at 10.60%*
1988	132466	14045
1989	146512	15534
1990	162046	17181
1991	179228	19003
1992	198231	21018
1993	219250	23246
1994	242497	25711
1995	268209	28438
1996	296647	31453
1997	328100	34788
1998	362888	38476
1999	401365	42556
2000	443922	47068
2001	490991	52059
2002	543050	57579
2003	600630	63684
2004	664314	70437
2005	734751	77905
2006	812657	86165
2007	898823	95301

take the profit. These bonds are currently yielding 10.76 percent and Mr. Smith must decide where he will invest the money *before* selling the bonds. Should Mr. Smith not find other investments that are paying 10.75 percent or more, then the bonds should not be sold. If Mr. Smith has losses of approximately $800, however, then he might use the sale of these bonds to offset the losses.

Table 8-8 can be used to show Mr. Smith what funds will be available in each year should all bonds go the full term to maturity without any early redemption. Ideally, with all other things being equal, Mr. Smith purchases bonds that mature in those years where minimum bond maturities occur. This serves two purposes. First, Mr. Smith's reinvestment interest rate risk will be minimized and second, Table 8-8 identifies the maturity cash flow should Mr. Smith decide that he needs to withdraw principal as well as interest.

Table 8-9 shows the portfolio quality breakdown. In Table 8-9, 69.1 percent of the portfolio is investment grade. This table can be used to identify the risk or exposure in a given quality rating level. The last column, "average yield %," shows the current yield for each quality rating level. As expected, the average yields increase as the quality level decreases.

Table 8-10 shows the breakdown by industry. The benefit of this table is that it shows Mr. Smith whether he has too many bonds in a specific industry. For example, 52 percent of Mr. Smith's portfolio is invested in two industries: bank-

TABLE 8-7
Total Portfolio Listing

Bond Title	*Quality*	*Coupon*	*Maturity*	*Quantity*	*Bond Cost*	*Last Sale*	*Current Yield*	*Total Profit Loss*	*Weekly Profit Loss*
Amer Medical	BB+	11.000	1998	2	105.000	98.500	11.17	-130.00	-37.50
Asarco	BBB	9.750	2000	7	92.393	97.750	9.97	374.99	-52.50
Ashland Oil	A-	11.100	2004	2	106.500	102.375	10.84	-82.50	-20.00
Athlone	CCC+	11.000	1993	2	97.500	96.625	11.38	-17.50	32.50
Balfour	NR	13.500	1998	2	100.750	94.000	14.36	135.00	20.000
Bank America	BBB-	8.875	2005	2	84.500	89.500	9.92	100.00	10.00
Bank America	BBB-	8.350	2007	2	81.250	85.500	9.77	85.00	25.00
Beth Steel	B	8.450	2005	5	60.725	78.500	10.76	888.75	-37.50
BPNA	AA	10.000	2000	1	100.750	101.000	9.90	2.50	.00
CEI	BBB-	9.850	2010	5	96.500	95.750	10.29	-37.50	12.50
CEI	AA	8.125	2007	2	83.750	86.750	9.37	60.00	-25.00
Citicorp	BBB-	9.250	2009	5	90.950	92.000	10.05	52.50	62.50
Comdisco	BBB-	9.650	2002	3	93.167	91.875	10.50	-38.76	-3.75
Comm Edison	BBB+	8.250	2007	1	81.625	85.750	9.62	41.25	2.50
Comm Edison	BBB+	12.125	2013	2	107.000	108.500	11.18	30.00	5.00
Cons Power	BBB-	9.750	2006	2	95.000	97.500	10.00	50.00	-10.00
Detroit Ed	BBB	9.875	2004	8	97.063	99.000	9.97	154.96	20.00
Duquesne Lt	BBB	10.125	2009	3	98.250	99.875	10.14	48.75	-48.75
Fairchild	B+	9.750	1998	3	89.917	88.000	11.08	-57.51	240.00
Fireman Fund	AA-	9.625	2016	1	97.000	94.500	10.19	-25.00	.00
Fuqua	B	9.875	1997	1	99.000	97.000	10.18	-20.00	.00
Georgia Pwr	BBB	9.875	2006	1	98.500	97.000	10.18	-15.00	.00
Georgia Pwr	BBB	10.500	2009	3	100.375	101.250	10.37	26.25	41.25
Georgia Pwr	BBB	11.000	2009	1	99.000	102.250	10.76	32.50	-2.50
GMAC	AA-	9.750	2003	2	98.500	99.750	9.77	25.00	-2.50
Inland Steel	BB-	7.900	2007	4	76.500	78.750	10.03	90.00	70.00

TABLE 8-7 continued

Bond Title	*Quality*	*Coupon*	*Maturity*	*Quantity*	*Bond Cost*	*Last Sale*	*Current Yield*	*Total Profit Loss*	*Weekly Profit Loss*
Integr Res	BBB–	10.750	1996	4	98.500	94.000	11.44	–180.00	40.00
Jersey Power	BBB+	9.000	2008	1	91.000	92.000	9.78	10.00	6.25
Manu Hanover	BBB	8.125	2004	3	77.000	83.125	9.77	183.75	–7.50
Manu Hanover	BBB	8.125	2007	6	81.250	81.750	9.94	30.00	–15.00
Marathon Oil	B+	8.500	2006	2	85.500	87.500	9.71	40.00	55.00
Mattel	CCC+	11.625	2003	3	97.000	92.000	12.64	–150.00	60.00
McDermott	BB+	10.000	2003	7	99.268	86.500	11.56	–893.76	–35.00
Mellon	A–	8.600	2009	3	81.250	86.250	9.97	150.00	15.00
Nat Medical	BBB+	12.000	2000	1	106.000	102.000	11.76	–40.00	–5.00
Niag Mohawk	BBB+	10.200	2005	3	99.542	101.500	10.05	58.74	15.00
Occidental	BBB	10.000	1991	5	101.475	101.500	9.85	1.25	18.75
Ohio Edison	BBB	11.875	2010	2	104.375	106.000	11.20	32.50	–20.00
Oppenheimer	NR	12.750	2002	2	99.000	95.000	13.42	–80.00	–20.00
Pac Gas/Elec	A+	9.125	2006	1	91.875	95.000	9.61	31.25	5.00
Phil Electr.	BBB–	11.000	2011	2	98.625	99.625	11.04	20.00	–2.50
Phil Electr.	BBB–	9.625	2002	2	96.125	95.250	10.10	–17.50	.00
Pier One	B	11.500	2003	2	99.875	95.000	12.11	–97.50	.00
Ramada	B–	10.000	1993	2	95.500	93.000	10.75	–50.00	17.50
Rochestr Gas	BBB+	8.375	2007	1	84.250	83.500	10.03	–7.50	.00
Shearson	A	10.750	2003	3	96.375	100.375	10.71	120.00	3.75
So. Pacific	BBB	10.350	1994	1	104.875	101.125	10.23	–37.50	7.50
St. Regis	BBB	10.625	2010	1	101.000	100.000	10.63	–10.00	.00
Toledo Edisn	BBB–	9.625	2008	2	94.000	93.375	10.31	–12.50	–22.50
Union Carbid	BB+	8.500	2005	5	81.375	83.000	10.24	81.25	25.00

TABLE 8-8
Funds Availability

Year	*Bonds Maturing*
1988	0
1989	0
1990	0
1991	5000
1992	0
1993	4000
1994	1000
1995	0
1996	4000
1997	1000
1998	7000
1999	0
2000	9000
2001	0
2002	7000
2003	17000
2004	13000
2005	15000
2006	6000
2007	16000
2008	3000
2009	15000
2010	8000
2011	2000
2012	0
2013	2000
2014	0
2015	0
2016	1000
2017	0
2018	0
2019	0
2020	0

ing and electric utilities. This might seem risky, but using the industry quality breakdown in Table 8-11, all of the bonds in these two industries are investment grade. (The "code" column in Table 8-11 comes from the classifications of Table 5-1.)

Table 8-12 shows Mr. Smith the yield to maturity, margin yield to maturity (based upon current borrowing rate), and yield to call date. The critical decision column in Table 8-12 is the "past call date." There are several critical decisions Mr. Smith must make:

- The current yield is greater than the yield to call date and the call date has past. In this case, the bond is probably selling over par and there is a risk of losing money should the redemption occur.

- The current yield is greater than the yield to maturity but the call date has not arrived. The critical question is whether or not the early call date will be executed. This depends upon the current interest rates and the coupon. For example, Standard Oil of Ohio has a bond with a coupon of 13$^{3}/_{8}$ percent and maturing in 1992. The bond has an early call date of September 15, 1989 at par. In December 1988, the bond was selling for $1,040 at a time when the prime rate was 9 percent. If you own this bond, should you sell it knowing that in nine months the bonds will almost assuredly be called in at par and refinanced at a lower interest rate?
- The current yield is greater than the yield to maturity and the call date has past. The decisions here are the same as the situation above.

TABLE 8-9
Quality Breakdown

Bond Quality	*Bond Quantity*	*Percent of Portfolio*	*Cumulative Percentage*	*Average Yield%*
AAA	0	.0	.0	.00
AA+	0	.0	.0	.00
AA	3	2.2	2.2	9.54
AA−	3	2.2	4.4	9.91
A+	1	.7	5.1	9.61
A	3	2.2	7.4	10.71
A−	5	3.7	11.0	10.32
BBB+	9	6.6	17.6	10.41
BBB	41	30.1	47.8	10.09
BBB−	29	21.3	69.1	10.39
BB+	16	11.8	80.9	10.87
BB	0	.0	80.9	.00
BB−	4	2.9	83.8	10.03
B+	3	2.2	86.0	11.08
B	8	5.9	91.9	11.03
B−	2	1.5	93.4	10.75
CCC+	5	3.7	97.1	12.14
CCC	0	.0	97.1	.00
CCC−	0	.0	97.1	.00
CC	0	.0	97.1	.00
C	0	.0	97.1	.00
D	0	.0	97.1	.00
NR	4	2.9	100.0	13.89
	136			10.54

Total Bonds Owned 136
Total Appreciation $686.16
Weekly Gain/Loss $547.50

TABLE 8-10
Industry Breakdown

Industry Code	*Bonds Owned*	*Percent of Portfolio*	*Industry Return*
Aerospace	3	2.21	11.08
Banking	18	13.24	9.83
Chemicals	5	3.68	10.24
Conglomerates	1	.74	10.18
Data Processing	3	2.21	10.50
Finance	6	4.41	10.88
Health Care Centers	3	2.21	11.37
Hotels/Motels/Inns	2	1.47	10.75
Insurance	1	.74	10.19
Jewelry/Silverware	2	1.47	14.36
Leisure/Amusement	3	2.21	12.64
Mining	7	5.15	9.97
Oil & Gas	17	12.50	10.66
Paper/Products	1	.74	10.63
Railroads	1	.74	10.23
Retail stores	2	1.47	12.11
Securities	5	3.68	11.79
Steel-Iron	11	8.09	10.61
Utilities-Electric	34	25.00	10.26
Utilities-Diversify	11	8.09	10.19
	136	100.00	

In almost all situations, the critical decision is what to do with the money should you liquidate. Obviously, if you receive a greater return for the same money without sacrificing quality, then you should sell.

Sometimes there are indications that a bond might decrease in price to a point where it is better to sell now. Table 8-12 indicates the bonds in Mr. Smith's portfolio that are on Standard and Poor's CreditWatch. The four bonds that are on CreditWatch with negative implications have the potential to be downgraded *below* investment grade. This might cause wholesale selling with a substantial decrease in price. Mr. Smith must consider these risks.

RISK ANALYSIS

Having analyzed his portfolio, Mr. Smith must now assess the risks in order to take any necessary corrective actions. The six risks to consider are:

- Interest Rate Risks
- Reinvestment Risks
- Inflationary Risks
- Liquidation (i.e., market) Risks
- Call Risks
- Default Risks

TABLE 8-11
Industry Quality Breakdown

Industry	*Code*	*Bonds Owned*	*Bond Rating Categories*									
			AAA	*AA*	*A*	*BBB*	*BB*	*B*	*CCC*	*CC,C*	*D*	*NR*
Aerospace	2	3	0	0	0	0	0	3	0	0	0	0
Banking	10	18	0	2	3	13	0	0	0	0	0	0
Chemicals	14	5	0	0	0	0	5	0	0	0	0	0
Conglomerates	17	1	0	0	0	0	0	1	0	0	0	0
Data Processing	20	3	0	0	0	3	0	0	0	0	0	0
Finance	26	6	0	2	0	4	0	0	0	0	0	0
Health Care Centers	31	3	0	0	0	1	2	0	0	0	0	0
Hotels/Motels/Inns	33	2	0	0	0	0	0	2	0	0	0	0
Insurance	35	1	0	1	0	0	0	0	0	0	0	0
Jewelry/Silverware	37	2	0	0	0	0	0	0	0	0	0	2
Leisure/Amusement	40	3	0	0	0	0	0	0	3	0	0	0
Mining	45	7	0	0	0	7	0	0	0	0	0	0
Oil & Gas	49	17	0	1	2	5	9	0	0	0	0	0
Paper/Products	50	1	0	0	0	1	0	0	0	0	0	0
Railroads	54	1	0	0	0	1	0	0	0	0	0	0
Retail stores	58	2	0	0	0	0	0	2	0	0	0	0
Securities	61	5	0	0	3	0	0	0	0	0	0	2
Steel-Iron	66	11	0	0	0	0	4	5	2	0	0	0
Utilities-Electric	72	34	0	0	0	34	0	0	0	0	0	0
Utilities-Diversify	75	11	0	0	1	10	0	0	0	0	0	0

TABLE 8-12
Yield Tables

Bond Title	*Quality*	*Coupon*	*Maturity*	*Quantity*	*Current Yield*	*Yield to Maturity*	*Yield to Call Date*	*Past Call Date*	*Margin Yield to Maturity*
Amer Medical	BB+	11.000	1998	2	11.17	11.32	11.32	yes	13.00
Asarco	BBB	9.750	2000	7	9.97	10.17	10.17	yes	9.42
Ashland Oil	A−	11.100	2004	2	10.84	10.70	9.68	no	12.03
Athlone	CCC+	11.000	1993	2	11.38	12.08	12.08	no	13.65
Balfour	NR	13.500	1998	2	14.36	15.00	15.00	yes	22.59
Bank America	BBB−	8.875	2005	2	9.92	10.61	10.61	yes	9.25
Bank America	BBB−	8.350	2007	2	9.77	10.66	10.66	yes	8.80
Beth Steel	B	8.450	2005	5	10.76	12.38	12.38	no	11.79
BPNA	AA	10.000	2000	1	9.90	9.82	9.82	yes	9.20
CEI	BBB−	9.850	2010	5	10.29	10.49	10.49	yes	10.36
Citicorp	AA	8.125	2007	2	9.37	10.17	10.17	yes	7.60
Clev El	BBB−	9.250	2009	5	10.05	10.47	10.47	yes	9.66
Comdisco	BBB−	9.650	2002	3	10.50	11.14	12.71	no	11.01
Comm Edison	BBB+	8.250	2007	1	9.62	10.50	10.50	yes	8.36
Comm Edison	BBB+	12.125	2013	2	11.18	10.86	10.86	yes	13.03
Cons Power	BBB−	9.750	2006	2	10.00	10.14	10.14	yes	9.50
Detroit Ed	BBB	9.875	2004	8	9.97	10.04	10.04	yes	9.42
Duquesne It	BBB	10.125	2009	3	10.14	10.14	10.14	yes	9.91
Fairchild	B+	9.750	1998	3	11.08	12.44	12.44	yes	12.74
Fireman Fund	AA−	9.625	2016	1	10.19	10.39	10.83	no	10.06
Fuqua	B	9.875	1997	1	10.18	10.52	10.52	yes	10.04
Georgia Pwr	BBB	9.875	2006	1	10.18	10.35	10.35	yes	10.04
Georgia Pwr	BBB	10.500	2009	3	10.37	10.31	9.14	yes	10.61
Georgia Pwr	BBB	11.000	2009	1	10.76	10.65	8.56	yes	11.77
GMAC	AA−	9.750	2003	2	9.77	9.79	9.79	yes	8.82
Inland Steel	BB−	7.900	2007	4	10.03	11.45	11.45	yes	9.60
Integr Res	BBB−	10.750	1996	4	11.44	12.23	12.71	no	13.81

TABLE 8-12 continued

Bond Title	*Quality*	*Coupon*	*Maturity*	*Quantity*	*Current Yield*	*Yield to Maturity*	*Yield to Call Date*	*Past Call Date*	*Margin Yield to Maturity*
Jersey Power	BBB+	9.000	2008	1	9.78	10.22	10.22	yes	8.85
Manu Hanover	BBB	8.125	2004	3	9.77	11.04	11.04	yes	8.82
Manu Hanover	BBB	8.125	2007	6	9.94	11.11	11.11	yes	9.32
Marathon Oil	BB+	8.500	2006	2	9.71	10.51	10.51	yes	8.64
Mattel	CCC+	11.625	2003	3	12.64	13.22	13.22	yes	17.41
McDermott	BB+	10.000	2003	7	11.56	12.60	12.60	yes	14.18
Mellon	A−	8.600	2009	3	9.97	10.73	15.29	no	9.41
Nat Medical	BBB+	12.000	2000	1	11.76	11.60	10.78	no	14.79
Niag Mohawk	BBB+	10.200	2005	3	10.05	9.96	8.57	yes	9.65
Occidental	BBB	10.000	1991	5	9.85	9.36	9.36	no	9.06
Ohio Edison	BBB	11.875	2010	2	11.20	10.95	5.54	yes	13.11
Oppenheimer	NR	12.750	2002	2	13.42	13.80	13.80	yes	19.76
Pac Gas/Elec	A+	9.125	2006	1	9.61	9.90	9.90	yes	8.32
Phil Electr.	BBB−	11.000	2011	2	11.04	11.06	13.51	no	12.62
Phil Electr.	BBB−	9.625	2002	2	10.10	10.46	10.46	yes	9.81
Pier One	B	11.500	2003	2	12.11	12.46	12.46	yes	15.82
Ramada	B−	10.000	1993	2	10.75	12.26	12.26	yes	11.76
Rochestr Gas	BBB+	8.375	2007	1	10.03	11.07	11.07	yes	9.59
Shearson	A	10.750	2003	3	10.71	10.68	10.68	yes	11.63
So. Pacific	BBB	10.350	1994	1	10.23	10.05	9.12	yes	10.20
St. Regis	BBB	10.625	2010	1	10.63	10.63	13.63	no	11.38
Toledo Edisn	BBB−	9.625	2008	2	10.31	10.66	10.66	yes	10.42
Union Carbid	BB+	8.500	2005	5	10.24	11.45	11.45	yes	10.22

TABLE 8-13
Bonds that Have Been Placed on CreditWatch For Possible Upgrading or Downgrading

Bond Title	*Quality*	*Coupon*	*Maturity*	*Implication*
CEI	BBB–	9.850	2010	NEGATIVE
Clev El	BBB–	9.250	2009	NEGATIVE
Ramada	B–	10.000	1993	POSITIVE
So. Pacific	BBB	10.350	1994	NEGATIVE
Toledo Edis	BBB–	9.625	2008	NEGATIVE

All fixed-income securities are subject to interest rate risks. Interest rates and price volatility go hand-in-hand. If interest rates increase, Mr. Smith must expect the cash value of his portfolio to decrease. His annual interest income will not change, however. Mr. Smith's first reaction might be to sell some bonds and hold on to a cash reserve to buy better (i.e., higher yield) bonds. When you consider the buying/selling commissions, together with the loss of interest income during the waiting period, however, Mr. Smith is probably better off holding on to the bonds as long as the bonds are income producing.

Reinvestment risk must be considered if large sums of money come due on a given date. Mr. Smith has taken steps to minimize his reinvestment risks by spreading out his maturity dates. Should Mr. Smith believe that interest rates will decrease in the near term, then he might want to purchase good interest-earning bonds now with borrowed funds (perhaps on margin) and pay off the notes with coupon interest.

Inflationary risks can be planned for by developing a diversified portfolio. Inflationary pressure decreases when you purchase lower-quality bonds, but default pressures increase. Mr. Smith can partially compensate for inflationary pressures by properly reinvesting coupon interest.

Bonds that are listed on the New York and American Stock Exchanges are generally highly liquid. If Mr. Smith suddenly had a need for cash, he could easily sell his bonds, but perhaps at a slight loss. For non-listed bonds, the liquidity risk increases dramatically. Factors that affect liquidity include:[2]

1. Amount outstanding (dollar amount of the issue of bonds outstanding)—the more the better.
2. Amount closely held (dollar amount of issue)—the less, the better.
3. Coupon level—the closer to the current coupon level the better because there is an investor preference for current coupon securities.

[2]Fong, H.G. and Fabozzi, F.J., *Fixed Income Portfolio Management*, Dow Jones Irwin, 1985, p. 43.

4. Age of issue—recently issued securities tend to be more actively traded.
5. Quality—the higher the better.
6. Terms (such as callability or sinking-fund provisions)—tend to reduce liquidity but if a bond is redeemed by being called, the call feature provides a potential liquidity source.
7. Maturity (duration)—fixed income securities with a maturity or duration of less than one year tend to be more liquid than any longer maturity/duration securities for any given issue.

Call risks can be prevented by purchasing noncallable bonds or by purchasing bonds that sell sufficiently below par such that an appreciable gain would be made should the bond be called. Bonds with high coupons have a high risk of early redemption.

Default risk cannot be entirely eliminated, even if Mr. Smith had purchased only investment-grade securities. Even good quality bonds eventually get downgraded to "fallen angel" status. Therefore, Mr. Smith must realize that the portfolio must be monitored for those bonds whose quality rating might be lowered.

CORRECTIVE ACTION

Mr. Smith must be prepared to take corrective action should the need arise. Typical corrective action steps might be purchasing high-risk bonds to fight inflation, purchasing low-risk bonds to balance out a portfolio, or to sell bonds once a substantial profit has been made.

Mr. Smith must also be prepared to take a loss. Nobody wants to sell at a loss. If Mr. Smith believes that the situation is deteriorating, then he must take his lumps and liquidate. It is often better to liquidate a deteriorating asset in order to purchase a quality interest-bearing asset than to play the role of mind-reader hoping the company turns around. Should you sell, you can always repurchase the bond if more favorable conditions arise.

9

Selecting a Broker

NOT EVERYONE HAS THE GOOD FORTUNE TO FIND A TOP-NOTCH BROKER. IF you do your homework correctly, however, it is possible to succeed. If you want to find a broker that suits your needs, it will take time and effort. You should select a broker the same way you would select a physician. After all, isn't the broker partially responsible for your *"financial health?"*

Brokers work off of commissions. This poses a serious problem in finding a good broker for bonds. The commission on bonds runs $5 to $10 per bond. This is extremely low compared to the commission on stocks. Therefore, stockbrokers would rather sell you stocks where your capital will turn over several times in a given year rather than offer you long-term bond investments. For the simple investor, good bond brokers are hard to find.

THE SELECTION PROCESS

Selecting a stockbroker is easier to accomplish if the investor is interested in stocks. But to find stockbrokers that are exclusively or heavily involved in bonds (i.e., bondbrokers) is much more difficult. It is true that brokerage houses have bondbrokers. Unfortunately, these bondbrokers deal exclusively with super-large clients such as pension fund managers who can purchase $5 to $10 million worth of bonds in a given day. It is equally as true that most stockbrokers can sell you bonds as well as stocks. But how much of a commission will they make from the average investor who might save $1,000 per month for investment bonds? That's a commission of $10 per month.

Step 1: Do Your Homework. The worst mistake an investor can make is to simply walk into a brokerage house and ask for a broker to help you open up your account. If the investor intends to "call all of the shots himself," then this approach might be acceptable, but the smart investor shops around. The more information you have, the more often you will make the right decision.

There is nothing wrong with asking your relatives, friends, and colleagues what they think about their broker. Even if the broker handles only stocks for your contacts, you might be surprised to find that the broker has bond clientele also. This information will come out during your interview. Talking to people is a good way of getting references. Your main concern should be the relationship that your friend has with his or her broker.

Step 2: Prepare to Interview Brokers. As with any interview, you must be prepared not only for the questions that you want to ask your potential broker, but also for the questions that the broker will ask you. Most brokers will ask you three questions:

- How much money do you want to invest?
- Do you plan to "feed" your account periodically with additional funds?
- Do you want to take risks, and how much of a risk?

To answer these three questions you must prepare your financial goals. Your broker cannot prepare a portfolio for you until your objectives are known. These are the typical questions you should ask yourself:

- Is this money for my retirement or is it "mad" money?
- Do I have any large expenses planned that some of the money will have to be withdrawn for? (i.e., marriage, weddings, college, home purchase)
- What are the tax implications for the money in the account? (i.e., your present and future tax brackets)
- Is this account to be an IRA pension plan or profit sharing plan? (i.e., tax exempt until withdrawal)
- Will the account be a margin account?
- Do I have other accounts?
- How old am I and what risks do I want to take based upon my answers to the above questions?

It is normally advisable to determine your net worth before answering the above questions. You do not have to be a financial genius to determine your net worth. Most banks will provide you with net worth worksheets that are used to assess your financial position when you apply for certain types of loans. You should also project your salary expectations and gross income for at least the next three to five years so you can budget for your investments.

Step 3: Interview the Brokers. When interviewing brokers, prepare a well thought out list of questions that you would like to have answered. Do not be afraid to ask difficult questions. If the broker wants your business, he will answer the questions to the best of his ability.

Insist on a face-to-face interview with each broker. Sometimes, it is easy to sense distrust and incompatibility when talking face-to-face rather than by telephone. If you feel uncomfortable with this broker, then cross him off of your list and proceed to the next broker.

When you prepare your list of questions, they should be categorized into two groups: questions about the company itself and questions about the broker. The following six questions can be used as guidelines for evaluating a brokerage firm, regardless of the size?[1]

- Who are the principal partners or branch office managers, and how long have they been at this location? Rapid turnover is not a good sign.
- Do these principals engage in community activities? You want a broker and a firm who are interested in the welfare of your town.
- Are you treated courteously and in a friendly fashion as a prospective client, or does the staff seem too busy to take much time with you?
- Does the staff seem to "turn off" when they learn you are a beginning investor with modest means?
- Does the office appear neat and efficient? Is the reception room comfortable or just a place for the pizza delivery person to wait until he is paid?
- Is the person who meets with you a senior, experienced broker, or are you assigned to a young trainee? (You're not always given a choice, especially if you have a new or small account.)

The following are typical questions that you can ask to find out information on your broker himself:

- How long have you been a broker?
- How long have you been with this firm?
- Do you specialize in stocks, bonds, or both?
- What types of corporate bonds do you like?
- Do you handle only wealthy clients?
- Would you be willing to work with an inexperienced investor such as me?
- Do you have other clients like me who are inexperienced bond investors?
- Will you consult me on decision-making or do you want full discretionary power?
- What are your feelings on risk?
- Are you knowledgeable on the junk bond market?

---

[1]Jay J. Pack, *How to Talk to a Broker*, © 1985, The Cloverdale Press Publishers, New York, p. 37.

- What's your opinion on margin buying of bonds? Today? Six months from now? Next year?
- What returns can you get for me assuming a reasonable risk?
- Will the results of your firm's research department be made available to me?
- If your firm underwrites new issues of bonds, will they be made available to me?

If the first interview leaves you with a feeling of comfort, do not make the mistake of not interviewing two or three other brokers before making your final choice.

Step 4: Select the Broker. When selecting a broker, there is a natural tendency to look only at those brokerage houses that are close by. This is often a mistake. Most transactions take place by phone. Brokerage houses accept collect calls if you are out of town. Today, however, most firms have toll-free numbers. Do not let proximity stand in the way of selecting your financial advisor.

The broker you select should be someone whose professional ability you have confidence in. The broker should be willing to provide you with advice and guidance and should take the time to do so. In a good working relationship, your broker will understand your needs and find you quality bonds that satisfy your needs. For example, if your broker knows that your investments are for retirement, then your broker will probably recommend bonds rated BBB or better. Pack has developed a list of pitfalls to look for in broker selection.[2] Avoid a broker who:

- Is patronizing or condescending.
- Promises to make you rich.
- Won't give you references.
- Uses a lot of jargon.
- Doesn't take time to discuss your financial goals or your appetite for risk.
- Has changed firms three or four times in the same number of years.
- Has had no previous experience and is learning with your money.
- Seems poor—you don't want to hire a broker who appears down at the heels and seems not to have made a success of his own career.
- Suggests you put all of your money into stocks.
- Deals with clients who have much more money than you.
- Puts sales pressure on you to buy a product or open a certain account.
- Doesn't return your phone calls.

---

[2]Ibid; p. 51.

- Says he's an expert in all areas of finance.
- Won't refer you to other specialists or experts.

Step 5: Open Your Account. When you open your account, there are two critical questions that must be considered:

- Should I open a discretionary account?
- Should the bonds be in my name or the "street" name?

Discretionary accounts allow the broker to buy and sell securities for your account. To do this, you must sign a *limited trading authority* letter, which will be kept on file by the broker. This letter authorizes the broker to buy or sell bonds in your account but not to withdraw funds.

Discretionary accounts often create headaches for stock investors because of fears that the broker will continuously buy and sell stocks to generate commissions. With bonds, however, there is little fear of this because brokers recognize bonds as long-term securities. If you find that your account has perhaps $900 in idle cash, then there is nothing wrong in asking your bondbroker to buy you the best BBB or better bond and not to exceed the $900 limit. It is not practical to ask him to find five or six choices and then call you for the final selection. If you have a $100,000 inheritance to invest, however, and want a diversified account, then you might want to be more actively involved, and your broker should understand this. Your broker has access to much more information than you do concerning the best available bonds at the lowest price, so it's important to work well with him.

The biggest trouble with discretionary accounts for bonds is when you invest heavily in junk bonds, especially in a margin account. Good brokers will always want you to have some degree of protection from maintenance calls and will usually recommend a highly diversified portfolio.

When you purchase bonds, they can be either in your name or the name of the brokerage house, or the street name. If the bonds are in the street name, the bonds remain in the brokerage house vault and your monthly statements identify your ownership.

If the bonds are issued in your name, then the coupon interest payments are made to you directly rather than to the brokerage house who would then credit your account. Generally, there is no interest charge for asking the brokerage house to leave the bonds in the street name. Actually, this is more convenient for both you and your broker. If your monthly statement does not indicate interest that should have been paid, your broker will trace down the problem and correct the discrepancy.

Step 6: Develop a Meaningful Working Relationship with Your Broker. The best way to destroy a potentially good working relationship is to impose unrealistic demands and expectations on your broker. For example:

- Your broker is *not* responsible for reviewing your monthly financial statements. This is your job. Your broker could have 600 clients.
- Place realistic orders for bonds. You will not be able to always buy at the lowest possible price. Your broker is in the best position to tell you what is a realistic buy/sell price for the next few days. Simply because a bond dropped in price by $40 yesterday does not mean that you'll be able to purchase at that price. You should give your broker the discretion to raise or lower the price by up to $10. It is unfair to place unrealistic orders and expect your broker to continuously watch these orders for you.
- Fluctuations in bond prices do in fact occur. Do not ask your broker for explanations. He's not a mind reader. If your bond account contains junk bonds, you *must* expect large fluctuations.

Pack has compiled a list of additional telephone "Don'ts" when dealing with brokers.[3] These apply to bonds as well as stocks.

TELEPHONE DON'TS

- Don't call every day and ask for a lot of quotes. (It's perfectly all right to call once a week.)
- People who are not very busy might get into the habit of calling their broker as a daytime activity. Consult the newspaper instead, and don't let telephone calls become a recreation for you and a burden for your broker.
- Don't call to ask for explanations about your statement, confirmation, or other paperwork without first trying to figure it out yourself. Call only if necessary, and then be sure you call before or after market hours. Try asking the broker's assistant first.
- Don't tell your broker about other stocks you or your

TELEPHONE DO'S

- Ask your broker's secretary or assistant for help on small details about your account.
- Send articles, clippings, and any research that you feel will be of interest to your broker. Remember that you and he have a partnership that involves judgment, information and market perceptions; it isimportant that you work together in these three areas.
- Call and offer praise when things go well.
- Pay for your securities promptly.
- Inform your broker of changes in address and marital statusimmediately.
- Tell your broker if you're going to be out of the country or unreachable for a long time so

[3]Ibid, pp. 78–79.

friends own, through other brokers, that are doing brilliantly. It will make him feel uncomfortable and put him on edge. If you know someone else who is doingmuch better, simply switch your account to that broker.

- Don't nag your broker about stock selections he made that have since dropped in price. Ask politely if he still feels the fundamentals are in place and if he is willing to hold the stock for you, and for how long.
- Don't complain that the market has gone up and your stocks have not. Instead, ask your broker if his recommendations for you have been special situations, such as takeover candidates
- Don't take credit for good suggestions. You will improve your relationship if you praise your broker whenever possible
- Don't ask your broker to do the research on a tip or recommendation from another person. Instead, ask him if he has any information he can contribute and, if so, to send you the material so you can make the decision. Many people feel their broker is a research library that can be put to work trackingdown obscure ideas. If your broker is interested in your information, he will automatically volunteer to work on it and follow up on the idea.

you can delegate authority to him to act in your behalf.

- Telephone if you are worried about a sharply dropping stock market. Your broker's experience and perceptions will be better than yours in a crisis.
- As you gain more experience you will be more confident about calling your broker. Meanwhile, don't be inhibited about calling him—but do be sensitive about why, when, and how often you call
- Be certain that there is no misunderstanding when you place an order. Know precisely what you want and what type of order you are giving. Mistakes are very costly and often are charged to the broker, which does not help your relationship
- You might call as often as you want to request that publishedinformation be sent to you. This type of research is readily available and can usually be sent out by a secretary.

10

Bond Mathematics

FOR THE AVERAGE INVESTOR, THE WORDS, "BOND MATHEMATICS," APPEAR to have a mystique all to itself. You don't need to be a college professor with a Ph.D. in mathematics or finance in order to understand bond mathematics. Although there are equations involving complex financial formulas, they are most often used by pension fund managers of whom a fractional change in interest rates or bond selling prices could result in millions of dollars. There are, however, relatively simple mathematical formulas that the average investor can use.

The purpose of this chapter is to eliminate the mysticism and provide the average investor with the necessary simple mathematics to manage his own portfolio. All of the equations presented here can be executed on just about any business or scientific calculator. Consider the three bonds below:

Bond	*Coupon*	*Year*	*Quality*
Ches. Pot. Telephone, W.V.	9.25%	2019	AA
J. C. Penney Finance	10.20%	1994	A+
Southern Pacific Co.	10.35%	1994	BB+

If you purchase the Chesapeake Potomac Telephone and Telegraph of West Virginia bond, you will receive $92.50 each year. If the interest rates increase, you might still receive $92.50 each year. On the other hand, other issues could be paying more. Also, in the above example, the Southern Pacific bond pays more interest but has a much lower-quality rating. This bond matures in 1994, whereas the telephone bond matures in 2019. These examples illustrate that bond mathematics is *not* a replacement for making decisions. Bond mathematics is simply another tool to assist the investor in making the best decision.

FUTURE VALUE

The concept that money has a time value is fundamental to all investments. Money has a time value because of the opportunity for investing at some present or future interest rate. Consider again the three bonds just discussed. On August 11, 1989, all three bonds were selling at par. Suppose you purchase the telephone bond at par and hold it for one year. At the end of the first year the value of your account will be $1,000 plus $92.50 for a total of $1,092.50. (Note: We are assuming here that the bond pays interest annually.) Assuming that the interest can also be reinvested at the same 9.25 percent, the two-year value of the account will be $1,000 + 2 × $92.50 + 8.56 = $1,193.56. The value of $8.56 is called interest on interest.

End of Year	*Cash Value, $*
1	1,092.50
2	1,193.56
3	1,303.96
4	1,424.58
5	1,556.35
6	1,700.31

In other words, you can say that the future value of the 9.25 percent investment of $1,000 would be worth $1,700.31. Consequently, the investment grew by 70.031 percent or $700.31:

6 payments of $92.50	=	$555.00
interest on interest	=	145.31
		$700.31

The mathematical expression to show future value of an investment is:

$$F = A(1+i)^N$$

where

F = future value, $
A = amount invested, $
i = yearly interest rate, in decimal form
N = number of years

using the date from the Telephone Bond,

$$F = \$1{,}000\ (1 + 0.0925)^6$$
$$= \$1{,}700.31$$

There are two assumptions made in using this equation. First, assume there are annual coupon payments, and second we have not accounted for any taxes.

In the previous equation, the expression:

$$(1 + 0.0925)^6$$

is the future value of $1 invested at 9.25 percent for six years, with interest compounded annually.

At the beginning of this chapter you selected three bonds, all selling at par, and with a coupon spread of 1.1 percent. To illustrate the effect of "going for the gold" with higher interest rates, see the results of each investment for six years:

		Bond	
	Telephone	*Penney*	*South. Pac.*
Principal	$1,000.00	$1,000.00	$1,000.00
6 Coupons	555.00	612.00	621.00
Interest on Interest	145.31	178.98	184.65
Six-Year Total	$1,700.31	$1,790.98	$1,805.65

As expected, higher coupon rates not only give greater coupon payments, but greater interest on interest. Also, it should be apparent that the interest on interest can account for almost 22 percent of the total interest received.

Since most corporate bonds pay semiannual, or even quarterly, rather than annually, the equation for future value can be modified to the following:

$$F = A\left(1 + \frac{i}{m}\right)^{NXm}$$

where m = the number of times each year when coupon payments are received.

Applying this equation to the Telephone Bond, see the following table for holding the bond for six years.

Interest Compounded	*Year 6 Total*
Yearly	$1,700.31
Semiannually	1,720.39
Quarterly	1,730.97

As you can see, with all other things being equal, the greater the frequency of interest payment, the greater the future value. Of course, it could be argued that the difference between annual and semiannual is only $20. Holding bonds for 15 to 20 years, however, such as a retirement account and by owning a large amount of bonds, this "small" difference could be measured in hundreds or even thousands of dollars.

FUTURE VALUE OF AN ANNUITY

An annuity is a sum of money that the investor receives at periodic intervals. The annuity is most often a fixed amount and might be in the form of coupon payments. The future value of an annuity is, therefore, the total sum of money accumulated after a given time period, assuming that all of the annuities are reinvested at a fixed interest rate. If the annuity instrument is a bond, then the total price must include the maturity value of the instrument.

For example, assume the investor purchases a financial instrument that will generate a $2,000 per year annuity for six years, and the annuity is paid annually. How much money will the investor have at the end of the six year period, assuming the investor can reinvest the annuity at 9.25 percent?

One solution to the problem requires application of the future value equation presented in the previous example. At the end of the first year, the $2,000 annuity can be reinvested for five more years:

$$F_1 = \$2{,}000\ (1.0925)^5$$
$$= \$3{,}112.70$$

where F_1 = the future value of the year 1 annuity.

In similar fashion:

$$F_2 = \$2{,}000\ (1.0925)^4$$
$$= \$2{,}849.58$$

$$F_3 = \$2{,}000\ (1.0925)^3$$
$$= \$2{,}607.92$$

$$F_4 = \$2{,}000\ (1.0925)^2$$
$$= \$2{,}387.12$$

$$F_5 = \$2{,}000\ (1.0925)^1$$
$$= \$2{,}185.00$$

$$F_6 = \$2{,}000\ (1.0925)^0$$
$$= \$2{,}000$$

Future value of 1st $2,000	$ 3,112.70
Future value of 2nd $2,000	$ 2,849.58
Future value of 3rd $2,000	$ 2,607.92
Future value of 4th $2,000	$ 2,387.12
Future value of 5th $2,000	$ 2,185.00
Future value of 6th $2,000	$ 2,000.00
	$15,142.32

Therefore, the future value of this six-year, $2,000 annuity is $15,142.32, where $12,000 was due to annuity payments and $3,142.32 was the result of interest payments. This is rather tedious, but fortunately there is a formula that can be used to speed up the process:

$$F = A\left[\frac{(1 + i)^N - 1}{i}\right]$$

where: F = future value of annuity, \$
A = annuity \$
i = Interest rate in decimal form
N = number of yearly payments

Using this equation, the future value of the annuity will be \$15,142, which agrees with the previous method.

To consider a second example, assume the investor has sufficient funds in his retirement account to purchase 10 bonds, which mature in five years. The bonds are somewhat speculative in that the current purchase price is \$885 per bond, the coupon is 9.75 percent, and the bonds pay interest annually. Furthermore, the investor wants to reinvest the annuity in a safer investment instrument paying 8.5 percent interest.

In this example, the annuity is 10 annual coupon payments of \$97.50 for a total of \$975. Using the equation above:

$$\begin{aligned} F &= 975\,\frac{(1 + 0.085)^5 - 1}{.85} \\ &= \$5{,}777.24 \end{aligned}$$

At the end of five years, the future value of the annuity will be \$5,777.24, which includes \$4,875 in annuity payments and \$902.24 in interest on interest. The five-year cash value of the account will be:

Asset purchase price (10 × \$885)	\$ 8,850.00
Annuities	4,875.00
Interest on interest	902.24
Capital gains (10 × [\$1,000 – \$885])	1,150.00
	\$15,777.24

In this example, the interest on interest and capital gains are 42 percent of the annuities. Since most bonds pay interest semiannually, the equation for future annuity value can be modified as follows:

$$F = \frac{A}{M}\left[\frac{(1 + \frac{i}{m})^{N \times m} - 1}{i/m}\right]$$

where m = 2 for semiannually payments and m = 4 for quarterly payments. Applying this equation to the previous problem gives a future annuity value of \$5,921.28, which is an interest on interest increase of \$144.84.

Asset purchase price	$ 8,850.00
Annuities	4,875.00
Interest on interest	1,046.04
Capital gains	1,150.00
	$15,921.28

Capital gains/losses can be an important part of the total annuity cash value. Consider an annuity package composed of 10 bonds with a coupon of 13 percent, a maturity of five years, and is selling at $1,080. Assuming a reinvestment rate of 9 percent compounded annually, the total cash value is:

Asset purchase price	$10,800.00
Annuities	6,500.00
Interest on interest	1,280.12
Capital loss	– 800.00
	$17,780.12

In this example, the asset depreciates by $800 as the bonds reach maturity.

PRESENT VALUE OF A FUTURE RETURN

In previous sections, I discussed the computation of the future value of an investment. In this section, I will reverse the process by calculating how much money we must invest *today* in order to achieve the future value. The amount of money that must be invested today is called the present value.

The concept of present value is fundamental to all financial investments. It is particularly important in evaluating fixed-income securities, as you will see later in this section. Previously, I showed you how the future value of an investment with a fixed interest rate can be expressed mathematically as:

$$F = A\,(1 + i)^N$$

If this equation is rewritten to solve for A:

$$A = \frac{F}{(1 + i)^N}$$

where A is the amount to be invested today to produce a future value, F. The equation can also be written as:

$$A = F\left[\frac{1}{(1+i)^N}\right]$$

where the term in the square brackets represents the present value of $1 in the future. This process is often referred to as discounting, and the interest rate is often called the discount rate.

For example, consider this investor, who has a liability of $3,500, which must be paid in four years. If interest rates are 8.75 percent, how much money must be invested today to meet this liability?

$$A = \$3{,}500 \left[\frac{1}{(1.0875)^4} \right]$$
$$= \$2{,}502.37$$

Therefore, if the investor puts $2,502.37 into a four-year investment instrument that pays 8.75 percent interest annually, then in four years, the value of the account will be $3,500.

As another example, consider that this couple intends to buy a new home in 3.5 years. The down payment needed will be $40,000. Currently, the couple has $27,500 in their savings account that pays 9.0 percent interest. Will this be sufficient to cover the downpayment 3.5 years from now?

$$A = \$40{,}000 \left[\frac{1}{(1.09)^{3.5}} \right]$$
$$= \$29{,}584.70$$

Because $29,584.70 will be needed to satisfy the future liability of $40,000, the couple will need to increase their savings by $2,084.70 to meet the liability.

The two examples presented here are lump-sum annuities. Most investors have a series of future values that must be satisfied. Consider an investor who wants to finance his child's college education. The university has informed him that his liability stream will be:

Years from Now	*Liability*
1	$15,000
2	17,000
3	19,000
4	21,000

How much money must the investor have on hand today to satisfy this liability stream, assuming that the current interest rate for his investment is 9.25 percent? Using the equation for present value, you can apply it to each of the liabilities and generate a table such as the one shown below:

Years from Now	*Future Value of Liability*	*Present Value of Liability*
1	$15,000	$13,729.98
2	17,000	14,243.15
3	19,000	14,571.00
4	21,000	14,741.22
		$57,285.35

Therefore, if the investor has $57,285.35 and invests it at 9.25 percent, he will satisfy his liability stream exactly. In order to verify that this is true, conduct a cash flow analysis:

Year	*Amount at Start of Year*	*Interest Received*	*Year-end Liability*	*Amount at End of Year*
1	$57,285.35	5,298.89	15,000	$47,584.24
2	$47,584.24	4,401.54	17,000	$34,985.78
3	$34,985.78	3,236.18	19,000	$19,221.96
4	$19,221.96	1,788.04	21,000	0

As you can see, this provides exactly enough money to pay off the liability stream.

Preset value can also be used to determine whether or not the purchase price of a financial instrument is advantageous. For example, you have the opportunity to purchase a 7 percent coupon bond maturing in four years and currently selling for $940. Is this bond a good investment if your target return is 8 percent? (Assume coupon payments are annual and bonds mature at $1,000.)

Years from Now	*Future Value*	*Present Value of $1 at 8%*	*Present Value of Payment*
1	$ 70	0.9259	$ 64.81
2	70	0.8573	60.01
3	70	0.7938	55.57
4	$1070	0.7350	786.48
			$966.87

From the above analysis, the present value of the investment would be $966.87, which is more than the purchase price. Therefore, purchasing this bond would be a good investment and your return would be more than 8 percent. Had the bond been selling at $980, the investment would not be a good choice. This same process can be used as well for bonds selling over par.

PRESENT VALUE OF AN ANNUITY

When the same amount of money is received each year, the process is referred to as an annuity. The coupon payment from a bond can be considered an annuity.

One way to compute the present value of an annuity is to use the process described in the previous section where you must calculate the present value of each interest payment and then sum them up. This can be a tedious process when calculating the present value of a 20-year bond. Fortunately, there is a formula you can use to calculate the present value of an annuity:

$$P = F\left[\frac{1 - \frac{1}{(1+i)^N}}{i}\right]$$

where F = the annuity value and n = the number of years.

Consider a 10-year bond with a coupon payment of 6 percent and which is currently selling for $790. The coupon payment is assumed to be annual. The investor wants an annual interest rate of 8.2 percent. The problem can be solved in two parts. The first part is to calculate the present value of 10, annual annuity payments of $60. The second part is to calculate the present value of a lump sum of $1,000 in 10 years.

For the annuities:

$$P = \$60\left[\frac{1 - \frac{1}{(1.082)^{10}}}{0.082}\right]$$

$$= \$399.00$$

For the lump sum payment:

$$P = \$1{,}000\left[\frac{1}{(1.082)^{10}}\right]$$

$$= \$454.70$$

The future value of the investment is, therefore, the total of two parts:

Annuities	$399.00
Lump Sum	454.70
	$853.70

The present value is greater than the current selling price of the bond, and is a good investment because the actual return will exceed the desired 8.2 percent. The same equations can be used to calculate the present value of bonds with semiannual coupon payments. In this case, however:

A = semiannual coupon payment
N = number of semiannual payment periods
i = semiannual interest rate

Assume that in the previous example, the interest payments are semiannual. In this case, there would be 20 annuity periods of $30 each.

Annuities:

$$P = \$30 \left[\frac{1 - \dfrac{1}{(1.041)^{20}}}{0.041} \right]$$

$$= \$404.12$$

Lump sum payment:

$$P = 1000 \left[\frac{1}{(1.041)^{20}} \right]$$

$$= \$447.70$$

The total present value is:

Annuity:	$404.12
Lump Sum:	447.70
	$851.82

Notice that the net present value decreased by almost $2 because of the semiannual compounding effect. The more frequently interest is compounded, the greater the return on the investment, thus decreasing the net present value.

YIELD ANALYSIS

In Chapters 2 and 4 I discussed the importance of calculating the yield to maturity. For example, if you purchase a bond for $900 with a 9 percent coupon, your current yield will be 10 percent. But what if you hold the bond to maturity? What rate of return or yield will you earn?

To calculate yields, use the equations in the previous section on present values. Unfortunately, the process is trial-and-error and might require several iterations. Generally, computers are used for exact analysis.

For example, consider a bond that matures in 10 years, has an 8 percent coupon, which pays semiannually, and is currently selling for $840. If you purchase the bond and hold it until maturity, what is your yield?

1. Select a very low interest rate such as 4 percent and calculate the net present value. Using the equations from the previous section, you would have:

   $$P_L = \$1{,}327.03$$

   P_L is the present value for the low interest rate of 4 percent (i.e., i_L = 4.0%).

2. Select a very high interest rate such as 12 percent and calculate the net present value.

   $$P_H = \$770.60 \text{ for } i_h = 12\%$$

the subscript $_H$ indicates high value of interest rate.

3. Calculate a new interest rate, i_m, such that:

$$i_m = \frac{i_L + i_H}{2}$$

In this example, $i_m = 8\%$.

4. Calculate the net present value using the interest rate i_m.

$$P_m = \$1{,}000.00$$

5. Establish a test convergence interval for P_m. In this example, assume that the solution is acceptable if the value of F_m is within +/− $5 of the current price of the bond. Mathematically, if $835.00 \leq F_m \leq 845.00$. You can then assume that i_m is the approximate yield to maturity. If P_m does not fall within this range, then proceed to the next step.

6. In this step, you must find either a new value of i_L or i_H based on F_m. One of the following conditions must be met:

$$\text{IF } \{850 \leq P_M \leq F_L\}\ i_L = i_m$$
$$\text{IF } \{F_H \leq P_M \leq 850\}\ i_H = i_m$$

Because the value P_m satisfied the first inequality, you replace i_L by i_m and proceed to 3. Repeat steps 3, 4, 5, and 6 as many times as necessary until the present value converges to the current selling price. You can then generate the following table:

Iteration	i_L	i_H	i_M	P_M
1	4.0%	12.0%	8.0%	$1,000.00
2	8.0	12.0	10.0	875.38
3	10.0	12.0	11.0	812.75
4	10.0	11.0	10.5	847.47
5	10.5	11.0	10.75	833.96
6	10.5	10.75	10.625	840.68

After six iterations, the process converges to a yield of 10.625 percent. This process is referred to as the binary chop method. The amount of iterations depends on the convergence accuracy requested.

As a second example, look at a bond that is selling over par. Consider a bond selling at $1,160, with a coupon of 12 percent and 7.5 years to maturity. Interest payments are semiannual. The amount of iterations will depend on the convergence accuracy requested. For example, look at a bond that is selling over par at $1,160 with a coupon of 12 percent and 7.5 years to maturity. Interest payments are semiannual.

Iteration	i_L	i_H	i_M	P_M
1	4.0%	12.0%	8.0%	$1,223.36
2	8.0	8.0	10.0	1,103.80
3	8.0	10.0	9.0	1,161.09

If the investor is willing to accept a return on investment of 9 percent, then purchasing this bond for $1,160 and holding it 7.5 years until maturity will provide this return.

Unfortunately, yield-to-maturity calculations do not always provide the necessary decision-making information for the investor. Suppose in the above example that the bond has a call provision at par four years from now. What is the yield-to-call date, assuming that the call provision is executed? Using this same process with a five-year time frame, you have:

Iteration	i_L	i_H	i_M	P_M
1	4.0%	12.0%	8.0%	$1,134.65
2	4.0	8.0	6.0	1,210.59
3	6.0	8.0	7.0	1,171.85
4	7.0	8.0	7.5	1,153.07
5	7.0	7.5	7.25	1,162.40

If the bond were held until maturity, the return would be 9 percent, but if the bond is redeemed after four years, the return would be only 7.25 percent.

HOLDING PERIOD YIELD

In the previous section I showed you how to calculate the yield to maturity and yield-to-call date. There were "promised" yields assuming that:

1. The bond is held to either maturity or the earliest redemption date.
2. All coupon payments are paid.
3. All coupon payments are reinvested at the yield-to-maturity or yield-to-call interest rate.

Item 3 above is the focus of this section. Previously, I showed you that the interest-on-interest calculation can be a substantial portion of the bond's total return, perhaps by as much as 30 to 40 percent. But what if the coupon payments are reinvested at an interest that is less than the yield to maturity? Obviously, the bond's total return will be less. This is referred to as reinvestment risk. The period of time that the investor possesses the bond is referred to as the holding period and can be substantially less than the maturity period. Two mathematical formulas can be used to calculate the holding period.

$$\$_c = C\left[\frac{(1 + i_r)^n - 1}{i_r}\right]$$

where: $\$_c$ = coupon plus interest on interest, \$
C = semiannual coupon payment, \$
i_r = semiannual reinvestment rate, decimal form
n = number of semiannual periods in holding period

In the expression, the semiannual reinvestment rate is simple interest. The second formula is:

$$i_{hr} = \left[\frac{\text{Total Future Amount}}{\text{Bond Price}}\right]^{1/n} - 1$$

where: i_{hr} = semiannual horizon return, decimal form.

The total future amount is the total dollar return (coupon payment and interest-on-interest) plus the price of the price of the bond (including capital gains/losses). For example, consider a bond that is selling at par with a 10 percent coupon, a maturity of eight years, and the coupons are to be reinvested at 8.2 percent until maturity.

$$\$_c = \$50\left[\frac{(1.041)^{16} - 1}{.041}\right]$$
$$= \$1,100$$

Total future amount:

$$\$_c = \$1,100$$
$$\text{Par} = \underline{\ 1,000}$$
$$\$2,100$$

$$i_{hr} = \left[\frac{\$2,100}{1,000}\right]^{1/16} - 1$$
$$= 0.04746$$

Because the holding period return is semiannual, you must multiply by two. Therefore, the total holding period yield will be 9.59 percent. This is less than the yield-to-maturity, which is 10 percent, because the reinvestment rate is less than the yield-to-maturity rate.

In the next example, calculate the holding period return for a bond selling below par. Consider a 9 percent coupon bond that is selling at \$825 and held to maturity, which is in 15 years. The reinvestment rate is 7 percent.

$$\$_c = \$45 \left[\frac{(1.035)^{30} - 1}{0.035} \right]$$
$$= \$1{,}806.79$$

Total future amount:

$$\$_c = \$1{,}806.79$$
$$\text{Par} = \frac{1{,}000.00}{\$2{,}806.79}$$
$$i_{hr} = \left[\frac{\$2{,}806.74}{825.00} \right]^{1/30} - 1$$
$$= 0.04166$$

Because this is the semiannual rate, the total annual holding period return will be 8.33 percent.

In the previous two examples, I assumed that the bonds would be held until maturity. Now consider holding periods that are less than the maturity period. In this case, the equations must be modified as follows:

1. Coupon interest and interest-on-interest are calculated until the end of the holding period.
2. The expected selling price of the bond at the end of the holding period must be calculated.

To calculate the expected selling price of the bond at the end of the investment period requires an estimate or knowledge of the yield-to-maturity and use of the present value calculations discussed earlier in this chapter. In other words, knowing the yield to maturity and the time period ***between*** the holding period and the maturity point, you can calculate the net present value (at the end of the holding period) such that the yield-to-maturity will be met.

The equations to use are:

$$P = F \left[\frac{1 - \frac{1}{(1+i)^N}}{i} \right]$$

where: F = the semiannual coupon payment,
N = the number of semiannual time periods remaining, and
i = semiannual interest rate.

The second equation to be used is:

$$A = \frac{F}{(1+i)^N}$$

where: F = maturity value,
N = number of semiannual time periods remaining, and
i = semiannual interest rate.

Therefore, the expected price at the end of the holding period is the sum of the two present values A plus P.

Consider a bond with a 9 percent coupon that is selling at par, and has a maturity of 10 years. If the reinvestment rate is 7 percent, what is the yield for a six-year holding period, assuming that the yield to maturity will be 8.5 percent? Coupon plus interest on interest:

$$C_{\$} = \$45 \left[\frac{(1.035)^{2}}{0.035} - 1 \right]$$
$$= \$657.09$$

Expected price at end of the holding period:

To calculate the present value of coupon payments,

$$P = \$45 \left[\frac{1 - \dfrac{1}{(1.0425)^{8}}}{0.0425} \right]$$
$$= \$299.87$$

Holding period present value of maturity price is:

$$A = \frac{1000}{(1.0425)^{8}}$$
$$= \$716.79$$

$$\text{Expected price} = \$299.87 + \$716.79$$
$$= \$1{,}016.66$$

Total Future Amount:

$$C_{\$} = \$\ 657.09$$
$$\text{Expected Price} = \underline{\$1{,}016.66}$$
$$\$1{,}673.75$$

$$i_{hr} = \left[\frac{\$1{,}673.75}{\$1{,}000.00} \right]^{1/12} - 1$$
$$= 0.04386$$

The annual holding period return is 8.77 percent.

HOLDING PERIOD YIELD FOR CALLABLE BONDS

If the holding period of a bond is less than the call date, then the mathematical expressions in the previous section can be used. If the call date and the holding period are the same, then the call price will be the expected price at the end of the holding period. If the holding period extends beyond the call date, then all proceeds must be reinvested at the reinvestment rate.

Consider a 12 percent coupon bond with a maturity of 15 years and selling for $1,080. The bond is callable in five years at $1,060, and the reinvestment rate is 8 percent. Assume that the holding period is five years.

$$C_{\$} = \$60 \left[\frac{(1.04)^{10} - 1}{0.04} \right]$$
$$= \$720.37$$

The expected price at end of holding period is the call price, $1,060.

Total Future Amount:

$C_{\$}$	=	$ 720.37
Call Price	=	1,060.00
		$1,880.37

$$i_{hr} = \left[\left(\frac{\$1,880.37}{\$1,080} \right)^{1/10} - 1 \right]$$
$$= 0.057$$

Doubling this gives 11.4 percent as the holding period return.

The next problem is the same as the previous example, except that the holding period is eight years instead of five years. The total future amount up to the call date is still $1,880.37. There are still three years remaining, however, in the holding period. In these three years, the five-year future amount will be invested at 8 percent, which gives:

$$(\$1,880.37)\,(1.04)^{6}$$
$$= \$2,379.27$$

This value is the total future amount to the end of the holding period.

$$i_{hr} = \left[\frac{\$2,379.27}{\$1,080.00} \right]^{1/16} - 1$$
$$= 0.0506$$

Doubling this value provides a holding period return of 10.12 percent.

Appendix A
Debt Rating Revisions: Aftermath of Mergers*

MERGERS, ACQUISITIONS, AND DIVESTITURES REPRESENTED THE LARGEST single cause of changes in debt ratings of industrial companies by Standard and Poor's during 1984. Standard and Poor's upgraded or downgraded ratings of long-term debt issued by 146 industrial companies, and about 25 percent of the revisions stemmed directly from merger, acquisition, and divestiture activity, including leveraged buy outs. Obviously, not all mergers and acquisitions or redeployment projects provoke a rating change. Indeed, at least 15 companies that were involved in major acquisition or divestiture deals during 1984 sailed through with their ratings intact. But at the very least, companies that are active in buying and selling corporate properties should be advised that their activities will provoke a comprehensive and exhaustive review of the ratings of their debt securities.

The triggering mechanism for this examination is that the redeploying company is undergoing financial, structural, and sometimes, a strategic change that could influence the credit quality of its debt securities, as well as those issues of an acquired business that may still be outstanding after a merger. Moreover, for a divested property that gains independence, there is a need to inaugurate ratings of the "new" company on a stand-alone basis. Standard and Poor's determinations result from an extensive analysis that probes not only the financial aspects of the company, including its leverage posture, but its operations, strategies, objectives, mergers and acquisitions policies, and other key elements of its business plan. Since debt ratings (which can be a measure of the credit risk premium

* By Gail I. Hessol Senior Vice President, industrial ratings, for Standard and Poor's Corp., who heads a group with responsibility for debt ratings in several industries. Source: "*Debt Rating Revisions:* Aftermath of Mergers" *Mergers and Acquisitions*, Winter 1985, pp.42–47.

demanded by investors) can be instrumental in determining the cost of capital needed to carry out the program, they never should be overlooked by the redeploying company. Thus, it is valuable for the dealmakers, lenders, investors, and corporate executives to know exactly what Standard and Poor's is looking for in sizing up debt ratings.

Analyzing an acquisition is stickiest for Standard and Poor's when both the acquiring and acquired companies have rated debt outstanding. Some prominent examples were Texaco Inc.'s acquisition of Getty Oil Co. Beatrice Cos.' acquisition of Esmark Inc., and Lear Siegler Inc.'s acquisition of Bangor Punta Corp., all in 1984. In each case, both companies had different debt ratings at the time the transaction was announced. Thus, the first question Standard and Poor's had to address was whether the debt of the parent and subsidiary companies should continue to be rated differently. Only then could we determine which specific ratings be assigned.

We decided on the same rating for both companies, although the changes had varied effects on individual issues. For example, both Texaco and Getty were accorded post-merger ratings of AA– on senior debt and A-1+ on commercial paper, but in both cases the senior debt ratings were downgraded from AA+ for Texaco and AAA for Getty. Both Beatrice and Esmark wound up with ratings of A for senior debt and A-2 for commercial paper. Beatrice senior debt was downgraded from AA, while Esmark was upgraded from BBB. Esmark experienced no change in its commercial-paper rating but Beatrice's caliber was downgraded from A-1. Increased debt leverage and the expectation that heightened financial risk would continue figured prominently in the Texaco and Beatrice rating acquisitions. Both Lear Siegler and Bangor Punta were given post-merger ratings of A– on senior debt, unchanged for Lear but up from B+ for Bangor. Lear Siegler's commercial-paper rating was moved down a notch to A-2 from A-1.

If the acquiring company explicitly guarantees or assumes its new subsidiary's obligations, those issues will be rated the same as the parent's debt. Memorex Corp. was a financially troubled company, with a low, subordinated debt rating of B–, when it was acquired by Burroughs Corp. in 1982. Because Burroughs assumed the Memorex debt on a senior basis, however, the rating of the acquired company was raised to Burroughs' level of A. (Both ratings were subsequently lowered to A–.) More common, an explicit debt guarantee or assumption is not executed. Nevertheless, Standard and Poor's generally assigns the same rating to the debt of a parent and its subsidiary. In fact, this is the policy unless special circumstances demand otherwise. This does not, however, preclude a change in the parent's outstanding rating, as was demonstrated in the Texaco and Beatrice cases.

Our rationale is pragmatic and somewhat subjective. The 1984 mergers of Jones & Laughlin (LTV Corp. subsidiary) and Republic Steel, American Medical

International Inc. and Lifemark Corp., and Chevron Corp. and Gulf Oil Corp. illustrate our thinking. The purpose of the acquisitions was to integrate their operations, combining the best parts of each and realizing economies of scale. Over time, it would be impossible to separate the financial results of the acquiring and acquired companies. Accordingly, their debt was rated the same. Again, the shifts were varied as to direction. Chevron and Gulf were accorded senior debt ratings of AA, both down from AAA before their deal was announced, reflecting Chevron's higher financial leverage. Each firm's commercial paper was unchanged at A-1+. Jones & Laughlin and Republic received senior debt ratings of BB+, with Jones & Laughlin unchanged and Republic up a notch from BB. American Medical was unchanged with an A senior debt rating, but Lifemark advanced to A– from BB+.

WILLINGNESS TO SUPPORT DEBT

When operating synergies are not apparent, our analysis is a bit more difficult and depends on whether the acquiring (parent) company is a stronger or weaker credit than the acquired (subsidiary) company. When Standard Oil Co. of Ohio, with a solid AA debt rating, acquired Kennecott, the copper miner whose BBB debt rating was decidedly tenuous, an equalization of the two ratings was not considered appropriate. The size and scope of Sohio's original and planned investment in Kennecott certainly represented a significant commitment on its part. However, because Kennecott represented a diversification rather than an enhancement of Sohio's core business, there were significant questions about whether Kennecott's negative course could be reversed; since Sohio was not willing to explicitly support its new subsidiary's debt, the circumstances suggested that Sohio was not willing to bet its own solvency on behalf of Kennecott. Therefore, the rating gap was narrowed, and Sohio's debt was assigned an AA– rating (down from AA) and Kennecott's an A– (up from BBB), reflecting both the drain on Sohio's resources and the benefit these funds would provide for Kennecott. Subsequently, Sohio agreed to guarantee Kennecott's obligations and the Kennecott debt rating was raised to AA–.

When a parent company owns a subsidiary that is perceived to be a stronger credit, rating parity typically results. Reluctance to rate a subsidiary's debt higher than its parent's stems from a phenomenon apparent since the passage of the 1979 Bankruptcy Act. In bankruptcy filings such as those of White Motor Corp., Wicks Corp., and Manville Corp., apparently healthy subsidiaries were included in their parent's bankruptcy petitions. The lesson was that a subsidiary is usually as close to bankruptcy as its parent. Exceptions could be banking, utility, or insurance subsidiaries that are protected by special regulatory safeguards. Other possible exceptions arise when subsidiaries are operationally and financially independent or when a joint bankruptcy filing would be uneconomic or impractical.

TABLE A-1
What the Ratings Mean

Long-term Debt

AAA Debt rated AAA has the highest rating assigned by Standard & Poor's. Capacity to pay interest and repay principal is extremely strong.
AA Debt rated AA has a very strong capacity to pay interest and repay principal and differs from the highest rated issues only in small degree.
A Debt rated A has a strong capacity to pay interest and repay principal although it is somewhat more susceptible to the adverse effects of changes in circumstances and economic conditions than debt in higher rated categories.
BBB Debt rated BBB is regarded as having an adequate capacity to pay interest and repay principal. Whereas it normally exhibits adequate protection parameters, adverse economic conditions, or changing circumstances are more likely to lead to a weakened capacity to pay interest and repay principal for debt in this category than in higher rated categories.
BB, B, CCC, CC Debt rated BB, B, CCC, or CC is regarded, on balance, as predominantly speculative with respect to capacity to pay interest and repay principal in accordance with the terms of the obligation. BB indicates the lowest degree of speculation and CC the highest degree of speculation. While such debt will likely have some quality and protective characteristics, these are outweighed by large uncertainties or major risk exposures to adverse conditions.
C This rating is reserved for income bonds on which no interest is being paid.
D Debt rated D is in default, and payment of interest and/or repayment of principal is in arrears.
Plus(+) or minus(−) The ratings from AA to B may be modified by the addition of a plus or minus sign to show relative standing within the major rating categories.

Commercial Paper

A standard & Poor's commercial paper rating is a current assessment of the likelihood of timely payment of debt having an original maturity of no more than 365 days.
A Issues assigned this highest rating are regarded as having the greatest capacity for timely payment. Issues in this category are delineated with the numbers 1, 2, and 3 to indicate the relative degree of safety.
A-1 This designation indicates that the degree of safety regarding timely payment is either overwhelming or very strong. Those issues determined to possess overwhelming safety characteristics are denoted with a plus (+) sign designation.
A-2 Capacity for timely payment on issues with this designation is strong. However, the relative degree of safety is not as high as for issues designated A-1.
A-3 Issues carrying this designation have a satisfactory capacity for timely payment. They are, however, somewhat more vulnerable to the adverse effects of changes in circumstances than obligations carrying the higher designations.
B Issues rated B are regarded as having only an adequate capacity for timely payment. However, such capacity may be damaged by changing conditions or short-term adversities.
C This rating is assigned to short-term debt obligations with a doubtful capacity for payment.
D This rating indicates that the issue is either in default or is expected to be in default upon maturity.

Note: *Standard & Poor's* ratings using *Standard and Poor's* language.

EXAMINING A BUSINESS' RISK FACTORS

When a company whose debt already is rated accomplishes a major acquisition or divestiture, the focus of our analysis is: What has changed?

The starting point is the company's business risk. U.S. Steel Corp.'s acquisition of Marathon Oil Co. in 1982, Signal Co.s' divestiture of Mack Trucks in 1983, and Time Inc.'s sale of its forest-products businesses in 1984 markedly improved the business fundamentals of the acquiring or divesting companies. In fact, the changed business risk was the most critical rating factor in these situations. Reducing a company's dependence on the steel, truck, or lumber industries almost always is a good move. But we are mindful of the many unsuccessful acquisitions, particularly when the acquired firm is in an unfamiliar and rapidly changing industry. These risks are weighed in the initial evaluation of an acquisition. Therefore, if the acquired company proves to be a disappointment and its asset value subsequently is written down, a rating reduction may not be necessary. Ashland Oil's acquisition of Integon, an insurance company, is an example of this situation.

An acquisition might also change a company's business-risk profile by altering its competitive posture. The spectacular 1984 energy company mergers were simply the least expensive way for some firms to replace oil reserves or rationalize their refining and marketing activities. Ralston Purina's acquisition of Continental Baking provided a new bakery line for Ralston's healthy grocery-products division, although Ralston's senior debt rating was lowered slightly, to AA– from AA, immediately after the deal. Acquisitions that truly strengthen or broaden an existing business are viewed positively.

It is almost axiomatic that an acquisition is intended to improve business risk. The trade-off, however, is its effect on financial risk. The decision to raise, lower, or maintain the acquiring company's rating is clear-cut only when the effects on business and financial risk are the same—i.e., both simultaneously improve, deteriorate, or don't change.

Because large acquisitions rarely are paid for with common stock today, financial risk is typically heightened. The extreme case is a leveraged buy out. No matter how undervalued a company's assets were before the leveraged buy out, when those same assets, with the same earning and cash-generating power are suddenly forced to service mounds of new debt, financial risk must increase. Business risk is, of course, unchanged. Leveraged buy outs were responsible for many of the sharpest reductions in industrial debt ratings during 1984. Metromedia Inc.'s debt rating was cut to B– from BB+, and Amstar Corp.'s to B from BBB–. Cone Mills Corp.'s commercial-paper rating was downgraded to B from A-1. More typically, some new debt and other sources of funds are used to acquire a firm that enhances the acquiring company's business risk.

The assessment of the combined entity's business profile leads directly to the development of financial expectations for specific rating categories. For simplicity's sake, I will focus on the financial leverage parameter. On the day the merger is consummated, debt leverage, within the context of the company's new business profile, often suggests its rating should be lowered several notches.

Thus, it is critical to determine whether this higher level of debt leverage is permanent. If not, how will it be reduced? Management of the acquiring company usually presents Standard and Poor's with a plan for repaying the acquisition debt and returning leverage to historical levels. Evaluating the credibility of this plan becomes the next key step in our analysis of the acquisition.

There are usually two ways to repay debt: cash flow from operations and proceeds from asset disposals. The stability of earnings is examined with special emphasis on the near-term outlook. Often a sensitivity analysis is performed with various macroeconomic assumptions. Overly optimistic earnings forecasts for its own or the acquired company's business have stymied many companies' debt repayment plans. Fluor Corp., for example, encountered profitability problems at its St. Joe Minerals subsidiary that was acquired in 1981 at a price in excess of $2.3 billion. These difficulties subsequently contributed to a reduction in Fluor's senior debt rating to A from AA. Our assessment of asset disposal plans is also hard-nosed. Can the company provide tangible evidence to support its estimates of realizable proceeds? Are the assets profitable and attractive to others? Metallurgical coal properties, Northwest timberland, or an aging oil refinery probably won't pass these tests. Proceeds from their sales cannot be relied upon to repay debt.

ACQUISITION POLICY COMES UNDER REVIEW

If we assume that management's projected cash flow and asset disposal plans are reasonable, that leaves a more fundamental question. How much financial leverage does management truly want to employ? Is this acquisition a one-time blip or will it be followed by others? Has management fundamentally changed its financial-risk philosophy? Beatrice's long string of acquisitions, culminating in the Esmark purchase of 1984, clearly represented to us a philosophical change—a desire to incur greater financial risk. A management's stated interest in sizeable acquisitions or a merger bid that fails might be sufficient evidence for Standard and Poor's to decide that financial policies have become more aggressive and that a rating change is warranted.

In a similar view, we might determine that an acquisition is not a luxury. Rather, it might be essential to achieve real earnings growth and to maintain an adequate return on capital. Most of the large energy company mergers in 1984 were simply substitutes for capital spending, and the resulting increases in debt leverage reflected the growing costs of finding hydrocarbons. Even without buying entire companies, few of the major energy concerns would have been able to maintain pre-1983 capital structures.

BALANCING THE SCALES

Occidental Petroleum Corp.'s acquisition of Cities Service Co. offers a good example of the analytical process Standard and Poor's puts into play in a major merger situation. When the acquisition was announced in 1982, Oxy's senior debt was rated BBB+ and Cities Service's was rated A+.

First, we concluded that both companies should be rated the same. They were both primarily in the energy business, and no legal arguments were offered supporting the segregation of Cities Service's operations, earnings, or cash flow. Oxy's business risk clearly was improved by the transaction. Although its earnings record had been good, the lion's share of profits had come from risky foreign oil properties concentrated in Libya, Peru, and Bolivia. Its domestic businesses included lackluster chemical and coal operations, and a leading meat processor. Cities Service was a U.S.-based integrated energy company. It's low-margin marketing arm was slated for sale. Cities Service would provide Oxy with a strong, predictable source of domestic earnings and cash flow, and was in a familiar business.

The financial-risk profile was less sanguine. Prior to the acquisition. Oxy's total debt ratio was 31 percent. This conservative leverage for a BBB+ senior debt rating was deemed necessary to offset the business risks cited above. The $4.1 billion Cities Service acquisition was to be financed with $2.4 billion of new debt and $1.3 billion of long-lived preferred stock. Oxy's pro forma debt ratio jumped to 43 percent. Its pro forma coverage of interest expense and preferred dividends was only 1.2 times, compared to actual fixed-charge coverage of seven times in 1981. The company did have a plan for reducing these obligations. Asset disposals estimated at $2.7 billion were planned for the next couple of years. The company already had offers in hand for certain key properties and others were considered highly marketable. Proceeds from asset sales plus cash flow from operations could reduce debt leverage to 40 percent within two years. Management insisted that all necessary steps would be taken to restore a sound capital structure.

CHANGE IN COURSE

In view of the improved business risk, we determined that debt leverage near 40 percent would be acceptable and that management was committed to quickly paring leverage to this level. Accordingly, we affirmed Oxy's BBB+ senior debt rating and brought the Cities Service rating into line with it.

Curiously, there is another chapter to this story. Oxy's earnings for 1982 and 1983 did not meet expectations. But management restrained capital expenditures and aggressively followed its asset disposal plan. But during 1984, management changed its course. Changes in the company's tax posture, dissension within the Oxy boardroom, and intense pressure on all energy companies to maximize shareholder value led to a series of financial transactions. Oxy repurchased $650 million of preferred stock and $194 million of common stock and sold $900 million of new long-term debt and $300 million of new preferred stock. The result was a total debt ratio of 48 percent. Moreover, management was contemplating the repurchase of additional preferred shares that would further weaken the capital structure. This suggested that preferred stock should be ana-

TABLE A-2
Debt Rating Status of Selected Companies Following Mergers and Acquisitions Transactions 1984

Acquiring and Divesting Companies

Company	*Senior Debt/ Commercial-Paper Rating* *Before Deal*	*After Deal*
American Medical Int'l. Inc.	A/NR	A/NR
American Standard Inc.	A+/NR	A+/NR
American Stores Inc.	A/A-1	A/A-1
Bally Manufacturing Corp.	*BBB−/NR	*BB−/NR
Beatrice Cos.	AA/A-1+	A/A-2
Black & Decker Mfg. Co.	A+/A-1	A+/A-1
CBI Industries Inc.	NR/A-1	NR/A-2
Carter Hawley Hale Stores Inc.	BBB/NR	BBB−/NR
Champion Int'l. Corp.	BBB+/A-2	BBB+/A-2
Circle K Corp.	*BB−/NR	*BB−/NR
Crane	BBB−/NR	BB+/NR
Damson Oil Corp.	*B−/NR	*B−/NR
Kerr Glass Mfg. Corp.	BBB/NR	CW
Kiewit U.S. Co.	NR/A-1+	NR/NR
LTV Corp.	BB−/NR	BB−/NR
Lear Siegler Inc.	*A−/A-1	*A−/A-2
McKesson Corp.	A−/A-2	A/A-1
Mobil Corp.	AA/NR	AA−/NR
Mobil Oil Corp.	AAA/A-1+	AA/A-1+
NVF Co.	*B/NR	CW
RCA Corp.	BBB+/A-2	A−/A-2
Rykoff (S.E.) & Co.	*BB+/NR	*B+/NR
SFN Companies Inc.	NR/A-1	NR/A-3
Sharon Steel Corp.	*B/NR	CW
Smith International Inc.	A/A-1	CW
Southland Corp.	A/A-1	A−/A-2
Standard Oil Co. of Calif.	AA/A-1+	AA/A-1+
Texaco Financial Services	NR/A-1+	NR/A-1+
Texaco Inc.	AA+/A-1+	AA−/A-1+
Texas Pipeline Co.	NR/A-1+	NR/A-1+
U.S. Gypsum Co.	AA/A-1+	AA−/A-1+
Walt Disney Productions	NR/A-1+	NR/A-1
Warner Communications Inc.	BBB−/A-3	BBB−/B
Williams Companies	BB+/NR	BB−/NR

(Table A-2. continues.)

Acquiring and Divesting Companies

Company	*Senior Debt/ Commercial-Paper Rating* *Before Deal*	*After Deal*
Amerace Corp	*BBB – /NR	NR/NR
Amstar Corp.	*BBB – /A-2	*B/B
Avis Leasing Corp.	NR/A-2	NR/A-2
Bangor Punta Corp.	*B + /NR	*A – /NR
Cole National Corp.	*BB – /NR	CW
Cone Mills Corp.	NR/A-1	NR/B
Continental Group Inc.	A/A-2	BB/NR
Dorchester Gas Corp.	*BBB – /NR	NR/NR
Esmark Inc.	BBB/A-2	A/A-2
Geosource Inc.	NR/A-1 +	NR/NR
Getty Capital Corp.	NR/A-1 +	NR/A-1 +
Getty Oil Co.	AAA/A-1 +	AA – /A-1 +
Guardian Industries Inc.	BBB/A-2	CW
Gulf Oil Corp.	AAA/A-1 +	AA/A-1 +
Gulf Oil Financial Corp.	AAA/A-1 +	AA/A-1 +
Jewel Cos.	A/A-1	A/NR
Jones & Laughlin Steel Inc.	BB + /NR	BB + /NR
Lifemark Corp.	*BB + /NR	*A – /NR
Masonite Corp.	NR/A-1	NR/NR
Metromedia Inc.	*BB + /NR	*B – NR
Milton Bradley Co.	NR/A-2	NR/NR
Moran Energy Inc.	*B + /NR	*BBB – /NR
National Can Corp.	A – /A-2	CW
Norton Simon Inc.	BBB/A-2	A/A-2
Palm Beach Inc.	*B + /NR	CW
Pembroke Capital Co.	AA + /NR	AA – /NR
Peoples Drug Stores Inc.	*B/NR	NR/NR
Petrolane Inc.	A/A-1	A – /A-1
Republic Steel Corp.	BB/NR	BB + /NR
Reserve Mining Co.	BB/NR	BB + /NR
St. Regis Corp.	A – /NR	BBB + /NR
Superior Oil Co.	AA/A-1 +	AA/A-1 +
Trane Co.	A/A-2	A + /NR
U.S. Industries	BBB/A-2	CW/NR

Subordinated debt. NR = No rating. CW = Still on CreditWatch.

Source: Standard and Poor's.

lyzed as debt rather than equity. Additionally, a major new oil find in Colombia will require a substantial capital investment. As a result of these developments, Standard and Poor's lowered Oxy's senior debt rating to BBB from BBB + , concluding that management's commitment to credit quality was not as strong as we had perceived it to be when Cities Service was acquired.

As soon as an acquisition is announced publicly, we make a preliminary assessment of its impact on the ratings of both the acquiring and acquired companies, as well as any ratings of their subsidiaries. At this stage, we rely on the publicly reported terms of the transaction, which may be incomplete, and our current knowledge of both companies' businesses. If there is a reasonable chance that the acquisition will result in a rating change, upward or downward, we will notify the issuer that the rating is being placed on CreditWatch, a Standard and Poor's service that highlights potential changes in ratings of debt securities. If an important acquisition is not expected to alter a company's rating, Standard and Poor's typically publishes a rating affirmation shortly after the transaction is announced. We were able to affirm International Business Machines Corp.'s AAA debt rating only a few days after its acquisition of ROLM Corp. was announced in 1984. Standard and Poor's determined the deal would have only a modest impact on IBM's balance sheet and offered potential operating synergies that would sufficiently offset any risks resulting from the debt securities issued to complete the acquisition.

Additions to CreditWatch are released to the press every Friday afternoon. All CreditWatch listings clearly state whether the rating implication is positive, negative, or developing. "Developing" means that the rating could go up or down. This rare situation might occur, for example, if there are competing tender offers for the same firm with one bidder rated higher and one lower than the target company.

PATH TO RATING DECISION

A rating decision is usually made within 90 days. To complete our review, we analyze the short-term and long-term financing plan for the acquisition, pro forma combined earnings and cash flow projections, and any planned asset disposals. We recognize that a company may need time to prepare this information, and busy schedules may not permit us to meet with management until several weeks after the acquisition is announced. We strongly urge the acquiring company to meet with Standard and Poor's. Only through a candid face-to-face exchange with executives can we evaluate a company's long-term plans for the acquired business and gauge management's commitment to credit quality.

If the takeover is friendly, and the antitrust review perfunctory, a rating committee will be convened shortly after our meeting with management. The rating decision is then communicated to the company, followed by our public rating announcement, and the issue is then removed from CreditWatch.

Our rating decision normally is announced prior to the consummation of the acquisition, which facilitates the pricing of any securities to be issued in the transaction. We will postpone our rating decision only if, in our judgment, there is a serious legal challenge to the acquisition.

The growing magnitude and frequency of acquisitions, the creation of CreditWatch, and our increased understanding of the role of ownership in credit analysis have heightened Standard and Poor's awareness of acquisitions. The more we demystify our analytical process, the better prepared redeploying executives will be to face the consequences of rating changes and their impact on capital cost.

Appendix B
Credit Analysis for Corporate Bonds*

TRADITIONALLY, CREDIT ANALYSIS FOR CORPORATE BONDS HAS FOCUSED almost exclusively on the default risk of the bond. That is, what is the chance that the bondholder will not receive the scheduled interest payments and/or principal at maturity. This one-dimensional analysis concerned itself primarily with straight ratio analysis. This approach was deemed appropriate during the time when interest rates were stable and investors purchased bonds with the purpose of holding them to maturity. At that time fluctuations in the market value of bonds because of interest-rate changes were minimal, and fluctuations due to credit changes of the bonds were mitigated by the fact that the investor had no intention of selling the bond before maturity. During the past decade, however, the purpose of buying bonds has changed dramatically. Investors still purchase bonds for security and thereby forego the higher, expected return of other assets such as common stock. However, an increasing number of investors buy bonds to actively trade them with the purpose of making a profit on changes in interest rates or in absolute or relative credit quality. The second dimension of corporate bond credit analysis addresses the latter purpose of buying a bond. What is the likelihood of a change in credit quality that will affect the price of the bond? This second dimension of corporate bond analysis deals primarily with the ratios and profitability trends, such as return on equity, operating margins, and asset turnover, generally associated with common stock analysis. In practice,

*I wish to thank Richard S. Wilson, vice president, fixed income research, Merrill Lynch, Pierece, Fenner & Smith, for his helpful comments and suggestions.

Reprinted from *The Handbook of Fixed Income Securities*, edited by Frank J. Fabozzi and Irving M. Pollack. (Homewood: Dow-Jones Irwin, 1987). Reprinted with permission.

both dimensions of analysis should be applied in corporate bond analysis because, in a sense, both dimensions are addressing the same issue—default or credit risk. Only by using both dimensions of credit analysis, however, will the analyst address the dual purpose of a bondholding: security of interest and principal payments and stability or improvement of credit risk during the life of the bond.

Historically, common stock and bond research areas have been viewed as separate. With the development of the options theory, however, the two disciplines are beginning to be viewed as complementary.

The value of the option is a direct function of the company's aggregate equity valuation. As the market value of a company's stock increases, the value of the option increases. Conversely, as the market value of a company's stock declines, so does the value of the option. The practical implication of this theory for corporate bond analysis is that the perceptions of both markets should be compared before a final credit judgment is rendered. An analyst who believes that there is a higher level of efficiency in the stock market than in the bond market should pay particular attention to the stock price of the company being analyzed, especially in situations where the judgment of the two markets differ substantially.

For example, in each 1981, the market to book values of the major chemical companies ranged from .77 to 2.15. The bond ratings of these same companies ranged from Baa/BBB to Aaa/AAA. The interesting point is not the range of either the market to book values or bond ratings, but rather that, although there was some correlation between the market/book ratios and bond ratings, there were instances in which there was little or no correlation. The options theory would suggest that there should be more of a relationship between the two. When the relative valuation of the bond as measured by the rating is low compared with the equity valuation as measured by market/book, one or both markets might be incorrectly valuing the company. Because bond-rating changes are generally slower than market moves, it is likely that the bond market is undervaluing the company.

Although there are numerous types of corporate bonds outstanding, three major issuing segments of bonds can be differentiated: industrials, utilities, and finance companies, all of which are discussed in this section.

INDUSTRY CONSIDERATIONS

The first step in analyzing a bond is to become familiar with the industry. Only within the context of an industry is a company analysis valid. For example, a company growing at 15 percent annually might appear attractive. If the industry is growing at 50 percent annually, however, the company is competitively weak. Industry considerations can be numerous, however, and an understanding of the following eight variables should give the general, fixed-income analyst a sufficient framework to properly interpret a company's prospects.

Economic Cyclicality

The economic cyclicality of an industry is the first variable an analyst should consider in reviewing an industry. Does the industry closely follow gross national product (GNP) growth, as does the retailing industry, or is it recession resistant but slow growing, such as the electric utility industry? The growth in earnings per share (EPS) of a company should be measured against the growth trend of its industry. Major deviations from the industry trend should be the focus of further analysis. Some industries can be somewhat dependent on general economic growth but be more sensitive to demographic changes. The nursing home industry is a prime example of this type of sensitivity. With the significant aging of the U.S. population, the nursing home industry is projected to have above average growth for the foreseeable future. Other industries, such as banking, are sensitive to interest rates. When interest rates are rising, the earnings of banks with a high, federal-funds exposure underperform the market because their loan rates lag behind increases in the cost of money. Conversely, as interest rates fall, banking earnings outperform the market because the lag in interest change works in the banks' favor.

In general, however, the earnings of few industries perfectly correlate with one economic statistic. Not only are industries sensitive to many economic variables, but often various segments within a company or an industry move countercyclically, or at least with different lags in relation to the general economy. For example, the housing industry can be divided between new construction and remodeling and repair. New construction has historically led GNP growth, but repair and remodeling has exhibited less sensitivity to general trends. Therefore, in analyzing a company in the construction industry, the performance of each of its segments must be compared with the performance of the subindustry.

Growth Prospects

A second industry variable related to economic cyclicality is the growth prospects for an industry. Is the growth of the industry projected to increase and be maintained at a high level, such as the nursing industry, or is growth expected to be stable? Each growth scenario has implications for a company. In the case of a fast-growth industry, how much capacity is needed to meet demand, and how will this capacity be financed? In the case of slow-growth industries, is there a movement toward diversification and/or a consolidation within the industry, such as in the brewing industry? A company operating within a fast-growing industry often has a better potential for credit improvement than a company whose industry's growth prospects are below average does.

Research and Development Expenses

The broad assessment of growth prospects is tempered by the third variable—the research and development expenditures required to maintain or expand market position. The technology field is growing at an above-average rate, and the companies in the industry should do correspondingly well. Highly technical products, however, can become dated and obsolete quickly. Therefore, although a company might be situated well in an industry, if it does not have the financial resources to maintain a technological lead, or at least expend a sufficient amount of money to keep technologically current, its position is likely to deteriorate in the long run. In the short run, however, a company whose research and development expenditures are consistently below industry averages might produce above-average results because of expanded margins.

Competition

Competition within an industry also directly relates to the market structure of an industry and pricing flexibility. An unregulated monopoly is in an enviable position because it can price its goods at a level that will maximize profits. Most industries encounter some free market forces and must price their goods in relation to the supply and demand for their goods as well as the price charged for similar goods. In an oligopoly, a pricing leader is not uncommon. General Motors Corporation, for example, performs this function in the automobile industry. A concern arises when a small company is in an industry that is trending toward oligopoly. In this environment, the small company's costs of production might be higher than those of the industry leaders, and yet it might have to conform to the pricing of the industry leaders. In the extreme, a price war could force the smaller companies out of business. This situation is present now in the brewing industry. For the past two decades, as the brewing industry has become increasingly concentrated, the leaders have gained market share at the expense of the small, local brewers. Many small, local brewers have either been acquired or have gone out of business. These local brewers have been at a dual disadvantage: They are in an industry that is moving toward oligopoly, and yet their weak competitive position within the industry largely precludes pricing flexibility.

Sources of Supply

The market structure of an industry and its competitive forces have a direct impact on the fifth industry variable—supply sources of major production components. For example, a company in the paper industry that has sufficient timber acreage to supply 100 percent of its pulp is preferable to a paper company that must buy all, or a large percentage, of its pulp. A company that is not self-sufficient in its factors of production but is sufficiently powerful in its industry to pass along increased costs is also in an enviable position. R. J. Reynolds is an example of the latter type of company. Although R. J. Reynolds has major exposure to commodity prices for ingredients, its strong market position has enabled it to pass along increased cost of goods sold.

Degree of Regulation

The sixth industry consideration is the degree of regulation. The electric utility industry is the classic example of regulation. Nearly all phases of a utility's operations are regulated. An analyst should not be as concerned with the existence or absence of regulation per se, but rather with the direction of regulation and the effect it has on the profitability of the company. For the electric utility industry, regulation generally places a cap on earned returns. Other industries, such as the drug industry, also has a high, though less pervasive, degree of regulation. In the drug industry, however, the threat of increased regulation has been a negative factor in the industry for some time.

Labor

The labor situation of an industry should also be analyzed. Is the industry heavily unionized? If so, what has been the historical occurrence of strikes? When do the current contracts expire, and what is the likelihood of timely settlements? The labor situation is also important in non-unionized companies, particularly situations where labor is tight. What has been the turnover of professionals and management in the firm? What is the probability of a firm's employees, such as highly skilled engineers, being hired by competing firms? The more labor intensive an industry, the more significance the labor situation assumes.

Accounting

A final industry factor to consider is accounting. Does the industry have special accounting practices, such as those in the insurance industry or the electric utility industry? If so, an analyst should become familiar with industry practices before proceeding with a company analysis. Also important is whether a company is liberal or conservative in applying the generally accepted accounting principles. The norm of an industry should be ascertained, and the analyst should be sure to analyze comparable figures.

FINANCIAL ANALYSIS

Once an analyst understands an industry, he can proceed with a financial analysis. The financial analysis should be conducted in three phases. The first phase consists of traditional ratio analysis for bonds. The second phase, generally associated with common stock research, consists of analyzing the components

TABLE B-1
Exhibit 1. Three-Year (1981 – 1983)
Medians of Key Ratios by Rating Category

	AAA	*AA*	*A*	*BBB*	*BB*	*B*
Pretax interest coverage	14.84	6.49	4.65	2.87	2.10	1.55
Pretax interest and full rental coverage	8.38	3.97	2.81	2.07	1.73	1.39
Funds from operations/long-term debt	261.61	111.64	62.60	40.61	24.79	16.46
Funds from operations/total debt	162.09	79.43	53.33	36.34	22.65	13.74
Pretax return on average long-term capital employed	26.82	20.68	16.87	12.41	13.73	10.53
Operating income/sales	17.63	13.19	11.24	8.10	10.23	9.65
Long-term debt/capitalization	8.81	19.23	26.73	33.54	46.16	55.37
Total debt/capitalization including short-term debt	14.67	24.40	30.22	36.25	50.07	59.03
Total debt/capitalization including short-term debt (including 8X rents)	25.62	37.64	43.49	48.13	59.05	68.23
Total liabilities/tangible shareholders' equity and minority interest	65.44	101.57	115.47	127.40	197.54	268.95

Note: These are not meant to be minimum standards.

SOURCE: Standard & Poor's Corporation, 1985.

of a company's return on equity (ROE). The final phase considers such nonfinancial factors as management and foreign exposure and includes an analysis of the indenture.

Traditional Ratio Analysis

There are numerous ratios that can be calculated in applying traditional ratio analysis to bonds. Of these, eight will be discussed. Those selected are the ratios with the widest degree of applicability. In analyzing a particular industry, however, other ratios assume significance and should be considered. For example, in the electric utility industry, allowance for funds used in construction as a percent of net income is an important ratio that is inapplicable to the analysis of industrial or financial companies.

Pretax interest coverage. Generally, the first ratio calculated in credit analysis is pretax interest coverage. This ratio measures the number of times interest charges are covered on a pretax basis. Fixed-charge coverage is calculated by dividing pretax income plus interest charges by total interest charges. The higher the coverage figure, the safer the credit. If interest coverage is less than 1X, the company must borrow or use cash flow or sell assets to meet its interest payments. Generally, published coverage figures are pretax as opposed to aftertax because interest payments are a pretax expense. Although pretax interest coverage ratio is useful, its utility is a function of the company's other fixed obligations. For example, if a company has other significant fixed obligations, such as rents or leases, a more appropriate coverage figure would include these other fixed obligations. The retail industry is a good example because companies typically have significant lease obligations.

A calculation of simple pretax interest coverage would be misleading in this case because fixed obligations other than interest are significant. The analyst should also be aware of any contingent liabilities, such as a company's guaranteeing another company's debt. For example, there has been a dramatic increase in the insurance industry's guaranteeing of other companys' debt. Today, this guaranteed debt exceeds the debt of the industry. Although the company being analyzed might never have to pay interest or principal on the guaranteed debt, the existence of the guarantee diminishes the quality of the pretax coverage. In addition, the quality of the guaranteed debt must be considered.

Once pretax interest coverage and fixed-charge coverage are calculated, the ratios' absolute levels and the numbers relative to those of the industry must be analyzed. For example, pretax interest coverage for an electric utility of 4.5X is consistent with an AAA rating, whereas the same coverage for a drug company would indicate a lower rating.

Standard and Poor's 1981–1983 median ratios of pretax interest coverage ranges for the senior debt of industrial companies were as follows:

Rating Classification	*Pretax Interest Coverage*
AAA	14.84
AA	6.49
A	4.65
BBB	2.87

Leverage. A second important ratio is leverage, which can be defined in several ways. The most common definition is long-term debt as a percent of total capitalization. The higher the level of debt, the higher the percentage of operating income that must be used to meet fixed obligations. If a company is highly leveraged, an analyst should also look at its margin of safety. The margin of safety is defined as the percentage that operating income could decline and still be sufficient to allow the company to meet its fixed obligations. Standard and Poor's 1981–1983 median ratios of leverage for the senior debt of industrial companies were as follows:

Rating Classification	*Long-Term Debt/Capitalization*
AAA	8.81
AA	19.23
A	26.73
BBB	33.54

The most common way to calculate leverage is to use the company's capitalization structure as stated in the most recent balance sheet. In addition to this measure, capitalization should be calculated using a market approximation for the value of the common stock. When a company's common stock is selling significantly below book value, leverage will be understated by the traditional approach.

The degree of leverage and margin of safety varies dramatically among industries. Finance companies have traditionally been among the most highly leveraged companies, with debt to equity ratios of 10/1. Although such leverage is tolerated in the finance industry, an industrial company with similar leverage would have a difficult time issuing debt.

In addition to considering the absolute and relative level of leverage of a company, an analyst should evaluate the debt itself. How much of the debt has a fixed rate, and how much has a floating rate? A company with a high component of debt tied to the prime might find its margins being squeezed as interest rates rise if there is no compensating increase in the price of the firm's goods. Such a debt structure could be beneficial during certain phases of the interest rate cycle, but it has the disadvantage of precluding a precise estimate of what interest charges for the year will be. In general, a company with a high percentage of floating-rate debt is less preferable than a similarly levered company with a small percentage of floating-rate debt.

The maturity structure of the debt should also be evaluated. What is the percentage of debt that is coming due within the next five years? As this debt is refinanced, how will the company's embedded cost of debt be changed? In this regard, the amount of original-issue discount (OID) debt should also be considered. High quality OIDs were first issued in sizeable amounts in 1981, although lower-quality OIDs have been issued for some time. This debt is issued with low or zero coupons and at substantial discounts to par. Each year the issuing company expenses the interest payment (coupon times the total principal amount due at maturity) as well as amortization of the discount. At issuance, only the actual bond proceeds are listed as debt on the balance sheet. However, because this payable debt will increase annually, an analyst should consider the full face amount due at maturity when evaluating the maturity structure and refinancing plans of the company.

Cash flow. A third important ratio is cash flow as a percent of total debt. Cash flow is often defined as net income plus depreciation, depletion, and deferred taxes. In calculating cash flow for credit analysis, the analyst should also subtract noncash contributions from subsidiaries. In essence, an analyst should be concerned with cash from operations. Any extraordinary sources or uses of funds should be excluded when determining the overall trend of cash flow coverage. Cash dividends from subsidiaries should also be questioned in terms of their appropriateness (too high or too low relative to the subsidiary's earnings) and also in terms of the parent's control over the upstreaming of dividends. Is there a legal limit to the upstreamed dividends? If so, how close is the current level of dividends to the limit? Standard and Poor's 1981 – 1983 Median Ratios of Funds From Operations/Long-Term Debt for the senior debt of industrial companies were as follows:

Rating Classification	*Funds From Operations/ Long-Term Debt*
AAA	262
AA	112
A	63
BBB	41

Net assets. A fourth significant ratio is net assets to total debt. When analyzing this facet of a bond's quality, the liquidation value of the assets should be considered. Liquidation value often differs dramatically from the value stated on the balance sheet. At one extreme, consider a nuclear generating plant that has had operating problems and closed down, and whose chance of receiving an operating license is questionable. This asset is likely overstated on the balance sheet, and a bondholder should take little comfort in reported asset protection. On the other hand, is a forest products company whose vast timber acreage is significantly understated on the balance sheet. In addition to the assets' market value, some consideration should also be given to the liquidity of the assets. A company with a high percentage of its assets in cash and marketable securities is in a much stronger asset position than a company whose primary assets are illiquid real estate.

In addition to the major variables discussed above, an analyst should also consider several other financial variables including intangibles, unfunded pension liabilities, the age and condition of the plant, and working capital adequacy.

Intangibles. Intangibles often represent a small portion of the asset side of a balance sheet. Occasionally, however, particularly with companies that have or have had an active acquisition program, intangibles can represent a significant portion of assets. In this case, an analyst should estimate the actual value of the intangibles and determine whether this value is in concert with the balance sheet valuation. A carrying value significantly higher than market value indicates a potential for a write-down of assets. The actual write-down might not occur until the company actually sells the subsidiary that the intangibles are identified with. However, an analyst should recognize the potential, and adjust capitalization accordingly.

Unfunded pension liabilities. Unfunded pension liabilities can also affect a credit decision. Although a fully funded pension is not necessary for a high credit assessment, a large unfunded pension liability that is 10 percent or more of net worth can be a negative. A company whose unfunded pension liabilities are sufficiently high enough to interfere with corporate planning should be considered carefully. For example, a steel company with high unfunded pension liabilities might delay or decide against closing an unprofitable plant because of the pension costs involved. An analyst should also be aware of a company's assumed rate of return on its pension funds and salary increase assumptions. The higher the assumed rate of return, the lower the contribution a company must make to its pension fund, given a set of actuarial assumptions. Occasionally, a company having difficulty with its earnings will raise its actuarial assumption and thereby lower its pension contribution and increase earnings. The impact on earnings can be dramatic. In other cases, companies have attempted to "raid" the excess funds in an overfunded retirement plan to enhance earnings.

Age and condition of plant. The age of a company's plant should also be estimated, if it differs dramatically from industry standards. A heavy, industrial company, whose plants average age is well above that of its competitors, is probably already paying for its aged plant through operating inefficiencies. In the longer term, however, the age of net plant is an indication of future capital expenditures for a more modern plant. In addition, the underdepreciation of the plant significantly lowers inflation-adjusted earnings.

The Financial Accounting Standards Board Statement Number 33 requires extensive supplementary information from most companies on the effect of changing prices. This information is generally unaudited and there is still no consensus on the best presentation of such data. The supplementary information provision does, however, give the analyst an indication of the magnitude of the effects of inflation on a given company. The effects differ dramatically from industry to industry. At one extreme are the high technology and financial terms where the effects are nominal. At the other extreme are capital-intensive industries where the effects are major.

Working capital. A final variable in assessing a company's financial strength concerns the strength and liquidity of its working capital. Working capital is defined as current assets less current liabilities. Working capital is considered a primary measure of a company's financial flexibility. Other such measures include the current ratio (current assets divided by current liabilities) and the acid test (cash, marketable securities, and receivables divided by current liabilities). The stronger the company's liquidity measures, the better able it is to weather a downturn in business and cash flow. When assessing this variable, an analyst should consider the normal working capital requirements of a company and industry. The components of working capital should also be analyzed. Although accounts receivables are considered to be liquid, an increase in the average days a receivable is outstanding might be an indication that a higher level of working capital is needed for the efficient running of the operation.

Analyzing the Components of Return on Equity

Once the financial analysis is complete, a bond analyst traditionally examines the earnings progression of the company and its historical return on equity (ROE). This section of analysis often receives less emphasis than the traditional ratio analysis. It is equally important, however, and demands equal emphasis. An analysis of earnings growth and ROE is vital in determining credit quality because it gives the analyst necessary insights into the components of ROE and indications of the sources of future growth. Equity analysts devote a major portion of their time examining the components of ROE, and their work should be recognized as valuable resource material.

A basic approach to examining the components of return on equity is presented in a popular investment textbook by Jerome B. Cohen, Edward D. Zinbarg, and Arthur Zeikel.[1] Their basic approach breaks down return on equity into four principal components: pretax margins, asset turnover, leverage, and the tax rate. These four variables multiplied together equal net income/stockholders' equity, or return on equity.

$$\left[\frac{\text{Nonoperating pretax income}}{\text{Sales}} + \frac{\text{Operating pretax income}}{\text{Sales}}\right] \times \frac{\text{Sales}}{\text{Assets}} \times \frac{\text{Assets}}{\text{Equity}} \times (1 - \text{Tax rate}) = \text{Net Income/Equity}$$

In analyzing these four components of ROE, the analyst should examine their progression for a minimum of five years and at least through a business cycle. The progression of each variable should be compared with the progression of the same variables for the industry, and deviations from industry standards should be further analyzed. For example, perhaps two companies have similar ROE's, but one company is employing a higher level of leverage to achieve its results, whereas the other company has a higher asset-turnover rate. As the degree of leverage is largely a management decision, an analyst should focus on asset turnover. Why have sales for the former company turned down? Is this downturn a result of a general slowdown in the industry, or is it that assets have been expanded rapidly and the company is in the process of absorbing these new assets? Conversely, a relatively high rise in asset-turnover rate

[1] *Investment Analysis & Portfolio Management* (Homewood, IL: Richard D. Irwin, 1977).© Richard D. Irwin, Inc., 1977.

could indicate a need for more capital. If this is the case, how will the company finance this growth, and what effect will the financing have on the firm's embedded cost of capital?

An analyst should not expect similar components of ROE for all companies in a particular industry. Deviations from industry norms often indicate management philosophy. For example, one company might emphasize asset turnover, and another company in the same industry might emphasize profit margin. As in any financial analysis, the trend of the components is as important as the absolute levels.

In order to give an analyst a general idea of the type of ratios expected by the major rating agencies for a particular rating classification, see the Standard and Poor's medians of key ratios for 1981 – 1983 by rating category earlier in this section. An analyst should only use this table in the most general applications, however, for two reasons. First, industry standards vary considerably. Second, financial ratios are only one part of the analysis.

Nonfinancial Factors

After the traditional bond analysis is completed, an analyst should consider some nonfinancial factors that might modify the evaluation of the company. Among these factors are the degree of foreign exposure and the quality of management. The amount of foreign exposure should be ascertainable from the annual report. Sometimes, however, specific country exposure is less clear because the annual report often lists foreign exposure by broad geographic divisions. If there is concern that a major portion of revenue and income is derived from potentially unstable areas, an analyst should carefully consider the total revenue and income derived from the area and the assets committed. Further consideration should be given to available corporate alternatives in case assets are nationalized. Additionally, the degree of currency exposure should be determined. If currency fluctuations are significant, has management hedged its exposure?

The quality and depth of management is more difficult to evaluate. Earnings progress at the firm is a good indication of the quality of management. Negative aspects would include a firm founded and headed by one person who is approaching retirement and has made no plan for succession. Equally negative is the firm that has had numerous changes of management and philosophy. On the other hand, excessive stability is not always desirable. If one family or group of investors owns a controlling interest in a firm, they might be too conservative to react to changes in the markets. Characteristics of a good management team should include depth, a clear line of succession if the chief officers are nearing retirement, and a diversity of age within the management team.

INDENTURE PROVISIONS

An indenture is a legal document that defines the rights and obligations of the borrower and the lender with respect to a bond issue. An analysis of the indenture should be a part of a credit review because the indenture provisions establish rules for several important spheres of operation for the borrower. These provisions, which can be viewed as safeguards for the lender, cover such areas as the issuance limit of additional debt, sale and leasebacks, and sinking-fund provisions.

The indentures of bonds of the same industry are often similar in the areas they address. Correlation between the quality rating of the senior debt of a company and the stringency of indenture provisions is not perfect. For example, the debt test is more severe in A securities than in BB securities. However, subordinated debt of one company will often have less restrictive provisions than will the senior debt of the same company. In addition, more restrictive provisions are also generally found in private placement issues. In analyzing a company's indenture, the analyst should look for the standard industry provisions. Differences in these provisions (either more or less restrictive) should be examined more closely. In this regard, a more restrictive nature is not necessarily preferable if the provisions are so restrictive that they hinder the efficient operation of the company.

Below are the provisions most commonly found in indentures. These provisions are categorized by industry because the basic provisions are fairly uniform within an industry. A general description of the indenture is found in a company's prospectus. However, notification is generally given that the indenture provisions are only summarized. A complete indenture can be obtained from the trustee who is listed in the prospectus.

Utility Indentures

Security. The security provision is generally the first provision in a utility indenture. This provision specifies the property on which there is a mortgage lien. In addition, the ranking of the new debt relative to outstanding debt is specified. Generally, the new bonds rank equally with all other bonds outstanding under the mortgage. This ranking is necessary, but it has created difficulty for the issuing companies because some mortgage indentures were written more than 40 years ago. Specifically, because all bondholders must be kept equal, companies must often retain antiquated provisions in their indentures. Often, these provisions hinder a company from running efficiently because of structural changes in the industry since the original writing of the indenture. Changes in these provisions can be made, but changes have occurred slowly because of the high percentage of bondholders that must approve a change and the time and expense required to locate the bondholders.

Issuance of additional bonds. The "Issuance of Additional Bonds" provision establishes the conditions under which a company can issue additional first mortgage bonds. Often, this provision contains a debt test and/or an earnings test. The debt test generally limits the amount of bonds that might be issued under the mortgage to a certain percentage (often 60 percent) of net property or net property additions, the principal amount of retired bonds, or deposited cash. The earnings test, on the other hand, restricts the issuance of additional bonds under the mortgage unless earnings for a particular period cover interest payments at a specified level.

Although both of these tests might appear straightforward, an analyst must carefully study the definitions contained in the tests. For example, net property additions might be defined as plants that have operating licenses.

Although there has been a great deal of nuclear construction, few operating licenses have been granted over the past decade. Therefore, there is a significant backlog of construction work in progress (CWIP) that has had to be financed and yet might not be operational for some time. This situation can present problems for a company whose indenture requires net plant additions to be licensed and/or used and useful assets. In the extreme case, a company with a heavy nuclear construction program might find itself unable to issue bonds under its mortgage agreement.

In a similar circumstance, a company whose regulatory commission requires a substantial write-down related to nuclear construction may find itself unable to meet a debt test for several years if the write-down is taken in one quarter.

Maintenance and replacement fund. The purpose of a maintenance and replacement fund (M&R) is to assure that the mortgaged property is maintained in good operating condition. To this end, electric utility indentures generally require that a certain percentage of gross operating revenues, a percentage of aggregate bonded indebtedness, or a percentage of the utility's property account be paid to the trustee for the M&R fund. A major portion of the M&R requirement has historically been satisfied with normal maintenance expenditures. To the extent there is a remaining requirement, the company might contribute cash, the pledge of unbonded property additions, or bonds.

The rapid escalation of fuel costs during the 1970s has greatly raised the required levels of many M&R funds that are tied to operating revenues. This situation precipitated a number of bond calls for M&R purposes. Bonds can still be called for this purpose, but investors are more cognizant of this risk and are less likely to pay a significant premium for bonds subject to such a call. Furthermore, M&R requirements are slowly being changed toward formulas that exclude the large portion of operating income attributable to rises in fuel costs. Finally, a number of companies have indicated that they have no intention of using M&R requirements for calling bonds because of the original intent of the provision and also because of the disfavor such an action would generate among bondholders. However, the intent of companies in this regard would certainly be secondary if a call for M&R requirements were ordered by a commission.

Redemption provisions. The redemption, or call, provision specifies during what period and at what prices a company might call its bonds. Redemption provisions vary. Currently, long-term bonds are generally callable but nonrefundable for five years. Exceptions to this statement are the longer—term issues of the AT&T System, which are noncallable for five years. In the case of intermediate and short-term issues, the noncall provisions generally extend to a year or two prior to maturity. Refunding is an action by a company to replace outstanding bonds with another debt issue sold at a lower interest expense. (Refunding protection does not protect the bondholder from refunding bonds with equity or short-term debt.) The refunding protection is a safeguard for bondholders against their bonds being refunded at a disadvantageous time.

Sinking fund. A sinking fund is an annual obligation of a company to pay the trustee an amount of cash sufficient to retire a given percentage of bonds. This requirement can often be met with actual bonds or with the pledge of property. In general, electric utilities have 1 percent sinking funds that commence at the end of the refunding period. There are, however, several variations of the sinking-fund provision with which an analyst (and bondholder) should be familiar with because they could directly affect the probability of bonds being called for sinking-fund purposes. Some companies have nonspecific, or funnel, sinkers. This type of sinker often entails a 1 or 1½ percent sinking fund applicable to all outstanding bonds. The obligation can be met by the stated percentage of each issue outstanding, by cash, or by applying (or funneling) the whole requirement against one issue or several issues.

Other provisions. In addition to the provisions discussed above, the indenture covers the events of default, modification of the mortgage, and the powers and obligations of the trustee. In general, these provisions are fairly standard, although differences occur that should be evaluated.

Industrial Indentures

Many of the provisions of an industrial indenture are similar to a utility's indenture, although some items might be changed. For example, sinking-fund and redemption provisions are part of an industrial indenture. However, refunding protection for an industrial is generally 10 years (as opposed to 5 years for an electric utility), and sinking funds often have the option to double or more than double their requirements on an annual basis at the option of the company.

In general, there are five indenture provisions that have historically been significant in providing protection for the industrial bondholder.

Negative pledge clause. The negative pledge clause provides that the company cannot create or assume liens to the extent that more than a certain percentage of consolidated net tangible assets (CNTA) is so secured without giving the same security to the bondholders. This provision is important to the bondholders because their security in the specific assets of the company establishes an important protection for their investment. The specific percentage of CNTA that is exempted from this provision is referred to as exempted indebtedness, and the exclusion provides some flexibility to the company.

Sale and lease-back transaction limits. The indenture provision that limits sales and lease-backs parallels the protection offered by the negative pledge clause, except that it provides protection for the bondholder against the company selling and leasing back assets that provide security for the debtholder. In general, this provision requires that assets or cash equal to the property sold and leased back be applied to the retirement of the debt in question or used to acquire another property for the security of the debtholders.

Sale of assets or merger. The sale of assets or merger provision protects the debtholder in the event that a substantial amount of all of the assets of the amount or company are sold or merged into another company. Under these circumstances, the provision generally states that the debt be retired or be assumed by the merged company.

Dividend test. The dividend test provision establishes rules for the payment of dividends. Generally, it permits a company to pay dividends to the extent that they are no greater than net income from the previous year, plus the earnings of a year or two before. Although this provision allows the company to continue to pay dividends when there is a business decline, it assures the debtholders that the corporation will not be drained by dividend payments.

Debt test. The debt test limits the amount of debt that can be issued by establishing a maximum debt/assets ratio. This provision is generally omitted from current public offerings. There are, however, numerous outstanding indentures that include this provision. In addition, private placements often include a debt test. When present, the debt test generally sets a limit on the amount of debt that can be issued per dollar of total assets. This limit is sometimes stated as a percentage. For example, a 50 percent debt/asset limit restricts debt to 50 percent of total assets.

Financial Indentures

Sinking-fund and refunding provisions. Similar to industrial indentures, indentures for finance issues specify sinking-fund and refunding provisions. In general, finance issues with a short maturity are noncallable, whereas longer issues provide 10-year call protection. Occasionally, an issue can be called early in the event of declining receivables. Sinking funds are not as common in finance issues as they are in industrial issues, although they are standard for some companies.

Dividend test. Perhaps the most important indenture provision for a debtholder of a finance subsidiary is the dividend test. This test restricts the amount of dividends that can be upstreamed from a finance subsidiary to the parent, thereby protecting the debtholder against a parent draining the subsidiary. This provision is common in finance indentures, but it is not universal. (One notable exception is International Harvester Credit.)

Limitations on liens. The limitation on liens provision restricts the degree to which a company can pledge its assets without giving the same protection to the bondholder. Generally, only a nominal amount can be pledged or otherwise liened without establishing equal protection for the debtholder.

Restriction on debt test. The debt test limits the amount of debt the company can issue. This provision generally is stated in terms of assets and liabilities, although an earnings test has occasionally been used.

UTILITIES

Utilities are regulated monopolies. These companies generally operate with a high degree of financial leverage and low, fixed-charge coverage (relative to industrial companies). These financial parameters have been historically accepted by investors because of the regulation of the industry and the belief that there is minimal, if any, bankruptcy risk in those securities because of the essential services they provide. The changing structure of the electric utility industry because of increasing investment in nuclear generating units and their inherent risk has changed this belief. Initially, the faltering financial position of General Public Utilities, precipitated by the Three Mile Island nuclear accident and the regulatory delays in making a decision regarding the units, highlighted the default risk that does exist in the industry. More recently, the default of several Washington Public Power Supply System issues reemphasized the default risk. In addition, the industry is faced with the acid rain issue and increased uncertainty in construction costs and growth rates. In 1985, Standard and Poor's developed more conservative financial benchmarks for a given rating to reflect the increased risk in the industry.

Segments within the Utility Industry

There are three major segments within the utility industry: electric companies, gas companies, and telephone companies. This section will deal primarily with the electric utilities. This segment encompasses most of the variables affecting the industry in general.

FINANCIAL ANALYSIS

There are four major financial ratios that should be considered in analyzing an electric utility: leverage, pretax interest coverage, cash flow/spending, and cash flow/capital.

Leverage in the electric utility industry is high considering industrial concerns. This degree of leverage is accepted by investors because of the historical stability of the industry. The expected ranges for AAA, AA, A, BBB, and BB companies are outlined below:

Rating Classification	*Debt Leverage*
AAA	Less than 41 percent
AA	39-46 percent
A	44 to 52 percent
BBB	50 to 58 percent
BB	Greater than 56 percent

In calculating the debt leverage of an electric utility, long-term debt/capitalization is standard. The amount of short-term debt should also be considered, however, because this is generally variable-rate debt. A high proportion of short-term debt might also indicate the possibility of the near-term issuance of long-term bonds. In addition, several companies guarantee the debt of subsidiaries (regulated or nonregulated). The extent of these guarantees should be considered in calculating leverage.

Fixed-charge coverage for electric utilities is also low relative to coverage for industrial companies. Standard and Poor's expected ranges for coverage are as follows:

Rating Classification	*Expected Pretax Fixed-Charge Coverage*
AAA	Greater than 4.5X
AA	3.5-5.0X
A	2.5-4.0X
BBB	1.5-3.0X
BB	Less than 2.0X

These ranges are accepted by investors because of the stability of the industry. Because of the changing fundamentals of the industry discussed above, however, perhaps less emphasis should be placed on the exact coverage figures and more on the trend and quality of the coverage.

The utility industry is unique because its earnings include allowance for funds used during construction (AFUDC). AFUDC is an accounting treatment that allows utilities to recognize income (at a rate determined by individual regulatory commissions) on the amount of funds employed in construction. The percentage that AFUDC represents of total earnings varies significantly from almost zero to well in excess of 70 percent of earnings. Currently, AFUDC generates more than 50 percent of industry earnings. Obviously, the higher the percentage that AFUDC represents of net earnings, the lower the quality of earnings. This becomes evident when the cash flow of a utility is calculated. Often, the cash flow of a utility with substantial AFUDC is less than the dividend requirements of the company. In this instance, the company is returning the capital of the shareholders!

In calculating fixed-charge coverage, the analyst should calculate two sets of coverage figures—fixed-charge coverage, including AFUDC and fixed-charge coverage, and excluding AFUDC, with the latter being more important.

A third important ratio is cash flow/spending. This ratio should be approximated for three years (the general range of an electric company's construction forecast). The absolute level as well as the trend of this ratio provides important insights into the trend of other financial parameters. An improving trend indicates that construction spending is probably moderating, whereas a low cash flow/spending ratio might indicate inadequate rates being approved by the commissions and a heavy construction budget. Estimates for construction spending are published in a company's annual reports. Although these are subject to revision, the time involved in building a generating unit makes these forecasts reasonably reliable. In 1985, Standard and Poor's de-emphasized this ratio primarily because of its volatility. Although it will still be considered, Standard and Poor's now emphasizes cash flow/capital as a preferable indicator of cash flow adequacy.

Standard and Poor's ranges for cash flow/spending (suspended in January 1985) and its expected ranges for net cash flow/permanent capital are as follows:

Rating Classification	*Expected Cash Flow/ Spending*	*Net Cash Flow/ Permanent Capital*
AAA	—	Greater than 10 percent
AA	More than 40 percent	7.0-11.0 percent
A	20-50 percent	5.0-8.0 percent
BBB	Less than 30 percent	2.5-6.0 percent
BB	—	Less than 3.0 percent

In calculating cash flow, the standard definition outlined above should be followed. However, AFUDC should also be subtracted, and any cash flow from nonregulated subsidiaries should be segregated and analyzed within the total context of the company. The regulatory commissions take divergent views on nonutility subsidiaries. Some commissions do not regulate these subsidiaries at all, but other commissions give inadequate rate relief to an electric utility with a profitable nonutility subsidiary under the premise that the company should be looked at as a whole. In the extreme, the latter view has encouraged companies to sell or spin off some subsidiaries.

Nonfinancial Factors

Although financial factors are important in analyzing any company, nonfinancial factors are particularly important in the electric utility industry and may alter a credit assessment. The five nonfinancial factors outlined below are of particular importance to the utility industry. These are in addition to the nonfinancial factors discussed earlier.

Regulation is perhaps the most important variable in the electric utility industry. All electric companies are regulated. Most are primarily regulated by the state or states in which they operate. If a company operates in more than one state, the analyst should weigh the evaluation of the regulatory atmosphere by revenues generated in each state. In addition, the Federal Energy Regulatory Commission (FERC) regulates interstate operations and the sale of wholesale power. Currently, FERC regulation is considered to be somewhat more favorable than that of the average state regulatory commission.

Regulation is best quantified by recent rate decisions and the trend of these decisions. Although a company being analyzed might not have had a recent rate case, the commission's decisions for other companies operating within the state might be used as a proxy. Regulatory commissions are either appointed or elected. In either case, the political atmosphere can have a dramatic effect on the trend of decisions.

The regulators determine innumerable issues in a rate decision, although analysts often mistakenly focus only on the allowed rate of return on equity or the percentage of request granted. In particular, the commissions determine how much of construction work in progress (CWIP) is allowed into the rate base. A company might appear to have a favorable allowed ROE but be hurt because only a small portion of the company's capital is permitted to earn that return, while the CWIP earns nothing. Due to the high construction budgets for nuclear-generating plants and the length of time these plants are under construction, allowance of CWIP in the rate base is of critical importance. Some companies have more than half of their capital in CWIP that is not permitted to earn a return.

In addition, regulators have a high degree of control over the cash flow of a company through the allowance or disallowance of accounting practices and the speed with which decisions are made on cases.

The source of a company's energy is a second important variable. Currently, a company with a heavy nuclear construction budget is viewed negatively compared to a company with coal units under construction. Not only are the lead times for nuclear construction much longer than for other generating plants, but the risk of licensing delays are significant in nuclear construction. The energy source variable relates to a third variable, the growth and stability of the company's territory. Although above-average growth is viewed positively in an industrial company, it is viewed negatively with respect to an electric utility. An electric utility with above-average growth must necessarily have a high construction budget. To the extent that CWIP is disallowed or only partially allowed in the company's rate base, the company is likely to have declining financial parameters until the unit is operational. A fourth variable that should be considered is whether a company is a subsidiary of a holding company. Holding company status permits non-utility subsidiaries, but it is not universal that these subsidiaries (if successful) will improve the overall credit quality of the company. This depends on the regulatory atmosphere. Furthermore, when there are several electric utility subsidiaries, the parent is more likely to give relatively large equity infusions to the relatively weak subsidiaries. The stronger subsidiary might have to "support" the other subsidiaries. Finally, holding companies should be analyzed in terms of consolidated debt. Although a particular subsidiary might have relatively strong financial parameters, off-balance sheet financing may lower the overall assessment.

A final nonfinancial factor is the rate structure of a utility. An electric utility with a comparatively low rate structure is generally in a stronger position politically to request rate increases than one with rates higher than national averages, and particularly one with rates higher than regional averages.

FINANCE COMPANIES

Finance companies are essentially financial intermediaries. Their function is to purchase funds from public and private sources and to lend them to consumers and other borrowers of funds. Finance companies earn revenue by maintaining a positive spread between what the funds cost and the interest rate charged to customers. The finance industry is highly fragmented in terms of type of lending and type of ownership. This section will briefly outline the major sectors in the industry and then discuss the principal ratios and other key variables used in the analysis of finance companies.

Segments within the Finance Industry

The finance industry can be segmented by type of business and ownership. In order to accommodate the diverse financial needs of the economy, finance companies lend in numerous ways. Five of the major lending categories are:

1. Sales Finance
2. Commercial Lending
3. Wholesale or Dealer Finance
4. Consumer Lending
5. Leasing

Most often, companies are engaged in several of these lines rather than one exclusive line. Sales finance is the purchase of third-party contracts that cover goods or services sold on a credit basis. In most cases, the sales finance company receives interest on the goods or services sold. Commercial finance is also generally on a secured basis. With this type of financing, however, the security is most often the borrower's account receivables. In factoring, another type of commercial lending, the finance company actually purchases the receivables of a company and assumes the credit risk of the receivables.

Dealer or wholesaler finance is the lending of funds to finance inventory. This type of financing is secured by the financed inventory and is short-term in nature. On the other hand, leasing is intermediate to long-term lending—the lessor owns the equipment, finances, the lessee's use of it, and generally retains the tax benefits related to ownership.

Consumer lending has historically involved short-term, unsecured loans of relatively small amounts to individual borrowers. This is, in part, because of the more lenient bankruptcy rules and higher default rates on consumer loans, consumer finance companies have dramatically expanded the percentage of their loans for second mortgages. The lower rate charged individuals for this type of loan is offset by the security and lower default risk of the loan.

There are many other types of lending in addition to those described above. Among these are real estate lending and export/import financing.

The ownership of a finance company can significantly impact how a company is evaluated. In some instances, ownership is the most important variable in the analysis. There are three major types of ownership of finance companies:

1. Captives
2. Wholly Owned
3. Independents

Captive finance companies, such as General Motors Acceptance Corporation and J. C. Penney Financial, are owned by the parent corporation and are engaged solely or primarily in financing the parent's goods or services. Generally, maintenance agreements exist between the parent and the captive finance company under which the parent agrees to maintain one or more of the finance company's financial parameters, such as fixed-charge coverage, at a minimum level. Because of the overriding relationship between a parent and a captive finance subsidiary, the financial strength of the parent is an important variable in analyzing a finance company. Captive finance companies can, however, have ratings either above or below those of the parent.

A wholly-owned finance company such as Associates Corporation of North America differs from a captive in two ways. First, it primarily finances the goods and services of companies other than the parent. Second, maintenance agreements between the parent and the subsidiary are generally not as formal. Frequently, there are indenture provisions that address the degree to which a parent can upstream dividends from a finance subsidiary. The purpose of these provisions is to prevent a relatively weak parent from draining a healthy finance subsidiary to the detriment of the subsidiary's bondholders.

Independent finance companies are either publicly owned or closely held. Because these entities have no parent, the analysis of this finance sector is strictly a function of the strengths of the company.

Financial Analysis

In analyzing finance companies, several groups of ratios and other variables should be considered. There is more interrelationship between these ratios and variables than for any other type of company. For example, a finance company with a high degree of leverage and low liquidity might be considered to be high investment quality if it has a strong parent and maintenance agreements. No variable should be viewed in isolation, but within the context of the whole finance company/parent company relationship.

Loan loss. The most important ratio in analyzing a finance company is the relationship of the company's loan loss experience and related variables. Net loan losses are defined as loans deemed uncollectible and therefore written off, less recoveries of loans previously written off. The importance of this ratio is twofold. First, the net loan loss is a major and unpredictable expense variable. Second, a company with an above average loan loss record has the necessary business expertise to create a loan portfolio of above-average quality. A related variable that should also be evaluated is the company's provision for these losses. If a company's loss provisions are consistently inadequate, they should be explored further for other indications of liberal accounting.

In evaluating the company's loan loss experience, an analyst must also necessarily consider the quality of the portfolio. Diversification is one measure of portfolio quality. Is the portfolio diversified across different types of loans? If the company is concentrated in, or deals exclusively in, one lending type, is there geographic diversification? For example, a company that deals exclusively in consumer loans in the economically sensitive Detroit area would not be as favorably viewed as a company with broad geographic diversification.

Accounting quality is also an important factor in assessing portfolio quality. The more conservative the accounting for income, revenue, and loan losses, the better. The security for the loans is also an important variable in portfolio quality. The stronger the underlying security, the higher the loan quality. Analysts should be primarily concerned with the level of loans compared with levels of similar companies and the risk involved in the type of lending. For example, the expected loan loss from direct, unsecured consumer loans is higher than for consumer loans secured by second mortgages. However, the higher fees charged for the former type of loan should compensate the company for the higher risk.

Leverage. Leverage is a second important ratio used in finance company analysis. By the nature of the business, finance companies are typically and acceptably more highly leveraged than industrial companies. The leverage is necessary to earn a sufficient return on capital. The acceptable range of leverage, however, is dependent on other factors, such as parental support, portfolio quality, and type of business. The principal ratio to determine leverage is total debt to equity, although such variations as total liabilities to equity might also be used. For a diversified company with a high portfolio quality, a leverage ratio of five to one is acceptable. On the other hand, a ratio of 10 to 1 is also acceptable for a captive with a strong parent and maintenance agreements. The analyst should always compare the leverage of a finance company with similar companies.

Liquidity. The third important variable in analyzing a finance company is liquidity. Because of the capital structure of finance companies, the primary cause of bankruptcies in this industry is illiquidity. If for some reason a finance company is unable to raise funds in the public or private market, failure can quickly result. This inability to raise funds could result from internal factors such as a deterioration in earnings, or from external factors such as a major disruption in the credit markets. Whatever the cause, a company should have some liquidity cushion. The ultimate liquidity cushion, selling assets, is only a last resort because these sales could have long-term, detrimental effects on earnings. The traditional liquidity ratio is cash, cash equivalents, and receivables due within one year divided by short-term liabilities.The higher this ratio, the higher the margin of safety. Also the liquidity of the receivables themselves and the existence of bank lines of credit to provide a company with short-term liquidity during a financial crisis should be considered. In general, smaller and weaker companies should have a higher liquidity cushion than companies with strong parental backing and who can rely on an interest-free loan from the parent company in times of market stress.

Asset coverage. A fourth important variable in analyzing finance companies is the asset coverage afforded the bondholder. In assessing asset protection, an analyst should consider the liquidation value of the loan portfolio.

Earnings record. The fifth variable to be considered is the finance company's earnings record. The industry is fairly mature and is somewhat cyclical. The higher the annual earnings-per-share growth, the better. Some cyclicality should be expected, however. In addition, an analyst should be aware of management's response to major changes in the business environment. Recent, more lenient personal bankruptcy rules, and the fact that personal bankruptcy is becoming more sociably acceptable, have produced significantly higher loan losses in direct, unsecured consumer loans. Many companies have responded to this change by contracting their unsecured personal loans and expanding their portfolios invested in personal loans secured by second mortgages.

Size. A final factor related to the finance company or subsidiary is size. In general, larger companies are viewed more positively than smaller companies. Size has important implications for market recognition in terms of selling securities, as well as diversification. A larger company is better able to diversify in terms of type and location of loan than a smaller company, and thereby reducing the risk of the portfolio.

In addition to analyzing the financial strength of a company according to the above variables, an analyst must incorporate the net effect of any affiliation the finance company has with a parent. If this affiliation is strong, it might be the primary variable in the credit assessment. The affiliation between a parent company and a finance subsidiary is straightforward; it is captive, wholly owned, or independent. The degree to which a parent will support a finance subsidiary, however, is not as straightforward. Traditionally, the integral relationship between a parent and a captive subsidiary indicated the highest level of potential support. It is becoming increasingly clear, however, that a wholly-owned finance subsidiary can have just as strong of an affiliation. For example, General Electric Credit Corporation (GECC) finances few products manufactured by its parent, General Electric Company. However, General Electric receives substantial tax benefits from its consolidation of tax returns with GECC. Additionally, General Electric has a substantial investment in its credit subsidiary. Therefore, although there are no formal maintenance agreements between General Electric and GECC, it can be assumed that General Electric would protect its investment in GECC if the finance subsidiary were to need assistance. In other instances, it might be that the affiliation and maintenance agreements are strong, but the parent itself is weak. In this case, the strong affiliation would be discounted to the extent that parent profitability is below industry standards.

In addition to affiliation, affiliate profitability, and maintenance agreements, analysts should also examine any miscellaneous factors that could affect the credit standing of the finance company. Legislative initiatives should be considered to determine any significant changes in the structure or profitability of the industry.

RATING AGENCIES AND BROKERAGE HOUSES

There is no substitute for the fundamental analysis generated by a fixed-income analyst. An analyst has many sources of assistance, however, the major sources of assistance are the public rating agencies and brokerage houses that specialize in fixed-income research.

Rating Agencies

Three major rating agencies provide public ratings on debt issues: Standard and Poor's Corporation, Moody's Investors Service, and Fitch Investors Service. In particular, Fitch rates a number of banks unrated by the other agencies. In addition, Duff & Phelps, Inc., a Chicago-based research house, has recently begun to offer public ratings.

Standard and Poor's (S&P) and Moody's are the most widely recognized and used of the services, although Duff & Phelps and Fitch are frequently cited. Standard and Poor's and Moody's are approximately the same size, and each rates the debt securities of approximately 2,000 companies. If a company desires a rating on an issue, it must apply to the rating agency. The agency, in turn, charges a one-time fee of generally \$5,000 to \$20,000. For this fee, the issue is reviewed periodically during the life of the issue and at least one formal review is made annually.

Three of the rating agencies designate debt quality by assigning a letter rating to an issue. Standard and Poor's ratings go from AAA to D, with AAA obligations having the highest quality investment characteristics and D obligations being in default. In a similar fashion, Moody's ratings extend from Aaa to C, and Fitch's, from AAA to D. Duff & Phelps, on the other hand, assigns numerical ratings from 1 to 14, with 1 analogous to an AAA rating.

Public ratings are taken seriously by corporate managements, because a downgrade or an upgrade by a major agency can cost or save a corporation thousands of dollars in interest payments over the life of an issue. In the event of a downgrade below the BBB or Baa level, a corporation could find its bonds ineligible for investment by many institutions and funds, either by legal or policy constraints. Therefore, corporations strive to maintain at least an investment-grade rating (Baa or higher) and are mindful of the broad financial parameters that the agencies consider in deriving a rating.

Many factors promote the use of agency ratings by investors, bankers, and brokers. Among these strengths are the breadth of companies followed, the easy access to the ratings, and the almost universal acceptance of the ratings. On the other hand, the ratings are criticized for not responding quickly enough to changes in credit conditions and for being too broad in their classifications.

The slow response time of the agencies to changes in credit conditions is certainly a valid criticism. There are few instances in which the lag is significant in terms of a dramatic change, but the market generally anticipates rating changes. The rating agencies have become increasingly sensitive to this criticism and have been quicker to change a rating in light of changing financial parameters. On the other hand, the agencies recognize the financial impact of their ratings and their obligation to rate the long-term (as opposed to the short-term) prospects of companies. Therefore, they have a three- to five-year perspective and purposefully do not change a rating because of short-term fluctuations.

Standard and Poor's has addressed this criticism directly by creating CreditWatch, a weekly notice of companies whose credit ratings are under surveillance for rating changes. These potential rating changes can be either positive or negative. The basis for potential change can emanate from a variety of sources, including company and industry fundamentals, changes in the law, and mergers. Duff & Phelps also has a "Watch List" of companies that are potential upgrades or downgrades. Additionally, subscribers to the agencies' services have access to agency analysts to discuss individual companies or industries.

Investors who are concerned that the ratings are too broad in their classifications have several options among the brokerage house services that offer more continuous ratings.

Brokerage-House Services

Many brokerage houses specialize in fixed-income research, however, these services are generally available only to institutional bond buyers. The strength of the research stems from the in-depth coverage provided, the statistical techniques employed, and the fine gradations in ratings. On the other hand, the universe of companies that these firms follow is necessarily smaller than that followed by the agencies.

Of particular interest is the methodology employed by Kidder Peabody to quantify risk. Kidder Peabody performs Financial Quality Profiles (FQP) on approximately 200 non-oil industrial companies, a universe of oil companies, and a growing number of finance companies. The FQP analysis concentrates on inflation-adjusted financial parameters. In particular, FQP quantifies the "unit growth fundable" of a company, which is the real growth rate of unit production that a company can sustain without a significant deterioration in its balance sheet. The result of an FQP analysis is a numerical rating ranging from 0 to 125 (93 – 125 is roughly equivalent to an AAA). The numerical ratings are the quantitative assessment of the firm's financial parameters. Kidder Peabody tempers these ratings with its assessment of other nonfinancial factors, such as management and industry outlook. In 1981, FQP analysis was extended to include forecasted FQP scores. Although several firms will qualitatively discuss the long-term outlook for a company, only FQP quantifies the evaluation.

In spite of the numerous services available, the market continues to demand more fixed-income research. To partially satisfy this demand, many independent analysts are evaluating segments of the market previously not covered or inadequately covered. This research is frequently supplied by specialists in independently originated research such as Autranet.

A format for analysis is essential. But keep in mind that securities analysis cannot be totally quantified, and an experienced analyst will develop a second sense about whether to delve into a particular aspect of a company's financial position or whether to take the financial statements at face value. All aspects of credit analysis, however, have become increasingly important as rapidly changing economic conditions and increasingly severe business cycles change the credit quality of companies and industries.

Bibliography

Altman, E.I., and Nammacher, S.A., *Investing in Junk Bonds*, John Wiley, New York, 1987.

Altman, E.I., and Nammacher, S.A., "The Default Rate Experience of High-Yield Corporate Debt," *Financial Analysts Journal*, July–August, 1985, pp. 25–41.

Bladen, Ashby, "High Noon in the Junk Bond Market," *Forbes*, May 21, 1984, p. 262.

Boyer, Edward, "Buying Bonds for Income, Not Safety," *Fortune*, 1986 Investor's Guide, pp. 49–51.

Carey, David, "Locking in the Best Returns," *Financial World*, October 14, 1986, pp. 23–25.

Consumer Guide, *Best Rated Investments for 1988*, Consumer Guide, 1987.

Darst, David, *The Complete Bond Book*, McGraw Hill, New York, 1975.

Douglas, Livingston, G., *Yield Curve Analysis*, New York Institute of Finance, New York, 1988.

Fabozzi, F.J., and Garlick, T.D., *Advances in Bond Analysis and Portfolio Strategies*, Probus Publishers, Chicago, 1987.

Fabozzi, F.J., and Pollack, I.M., *Handbook of Fixed Income Securities*, Dow Jones-Irwin, Homewood, Illinois, 1987.

Farrell, James L., Jr., *Guide to Portfolio Management*, McGraw Hill, New York, 1983.

Fong, H.G., and Fabozzi, F.J., *Fixed Income Portfolio Management*, Dow Jones-Irwin, Homewood, Illinois, 1985.

Francis, Jack C., *Investments*, McGraw-Hill, New York, 1986.

Hessol, Gail I., "Debt Rating Revisions: Aftermath of Mergers," *Mergers and Acquisitions*, Winter 1985, pp. 42–47.

Holt, Robert L., *The Complete Book of Bonds*, Harper and Row, New York, 1985.

Homer, S., and Leibowitz, M.L., *Inside the Yield Book*, Prentice Hall and The New York Institute of Finance, Englewood Cliffs, NJ, 1972.

Howe, Jane Tripp, *Junk Bonds*, Probus Publishers, Chicago, 1988.

Kaplan, Elizabeth, "The Waning of the Long-Term Bond," *Dunn's Business Month*, June 1985, pp. 40–42.

Kaplan, R.S., and Urwitz, G., "Statistical Models of Bond Ratings," *Journal of Business*, Vol. 52, No. 2, 1979, pp. 231–261.

Malitz, Illen, "On Financial Contracting: The Determinants of Bond Covenants," *Financial Management*, Summer 1986, pp. 18–24.

Noddings, Thomas, *Low Risk Strategies for the High Performance Investor*, Probus Publishing, Chicago, 1985.

Pinches, G.E., and Mingo, K.A., "Role of Subordination and Industrial Bond Ratings," *The Journal of Finance*, Vol. 30, No. 1, March 1975, pp. 201–206.

Platt, Harlan D., *Why Companies Fail*, Lexington Books, Lexington, Massachusetts, 1985, pp. 9–12.

Sherwood, Hugh C., *How to Invest in Bonds*, Walker Publishing, New York, 1983.

Solomon, Steven, "The Art of Managing Junk Bonds," *Institutional Investor*, Vol. 18, May 1984, pp. 133–135.

Stigum, M., and Fabozzi, F.J., *Bond and Money Market Investments*, Dow Jones-Irwin, Homewood, Illinois, 1987.

Veale, Stuart R., *Bond Yield Analysis*, The New York Institute of Finance, New York, 1988.

Index

Index